Through the Screen Door

*What Happened to the
Broadway Musical When
It Went to Hollywood*

Thomas S. Hischak

THE SCARECROW PRESS, INC.
Lanham, Maryland • Toronto • Oxford
2004

SCARECROW PRESS, INC.

Published in the United States of America
by Scarecrow Press, Inc.
A wholly owned subsidary of
The Rowman & Littlefield Publishing Group, Inc.
4501 Forbes Boulevard, Suite 200, Lanham, Maryland 20706
www.scarecrowpress.com

PO Box 317
Oxford
OX2 9RU, UK

British Library Cataloguing in Publication Information Available

Library of Congress Cataloging-in-Publication Data

Hischak, Thomas S.
  Through the screen door : what happened to the Broadway
musical when it went to Hollywood / Thomas S. Hischak.
      p. cm.
  Includes bibliographical references and index.
  ISBN 0-8108-5018-4 (pbk. : alk. paper)
  1. Musicals—United States—History and criticism. 2.
Musical films—United States—History and criticism. I. Title.
ML1711.H42 2004
791.43'6—dc22

                                        2004004067

⊗™ The paper used in this publication meets the minimum requirements of
American National Standard for Information Sciences—Permanence of Paper
for Printed Library Materials, ANSI/NISO Z39.48-1992.
Manufactured in the United States of America.

For Richard and Nancy Kroot

Contents

~

The Swinging Door:
An Introduction

When George S. Kaufman and Edna Ferber's 1936 Broadway play *Stage Door* was filmed by RKO in 1937, so many changes were made in the script that Kaufman wryly noted they should have renamed it *Screen Door*. Screenwriters Morrie Ryskind and Anthony Veiller didn't destroy the stage work, but they did open up the script, built up the roles that Katharine Hepburn and Adolph Menjou played, and softened some of the play's grittier edges. It was the usual Hollywood treatment. How many witty Broadway scripts were bought by the movies only to have most of the lines thrown out and replaced by "cinematic" dialogue! The same thing happened with Broadway musicals. A hot property with a score by Cole Porter or Rodgers and Hart starring a stage celebrity like Ethel Merman or Marilyn Miller would be sold to Hollywood, only to have the songs discarded and the leading lady replaced by a movie star. The result was sometimes a travesty of the original, but sometimes a whole new delight. Everyone on both coasts understood that plays and movies were not the same thing and what worked on Broadway didn't always play on screen in Peoria. The changes from one medium to the other resulted in many interesting surprises.

Yet from the early silent days, the movies have always turned to Broadway for material, actors, directors, and, later, songs. Musicals and talkies were made for each other. The very first "sound" film, *The Jazz*

Singer (1927), was based on a 1925 play by Samson Raphaelson that was not a musical. But when Jolson was cast as the struggling entertainer Jakie Rabinowitz, the producers knew he had to sing. In fact, the only sound portions of this legendary talkie were Jolson's songs. Hollywood's first musical was a Broadway product changed for the screen.

And so the pattern would continue for the next five decades until the filming of Broadway musicals became unprofitable in the 1970s. After a half dozen colossal flops based on Broadway shows, Hollywood turned its back on the Great White Way. Ironically, about the time that Broadway was becoming a no-go in Tinsel Town, film musicals started to travel east and became stage shows. With the traffic flowing in the opposite direction, the crossover between the stage and the screen was more complex than ever. It turned out that Kaufman's screen door could swing in both directions.

Through the Screen Door looks at 176 Broadway and Off-Broadway musicals that went to Hollywood. Some arrived there pretty much intact, others were altered beyond recognition, and still others became a sparkling new creation. The transition that each musical went through and the results of that changeover are the subject of this book. While the facts behind these changes, from the songs cut to the characters added, are a matter of record, evaluating the results is very subjective. Whether the film version of a Broadway musical was a hit or not is of no little interest. But *Through the Screen Door* is a highly personal and admittedly opinionated look at what happened to those musicals in terms of artistic achievement and audience satisfaction. Was a stage masterpiece destroyed, or was a film masterpiece created? Is the stage version better than the film version? Is different better or just different? These questions cannot be answered objectively, and I have no intention of doing so. But I will state that there is something unique and immediate about a Broadway musical just as there is something wonderfully thrilling about a film musical. I don't consider one medium superior to the other.

I have limited myself to American musicals on and off Broadway and to Hollywood films in this work. Chapter 8 looks at ten British musicals that were popular in New York and were later filmed with Hollywood connections. But there are dozens of British film versions of London stage hits that are not very familiar to American audiences, myself included. Also, some West End musicals have been made from Holly-wood films, such as *Hans Christian Andersen* and *Bugsy Malone*, that have yet to arrive on Broadway; these are not included, either. I have used the American titles for the films (many were retitled in Great Britain) but have made note when a film musical was retitled for tele-vision showing in the States. The dates used for the Broadway shows are those of the official opening of the musical in New York, and the film dates (always a matter of confusion) are the release dates in Cali-fornia. Finally, the movie versions discussed are those initially released by the studios. Many a film musical was butchered by the networks for television viewing. But now, thanks to videotapes and DVDs, most movies can again be seen in their original cutting.

Discovering or returning to the musicals covered in this book has been a joyful experience. The days of the classic film musical are over, but what a wonderful legacy celluloid provides! And the Broadway shows discussed, whether they are frequently revived today or only a memory for past generations, still can enthrall. What bountiful days those were when the Broadway musical went through the screen door and all the world could see what Hollywood hath wrought. The movie musical today, when it rarely happens, is not the same. Neither is Broadway, for that matter. But for a time the two worked together and often provided magic in two very different media.

CHAPTER ONE

~

Sometimes the Melody
Doesn't Linger On

Is there a difference between a Broadway score and the set of songs in a film musical? Both are hoping for variety, enough repetition to breed familiarity, and a few hit tunes. The songs, critics keep telling us, are the core of the musical, on both stage and screen. Shows were often identified by their popular songs (*Gay Divorce* was hawked as the "Night and Day Show"), and when a stage musical closed, sometimes only a handful of songs was all that survived. The songwriters have always been more visible than other writers; it was a Cole Porter musical, not a Herbert Fields or a Bella and Samuel Spewack musical. The songs are king. Yet a curious thing happened to Broadway scores when the shows were filmed. There is indeed a difference between the two kinds of scores, and it is this distinction that we will look at first.

The usual Broadway score has about a dozen songs, not counting reprises. In the 1920s and 1930s, each act often ended with a recap of the score as several melodies were worked into an act finale. Opening chorus numbers were requisite, torch songs always followed the (temporary) breakup between boy and girl about two-thirds of the way through the plot, and large dance numbers were nicely spaced apart, leaving room for more intimate songs. While the focal lovers of the piece had plenty of solos and the expected duet or two each act, there were often similar numbers in a lighter vein for the secondary comic couple, and sometimes a mismatched character (usually a clownish type) got a comic number with or without the chorus. When the more sophisticated Rodgers and Hammerstein model emerged in the 1940s, the plotting improved, but many of the unwritten rules remained. In modern musicals, the score continues to take up a substantial portion of stage time. In the more recent sung-through musicals, the score becomes the libretto. The songs remain king.

In film musicals, this approach is not necessarily the case. Consider some of the musicals not based on Broadway shows. Movie musicals have fewer songs, and less playing time is spent on them. While some films were stuffed with plenty of hits offered in abbreviated form (the George Gershwin biography *Rhapsody in Blue* managed to squeeze twenty-four Gershwin numbers into its 139 minutes), most got by with a fourth of that amount. *Swing Time*, for example, only has six songs, and one of those is an instrumental. And there are musical classics with even less: *42nd Street* and *Flying Down to Rio* each has only four songs, and some of those are primarily dance numbers. The original screen musical does not require a large number of songs, so it is no wonder that Broadway scores were often slashed to half their length for the movie versions.

Also, the emphasis within a song changed. A rhapsodic duet in the theater may go on for three minutes, but on the screen it could only last that long if the number moves into dance or some other appealing visuals. While it is true that film musicals (especially before the 1950s) ran roughly half the length of stage musicals, there is more to this abridging of music than just a matter of running time.

To tell the truth, Hollywood was wary of songs. It didn't know at first exactly what to do with them. Film tends to be realistic, and the narrative is primary. Songs are not realistic and, until the fully integrated musicals of the 1940s, did not advance the story. The studios knew the songs were the heart of the musical, yet they were suspicious of them. An actor bursting out in music because an emotion had overcome him was what made the theater songs soar. But would audiences as easily accept screen characters in realistic settings breaking into music? How does one move from dialogue into a song lyric? And where was the music coming from?

These questions, which seem superfluous today, were a great bother during the early talkies. Hollywood was worried that audiences would not believe stage conventions on the screen, and for the first decade or so a song had to be "explained." No wonder the setting for a musical number was always a nightclub or a stage show and the situation a rehearsal or a performance. That was easy to explain. But for two lovers to sing a duet in a nontheatrical setting was tricky. Sometimes one member of the twosome told the other about a particular song and then proceeded to sing it; consider Nelson Eddy telling Jeanette MacDonald about the "Indian Love Call" and then the two of them eventually harmonizing it together in *Rose Marie*. Other times the duet was turned into a musical conversation, trying to bridge the gap between dialogue and lyric. Often this was awkward and laughable, but sometimes it was inspired joy; recall Fred Astaire and Ginger Rogers grumbling about "A Fine Romance" in *Swing Time*. Solo numbers were frequently the most difficult. A torch song given a heartrending performance on stage could enthrall a live audience for three minutes. On screen the camera had to cut away for reaction shots or, worse, show a montage of images to make the number visually interesting. Broadway's act finales took too long, leading up to intermissions that weren't there, and minor characters getting their own songs were considered extraneous. So they were all cut. It took Hollywood a long time to get over its neurosis about songs on the screen.

When the first Broadway musicals were filmed, the hit songs were retained, but much of the score was abridged. Since movies thrived on plot, more emphasis was put on the story. Ironically, the libretto was usually the least impressive aspect of most stage musicals at the time. But Hollywood knew how to tell a story, so plot was given much more playing time in the early film musicals, and the score, what remained of it, was used as entertaining frosting on the cake. Obviously a Broadway score diminished by half is going to result in a truncated version of the original show. It was nothing to toss out six Cole Porter gems and then add tiresome scenes to the ridiculous storyline. That Porter score was probably the reason the studio bought the property in the first place, but in Hollywood nothing is sacred, especially a New York songwriter. Irving Berlin, the Gershwins, Jerome Kern, and all the great songwriters saw their Broadway scores skewered beyond recognition, but none, I think, were more abused than Rodgers and Hart. Looking closely at their Hollywood careers will illustrate the unhappy side of Broadway scores in Tinsel Town.

Composer Richard Rodgers and lyricist Lorenz Hart first found success on Broadway with *The Garrick Gaieties* in 1925. The next year they had four shows on Broadway and one in London, each one providing a sparkling score with more than its fair share of hits. Rodgers and Hart quickly became the most recognized, lauded, and performed songwriting duo yet seen on Broadway. Of course, Hollywood was interested, and in 1930 three film versions of their stage musicals were released, each one a box office failure. On Broadway, *Present Arms* (1928) was a pleasant yarn set in Hawaii about an uncouth marine (Charles King) who poses as a captain to win an aristocratic Lady (Flora LeBreton) away from a wealthy German suitor. Naturally, the marine is found out, but his valiant rescue during a yachting accident allows him to save face and get the gal. The Rodgers and Hart score of eleven songs was sprightly and playful: "Hawaii," "Down by the Sea," and "Blue Ocean Blues" providing the local color; the dance number "Crazy Elbows"; the torchy "I'm a Fool, Little One"; the narrative saga "A Kiss for Cinderella"; and the sassy song of regret "You Took Advantage of Me," which became a standard. Only the last two were retained for the 1930 film version retitled *Leathernecking* (but retaining its Broadway title in Great Britain where few knew that a marine was called a leatherneck). Six new numbers by various studio songwriters were added, and the plot was filled out with some comic cronies for the hero, played as a kind of nebbish by Ken Murray, who woos Irene Dunne. One of the highlights of the Broadway show was the choreography by Busby Berkeley, praised by one critic for its "aerial formations." Berkeley was not involved with the film version but would soon relocate to Hollywood, where his "aerial formations" would transform the movie musical.

Spring Is Here (1929) was leaner on plot but richer in its songs, the standard "With a Song in My Heart" leading the way. The story concerned a heroine (Lilian Taiz) who tries to go against her father's wishes and marry the man she loves. But when their elopement is foiled, she settles for her friend Terry Clayton (Glenn Hunter), a reliable guy whom her sister Mary Jane (Inez Courtney) knew was the better choice all along. Five of the fourteen stage songs were retained for the 1930 film, as was Courtney, whose rendition of the hedonistic "Baby's Awake Now" proved to be the vivacious high point in both the stage and screen versions. Courtney also reprised "Rich Man, Poor Man" in which Hart was at his sarcastic best. Bernice Claire played the troubled heroine and got to sing the lush "With a Song in My Heart," which was already very popular. The title song for both play and movie is a forgotten ditty fully titled "Spring Is Here in Person" and not the beloved favorite "Spring Is Here (Why Doesn't My Heart Go Dancing?)" that Rodgers and Hart later wrote.

Their score for *Heads Up!* (1929) was not as accomplished as those for *Present Arms* and *Spring Is Here*, but surely it deserved better when the 1930 film version cut all but two of the songs. The convoluted plot for Broadway's *Heads Up!* (totally rewritten after a disastrous tryout in Detroit) dealt with rum running and a stalwart Coast Guard lieutenant (Jack Whiting) who falls for the daughter of a wealthy yacht owner. Victor Moore stole the show (as he often did) as Skippy Dugan, the ship's cook who is also a crackpot inventor. The movie version wisely retained Moore and then rewrote the story as a romantic tale of coast guarder Charles "Buddy" Rogers trying to win a rich girl from a slick bootlegger. The lovely ballad "A Ship without a Sail" managed to make it to the screen, but the Broadway show's most popular number, the sprightly love song "Why Do You Suppose?" was dropped.

It is not surprising, after three dismissed film versions of their work, that Rodgers and Hart carried little clout in Hollywood. Yet the team went west during the Depression and scored eight original musicals. Their innovative and marvelous scores for *Love Me Tonight* and *Hallelujah, I'm a Bum*, for example, are today considered triumphs in rethinking the movie musical, but in their day, they were labeled interesting but modest achievements. By the end of the 1930s, when other Rodgers and Hart Broadway hits were filmed, the results were more satisfying, though often the scores still suffered. Consider *Babes in Arms* (1937), which introduced more standards than any other Broadway show after Irving Berlin's *Annie Get Your Gun*. From such a dazzling collection including "My Funny Valentine," "The Lady Is a Tramp," "Way Out West," "Johnny One Note," "I Wish I Were in Love Again," "All at Once," "Imagine," "Where or When" and the title march song, only the last two showed up in the 1939 movie version! Was this lack of foresight on the studio's part or just pigheadedness? Since several of these songs were already far along their way to becoming standards, one cannot help but think that MGM was hell-bent on creating a hit *despite* Rodgers and

Hart. Old favorites like "You Are My Lucky Star" and "I'm Just Wild about Harry" were pulled from the files, and Harold Arlen, E. Y. Harburg, Roger Edens, and others were commissioned to fill out the film score. The result, the first in a series of popular "Let's put on a show!" musicals featuring Mickey Rooney and Judy Garland, was a hit but could hardly be called a Rodgers and Hart show anymore.

The team's *The Boys from Syracuse* (1938) also contained a hefty supply of hits—"This Can't Be Love," "Sing for Your Supper," "Dear Old Syracuse," "Oh, Diogenes!," and "Falling in Love with Love"—but the 1940 Hollywood version decimated the score; some songs were cut, some numbers reduced to background music, and others edited to the point of teasers. The original was a playful take on Shakespeare's *The Comedy of Errors* filled with merry anachronisms and bright tunes. The film is rather vulgar and humorless and was not popular. In fact, it just about buried the show in the minds of many, and not until a successful 1963 revival Off Broadway did *The Boys from Syracuse* reenter the ranks of oft-produced musicals. The same cannot be said for *Too Many Girls* (1939), a delightful collegiate romp that was a hit on Broadway but is never done today.

Four bodyguards disguised as football players (Richard Kollmar, Eddie Bracken, Hal Le Roy, and Van Johnson) accompany the high-spirited heiress Consuelo (Marcy Westcott) to Pottawatomie College in New Mexico to keep an eye on her for her rich daddy. She falls for Kollmar, and both their romance and the big football game are in jeopardy when Consuelo learns the truth. Before things are sorted out, there's time for such vibrant Latin numbers as "All Dressed Up (Spic and Spanish)" and "She Could Shake Her Maracas" (both led by Desi Arnaz) and the standard "I Didn't Know What Time It Was." Hart wrote two brilliant comic lyrics: "I Like to Recognize the Tune," bemoaning the way swing orchestras bury the melody, and "Give It Back to the Indians," a wry listing of the ills of modern Manhattan. Both numbers were cut from the 1940 film version, but, surprisingly, much else remained, including Bracken, Le Roy, Johnson, Arnaz, and seven songs from the stage. Lucille Ball, in the ingenue phase of her career, played Consuelo opposite Richard Carlson as the love interest; Ann Miller was also added for spice. This time when a new number was added, it was actually by Rodgers and Hart: the lovely ballad "You're

Nearer." *Too Many Girls* is a very satisfying movie and probably the most accurate cinema record of a Rodgers and Hart Broadway musical.

The stage hit *I Married an Angel* (1938) actually started as a Hollywood project with the team writing much of the score in 1933 before the movie was canceled. When it arrived on Broadway five years later, it was a delicious mishmash of a show, with ballet sequences for Vera Zorina, a plot filled with fantasy and sexual innuendo, and the Hungarian characters inexplicably singing a celebratory number called "At the Roxy Music Hall." The Budapest banker Willie Palaffi (Dennis King) has girlfriend troubles and in disgust swears he will marry no one but an angel from heaven. Zorina arrives on cue and they wed, but the marriage is a bit rocky until a worldly-wise countess (Vivienne Segal) teaches the celestial bride a thing or two about the modern, earthly ways of doing things. George Balanchine staged the romantic and satiric ballets, and Rodgers and Hart provided nine delightful songs led by the flowing title number and the standard "Spring Is Here." Unique in the score were sections of rhymed dialogue that led into some of the songs or dance pieces.

Of course, all this disappeared in the 1942 film version that turned out to be a critical and financial dud. The urbane wit and sly, knowing characters and dialogue were turned into a lumbering romance (Nelson Eddy as the banker dreams that he marries angelic Jeanette MacDonald), and only four of the songs were retained, one of them ("At the Roxy Music Hall") rewritten by others until it became impotent. This celluloid flop put an end to the string of MacDonald–Eddy films, and it did nothing for the team of Rodgers and Hart either.

Neither did *Higher and Higher* (1940), a rare stage failure for the songwriting team. All the same Hollywood bought it, tossed out all the songs, then hired Harold Adamson and Jimmy McHugh to write a whole new score for the 1944 film version. While the stage *Higher and Higher* did not boast a top-notch Rodgers and Hart score, it did contain the late-blooming standard "It Never Entered My Mind."

An even more embarrassing transition from stage to screen was the team's *On Your Toes* (1936), the vibrant, innovative musical that employed dance in ways never seen before on Broadway. When it was filmed in 1939, the score was reduced to background music!

Lorenz Hart died in 1943, and the illustrious collaboration came to an end. But three film musicals featuring Rodgers and Hart songs were made after his death, and each one was successful. *Words and Music* (1948), Hollywood's sanitized biography of the team's career, featured over a dozen of their songs, the striking "Slaughter on Tenth Avenue" ballet, and hardly an ounce of truth about the two men's lives. The homosexual Hart, who was plagued with feelings of inferiority and alcoholism, was played by Mickey Rooney as a cheerful fellow who is often depressed because he's short, and Tom Drake's Richard Rodgers was duller than any composer ever was. The movie's saving grace was the score, filled with songs that had not survived earlier film transitions: "There's a Small Hotel," "I Wish I Were in Love Again," "Way Out West," "The Lady Is a Tramp," "Johnny One-Note," and others.

The uncompromising Broadway musical *Pal Joey* (1940) was much too adult to transfer to the screen as written and will be discussed later, but it is worth pointing out that of the dozen songs that Rodgers and Hart wrote for the show, only four ended up in the 1957 film. The rest of the score was filled out with standards written by the team for lighthearted musical comedies and were totally out of place in the seedy world of *Pal Joey*.

Rodgers and Hart's circus musical *Jumbo* (1935) did not reach the screen until 1962. Five songs from the original score were retained, including the waltzing ballad "The Most Beautiful Girl in the World," the tender "Little Girl Blue," and the lush "My Romance." The rest of the movie's score was made up of either numbers pulled from different Rodgers and Hart shows or new songs by others. The original *Jumbo* had been a mammoth production at the Hippodrome where the songs were sometimes dwarfed by a spectacular circus. The film also seeks spectacle and pretty much sticks to the plot of rival circus owners and the title elephant. Some of the screen performers are enjoyable, particularly Doris Day, Jimmy Durante, and Martha Raye, and the songs are well served for the most part. Not too bad for the last film of the team's stage works.

Rodgers and Hart's experience with Hollywood was not fortuitous, and Rodgers never forgot it. That was why in his second and very different career with Oscar Hammerstein, he was much more cautious, not selling his shows to the movies without having a large say in how the films were made. He had been burnt by Hollywood and was very suspicious of the screen door.

Cole Porter, on the other hand, acted nonplused about the treatment his scores got in Tinsel Town. The Porter shows on Broadway usually had even thinner plots than Rodgers and Hart's experimental musicals, and songs were bounced back and forth between shows without a problem. They still are; one never knows what Porter song will pop up in which revival. He did not seem too concerned about which songs they used in which film as long as they were Porter tunes. But even he must have been aghast at what happened to some of his Broadway scores.

Let's consider his first New York hit, *Paris* (1928), which introduced the sly "Let's Do It (Let's Fall in Love)." *Paris* was a frothy piece of musical comedy with the Parisian beauty Irene Bordoni pursuing the son of a straight-laced New England family. Porter only contributed three songs to the multiauthored Broadway score, but his and all the other numbers were dropped from the 1929 film version, and only Bordoni made it to Hollywood. The new screen score by Al Bryan and Ed Ward was as forgettable as the rest of the film, which is only recalled today as Bordoni's first talkie.

Porter fared no better with *Fifty Million Frenchmen* (1929). This delectable musical comedy posed William Gaxton as an American playboy in Paris who disguises himself as a tour guide to win the love of Genevieve Tobin (and a bet with his pal). The scintillating score was Porter's finest yet: "You Do Something to Me," "Find Me a Primitive Man," "You've Got That Thing," "Paree, What Did You Do to Me?" and some cult favorites such as "The Tale of the Oyster" (which was cut out of town). The various Paris landmarks re-created on the stage fairly cried out to be filmed. But Hollywood thought otherwise, the 1931 movie version retaining Gaxton and the plot premise but eliminating all of the score, save a few tunes for background music. (The same thing would happen to Porter's 1944 show *Mexican Hayride*, which also had its songs turned into underscoring when the play was filmed as an Abbott and Costello vehicle in 1948.)

Porter's *Panama Hattie* (1940) fared better only in terms of the score. Hattie is a nightclub owner in Panama City who must befriend her millionaire boyfriend's young daughter before they can tie the knot. The Broadway show was a well-crafted vehicle for Ethel Merman as Hattie, and Porter, who had written songs for her before, provided a brassy Merman-like score. *Panama Hattie* was filmed in 1942 without Merman, and the result was rather bland and not very popular. Such wonderful Porter songs as "Just One of Those Things," "I've Still Got My Health," and "Let's Be Buddies" were mixed into an eclectic score by everyone from Burton Lane and E. Y. Harburg to Gilbert and Sullivan. Porter was at least well represented, but without Merman, the whole project was a misfire.

History repeated itself in spades when Porter's *Something for the Boys* (1943), another Broadway hit with Merman, arrived on the screen in 1944 without star or score except the title song. On stage, Merman played defense plant worker Blossom Hart whose dental fillings start to pick up aircraft messages. It was that kind of show. But with Merman, who sent out her own special signals when she sang, it was musical comedy gold. The show's two hits, "Hey Good Lookin'" and "Could It Be You?" fell by the wayside when the movie was made, as well as the odd and naughty favorite "By the Mississinewah."

Not only Merman but also her costar Bert Lahr were dropped when Porter's *DuBarry Was a Lady* (1939) was filmed in 1943. This entertaining piece, about a washroom attendant (Lahr) who drinks a Mickey Finn and dreams he is King Louis XV of France, was tailor made for its stars. Merman plays a nightclub singer who becomes Lady DuBarry in the dream. Two Porter tunes survived the transition to film this time: "Katie Went to Haiti" and "Friendship." Again a risqué number, "But in the Morning, No," was dropped, which is understandable; but why the harmonizing "Do I Love You?" and the catchy "Well, Did You Evah?" disappeared is not so easily explained. (The last was finally heard on screen when Bing Crosby and Frank Sinatra sang it thirteen years later in *High Society*.) Some of these and other Porter shows will be discussed later, but the pattern remains the same: even the best Cole Porter song was expendable in Tinsel Town.

Of the many films made from Broadway musicals scored by the Gershwin brothers, two were particularly fleeced of their songs when they were filmed. *Strike Up the Band* (1930) was a political satire with lots of rhythmic dialogue and a score that included the standard "I've Got a Crush on You" and the lyrical "Soon." But only the title march number made it to the screen when the show became another Rooney–Garland "Let's put on a show!" rouser in 1940.

The Gershwins' jazzy, innovative *Lady, Be Good!* (1924) saw its two best songs, "Fascinating Rhythm" and "Oh, Lady, Be Good!" filmed in 1941, but gone were "Little Jazz Bird," "So Am I," and "The Half of It, Dearie Blues."

Jerome Kern spent many years in Hollywood and provided plenty of song gems in the 1930s, yet even he saw his Broadway scores tampered with. His stage classic *Show Boat* (1927) arrived on the screen pretty much unscathed on two occasions, but few of his other Broadway shows were as fortunate. Consider the sublime *Roberta* (1933). It had an old-fashioned plot about an American football player inheriting a dress shop in Paris and a clerk who turns out to be a princess in disguise. But the score included a handful of song favorites written with lyricist Otto Harbach. The 1935 screen version was rewritten as a Fred Astaire–Ginger Rogers vehicle, and only four songs from the stage were retained: "Let's Begin," "Yesterdays," "Smoke Gets in Your Eyes," and "I'll Be Hard to Handle" (lyric by Bernard Dougall). Three other Broadway numbers were only used as background music ("You're Devastating," "Don't Ask Me Not to Sing," and the unforgettable "The Touch of Your Hand"), and Kern provided new numbers with lyricist Dorothy Fields, most memorably "Lovely to Look At" and "I Won't Dance." The film of *Roberta* overflows with marvelous music (though the screenplay was not much of an improvement on the stage libretto), and it is all Kern. (*Roberta* was remade in 1952 as *Lovely to Look At,* and only three of the stage songs were used.)

Kern was not so lucky with *Very Warm for May* (1939), his last Broadway musical. Oscar Hammerstein provided the lyrics this time, and the superb score included the classic "All the Things You Are" as well as "Heaven in My Arms" and "In the Heart of the Dark." The musical was a backstager with a tired plot about the romantic doings at a summer stock theater. *Very Warm for May* was far from a hit but "All the Things You Are" was, and it was the only song retained when the show was filmed as *Broadway Rhythm* in 1944. This time the rest of the score was filled out with old songs by George Gershwin, Sunny Skylar, Louis Alter, and many others—but not one by Kern

The popular 1920s team of DeSylva, Brown, and Henderson saw all their major Broadway hits filmed in the 1930s, but again Hollywood was rather cavalier about the scores. *Good News* (1927) was the team's first book musical, with Ray Henderson composing the music and B. G. DeSylva and Lew Brown contributing to the libretto and lyrics. Not the first collegiate musical built around a football game (nor the last), *Good News* boasted a merry score that included such hits as "The Best Things in Life Are Free," "Lucky in Love," "Just Imagine," "The Varsity Drag," and the happy title song. The show was filmed twice with widely different results. The 1930 version inexplicably cut the first three songs listed here and added a handful by various studio tunesmiths. The film was rather lifeless and not very popular, due somewhat to the avalanche of mediocre movie musicals that year. When it was remade in 1947, all of the major songs were used, as well as some excellent new ones by Roger Edens, Betty Comden, Adolph Green, and others. This time it was a rousing hit at the box office.

DeSylva, Brown, and Henderson were not so lucky with *Hold Everything* (1928), a daffy musical comedy about boxing that featured Bert Lahr as a punch-drunk pug. The 1930 movie dropped Lahr and all of the score save two minor efforts. Left on the cutting room floor (if indeed they were ever filmed at all) were such delights as "To Know You Is to Love You," "Don't Hold Everything," "Too Good to Be True," and "You're the Cream in My Coffee."

When the trio turned to the sport of golf in *Follow Thru* (1929), they had another Broadway hit with two rival lady golfers fighting over Jack Haley and song hits like "Button Up Your Overcoat," "I Want to Be Bad," "You Wouldn't Fool Me, Would You?" and "My Lucky Star." Haley made it to the screen version, but only the first two mentioned songs did.

Flying High (1930) completed the team's quartet of Broadway hits. Its score was less impressive even though it included the sly "Thank Your Father," "Good for You—Bad for Me," and "Red Hot Chicago." Bert Lahr starred as a wacky airplane mechanic who was terrified of flying but managed to break a world aviation record by default. The 1931 movie kept Lahr (it was his film debut) but cut all the stage songs except the cheery title number. The team of DeSylva, Brown, and Henderson broke up in the 1930s and each went his separate way, but most of their finest songs were finally heard on screen in their musical bio *The Best Things in Life Are Free* (1956).

Of all the Broadway composers, none had more success in Hollywood than Irving Berlin. His "Blue Skies" was heard in the first talkie,

The Jazz Singer, and he saw dozens of his stage and Tin Pan Alley songs make it to the screen. Berlin also contributed dozens of new numbers for the movies. As America's favorite songwriter, he got more respect in Tinsel Town than any other songsmith. Yet even Berlin was powerless when it came to his Broadway scores on the screen. Several of his filmed stage shows will be looked at elsewhere but it is worth examining one at this point. *Louisiana Purchase* (1940) was Berlin's first Broadway musical in nearly seven years and at 444 performances his biggest hit yet. Inspired by the recent investigations into the corrupt doings of southern politico Huey Long, the libretto concerned a fraudulent New Orleans company run by William Gaxton that is under investigation by a bumbling but honest senator played by beloved comic Victor Moore. Gaxton tries to get the squeaky clean senator into a compromising position with two local femme fatales, Irene Bordoni and Vera Zorina, but honesty wins out, and the senator ends up marrying one of them. It was a sly and funny libretto by Morrie Ryskind and Berlin matched it with some satirical songs as well as catchy duets and contagious chorus numbers. It is, after *Annie Get Your Gun,* Berlin's most sparkling stage score, but, because it is not revived like the later show, the songs are not as well known today. After a rhymed prologue in which the lawyers argue about doing a musical that resembles current events, Berlin raises eyebrows with a very funny group number "Sex Marches On," followed by the simple but insistent title song. There are such expert duets as the comic "Outside of That I Love You," the pseudoromantic "You're Lonely and I'm Lonely," and the worldly-wise "It'll Come to You." "Fools Fall in Love" and "It's a Lovely Day Tomorrow" were the hit ballads but vivacious numbers like "Latins Know How" and "Wild about You" also brought down the house. Finally, there is one of Berlin's finest comic songs, "What Chance Have I with Love?" in which the meek senator looks at the great lovers of history and realizes he is way out of his league.

When Hollywood made a film of *Louisiana Purchase* in 1942, it gave the show top production values, but the result is rather lame. Moore, Bordoni, and Zorina reprised their roles, and the up-and-coming star Bob Hope was put in the Gaxton role. The screenplay toned down the satire and added a filibuster scene that worked for Hope but sunk the movie. All but four of the score's fifteen songs were cut. What remained were the duet "I'm Lonely and You're Lonely" that was staged so that it was neither funny nor sentimental, Bordoni's solo "It's a Lovely Day Tomorrow," the title song played under a garish Mardi Gras parade, and (surprisingly) an adapted version of the rhymed prologue now titled "Take a Letter to Paramount Pictures." One other stage song, the unimpressive "Dance with Me (At the Mardi Gras)," was used as an in-strumental in a ballroom scene. No new songs were added, so *Louisiana Purchase* on screen comes across as a drawn-out, unfunny comedy with a couple of songs awkwardly stuck in. Needless to say, the film was not popular, and its failure helped bury the stage show for future audiences. Berlin must have been disappointed to watch his greatest stage triumph (to date) become celluloid dead weight, and he later saw to it that his next hit, *Annie Get Your Gun*, was better treated by the studios.

Composer Vincent Youmans saw his two biggest Broadway hits, *No No Nanette* (1925) and *Hit the Deck!* (1927), each filmed twice. *No No Nanette* is considered the quintessential Roaring Twenties musical com-edy, and Youmans's score (with lyricists Otto Harbach and Irving Cae-sar) is filled with musical gems. "I Want to Be Happy" and "Tea for Two" were the standout hits, but also top-notch were "Too Many Rings around Rosie," "Where Has My Hubby Gone? Blues," "You Can Dance with Any Girl at All," and the sprightly title number. The 1930 screen version adhered pretty closely to the original plot about a married Bible salesman who gets into a compromising position with three ladies he's been helping financially. Yet when it came to the score, the studio only retained the two hits, kept the title number, and added a handful of for-gettable tunes by others. When *No No Nanette* was remade in 1940 the result was even less satisfying. More time was spent on the predictable storyline, and the songs (only five of them) were mostly used as back-ground scoring.

Hit the Deck! was also a Broadway smash even though its libretto was even thinner than *Nanette*'s. Café owner Looloo loves the sailor Bilge Smith (Charles King) so much she follows the fleet all the way to China to present him with his own boat that she refurbished with her life's savings. Louise Groody, who had charmed audiences as Nanette, played Looloo, and the success of the earlier show was repeated. Youmans' score (with lyricists Clifford Grey and Leo Robin) again pro-vided two standards, "Hallelujah" and "Sometimes I'm Happy" (lyric by

Irving Caesar), but there was much to be said for "Why, Oh Why?" "The Harbor of My Heart," "Lucky Bird," and "What's a Little Kiss between Friends." Only the first three numbers were used in the 1930 film treatment, but the score was augmented with other Youmans tunes, most memorably "Keeping Myself for You" (lyric by Sidney Clare) and "More Than You Know" (lyric by Edward Eliscu and Billy Rose). When *Hit the Deck!* was remade in 1955, the plot was greatly altered, but seven of the Broadway songs survived. With its bright cast (Jane Powell, Tony Martin, Debbie Reynolds, Ann Miller, etc.) and its slick MGM treatment, it was a success. Another movie version of *Hit the Deck* came out between these two films: *Follow the Fleet* (1936). It used only the barest thread of the original story and boasted a totally new (and totally superb) score by Irving Berlin.

Because he was an international celebrity in the world of classical music, conductor-composer Leonard Bernstein would seem a likely prospect for a tunesmith who got a little respect from Hollywood. But Bernstein's score for the stage hit *On the Town* (1944) was treated no better on the screen than if it had been composed by any New York hack songwriter. Betty Comden and Adolph Green provided the simple but effective stage libretto and the lyrics for Bernstein's challenging music. The plot, about three sailors on twenty-four-hour leave in New York City, was a descendant of *Hit the Deck!*, but it was the score and Jerome Robbins's exciting choreography that made *On the Town* special. In addition to some jazzy and very urban-sounding ballet pieces, the score included such outstanding numbers as the celebratory "New York, New York"; the comic seduction song "Come Up to My Place"; the bluesy, operatic "I Feel Like I'm Not Out of Bed Yet"; the catchy "I Get Carried Away"; the somber "Lonely Town"; the swinging "Ya Got Me"; the quietly blissful "Lucky to Be Me"; and the wistful farewell quartet "Some Other Time." It was a score overflowing with marvelous music in its songs and dance instrumentals. Yet movie producer Arthur Freed admitted he didn't like the score (too dissonant, too unpredictable, too edgy, he said), so the 1949 movie version only kept the first three songs listed here and sections of Bernstein's ballet music. It was probably the cinematic butcher job of the decade. Yet *On the Town* turned out to be a highly enjoyable movie and was very successful. It was the first film musical to extensively use actual New York locations, and it certainly looked like no other. The cast was uniformly excellent, as was Gene Kelly and Stanley Donen's direction and Robbins's choreography. But the songs mostly fell flat, both Bernstein's and new ones by Roger Edens (lyrics by Comden and Green). Only the theme song "New York, New York" comes alive on screen, probably because of the quick cutting and innovative use of Manhattan locations. One can enjoy the added number "Prehistoric Man," for example, for its clever staging even though the song itself is instantly forgettable. One of the great Broadway scores was lost when it went through the screen door, a collection of wonderful songs still to be heard in movie houses.

Many other stage musicals ought to be considered when discussing how Broadway scores were altered for the screen, but I will limit myself to five that are of special interest. Consider, for example, *Guys and Dolls* (1950). If ever a musical comedy instantly became a classic, it was this delectable show about gamblers, chorines, and religious rescuers inhabiting a fictionalized Broadway. Frank Loesser wrote sixteen songs for the musical (and not a one of them less than excellent), and the libretto, mostly by Abe Burrows, remains one of the sharpest and funniest in the annals of musical comedy. *Guys and Dolls* was a huge hit on Broadway, and movie producer Samuel Goldwyn paid a record $1 million for the movie rights and spent over $4 million to make it in 1955. But what an odd film musical it turned out to be with nonsingers Marlon Brando and Jean Simmons cast as the romantic singing couple and Frank Sinatra as the nonsinging gambler Nathan Detroit. At least Vivian Blaine got to reprise her funny, endearing Miss Adelaide from the original stage production. The sets and staging were in a colorful theatrical style that pretty much worked, and there is a lot to enjoy in *Guys and Dolls*. But the score? Fortunately eleven songs from Broadway were retained, but the very popular "Bushel and a Peck" was replaced by the predictable "Pet Me, Poppa" and the hit ballad "I've Never Been in Love Before" with the wan Latin number "A Woman in Love." To beef up Sinatra's role, the dull ballad "Adelaide" was added. All the new songs were by Loesser, but none came close to the quality of his stage score.

Stephen Sondheim didn't even get the chance to add new songs when Hollywood sliced up his brilliant score for *A Funny Thing Happened on the Way to the Forum*. The 1962 Broadway hit boasted a rich and varied set of songs that, admittedly, were not fully appreciated until years later. Yet there was no question about the contagious fun in numbers like "Comedy Tonight" and "Everybody Ought to Have a Maid." Both were kept in the 1966 movie version along with bits of "Lovely," "Bring Me My Bride," and the "Funeral Dirge." Moviegoers never got to hear such admirable songs as the merry trio "Pretty Little Picture," the insistent "I'm Calm," the wry duet "Impossible," and others. So little of the film's running time is devoted to music that it comes across as a comic race with a few abrupt stops for singing. As a comedy, the movie *Forum* is fun; as a musical, it is a major disappointment.

Yet sometimes Hollywood surprises and goes in the other direction. The smash hit melodrama *Broadway* (1929) was about a nightclub hoofer who gets mixed up with underworld figures and chorus girls in a seedy Broadway haunt. The Philip Dunning–George Abbott play had no songs per se though an offstage nightclub orchestra played throughout most of the evening. The 1929 movie version added five songs by Con Conrad, Sidney Mitchell, and Archie Gottler, and the melodrama became a musical. When *Broadway* was remade in 1942, those songs were tossed out and replaced with a half dozen 1920s standards. Songs were sacrificed for the plot in *Forum*, yet the plot-driven *Broadway* was abridged for its added songs. Go figure.

Probably the longest wait to be filmed goes to the 1897 musical play *The Belle of New York*. This breezy show, about a Manhattan playboy who is "saved" by a Salvation Army lass, only managed a short run in New York but was a big hit in London, Berlin, and Paris, with subsequent revivals in Europe. The tuneful score by Gustav Kerker and Hugh Morton included such ditties as "At Ze Naughty Folies Bergere" and "The Purity Brigade," early forerunners of Loesser's songs in *Guys and Dolls*. In 1952, MGM threw out the score and most of the plot of *The Belle of New York* and fashioned the tale into a period piece for Fred Astaire and Vera-Ellen. The new songs by Johnny Mercer and Harry Warren were sometimes enjoyable, though hardly from those two masters' top drawer. Kerker and Morton were long dead, and the original show was unknown to Americans.

But what of *Fanny* (1954), which *was* a Broadway hit, and composer-lyricist Harold Rome, who *was* very much alive when the film version came out in 1961? *Fanny* is Rome's richest score, filled with touching numbers like "Welcome Home" and "Be Kind to Your Parents," the catchy "Why Be Afraid to Dance?" and "Never Too Late for Love," the intriguing "Restless Heart," and the soaring title song. This tale set in a French fishing village was a charmer and the gentle score was all of a piece. Well, it remained together when the studios threw out every song and filmed *Fanny* as a nonmusical drama. (The story had already been made as a trilogy of movies in France.) So what's worse: a score decimated or a score totally ignored? Probably Rome was one of the few to know the answer to that uncomfortable question.

One could be optimistic, I suppose, and consider all the great scores that Hollywood created and weigh them against all the Broadway songs discarded. The two might well balance out. But with few exceptions, the studios never came up with new songs in filming Broadway shows that matched the quality of those eliminated. The choice to scale down the number of songs, we have seen, is understandable. So is the tailoring of songs to a star's particular talents. But what puzzles is how good songs were so often replaced by mediocre ones. It seems as though the studios, battling their inferiority complex regarding stage art and the movie business, had to prove themselves as creative makers of musicals, and one way of doing this was "improving" the Broadway shows they purchased. Ironically, the Hollywood-originated musicals were often as wonderful as the stage hits in New York. So why worry and tamper with proven Broadway scores? Irving Berlin wrote that "the song is ended but the melody lingers on" in the memory of all those who heard it. Perhaps. But sometimes Hollywood had a short memory.

CHAPTER TWO

~

How Boy Met Girl

Until the mid-1950s, when musicals by Rodgers and Hammerstein and others were given the prestige treatment by Hollywood and were brought to the screen pretty much intact, it was not uncommon to rewrite the Broadway libretto for the film version. In fact, it was expected. Movie musicals are limited in their running time and in the amount of songs that can be included. A two-and-a-half-hour stage musical with approximately half of its playing time spent on singing and dancing could not be turned into a hundred-minute movie without some major abridgement.

We have seen how the scores were often sacrificed in this process, but the plots often underwent a similar transition. The clichéd pattern for most Broadway librettos was simple. Act I: boy meets girl; Act II: boy loses girl; Act III: boy gets girl. The same pattern was transferred to the screen, but more was riding on the plot in Hollywood. Movies (at least those before the 1960s) were more interested in story than anything else. Even if the movie was a vehicle for stars, plot was still central. Since most Broadway musicals before the 1940s had pretty thin plots, it would seem that writing the screenplay for the film version would not be all that difficult. But again, Hollywood was wary of Broadway, afraid the storylines were too talky, too New York, too highbrow even. And rarely did the studios hire theater librettists for musical screenplays. They trusted their own writers more, people who knew how to write for the screen. Whether to justify their salaries or just to be different, many screenwriters went out of their way to turn proven stage librettos into totally new movie scenarios.

Something else was also at work that Hollywood could not ignore: movies could do things and go places that the stage shows couldn't. It was the magic of the medium. One could go anywhere and show anything without leaving the back lot. The major studios were elaborate factories for creating different worlds, either realistically or romantically. Location shooting, especially for musicals, was usually not necessary. The factories could recreate anything in-house. As for the public, they reveled in being taken on a phony but exhilarating journey to just about anywhere when they watched a film. They knew movies could go to wonderful places, and they anticipated the trip. While a theater audience will accept certain activities happening offstage in a Broadway show, moviegoers expect—even insist—to see it happen on screen. The stage convention of offstage action disappears in the cinema. No one exits in a movie; a character is on screen as long as the camera chooses him or her to be. The invisible fourth wall of the theater is a ridiculous conceit in a film. We expect to see places and people from every direction; it is not necessary to use one's imagination when watching a movie. So stage musicals, which have more conventions and demand more imagination than any other form of theater, cause special problems in cinematic storytelling.

When a Broadway show is filmed without altering the stage conventions, the result may be ludicrous. The horse race at Ascot in My Fair Lady is an obvious example. On stage, the Edwardian spectators looking out into the theater audience as they view the race not only is believable but enhances the experience; the reaction of the crowd is more important than the event they are watching. Yet when the movie was made in 1964, the filmmakers unwisely tried to keep the Ascot scene within a theatrical convention rather than a cinematic one and just added an artificial blur of horses going past the spectators. The movie audience felt cheated, and the scene was not nearly as effective as it had been on Broadway. In a film, one expects offstage happenings to happen onstage. In a traditional screen handling of My Fair Lady, the camera would cut from real horses racing around the track to Eliza

Doolittle and the crowd, alternating long shots and close-ups. The cross cutting would give the scene added suspense and go where the stage version could not. That would have been a movie musical. What appeared on the screen in 1964 during that scene was a blatant example of poor filmmaking.

Hollywood learned early on that plays and stage musicals had to be "opened up" when they were filmed. The earliest screen efforts were pretty much in set stage pieces, such as the conventional sequence of scenes in *The Broadway Melody* (1929). Four years later, when *42nd Street* was made, the traditional confines of stage space were gone. No Broadway house could contain the activities of Busby Berkeley's cinematic shenanigans. The same was true of the plots and even the characters. A story involving the two main lovers no longer had to alternate with scenes for the supporting characters. Comic sidekicks and sassy secondary lovers were often reduced to a line here and there, their songs cut, and their specialty numbers incorporated into the large production numbers. Yet it worked on screen. Compare the time spent on the comic couple in the stage hit *No No Nanette* with the funny sidekicks in *42nd Street*. Both are effective, but the screen treatment manages it in a fraction of the time. So "opening up" the stage work was more than just adding exteriors or cutting back and forth between different locations. It was a way of rethinking the plot in cinematic terms. Sometimes the transition was successful; other times it was lacking.

Since just about every Broadway libretto before 1960 was changed when filmed, examining very many of them would be repetitive. So I have chosen a dozen musicals that might represent the many kinds of results, both satisfactory and not, that came from rewriting stage shows for the screen.

Because George M. Cohan pretty much invented the American musical libretto, we'll look at one of his musicals first. *Little Nellie Kelly* (1922) comes near the end of Cohan's remarkable career, and, though it was dismissed by many critics as old-fashioned, it was very popular. True, Cohan was still writing the same kind of plots in the 1920s as he had in 1904 with *Little Johnny Jones*. The man was inventive but not flexible. *Little Nellie Kelly* tells the familiar tale of an Irish-American lass Nellie (Elizabeth Hines), the daughter of a policeman, who works in Devere's Department Store and is wooed by two very different men:

the rich, slick Jack Lloyd (Barrett Greenwood) and the cocky, honest Irish rough Jerry Conroy (Charles King). Since Nellie will not accept his offer to go out, Jack throws a party in his mansion for all the employees at Devere's, and Nellie attends. But Jerry crashes the party, and, when jewels are stolen in the mansion, he is immediately accused of the crime. It being the Roaring Twenties when Irene, Sally, and other musical heroines of the decade won rich sweethearts, it was a little surprising that Cohan retained his old-fashioned philosophy and had Nellie prefer the wrongly suspected Jerry over the princelike Jack. But Jerry is Irish, down-to-earth, and sings songs to her like "You Remind Me of My Mother" and "Nellie Kelly, I Love You." Of course, she chooses him. Jerry is cleared of the crime, and the would-be princess forsakes the prince and gets the boy next door. *Little Nellie Kelly* ran longer than any other Cohan show (276 performances) and was also a hit in London (where he rarely found success).

The film version was not made until 1940 as a vehicle for Judy Garland (her first solo star feature and her first truly adult role), and the screenplay by Jack McGowan only kept the thread of Cohan's plot. In Ireland, Nellie Noonan wants to marry local boy Jack Kelly (George Murphy), but her father (Charles Winninger) is against it. They wed anyway and move to New York where Jack becomes a policeman. Papa follows them to America and sponges off the couple, never warming up to the husband. In a rather daring move on McGowan's part, Nellie dies in childbirth, but the baby lives. Little Nellie Kelly (also Garland) grows up and falls for Dennis Fogarty (Douglas MacPhail), but again Grandpa Winninger tries to stop it, so father and sweetheart have to save the day. Only the title song was kept from the Cohan score, and new and old numbers were added, including a lively rendition of "Singin' in the Rain" by Garland. The crusty Irish nature of the play also remains and the sentimentality and patriotism are pretty thick, but *Little Nellie Kelly* is a surprisingly effective movie. Perhaps the Cohan libretto was too old-fashioned for 1940, but then it was considered outdated in 1922 as well, and that certainly didn't hurt business. Yet McGowan's screenplay is a step above many in the early 1940s and is a good example of a Broadway show being rethought as a film.

The plot that Guy Bolton and Fred Thompson fashioned for the stage hit *Lady, Be Good!* (1924) was a jazzier version of Cohan's story about someone rejecting a rich partner for the sweetheart next door. Vaudevillian siblings Dick and Susie Trevor (Fred and Adele Astaire) are evicted from their Manhattan apartment because he has spurned the affections of wealthy Josephine Vanderwater (Jayne Auburn), who owns the building. The brother and sister set up house on the sidewalk and befriend a tattered outcast Jack Robinson (Alan Edwards), whom Susie falls for. When the talkative lawyer "Watty" Watkins (Walter Catlett) offers her a lot of money if she'll impersonate a Mexican widow who is to inherit a fortune, Susie agrees in order to help Jack and keep Dick from marrying the predatory Josephine. After some complicated ruses (and dazzling musical numbers), it is discovered that Jack is actually a millionaire heir who was temporarily out of favor with his rich uncle. Susie and Jack are united, and Dick is able to throw off Josephine for good and marry the sweet girl he prefers. It was already a tired plot, but the dialogue often sparkled, and the Astaires (who became Broadway stars with this show) were outstanding. *Lady, Be Good!* was also the first Broadway score for the Gershwin brothers together, and, as we saw earlier, the songs were exceptional. At 330 performances, the musical was one of the long-runs of the decade.

The 1941 film version of *Lady, Be Good!* was also written by *Little Nellie Kelly*'s Jack McGowan (with John McClain and Kay Van Riper), but this time his rethinking and rewriting of the play misfired. Had Astaire been teamed up with one of his beloved leading ladies and been permitted to reprise numbers from the stage like "Fascinating Rhythm" and the title song, the movie may have survived the dreary new plot that McGowan and company devised. In the screenplay, songwriters Dixie Donegan (Ann Sothern) and Eddie Crane (Robert Young) are romantic as well as professional partners, but when success goes to his head, the team breaks up. What follows is a series of reconciliations and further partings that try the patience of even the most stolid movie musical fan. Eleanor Powell, as a character who hardly entered the plot, gave the movie its most winning moments, such as the lavish production number that featured her, eight grand pianos, and a hundred men in white tie and tails tapping to "Fascinating Rhythm." Also effective was Sothern's rendition of "The Last Time I Saw Paris," a poignant ballad by Jerome Kern and Oscar Hammerstein that was interpolated into the film and won the Oscar for Best Song. As far-fetched as the stage libretto was, it certainly was superior to the movie's seesaw story. And with only five musical numbers to try and lift up the sagging plot, the film seems endless. When Sothern and Young finally get together at the end of the film, the audience is too tired to care. *Lady, Be Good!* is a potent example of an ineffective libretto adaptation for the screen.

The Gershwins (and everybody else, including the audience) had much more luck with *Funny Face* (1927). Fred Thompson and Robert Benchley wrote the stage libretto that again featured the Astaires, but the result, called *Smarty*, played so poorly in tryouts in Philadelphia that Benchley resigned, and play doctor Paul Gerard Smith worked on script revisions with Thompson. A handful of Gershwin songs were replaced by new ones, and comic Victor Moore was added to the cast to beef up the much-needed comedy. The show that opened in New York was a hit even though the libretto was surprisingly hackneyed, using the old stolen jewels plot device that had been seen in dozens of shows before. Even the central premise is contrived: Jimmy Reeve (Fred Astaire) has three wards, all pretty girls whose prize belongings he keeps in his safe. June Wynne (Gertrude MacDonald), for example, has a pearl necklace locked in there. Her sister Frankie Wynne (Adele Astaire) has a diary that is filled with personal thoughts so incriminating that she convinces her boyfriend, the aviator Peter Thurston (Allen Kearns), to steal it from the safe. Somehow he manages to steal the pearls instead, setting off a merry chase that takes the cast to the pier at Atlantic City. To make matters more complicated (and more fun), two bumbling crooks played by Moore and William Kent also try to break into the safe and are swept along in the chase. It was all delightful nonsense made palatable by the engaging players and a top-notch Gershwin score that included "He Loves and She Loves," "'S Wonderful," "The Babbitt and the Bromide," "My One and Only," "High Hat," and the engaging title song.

Hollywood planned on filming *Funny Face* in 1928 with the Astaires, but, sadly, it never happened; it would have been the only film record of Adele in one of her Broadway roles. The British made a movie version of the show in 1936 and called it *She Knew What She Wanted*, but by then Adele had retired and brother Fred was firmly settled in California. It wasn't until 1957 that Tinsel Town finally filmed *Funny Face* and then without any of the plot or characters. All that remained was Fred Astaire and four of the Gershwins' original songs. Leonard Gershe wrote the screenplay, and it was very much a product of its time, poking fun at the fashion industry, fashion photography, the existential movement, and even the old Cinderella premise. A Richard Avedon–like photographer named Richard Avery (Astaire) discovers the intellectual Jo Stockton (Audrey Hepburn) working in a Greenwich Village book shop and is smitten with her gamin looks if not her highbrow manner. He tries to whisk her off to Paris to make her an international model, but Jo only agrees to go in order to meet the celebrated Sartre-like philosopher Professor Fostre (Michel Auclair), who hangs out at the Parisian Café de Flore. Fashion editor Maggie Prescott (Kay Thompson) of *Quality* magazine, who urges the public to "Think Pink!" grooms Jo into a first-class model, but the new star resists falling in love with Avery until she discovers that the professor is an oversexed fraud. It's a tight, clever screenplay that doesn't take itself too seriously and the new and old songs are used effectively throughout. The real Avedon was "visual consultant" on the movie, and it must have rubbed off because *Funny Face* is one of the most beautifully filmed pictures of the decade. Here is a case of the movie script being a vast improvement over the original stage libretto, but one can hardly call it an adaptation. Gershe's script (originally written for another film that never got made) is pure cinema, from its dazzling fashion sequence in various Paris locations, to the arty, pretentious atmosphere of the "beatnik" Café de Flore, to a memorable scene with Astaire and Hepburn dancing in the morning mist. No one would mistake this for a Broadway show.

Hit the Deck opened on Broadway the same year that *Funny Face* did, but it had no trouble getting put on screen. In fact, it was filmed three times. We have already seen what happened to the score, but consider also the transformations the libretto underwent. Herbert Fields wrote the script for the 1927 musical, basing it on the 1922 play *Shore Leave* by Hubert Osborne. The original property centered on Connie Martin, a shy dressmaker in New England, who falls for a sailor on leave and dedicates all her time and money to get him get his own ship. Fields turned the heroine into the saucy, carefree Looloo Martin (Louise Groody) who runs a dockside coffeehouse. She loves the rough-and-ready gob Bilge Smith (Charles King), but when he goes off to sea, Looloo doesn't sit demurely at home and wait for him. She travels the seven seas looking for him, finds him in China, and presents him with his own boat. Bilge is suspicious of a gal rich enough to take care of him, so Looloo agrees to sign all her money away to their first child, and the twosome head to the altar. The songs by Vincent Youmans (music), Clifford Grey, and Leo Robin (lyrics) were far from integrated into the plot, but Fields's libretto provided great opportunities for song and dance.

The first film version came out in 1930 and adhered pretty closely to Fields's libretto, though most of the score was gone. Polly Walker and Jack Oakie as Looloo and Bilge are personable, and there is even a two-color Technicolor section that is interesting, but much of the film falls flat. In 1936, screenwriters Dwight Taylor and Allan Scott returned to the original *Shore Leave* and turned it into the popular Fred Astaire–Ginger Rogers vehicle *Follow the Fleet*. Oddly, the principal characters of Connie and Bilge were made the secondary couple, and Fred and Ginger took center stage, he as a navy man and she as his ex–dancing partner and old sweetheart. Harriet Hilliard played the quiet Connie and Randolph Scott the dense but likable Bilge. The story stays in San Francisco, either aboard ships or on land, and only Connie's desire to buy Bilge his own boat is retained from the original. It is a sloppy script with some contrived quarrels between the two sets of lovers, but much of the playing time is spent on song and dance, and the Irving Berlin score sparkles: "Let Yourself Go," "I'd Rather Lead a Band," "Get Thee behind Me, Satan," "I'm Putting All My Eggs in One Basket," "Let's Face the Music and Dance," and other gems. *Follow the Fleet* is some kind of movie classic, but its connection to Broadway's *Hit the Deck* is tenuous at best.

The same can be said for the third movie version in 1955, though much of the score showed up in this one. Screenwriters Sonya Levien and William Ludwig jettisoned much of Fields and Osborne's characters and plot and just kept the navy uniforms. Tony Martin, Russ Tamblyn, and Vic Damone are three sailors on leave but spend more time making trouble than romancing. Damone is smitten with Jane Powell, who is so anxious to get a part in the stage show *Hit the Deck* that she agrees to meet a womanizing producer in his hotel room. The three gobs try to save her virtue by destroying the hotel suite but only get in trouble with the admiral (Walter Pidgeon), who just happens to be the father of Powell and Tamblyn. All that mattered were the musical numbers, and they are top-notch, Hermes Pan's choreography giving Ann Miller, Tamblyn, and others a chance to shine while wooden actors Damone and Martin (along with Powell) handled the lovely ballads. Interpolated Youmans songs such as "More Than You Know," "Keeping Myself for You," and "Why, Oh Why?" made the movie a true Youmans musical if not quite his *Hit the Deck*.

Two Broadway musicals from the 1930s, a famous one and an obscure one, are good examples of libretto tampering. *Yokel Boy* (1939) is long forgotten now, but it ran six months in New York because its familiar plot (stolen shamelessly from 1931's *America's Sweetheart*) and likable (but not memorable) songs allowed such comic actors as Buddy Ebsen, Judy Canova, and Phil Silvers a chance to shine. The New England local yokel Elmer Whipple (Ebsen) has loved pretty Mary Hawkins (Lois January) since childhood, so when she goes off to Hollywood to become a star, he follows her and tries to keep her from falling into the clutches of an amorous cinema idol. But Mary's screen career flounders, and Elmer convinces her that life back in the sticks is the life for them. Canova stole the show as a hillbilly who sang three rowdy numbers by Sam Stept, Charles Tobias, and Lew Brown (who also wrote the libretto), and Silvers as Punko Parks was noticed for the first time on a Broadway stage. The second-class film studio Republic Pictures bought the show for only $5,000 because it liked Canova and wanted to feature her in the movie version. But by the time the film was made in 1942, Canova was out, and so was Brown's plot.

In Russell Rouse's screenplay, the yokel Joe Ruddy (Eddie Foy Jr.) has seen so many movies at the local picture palace that he can accurately predict audience attendance and satisfaction levels. A crooked studio assistant (Roscoe Karns) finds out about Joe and decides to use him to determine a picture's success before it is made, thereby saving Hollywood millions of dollars. But soon gangsters are in on the racket, and the plot loses any congruity, relying on its five songs (three from the stage score) to keep the audiences in their seats. *Yokel Boy* was not a hit, but Republic later used Judy Canova's contract and starred her in a handful of their own musical comedies.

While both stage and screen versions of *Yokel Boy* have passed out of memory, *Anything Goes* (1934) continues to be one of the most revived of all 1930s Broadway shows. It was filmed twice, and its songs appeared in other movies as well. The unusual history of how the stage musical came to be is that of Broadway legend and is worth repeating here.

P. G. Wodehouse and Guy Bolton wrote a libretto called *Bon Voyage* about a group of characters aboard an ocean liner, a bomb threat that led to a shipwreck, and some daffy adventures aboard a desert island. Cole Porter wrote the score, and a crackerjack cast including Ethel Merman, William Gaxton, Victor Moore, and Bettina Hall was assembled. With the sets and costumes begun and the show about to go into rehearsals, disaster struck in the form of a real sea tragedy: the liner S. S. *Morro Castle* caught fire off the coast of New Jersey, and 125 people died. Major rewriting was necessary, but Wodehouse and Bolton were in England, so director Howard Lindsey and the press agent Russel Crouse teamed up and devised a new libretto using the existing songs, sets, and cast. (The twosome would go on to become one of the most successful playwriting teams in the American theater with such hit plays as *Life with Father* and musicals such as *The Sound of Music*.) The new version, now titled *Anything Goes*, was still set aboard a ship, but the only threats were romantic triangles and a harmless gangster (Moore) disguised as a missionary. It is a chaotic libretto with some far-fetched contrivances (Merman played an evangelist turned nightclub singer), but it worked beautifully on stage and, with minor alterations, still does. Billy Crocker (Gaxton) stows away to be with his sweetheart Hope Harcourt (Hall), who is being taken to England to wed a silly-ass Brit (Leslie Barrie). Billy dons various disguises as he tries to change Hope's mind and even gets involved with the on-the-lam Moore and some Chinese passengers. To add to the merriment, the Porter score was chock full of song favorites, including "I Get a Kick Out of You," "All through the Night," "Blow, Gabriel, Blow," "You're the Top," and the zippy title tune.

Running 420 performances, *Anything Goes* was one of the top hits of the decade, and two years after its opening the first film version was released by Paramount. It took four screenwriters (Walter DeLeon, Sidney Salkow, John C. Moffitt, and Francis Martin) to come up with a shooting script that was pretty much an abridged version of the stage libretto. Ethel Merman got to reprise her evangelist Reno and sing "I Get a Kick Out of You" and "You're the Top" (both with some laundered lyrics), but much of the rest of the cast was disappointing. Bing Crosby made an amiable but unexciting Billy (farce was not Crosby's forte), Ida Lupino was the object of his affections (she was now an English heiress on the run), and Charles Ruggles took over the role of the harmless gangster when W. C. Fields dropped out of the picture. There is much to enjoy in the film, but it never captures the frivolous, carefree fun that made the Broadway show so special. Paramount used only the title and five Porter songs when *Anything Goes* was remade in 1956. Sidney Sheldon wrote an original screenplay about two Broadway stars, Bing Crosby and Donald O'Connor, who supposedly set out on a ocean voyage to find the female lead for their next Big Show. It was a more ridiculously contrived premise than the original, and Sheldon hadn't had to work around a shipwreck. The two men have each fallen in love with girls in Paris (Jeanmaire and Mitzi Gaynor) and promise her the leading role. On the shipboard journey back to New York, with the girls in tow, Crosby and O'Connor try to work up the strength to the tell the other what they've promised. Aside from some delightful musical numbers (by Porter and others), nothing much happens. It is one of those musicals that never seems to start, no less develop. Luckily, neither film version seems to have hurt *Anything Goes* on stage. It's still done all the time.

Jumping a few decades ahead, one would think that 1960s musicals would arrive on the screen with their librettos intact. Mostly they were and for two reasons: the librettos got much better in the 1940s and thereafter, and Hollywood gave many Broadway shows the prestige treatment in the 1960s. Some of these faithful (sometimes too faithful) screen versions will be looked at later, but there are four Broadway musicals from the decade that made interesting script transitions. *On a Clear Day You Can See Forever* (1965) had a problematic libretto by Alan Jay Lerner (who wrote the score with composer Burton Lane) that explored the dramatic ideas behind ESP and reincarnation. Daisy Gamble (Barbara Harris) is a kookie chain smoker who is engaged to an uptight corporate type who is more interested in retirement plans than romance. She goes to the psychologist Mark Bruckner (John Cullum) to hypnotize her out of her smoking habit, but the doctor soon discovers (under hypnosis) one of Daisy's former lives as Melinda, an elegant femme fatale in Regency England. Daisy, of course, is smitten with the dashing doctor, but Mark is infatuated with Melinda. Leave it to Lerner to come up with a whole new love triangle that late in the game. But the premise is the most intriguing thing in the musical's script, and the triangle is not resolved satisfactorily when Daisy's psychic vision saves Mark's life by keeping him off a plane that is destined to crash. Mark settles for the present-day Daisy, and the audience had to settle for a forced happy ending. Yet there were many wonderful things in *On a Clear Day*, including Harris's enervating performance and a charming score.

Lerner was never satisfied with his libretto and made some major changes when he scripted the 1970 film version. The movie was bought by Paramount as a vehicle for Barbra Streisand, and, love her or leave her, she dominates the musical to the point that she sings every song except for two given to nonsinger Yves Montand as Mark (now called Marc Chabot to explain the Gallic accent). Lerner sticks to his original story for the first third of the picture and then fills out the scenes in Regency England by showing more of Melinda's life, a pseudo–*Oliver Twist* tale about an illegitimate youngster who blackmails her way into society, marries a pudgy old aristocrat for his money, and has a tragic love affair with a high-class cad. It was entertaining enough as a flashback but never very gripping as a plot, so the movie ended up having *two* unsatisfying stories. In the screenplay, Daisy and Marc part at the end of the film, but we are told, through one of her hypnosis sessions, that the twosome will find married bliss in future lives. Leave it to Lerner to come up with a whole new kind of happy ending.

Like the stage work, there is much to recommend in the movie *On a Clear Day*. Vincente Minnelli directed, and, while much of it was staged rather perfunctorily, he still had an eye for making a movie musical look terrific. Streisand is in fine form, getting to show off her versatility and a lot of glitzy clothes. Half of the Lerner–Burton score was dropped, but one of the two new numbers by the team, "Go to Sleep," is a delicious duet for Daisy and her alter ego (a third Daisy!). It is difficult to determine whether the screenplay is an improvement over the stage libretto since neither is completely satisfying. But one must remember that the studio cut the final print mercilessly (including several scenes and a song by Jack Nicholson as Daisy's brother), and the disjointed feel of the musical is the result. Yet with all their faults, both play and movie manage to please many viewers.

Lerner also did a lot of rewriting when his stage hit *Camelot* (1960) was filmed in 1967. The Broadway show had a very difficult birth as Lerner tried to turn T. H. White's mammoth Arthurian epic *The Once and Future King* into a musical libretto. The project was so unwieldy that songs, characters, and scenes were dropped during previews in order to bring the show in under three hours. The result was an uneven but occasionally thrilling piece of theater that eventually became a popular favorite. The triangle of the idealistic King Arthur (Richard Burton), the knowing Queen Guenevere (Julie Andrews), and the cocky but likable Sir Lancelot (Robert Goulet) was ideal for musical theater, but there was so much more to contend with: lofty ideas about civilization, magical forces at work, political intrigue, and a tragic ending. White's book had dozens of subplots; *Camelot* was so crowded it didn't have room for one. There was also an imbalance in tone. The first act, about Arthur and Guenevere's courtship, marriage, and their promotion of the Round Table, was pretty much musical comedy. The second act, about infidelity, conspiracy, and war, was serious musical drama. Only the high quality of the Lerner–Loewe score and the fine cast were consistent. But *Camelot* has a charm and sense of importance that much tidier shows lack, and it is not hard to see its appeal.

Since the movie had to be even shorter than the play, Lerner again was faced with more cutting and rethinking the material. He solved some problems and created others. By starting the screenplay with the last scene (the eve of battle) and then telling the story in one long flashback, Lerner set the serious tone from the beginning. It was an old cinematic device and a legitimate one. But the early, playful scenes between Arthur and Guenevere suffered from the somber opening, and the musical comedy numbers "I Wonder What the King Is Doing Tonight," "The Simple Joys of Maidenhood," and the title song don't sparkle as they do on stage. Lerner cut Morgan Le Fay and much of the fantasy aspects of the story (Merlin was reduced to an even less important role than in the libretto), which was just as well because Joshua Logan's lumbering production looked ridiculous any time it strayed from realism, as in the embarrassing wedding scene. Much of Lerner's screenplay is admirable, and the story holds together a little better than the Broadway show did. But the production values on stage were impeccable, and Warner Brothers' expensive but artificial settings, costumes, and cheesy special effects (those damn Logan filters!) just about sunk the whole project. Richard Harris tended to overact a bit as Arthur (he was much better in the role on stage), and Franco Nero was a handsome but unexciting Lancelot, yet Vanessa Redgrave's Guenevere was a fresh and exuberant creation, hitting both the whimsical and tragic aspects of the character. Camelot was a box office flop, earning less than half of the $15 million it cost, but, like the play, it has its admirers. Few musicals aim as high as this one, and its ambitious vision cannot be ignored.

Idealism of a very different sort was on display in Hair (1968), the "American tribal love-rock musical" that introduced rock music to Broadway and changed theater orchestrations forever. Even the most conservative stage musical today has its musical roots in Hair, which electrified the musicians and, consequently, forced the singers to be wired for sound. You can't do Oklahoma! or an operetta today without using the techniques first employed in Hair. Some critics felt that the loose and audacious libretto would also affect later Broadway musicals, but such has not been the case.

Gerome Ragni and James Rado wrote the book and the lyrics for Galt MacDermot's music for Hair, and they were all of a piece. The songs were mostly commentaries rather than character numbers or ballads, and the libretto was similar in that it commented on America and the issues it was facing rather than developing story and characters. The major players had character names, and a few things did happen to them, most memorably the death of the Brit Claude in Vietnam. With a Broadway run of 1,750 performances, several road companies filling theaters across the country, and hit songs on the radio such as "Aquarius," "Good Morning Starshine," "Easy to Be Hard," and "Let the Sunshine In," Hair was bought up by United Artists with the hopes of making a youth-oriented musical blockbuster.

The trouble was, it took the studio eleven years to figure out how to film such a loosely structured theater piece, and by the time the movie was released in 1979, the Age of Aquarius had passed. Hair became a scrubbed-up, buttoned-down nostalgia piece that neither shocked nor stirred up anyone. All the same, it is a rather accomplished movie in its way. Playwright Michael Weller wrote the screenplay that turned Claude (John Savage) into a young Oklahoma cowboy who, for some reason, decides to vacation in New York City before enlisting in the military. There he is taken in by a group of harmlessly naughty hippies who prance around Central Park and celebrate more than they protest. He befriends their leader, Berger (Treat Williams), who eventually takes Claude's place and ends up dying for him in Vietnam. It was a vague and contrived premise but one that showed off the appealing cast, the vibrant songs (most of the Broadway score was retained and there were no interpolations), and some lively choreography by Twyla Tharp. Milos Forman directed with a soft, romantic look that was atypical of his work but right in keeping with the old school of movie musicals. Hair is a good example of how even later film musicals were tied to the Hollywood belief in plot. And in this case the old philosophy was correct.

Finally, let us look at Cabaret (1966), which reached the screen in 1972. Like many musicals in the 1960s, this one had a long and interesting pedigree: a series of stories by Christopher Isherwood turned into the play I Am a Camera by John Van Druten that was filmed in 1955. Joe Masteroff wrote the libretto and took liberties with the source material, in particular making the cabaret the focal point of the piece. Before he knew it, Masteroff was writing two scripts: the story of British singer Sally Bowles (Jill Haworth) in prewar Berlin and a series of cabaret numbers that commented on that story. Holding the show together was the slim and slimy Master of Ceremonies (Joel Grey), a character not found in the stories or the earlier play or film. Cabaret was both conventional and innovative as traditional book scenes (including a subplot about a Jewish fruit merchant and a gentile landlady) took on a Brecht-like tone when running side by side the musical commentary in the Kit Kat Klub. Even the John Kander (music) and Fred Ebb (lyrics) score divided into two halves: typical character songs for the plot and stinging pastiche numbers for the nightclub. The whole enterprise was bold, demanding, and surprisingly entertaining. Harold Prince's inspired direction, the mesmerizing sets by Boris Aronson, and the gritty choreography by Ron Field certainly helped, and Cabaret was a major hit at 1,165 performances.

Except for Joel Grey, none of the artists from the stage production were involved in the film version. Director Bob Fosse had a theater background but also had an instinctive talent for cinema and appreciation of the difference between the two. His idea of Cabaret was very different and, with screenwriter Jay Presson Allen, did a radical rewrite of the libretto. Going back to the original Isherwood stories, they created a new subplot about a wealthy Jewess (Marisa Berenson) being wooed by a "closet" Jew (Fritz Wepper), eliminating the libretto's middle-aged couple altogether. Sally (Liza Minnelli) became an American, and the writer Cliff became the British Brian (Michael York). A romantic triangle was a developed utilizing the two lovers and a rich German playboy (Helmut Griem) who, in keeping with the decadent nature of the piece, was sleeping with each of them. The two realities of Cabaret (the book scenes and the nightclub scenes) meshed more completely in the film, sometimes colliding together effectively thanks to some superior editing. Fosse and Allen threw out all the book songs, and the only number not sung at the Kit Kat Klub was "Tomorrow Belongs to Me," presented as a sing-along at a rural beer garden. Like all of the musical numbers, it was devastatingly effective. Each stage element that the film discarded was replaced by something just as powerful or even better, such as the three new Kander and Ebb songs. Over the years, these and other screen additions have been incorporated into stage revivals of Cabaret, making the show a flexible and ever-changing musical like Show Boat. Trying to decide whether the play or the film is more effective is a fruitless endeavor; a Broadway classic was turned into a different kind of screen classic.

Cabaret brings us back to the idea of "opening up" stage material for the screen, with which we started the chapter. Fosse rethought the stage piece in terms of cinema but took some unpredictable chances in many ways. Usually musical numbers expand and enlarge when they are transferred to the screen. Fosse did the opposite with the Cabaret numbers on film. The stage of the Kit Kat Klub was smaller and less dazzling in the movie than any Broadway theater. Busby Berkeley gave us stage productions too large and fantastical to fit in any New York theater; Fosse created one that is more intimate and unembellished than any Broadway show. The screen Cabaret is unusual in that, rather than opening up the show, Fosse narrowed it down to a smaller but just as effective sock in the eye. It remains one of the most intriguing transitions from stage to screen in the history of both media.

Stage librettists and Hollywood screenwriters are unique authors in that they must be collaborative in nature. Even a solo book writer for a stage musical has to work with the lyricist and composer, not to mention the director, actors, and everyone else. In Hollywood, especially during the heyday of movie musicals, solo screenwriting credits were rare. Often one group of writers developed the story and others wrote the shooting script. While a Broadway musical may be changed during rehearsals or tryouts, the librettist is always involved. But movies are edited without the collaboration of writers and actors, so the final cut of a movie may be very different from what the screenwriters intended.

All this is worth mentioning because looking at the scripts for movie musicals is not the best way to determine the picture's effectiveness. A weak libretto may keep a Broadway show from being revived even if the score is superior. But a poorly written film musical can still enthrall as long as the performers and the production numbers are entertaining. We accept a dated "boy meets girl" storyline in an old film and put up with it, waiting for the next production number or favorite performer. Theater audiences are more restless with a poor libretto, and many a revival with a great score but a hackneyed book has quickly closed. Plot is one area where the Broadway musical and the Hollywood musical separate. Boy still has to meet, lose, and get girl, but it has to happen differently in each medium.

CHAPTER THREE

~

Close Copies

Having looked at how Broadway musicals had their scores and scripts changed for the movies, it is now time to consider those film musicals that not only faithfully retained the same songs and librettos but also used the directors, choreographers, and/or actors from the original stage productions. These close copies are invaluable for theater historians looking for a cinematic record of past stage shows. But how successful are they as films? Is fidelity to the original a guarantee of re-creating the stage works' special magic?

I have chosen a dozen movies that offer a pretty accurate record of their Broadway originals. Some are highly satisfying, while others are only curiosity pieces. Filming a Broadway musical by ignoring all the cinematic elements available is often as dangerous as throwing everything out of a stage show that made it so enjoyable in the first place. But the most unsuccessful of these examples still has its own peculiar fascination. Even a poor copy reveals something interesting about the original.

Among the earliest close copies are the film records of the Marx Brothers musicals *The Cocoanuts* (1925) and *Animal Crackers* (1928). Both were filmed under primitive conditions in the Astoria Studios on Long Island, and, while they are technically rather crude, neither is a dull or dusty historical record. In fact, they are highly entertaining and intriguing to both theater and movie fans.

George S. Kaufman wrote the stage libretto and Irving Berlin the songs for *The Cocoanuts*, but both were liberally sacrificed by the zany Brothers as comic bits were added during performances and musical spoofs overshadowed the original songs. While the show had a plot with a pair of lovers, some villains, and a tidy ending, much of the evening was comic anarchy that often resembled a vaudeville show. Groucho played Henry W. Schlemmer who runs a faltering Florida hotel while trying to pass off suspicious real estate in the swamp-ridden neighborhood. The two lovers (Jack Barker and Mabel Withee) are temporarily torn asunder when thieves steal Margaret Dumont's jewels and the young man is falsely accused. Chico and Harpo, as two of Schlemmer's cronies, frequently interrupted this tired story and participated in many of the evening's most cherished moments (few of which were musical). *The Cocoanuts* was a major hit at 276 performances.

The brothers returned to Broadway two seasons later in *Animal Crackers*, an even better show that may have had a similar plotline (by Kaufman and Morrie Ryskind) but boasted a better score (by Bert Kalmar and Harry Ruby) and even more opportunity for clowning. The setting this time was the Long Island mansion of Mrs. Rittenhouse (Dumont), who is hosting a celebration to welcome back to civilization the famous African explorer Captain Jeffrey Spaulding (Groucho). This time thieves steal one of Dumont's priceless paintings, and again an innocent juvenile is suspected. Chico and Harpo were shady but harmless henchmen who also tried to steal the painting to help the two lovers. But one never questioned how the Marx Brothers were involved in the plot; their presence was the raison d'être for the show. "Hooray for Captain Spaulding" was Groucho's unforgettable comic number, while the lovers got the pleasant but forgettable duets "Watching the Clouds Roll By" and "Who's Been Listening to My Heart?" *Animal Crackers* was also a hit, but it was the Brothers' last Broadway appearance; by 1931, they went west to Hollywood and never returned to the stage.

In 1929, while performing *Animal Crackers* each evening on Broadway, the brothers spent their days in Astoria making the film version of *The Cocoanuts*. Only three songs from the show were retained, a catchy new love duet "When My Dreams Come True" was added, and the plot was cut down to leave room for the comic routines, most memorably a surreal conversation about a "viaduct" and a farcical land auction.

Stage actors Oscar Shaw and Mary Eaton now played the lovers, but much of the rest of the Broadway cast was reconvened, most importantly Dumont and the Brothers. The clanking, primitive sound cameras had to be enclosed in glass booths to cut down on the noise, so *The Cocoanuts* is rather static in its cinematography and artificial in its settings and dance sequences. But whenever the camera catches the Marx Brothers doing one of their polished routines, the film comes to life.

The next year *Animal Crackers* was filmed at the same studio and the result was even more entertaining. All of the show's score was tossed out (save Groucho's two show-stoppers), and one new number, "Why Am I So Romantic?" was added to give the movie the semblance of a musical. The camera work is a bit more sophisticated though still pretty stationary. A slapstick scene set in two adjacent bedrooms was filmed straight on with few cuts, allowing the well-timed piece to play exactly as it had on stage. The supporting actors (Lillian Roth and Kay Francis, in particular) were more interesting this time around, though only Dumont got to interact much with the brothers (if you can call her befuddled demeanor interacting). *Animal Crackers* still feels like a filmed stage show, but, nonetheless, it ranks as a cinema comedy classic.

What makes watching these two Marx Brothers films so fascinating is seeing early sound moviemaking forced to conform to the medium of theater. It was a losing battle, and Hollywood soon learned how to break away from those confines. But in the trial-and-error process, we see two of the earliest and funniest movie musicals being born. It was clear that being faithful to the stage show had its perils, and filmmakers saw few rewards in re-creating Broadway on the screen as it had appeared in the theater.

Yet later films still managed to capture the look and feel of the stage original while using all the wondrous techniques of the cinema. Consider the academic musical *Best Foot Forward* (1941), which was filmed in 1943 with most of the plot, score, cast, and spirit of the original intact. John Cecil Holm's libretto is set in a Pennsylvania prep school called Winsocki, where the big event in question is not a football game but the annual prom. On a whim, student Bud Hooper (Gil Stratton) writes to a famous movie starlet (Rosemary Lane) and invites her to be his date for the dance. As part of a much-needed publicity stunt, she accepts, which causes all kinds of problems with Bud's steady girlfriend

(Maureen Cannon). Also, chaos reigns at the dance when overanxious students practically strip the starlet of all her clothes in their attempt to get souvenirs. It was a lightweight musical comedy in the vein of *Good News, Leave It to Jane*, and other campus shows. The score by Ralph Blane and Hugh Martin boasted the hit fight song "Buckle Down, Winsocki" and some other pleasant numbers. Directed by George Abbott and choreographed by Gene Kelly, *Best Foot Forward* was a surprise hit with a new and engaging cast that also included Kenny Bowers, Tommy Dix, Jack Jordan, June Allyson, and, as the hilarious Blind Date, Nancy Walker. The 1953 MGM film version dropped Abbott and Kelly but kept the same plot, seven of the score's songs (with three new ones by Blane and Martin), and cast members Bowers, Allyson, Walker, Jordan, and Dix, who was elevated to the leading male role. The studio wanted Shirley Temple as the starlet but had to settle for Lucille Ball, then in the so-called glamorous period of her career. (She is actually quite funny as a fading movie star named, accurately enough, Lucille Ball.) The screenplay fiddled with details but was mostly faithful to the stage libretto. One significant change: Winsocki became a military academy to better appeal to wartime moviegoers. Former comic actor Edward Buzzell directed, Charles Walters choreographed the musical numbers, and there was nothing stage-bound about either. *Best Foot Forward* came to life on the screen—a good example of fidelity and success.

Top Banana is a painful example of fidelity and sterility. It is one of the oddest of all musical films, and to watch it is an almost surreal experience. Hy Kraft wrote the 1951 stage libretto, which was an unabashed vehicle for Phil Silvers. He played the Milton Berle–like television comic Jerry Biffle from burlesque whose weekly TV show is given a romantic twist by its soap sponsors, who insist on introducing a singing pair of lovers. Jerry falls for the girl (Judy Lynn), but she prefers her more handsome and better-voiced partner (Lindy Doherty). As with the Marx Brothers' vehicles, plot was secondary, and much of the evening featured some inspired clowning by Silvers and other veterans of vaudeville, most memorably Jack Albertson, Herbie and Joey Faye, and Rose Marie. Johnny Mercer wrote the score which, aside from the catchy title number, was only mildly interesting, but the production numbers were staged with panache on Jo Mielziner's cartoonish sets.

Top Banana ran for 350 performances on Broadway but failed to make a profit or join the ranks of revived musicals.

United Artists bought the screen rights and wisely secured the services of Silvers. But instead of making a real movie of the show, it was simply filmed in the Winter Garden Theatre in 1954 using the cast, musical numbers (minus a few), sets, and even the theatrical lighting of the original production. What they didn't keep was the live audience, which might have made an interesting record of a Broadway performance. But on the screen Silvers and his fellow comics go through their routines with absolutely no audio response from the empty house. There is even a silent curtain call at the end! It's like watching a ghostly rehearsal. (The editors did splice some footage of an audience applauding after each production number.) True, there is no audience for *The Cocoanuts* or *Animal Crackers*, but those were obviously done in a studio. *Top Banana* quite clearly happens on the stage of a theater and the effect is very discomforting. (Making the movie even more bizarre, it was filmed in 3-D with the cast poking their heads or other objects at the camera to show off the newfangled effect.) It has to be the closest copy of all, yet one has to stretch the imagination to begin to re-create what this must have been like on Broadway with a live audience.

Two of the brightest Broadway hits of the 1950s, *The Pajama Game* (1954) and *Damn Yankees* (1955), shared the same producers, director, librettist, choreographer, and songwriters. And both were brought to the screen with pretty much all of the production talent from Broadway. These two films may not be "opened up" as much as other movie musicals, and each shows its theater roots, but both are highly satisfying. *The Pajama Game* may be about labor–management relations in a pajama factory, but such issues are soft-pedaled in Richard Bissell and George Abbott's libretto. The new plant supervisor Sid Sorokin (John Raitt) and the union activist Babe Williams (Janis Paige) find themselves on opposite sides of the bargaining table even as they fall in love to the sounds of Richard Adler and Jerry Ross's merry songs. A subplot concerning the time efficiency expert Hines (Eddie Foy Jr.) and an oversexed secretary Gladys (Carol Haney) supplied the laughs, and both couples were matched up in time for the finale as the workers got a 7½ cent raise. It was all unpretentious fun, and, aided by such hit songs as "Hey, There," "Steam Heat," and

"Hernando's Hideaway" and Bob Fosse's dances, the show ran just over a thousand performances.

So did *Damn Yankees*, which opened on Broadway the next year. Adler and Ross again provided a sparkling score, Fosse did the choreography, and Abbott directed and cowrote the libretto with Douglass Wallop. This Faustian story about a pact with Satan centered on baseball, but the real slugger of the evening was Gwen Verdon who, as the devilish Ray Walston's assistant Lola, tried to seduce baseballer Joe Hardy (Stephen Douglass) away from domestic bliss and into fame and sexual bliss. It was not your usual boy-meets-girl story. Although the plot somewhat fell apart in the second act, *Damn Yankees* was filled with playful ideas and memorable songs and dances. Verdon was a dancing star, and Abbott and Fosse saw to it that this show really moved.

But what tended to get bogged down were the movie versions of these back-to-back hits. Abbott codirected both films with Hollywood veteran Stanley Donen, and there seems to be more Abbott theatrics than Donen cinematics in each effort. *The Pajama Game* is the livelier of the two. Just about the whole cast was reassembled for the 1957 movie, but with Doris Day now playing Babe. The interiors seem fairly realistic, but some of the exteriors have the feel of painted scenery. Fosse's dances remain thrilling, and the production number "Once a Year Day" at the company picnic seems to burst all over the landscape. Another number that translated well was "I'll Never Be Jealous Again," a merry soft-shoe with Foy and Reta Shaw that seemed to glide through the factory. Eleven of the stage score's fifteen songs made it to the screen, and each one works.

On the other hand, too much of *Damn Yankees* has the feel of a filmed play about it. The 1958 movie has a few requisite shots of crowds in the baseball stadium, but most of the other scenes are stagy. Wonderful vaudeville turns like the baseballers' quintet "(You Gotta Have) Heart," the devil's soft-shoe "The Good Old Days," and Lola's sexy "A Little Brains—A Little Talent" are delivered to the camera as the fourth wall in a theater, but, without an audience to play to, they seem forced. Verdon's vampy "Whatever Lola Wants" as she tries to seduce Joe (Tab Hunter) in the locker room works better because her focus is on a character. Also, the opening number "Six Months Out of Every Year" uses montage and split screen effectively to show various households in Washington, D.C., watching baseball on television.

Stagy or not, Fosse's choreography never disappoints, and two high-lights of *Damn Yankees* are the playful hoe-down number "Shoeless Joe from Hannibal, Mo." and the highly stylized pas de deux "Who's Got the Pain?" which Fosse himself danced with Verdon. He and Hunter were the only major cast additions to the film, the rest (including secondary players Rae Allen and Jean Stapleton) coming straight from the Broadway production. It was indeed another close copy. Since both *The Pajama Game* and *Damn Yankees* are shows that are often revised and revived on stage, audiences who have seen vibrant live productions may find the two movie versions a bit dated and static. But only in the films can you see some of the original players and choreography, and that alone is more than enough reason to cherish them.

Another 1950s hit that saw its star performance preserved on screen was *Bells Are Ringing* (1956) with the great Judy Holliday as the life-fulfilling telephone service operator Ella Peterson. In her finest musical role, Holliday dominated the Broadway production even with a top-drawer book and score by Betty Comden, Adolph Green, and Jule Styne and estimable staging by Jerome Robbins. Ella falls for one of her unseen clients, the playwright Jeff Moss (Sydney Chaplin), who is suffering from writer's block. It was a nice twist on the traditional boy-meets-girl formula, and big-hearted Ella's gullibility and resourcefulness kept the plot in motion. "Just in Time" and "The Party's Over" were the two standout hit songs, but it was delicious character numbers such as "It's a Perfect Relationship" and "I'm Going Back" that propelled the action.

The 1960 movie version wisely retained Holliday, a few supporting players (including Jean Stapleton again as the owner of the telephone service), much of the libretto, and twelve of the sixteen songs. Vincente Minnelli directed, and, using some actual Manhattan locations, the movie seems to flow all over town. But there are disappointments as well. Dean Martin as Jeff made his lightweight leading role so weightless it practically disappeared, and most of the show's dancing (devised by Robbins and Bob Fosse on Broadway) disappeared. Charles O'Curran was the film's choreographer, and one can almost taste his frustration as the play's big dance number "Mu-Cha-Cha" is reduced on screen to a few steps and then a quick exit. But *Bells Are Ringing* is still an enjoyable close copy and an admirable record of one of Broadway's best performances.

Li'l Abner (1956) opened the same year as *Bells Are Ringing*, and its 1959 film version is also an accurate re-creation of the stage show. Al Capp's politically potent, fantastical comic strip about the denizens of rundown, useless Dogpatch, USA, was turned into a raucous musical by librettists Norman Panama and Melvin Frank and songwriters Gene de Paul (music) and Johnny Mercer (lyrics). While the naive, full-bosomed Daisy Mae (Edith Adams) tries to get her lackadaisical sweetheart Abner Yokum (Peter Palmer) to marry her, the whole town is in an uproar because Dogpatch has been deemed by the U.S. government to be the ideal spot to test atomic bombs. Added to this is a subplot concerning the greedy General Bullmoose (Howard St. John) and his oversexed assistant Appassionata von Climax (Tina Louise) trying to steal a formula devised by Mammy Yokum (Charlotte Rae) that transforms weaklings into beefy hunks like her son. Michael Kidd directed and choreographed the production like one long Sadie Hawkins Day race that delighted audiences for 693 performances. It is a broad, obvious show, but, after all, it was based on a comic strip.

The 1959 film used Palmer, Louise, St. John, and others from the stage (most memorably Stubby Kaye as Marryin' Sam); rehired Kidd to direct and do the choreography with Dee Dee Wood; included a dozen songs from the Broadway score; and even kept William and Jean Eckart's cartoonish scenic designs and Alvin Colt's outrageous costumes. But this didn't look like *Top Banana*. Filmed in a studio, Dogpatch became a colorful world of cutout shanties and exaggerated flora and fauna; it wasn't real, but neither was it a theater set. *Li'l Abner* works as a film while being faithful to the stage production. The dances, for example, are not presented with one focal point, as though the camera was the audience. Such vivacious numbers as "(Don't That Take the) Rag Offen the Bush" and the "Sadie Hawkins Day" ballet move among the ragtag houses and oversized vegetation as only a movie can. (This was no happy accident; Kidd had choreographed the robust dances in *Seven Brides for Seven Brothers* five years earlier.) *Li'l Abner* is an odd, one-of-a-kind film that accurately re-creates an odd, one-of-a-kind Broadway musical.

Also odd, but more sentimental and heartwarming, is *Flower Drum Song* (1958), Rodgers and Hammerstein's only musical comedy. It is not the plot that is unusual (it has the traditional pair of lovers, one romantic and the other comic) but the milieu: contemporary Chinese Americans in San Francisco's Chinatown. It is one of the team's few shows set in the present, and its score might be considered their most "modern," even with all of the Asian influences in it. The Chinese immigrant Mei Li (Miyoshi Umeki) is contracted to wed nightclub owner Sammy Fong (Larry Blyden), but he has fallen for the fully Americanized entertainer Linda Low (Pat Suzuki), who sings songs like "I Enjoy Being a Girl" and dances half-naked at the club to numbers like "Fan Tan Fannie." Sammy tries to foist Mei Li on his pal Wang Ta (Ed Kenny), whose father is trying to find a nice, traditional girl for his son. The fact that Wang Ta is also smitten with Linda gives the plot its main complication, though the story might just as well be described as the conflict between one generation and another, of new American ways versus old Asian ways. Joseph Fields and Oscar Hammerstein wrote the libretto, which was lighthearted and filled with musical comedy jokes not usually found in Rodgers and Hammerstein's other works. Gene Kelly flew in from Hollywood to direct the glittering production, and Carol Haney staged the dances. The show was popular enough to play six hundred times (the team's biggest hit since *The King and I* seven years earlier), and some of the songs joined the ranks of R & H favorites, such as "A Hundred Million Miracles" "You Are Beautiful," and "Love, Look Away."

Despite its unlikely prospects for success in Peoria and other middle American markets, Universal bought the rights and gave the 1961 film version excellent production values. Chinatown was re-created on the soundstage, and the many locales gleamed with the bright colors of the Orient. Umeki and Juanita Hall (as Wang Ta's funny aunt) were the only original cast members hired for the screen, but the new players were just as pleasing: Nancy Kwan as Linda, James Shigeta as Wang Ta, and Benson Fong as his father. Non-Asian actor Larry Blyden had gotten away playing Sammy on stage with ethnic makeup, but (thankfully) Jack Soo was recruited for the role on screen; he is easily the best one in the picture. Hermes Pan choreographed the musical numbers (only one song was cut from the Broadway score), and, with several of the principals dubbed, it sounded as good as it looked. Fields and Hammerstein's screenplay is pretty close to their libretto, so, all in all, *Flower Drum Song* is a fairly accurate re-creation of the original. Some aspects of the film may seem a bit patronizing to Asian Americans today (the 2002 Broadway revival made major book and even character changes), but the movie does not offend. It still remains the only Hollywood musical overflowing with Asian talent, which gives it a distinction if not more than a touch of pride.

Another contemporary musical hit of the same era (and there aren't all that many of them) was *How to Succeed in Business without Really Trying* (1961). One of the few musical satires to find popularity on Broadway, this show veers away from sentimentality and the usual musical trappings and aims its delectable barbs at everyone in the world of big business. J. Pierpont Finch (Robert Morse) rises from window washer to chairman of the board of the World Wide Wicket Company, his tale a spoof on the old Horatio Alger lesson. Finch is not without charm (both Morse and the character used charm disarmingly) but, in truth, is devious, self-serving, and unfeeling. Finch sings the show's big love song, "I Believe in You," to himself in the mirror. His relationship with secretary Rosemary (Bonnie Scott) is a very off-handed one, as if she was there because musicals demand that there be a love interest. But Abe Burrows's libretto concentrates on the business types, from the ineffectual top boss J. B. Biggley (Rudy Vallee) to his backstabbing nephew Bud Frump (Charles Nelson Reilly) to the incompetent but overendowed secretary Hedy la Rue (Virginia Martin). Burrows also directed and the dances Bob Fosse devised were all in a satirical tone, such as the office workers' romp as they desperately sing of their caffeine addiction in "Coffee Break" and the stylized musical lesson "A Secretary Is Not a Toy." Frank Loesser wrote such an unsentimental and integrated score that none of the songs became a hit, save "I Believe in You" when sung out of context. There is even an anthem near the end of the show that satirizes the Rodgers and Hammerstein models like "You'll Never Walk Alone" or "Climb Ev'ry Mountain." Sung by the board members, "Brotherhood of Man" is just as insincere as the gamblers' revival number "Sit Down, You're Rockin' the Boat" in Loesser's *Guys and Dolls*. Both are eleven o'clock blockbusters, and both lie through their teeth. *How to Succeed* still succeeds on stage because it doesn't date. The roles of secretaries and women in business have altered somewhat, but the show was always about finessing your way through a rather arbitrary network of people to achieve success through manipulation rather than talent. *How to Succeed* stands with *Of Thee I Sing* as Broadway's two great musical satires.

Before considering the film version of *How to Succeed*, let us look at *Of Thee I Sing* for a moment. Although it was a major hit, won a Pulitzer Prize, and was profitably revived, the Gershwins' musical was never filmed. How could such a musical comedy masterpiece be ignored by Tinsel Town? Frankly, the studios didn't like satire, musical or not. They didn't trust it (often they didn't understand it), and they didn't know how to sell it. Sentiment is easy to measure and manufacture, but how do you anticipate the public's reaction to satire? If Hollywood wanted to satirize politics, business, high society, even moviemaking, it did so through screwball comedy or other forms of farce. The satirical aspects came *after* the laughs instead of causing the laughs. The cockeyed favorite *My Man Godfrey* (1936) is a good example. The movie is a vicious look at the Depression and the idle upper class, yet it doesn't seem vicious. The picture is a farce first, a satire second. *Of Thee I Sing* must have frightened the studios; it's *all* satire. Better to have Frank Capra make a preachy melodrama about political corruption and give it a happy ending. That they understood.

Thirty years later a different generation of movie moguls looked at *How to Succeed* on Broadway and had to consider how a film could be made of it. The big studios were wary, so the smaller Mirisch Corporation bought the rights, retained much of the talent from the stage production, and released it through United Artists. Although the screen adaptation and directing chores went to David Swift, the 1967 movie closely follows Burrows in word and manner. Dale Moreda re-created Fosse's choreography, three-fourths of the score was kept, and several players from Broadway were hired, including Morse and Vallee. The stage production used bright, cartoonish sets and primary colors in the costumes. The movie had to go with real offices and furniture, but the palette is delightfully garish, and the whole look of *How to Succeed* is dazzlingly 1960s. There were a few concessions made for film audiences, primarily having to do with the lack of sincere romance in the story. Rosemary (Michele Lee) sings a teary rendition of "I Believe in You" to her sweetheart Finch, suggesting that perhaps he possesses the warmth and affection that she displays. It is a false moment in the movie but one that many deemed necessary. Much of the difficulty over Finch's selfishness is solved by Morse's performance. He is so boyishly likable that audiences forgive his shortcomings and actually want him to succeed. Vallee comes across a bit tired and too low-key in the film, but he is a nice contrast to all those blustering bosses that Hollywood used to favor. Anthony Teague's Frump is not as funny as Reilly's was, but Maureen Arthur is marvelously transparent as Hedy, even if two of her songs were cut. *How to Succeed* is one of the most enjoyable of the close copies; the fact that the movie remains a potent satire makes it even more valuable.

Very few Off-Broadway musicals have been filmed, and *Godspell* (1971), with its cast of ten energetic players acting out parables and scenes from St. Matthew's Gospel, did not seem a likely candidate for the screen. But *Godspell* was so popular (over three thousand performances in New York and seven road companies touring the States) that a film version was made and released in 1973 when the original stage production was still running. John-Michael Tebelak wrote and directed the inventive Off-Broadway musical that used vaudeville, mime, acrobatics, improvisation, and whatever else to dramatize the last days of Jesus (Stephen Nathan). Stephen Schwartz's eclectic score was just as inventive, using folk, rock, soft-shoe, and gospel numbers with unpretentious abandon. The whole thing was staged with little scenery (a few large blocks and ladders in front of a chain link fence), a few hand props, and the cast dressed as 1960s flower children. *Godspell* is more a celebration than a narrative, but it is a contagious theatrical piece and still has wide appeal. Yet how does one capture a celebration on film? The Off-Broadway production involved the audience more than most musicals did (patrons were even invited on stage to partake of wine at intermission), and you found yourself participating rather than just watching it. But it is difficult to participate in a film (unless you are at a midnight showing of *The Rocky Horror Picture Show*). All the same, *Godspell* was so popular that the studios could not ignore it.

Director-writer David Greene took on the challenge and came up with a workable solution. Manhattan became the setting for the gospel story, and it was filmed on location, from under bridges to the middle of Times Square to the top of the World Trade Center. Jesus (Victor Garber) and his followers dashed about New York, stopping at interesting (and beautifully photographed) places to tell a parable or sing one of the vibrant songs. Never was a stage musical "opened up" like this one. The feeling was panoramic, so some of the intimate numbers suffered. Although the text itself was not altered much, the movie did sometimes seem more like a celebration of Manhattan than Jesus and his teachings. But the important moments still played, and the old story set in a modern city gave the movie a quirky juxtaposition that the play didn't have. So as different as it looked, *Godspell* turned out to be a close copy. Four of the Off-Broadway cast members were in the film, the score was kept intact (with a new Schwartz song, "Beautiful City," added to tie in the Manhattan concept), and even the stage's ragtag costumes were duplicated. Does the film have the look and feel of the theater piece? Not really. But a literal duplication of the Off-Broadway celebration onto film would have been rather ineffective. At least the *Godspell* that Greene made was a movie.

It's hard enough to film a musical with no defined scenery or locale, but how does one make a movie out of a show whose action mostly takes place in one room? That is one of the many problems *1776* (1969) had to face. The Broadway musical is unusual on several fronts. It has one of the longest librettos of any show—some dialogue scenes going on for nearly thirty minutes without music. The cast of characters, mostly delegates to the Continental Congress in Philadelphia in 1776, are historical figures who debate rather than meet, lose, and find the girl. There are only two women in the musical, both wives of delegates, so romance was limited to fond expressions of marital affection or coy references to sex. Sherman Edwards's songs include such unlikely styles as the minuet, folk ballad, and Gilbert and Sullivan choral pastiches. And the whole thing pretty much takes place in the meeting room in Independence Hall. Yet *1776* plays beautifully on stage, and it entertains and moves one even as it breaks so many rules. Much of the credit must go to Peter Stone's libretto. A musical play about the debates and conflicts leading up to the ratification and signing of the Declaration of Independence is an unlikely prospect for success. But Stone managed to blend history and showmanship into a funny, thought-provoking script that made the issues both clear and interesting. Edwards's songs range from clever to silly to enthralling, and they would not work without the beautifully written libretto. With an impressive cast featuring William Daniels as John Adams, Howard Da Silva as Benjamin Franklin, and

Ken Howard as Thomas Jefferson, and a handsome production (designed by Jo Mielziner) that re-created the famous meeting room even as it evoked the period, 1776 felt like a full-fledged Broadway musical. The unlikely hit ran 1,217 performances on Broadway and continues to be revived today. Still a curiosity, perhaps, but a popular one.

1776 obviously needed to be "opened up" for a film version. And that was what happened in 1972: it was opened up . . . obviously. Few movie musicals are more awkward in their attempt not to look like a play, all the time appearing as stagebound as one of the early talkies. Director Peter Hunt, who had helmed the Broadway production, and Stone's screenplay seem to bend over backward to find reasons to get the action out of that room. The characters dance up and down the staircase, frolic in nearby gardens, even sing while riding horseback, all in their effort to make us think this is a movie. But little of the opening up works. The exteriors look pretty and romantic but seem forced. The few shots of period streets and crowds soon lead into artificial cul de sacs where even the flowers and trees behave like extras used as set dressing. The attempts to portray flashbacks or letters to Mrs. Adams back in Boston result in confusing and annoying filmmaking. Even the scenes kept in the meeting room are filmed with frantic camera work, quick cutting, and arty gauzes and filters to keep the action cinematic. The heartbreaking solo "Momma Look Sharp" is ruined by theatrical follow spots and cross fading like one would find in a 1970s television variety show. Most disconcerting, sometimes Stone's theatrical scenes and juicy dialogue sound phony in a production where close-ups and obviousness abound.

1776 never feels like a movie, and neither does it conjure up the essence of the stage production. Yet it is, on the surface, a close copy. The three principals and ten other cast members from Broadway appear in the film. The entire score is kept (though the song criticizing the conservative right called "Cool, Cool, Considerate Men" was edited out at the suggestion of then-president Nixon!), and an awful lot of the dialogue remains. But this kind of fidelity brings little satisfaction. There are things to appreciate in 1776: some delightful performances, a few intriguing book scenes, the full-voiced singing, and the subject matter itself. But this is a copy that often comes out faded and out of focus.

For something completely different, and I do mean different, there is *Hedwig and the Angry Inch* (1998), an Off-Broadway cult hit that was filmed in 2001 with the complete score and all the principal artists on board. This rock musical takes the form of a concert with Hedwig (John Cameron Mitchell) narrating his/her tale between songs. And what a tale it is! Young Hansel is born in East Berlin the year the wall goes up, grows into a confused transexual, then marries an American GI to get to the States but has to have a sex change operation to qualify. The operation is botched, and Hedwig (he uses his mother's name and passport) is left with an inch of undetermined sexual embarrassment. Once in America, she is dumped by the GI, has an affair with a military brat named Tommy Gnosis who becomes a rock star using Hedwig's songs, and then he, too, abandons her. Left singing rock and roll dirges in third-class dives, Hedwig continues on, searching for a personal and sexual identity. The bewigged, heavily made-up Mitchell was amazing, singing the rock score by Stephen Trask, telling his/her story in a phony German accent (Mitchell also wrote the libretto), and exuding a strange sensuality that was sexy without knowing which sex it was. The little musical quickly caught on and ran over two years.

Mitchell not only wrote and starred in the film but also directed it, which may have been too much of a good thing because the movie often gets bogged down in the cinematic tricks, and the bizarre storyline is not always clear. Mitchell does have some good ideas, though, such as using a cockeyed kind of primitive animation to illustrate the songs, most effectively in "Origin of Love." People who were only talked about on stage, such as the GI and Tommy, were cast and given scenes in the film, yet the characters rarely seemed as interesting as they were when described by Hedwig in a concert setting. Andrea Martin is funny as the agent booking Hedwig and her band into the most unlikely places, and some of the movie's best camerawork is catching the bored or baffled patrons. Here is a case of opening up the action for the screen but only occasionally bringing anything new to light. But the things that made *Hedwig and the Angry Inch* rock on stage are still there: Trask's score, the weird concept, and Mitchell's astonishing performance. What more can you ask for in a close copy?

CHAPTER FOUR

~

Star Light, Star Bright

Is there a difference between a stage star and a movie star when it comes to musicals? Looking at how few were successful in both media, there must be. Al Jolson, Julie Andrews, Danny Kaye, Ray Bolger, Eddie Cantor, Barbra Streisand, and a handful of others managed to shine while singing both on stage and on the screen. But what of Ethel Merman, Carol Channing, Alfred Drake, Gwen Verdon, Richard Kiley, Barbara Cook, Jerry Orbach, and all the others who were rarely given the opportunity to re-create their stage performances on film? Was it lack of talent or movie politics? Or was it just a matter of who is photogenic and who isn't?

Determining why the camera loves some people while others fail to glitter has puzzled filmmakers from the days of the silents. Studios groomed and promoted certain stars only to find the public wasn't buying. It happened to Anna Sten, Marian Davies, and even Lucille Ball until television embraced her. Other times moviegoers themselves chose someone from the background and made him or her a star. It happened to Van Johnson, Audrey Hepburn, and others. But how do you explain a player who is already an established Broadway star but is denied cinema stardom? Or the stage celebrity who gets the part but doesn't light up the screen? The history of filmed Broadway musicals is filled with examples of both cases. Mistakes have been made by the studios that boggle the minds of those looking back with the luxury of hindsight. Yet for every mistake that was made, there was probably one that was avoided. We forget how close we came to seeing Cary Grant play Henry Higgins in *My Fair Lady* or Frank Sinatra as Billy Bigelow in *Carousel*. There was more than mere stupidity at work here. There *is* a difference between a stage star and a movie star.

The earliest silent screen idols were celebrated for either their attractiveness or their comic abilities. The same could pretty much be said for the early stage stars as well, though one can find more exceptions for Broadway than for the movies. When sound came in, new factors were added to the making of a screen star. The voice was now as important as the face, whether the movie was a comedy or a romance. A comic star did not have to look or sound attractive but a romantic leading player sure had to. This rule was broken frequently on Broadway, with stars like Helen Hayes, Ruth Gordon, Alfred Lunt, Lynn Fontanne, Colleen Dewhurst, and others rising above mediocre looks and radiating their own unique quality. But musicals demanded something different, particularly musical comedy. The biggest stage stars of this genre were actually disproportionate in their features. Without calling them unattractive, one would have to admit that there was something in the facial makeup that was almost freakish: the overextended cheeks of Mary Martin, the endless forehead of Al Jolson, the puffy face of Ethel Merman, the bulging eyes of Carol Channing, the long nose of Ray Bolger, and so on. In musical comedy, these deviations from the norm made the actors distinctive and memorable. They did not look like the average chorus player, and they weren't—they were special. On stage, such performers appeared to be attractive because such exaggerated features read well in a theater. But in the movies, "special' is something altogether different. Studios preferred the softer features of a Jeanette MacDonald or the solid profile of a Gordon MacRae. Perhaps audiences did as well, though in most cases the moviemakers made that decision for them.

Another difference between stage and screen stars is their recognition factor. Before the advent of the movies, Broadway stars toured the nation, bringing their famous performances to even small cities and rural theaters. Actors like William Gillette and Maude Adams were not just New York favorites; they were beloved across the country. But by the 1920s, the nationwide stars were movie stars. There were still tours with Broadway celebrities in them, but audiences made a clear distinction between a movie star and a stage actor. The fact that moviemaking was centered in California while the theater capital was New York City did not help matters. Unlike in London, Rome, Paris, and other cities abroad where theaters and film studios were close to each other, American actors had to concentrate on one medium or the other. Several managed to have careers in both but rarely simultaneously. So audiences tended to categorize Leslie Howard as a movie star (even though he appeared in many plays) and Jessica Tandy as a stage star (despite her many films). Movie studios made the same distinction, and when they cast their film musicals, they usually dismissed the Broadway name from the list of possibilities and went looking for a bankable cinema personality. The important word here is *bankable*. Most decisions in film casting were (and still are) a matter of finances. For example, in the late 1960s and early 1970s, Barbra Streisand was the only female on the list of the ten most popular movie stars. So she was cast in a series of musical films regardless of whether she was right for the role. That was a financial decision rather than an aesthetic one. Yet as much as Broadway tries to promote its stars, you'll rarely find such reasoning in theater casting.

Which brings us to another distinction between stage and movie performers. A long-running Broadway musical has to be more than one stellar performance. The show itself must be some sort of star if it hopes to survive cast changes on Broadway and future productions elsewhere. In the old days, an Ethel Merman vehicle could recoup its investment during the length of her contract. But by the 1970s, that was no longer possible with even the biggest names. Notice how the longest-running stage musicals, from *A Chorus Line* to *Cats* to *The Lion King*, are not star shows. Broadway hits need long legs, and no one star can run that long. Of course, there are no casting changes once a movie is made, and the star and the film are forever linked together. If you get Judy Garland or Gene Kelly once, you get them forever. One doesn't have to picture *Top Hat* without Fred Astaire and Ginger Rogers; it's never going to happen. Movie stars are eternal; stage stars are for the present, no matter how much they linger in one's memory. Yet you cannot dismiss the argument that a live stage performance is so much more involving than movie acting. Perhaps. What Jolson did with a packed Broadway theater could never be recreated in any movie house.

Maybe that is the final distinction between the two types of performers. Broadway stars must connect with the live audience; film stars only need to be observed in order to work their magic. It is hard to picture Nelson Eddy and Jeanette MacDonald playing off a live audience in a theater. But that wasn't their charm, just as the way Carol Channing worked the crowd can never really happen on the screen. That's her charm.

Let us look at some musical theater stars and their film careers, starting with the screen's first singing sensation, Al Jolson. *The Jazz Singer* was a 1925 nonmusical play starring George Jessel as a cantor's son who wants to go into show business. Warner Brothers probably chose the property for its first full-length experiment with sound because it was a strong story with a few opportunities for songs. Only these musical numbers were to have sound; the rest of the melodrama would remain silent with titles for the dialogue. Jessel was to repeat his performance on screen, but he demanded more money when he heard it was to have sound, so Jolson was hired. He was Broadway's biggest male star at the time, with whole musical shows written for him to play the black-face comic character Gus and sing his "Mammy" songs. The role of Jakie Rabinowitz in *The Jazz Singer* was ideal for Jolson (efforts had been made for him to do the play before Jessel was hired), and his screen performance still fascinates. Jolson burst into song in movie houses across the nation, and audiences were thrilled. They were just as amazed when he ad-libbed some lines of dialogue as they were to hear a screen character speak for the first time. In some ways the sound revolution came from this phenomenon rather than the singing portion of *The Jazz Singer*. But either way, the first talkie was also the first movie musical.

The next year Jolson made *The Singing Kid*, another silent melodrama with sound for the musical numbers only. He played singing waiter Al Stone whose life falls apart when his wife leaves him and his young son dies. The tearjerker had a hopeful ending (a good woman brings Al out of his stupor), and the film was an even bigger hit than *The Jazz Singer*. (Two songs written for the movie, "Sonny Boy" and "There's a Rainbow 'Round My Shoulder," were also huge hits.)

Jolson's movie career would never reach this level of success until the twin biopics *The Jolson Story* and *Jolson Sings Again* in the 1940s, and only his singing voice was heard in those. Most of his eleven movies in between were not successful, and Jolson never became a durable film star. Perhaps he was too big, too over-the-top for the screen. This quality became more obvious in the 1930s when his style seemed so brash compared to Bing Crosby's or Fred Astaire's.

Of Jolson's dozen Broadway hits, he only appeared in movie versions of two of them. *Big Boy* (1925) was a loosely structured stage vehicle in which Jolson's Gus was a put-upon Negro stable boy who ends up as a jockey winning the Kentucky Derby. Singing songs such as "Keep Smiling at Trouble" and "It All Depends on You," Jolson was the whole show. In fact, he was known to dismiss the rest of the cast early some nights and just entertain the audiences at the Winter Garden with a one-man singing extravaganza. Such high jinks were not possible in the 1930 movie version, but Jolson still dominates the picture, singing and joking his way through the thin plot. In fact, *Big Boy* on screen has the feel of a one-man show. But no one complained at the Winter Garden, and the box office was healthy in movie theaters as well.

Jolson returned to Broadway after his early film triumphs and starred in *The Wonder Bar* (1931), an adaptation of a German musical that had been a hit in London. No Gus, no blackface, no loose Jolson vehicle this time. He played another Al, the proprietor of a swanky Paris cabaret, who battles the dirty dealings of a male dancer out to steal away the club's female attraction. The show was not a success, so after ten weeks Jolson left and returned to Hollywood. (He would only appear in one more New York show nine years later.) The 1934 film version, shortened to *Wonder Bar*, featured Jolson, but this was no solo show, either. Dolores Del Rio, Dick Powell, Kay Francis, and Ricardo Cortez also starred, and the film gave Jolson only a few opportunities to break out and dominate the screen. One unfortunate Busby Berkeley production number, "Goin' to Heaven on a Mule," allowed Jolson to don blackface once again and ride up to St. Peter's gate, where hundreds of black angels frolicked through the clouds and ate watermelon and pork chops. It was offensive even in its day and did Jolson's career no good.

He made five more film musicals after *Wonder Bar* (three of them in cameo roles only), but none were major hits. Jolson was a stage star but had turned his back on Broadway; Hollywood soon turned its back on him. Only the twin biographies and his enduring recording career kept him in the limelight during his later years.

The top female Broadway star of the 1920s was Marilyn Miller, a diminutive blonde singer and dancer who lit up the stage with her endearing persona. She came from vaudeville and was featured in revues before becoming the Roaring Twenties' favorite ingenue; she was *Sally*, *Sunny*, *Rosalie*, and other Cinderella-like heroines. Miller only made three films, but two of them gave her the opportunity to re-create her stage performances.

Sally (1920) was a charming rags-to-riches Broadway musical scripted by Guy Bolton and scored by Jerome Kern, Clifford Grey, and others. Sally Green is an orphan who washes dishes in a Greenwich Village eatery and dreams of becoming a *Follies* star. It all comes true, of course, thanks to her pal "Connie," the ex–Duke Constantine of Czechogovinia (Leon Errol), the wily agent Otis Hooper (Walter Catlett) who passes her off as a foreign ballerina, and the handsome young heir Blair Farquar (Irving Fisher) who falls in love with her. The score was filled with such gems as "Whip-Poor-Will" and "Wild Rose," but the musical highlight of the evening was Miller's simple but penetrating rendition of "Look for the Silver Lining" as she washed dishes in the restaurant kitchen. *Sally* ran 570 performances.

Sally's follow-up, *Sunny* (1925), ran nearly as long. Kern again provided a superb score with Otto Harbach and Oscar Hammerstein penning the lyrics and the libretto. Sunny Peters is a feisty bareback rider in a circus in England. When she is smitten with the American tourist Tom Warren (Paul Frawley), Sunny stows away on his ship heading back to New York to be near him. But, to enter the country, she must have an American husband, so she weds Tom's pal Jim (Jack Donahue). A quick divorce and Sunny ends up with Tom. It was a weak narrative that was spiced up with circus acts, a hunting scene in Britain, and Miller's considerable talents.

Bolton and William Anthony McGuire came up with a far-fetched libretto for Miller's *Rosalie* (1928), which included songs by George and Ira Gershwin, Sigmund Romberg, and P. G. Wodehouse. This time Miller was Princess Rosalie of Romanza, who is so beloved by the West Point cadet Richard Fay (Jack Donahue) that he flies solo over the Atlantic to be with her. But as dashing as he is, Richard is a commoner, and only by having Rosalie's father (Frank Morgan) abdicate the throne can the couple be united. It was all nonsense, but Miller made it work, captivating audiences with her delectable dancing princess for 335 performances.

After *Rosalie*, Miller went west to try her luck in the movies. She made her film debut as *Sally* in 1929, and the camera managed to capture some of her stage luster. It is an overstuffed production with the tiny dancer surrounded by hundreds of extras, but Miller comes across well. Alexander Gray is Blair and Joe E. Brown is "Connie," and Miller has great rapport with both of them.

In 1930, Miller made *Sunny*, and she seemed even more comfortable on the screen. She was partnered with Lawrence Gray and Joe Donahue this time, and both her dancing and singing appeared more polished. Although neither film was a blockbuster at the box office, Miller was establishing herself as a screen star. But it was not to be. After appearing in the film musical *Her Majesty Love* in 1931 and two more stints on Broadway, Miller died of poisoning at the age of thirty-seven. Would she have joined Irene Dunne and Jeanette MacDonald as one of the queens of movie musicals? It is difficult to say. Miller was primarily a dancer rather than a singer, and she possessed a theater singing voice rather than an operatic one. But the camera liked her, and her three movie performances hold up well.

A year after Miller's death, MGM filmed *Rosalie* (1937) with tap dancer Eleanor Powell in the title role. The two women were quite the opposite in physical stature and dancing style, so it is hard to picture Miller in this rat-a-tat-tat production. But one cannot help but speculate what film performances Miller might have given had she lived.

Although Helen Morgan lived a few years longer than Miller, her life was much more tragic. She also came from vaudeville, and her first big break was playing the title role of *Sally* in the 1924 touring production. Morgan's emotional problems and bouts with alcoholism limited her career, yet she soon established herself as one of America's finest torch singers. Her most famous Broadway role (and the only one she got to recreate on film) was the mulatto Julie in *Show Boat* (1927). The character was as tortured as the actress herself, keeping her bloodlines a secret and turning to drink when her husband leaves her. Morgan's renditions of "Can't Help Lovin' Dat Man" and "Bill" were legendary, and she got to sing both in the 1936 film version of *Show Boat*. (It was the last of the ten movies she made.) Like Miller, Morgan was a small woman, and her voice was a thin but effective soprano. She managed to command attention in a large theater, but one suspects that film was the medium that captured her best.

Morgan's performance as the aging burlesque queen Kitty Darling in *Applause* (1929) even surpasses *Show Boat* for its raw power. That same year she had her other Broadway triumph as the beer hall waitress Addie Schmidt in *Sweet Adeline*, a dark musical drama about the rise and fall of a singing star. The Jerome Kern–Oscar Hammerstein score provided Morgan with one of her signature songs, "Why Was I Born?" as well as "Here Am I," "Some Girl Is on Your Mind," and "Don't Ever Leave Me."

Perhaps Morgan's difficulties were known around Hollywood, because when *Sweet Adeline* was filmed in 1935, Irene Dunne played Addie. It's a rather dull film even though the plot and most of the score from Broadway were used. But Dunne failed to capture the desperation of the character, and her interpretations of the torch songs were admirable but not scorching. Morgan died at the age of forty-one though she looked older than that six years earlier in the film of *Show Boat*. But on stage or screen, she was one of the giants of the musical form.

Two very popular male performers on Broadway during the early decades of the century had quite different experiences in Hollywood. George M. Cohan, the one-man dynamo who thought nothing of writing, directing, producing, and starring in his own Broadway musicals, never got to re-create any of his stage portrayals on screen. Cohan first became a major Broadway player as the cocky American jockey Johnny riding the Derby in London in *Little Johnny Jones* (1904). When a film version was made in 1929, Cohan was passed over for comic Eddie Buzzell even though Cohan was still a hot item on Broadway. It's an early and primitive movie saved only by Buzzell and his bouncy way of delivering "The Yankee Doodle Boy" and "Give My Regards to Broadway."

Cohan appeared in one film, *The Phantom President* (1932), and he is quite interesting to watch. But he preferred the stage. Despite their popularity, few of Cohan's other shows were filmed, though the songs popped up in numerous pictures. But he did live to see James Cagney impersonate him so well in the biopic *Yankee Doodle Dandy* (1942).

Eddie Cantor, on the other hand, had little difficulty crossing over to films. The thin, hyperactive comic with the protruding "banjo eyes" was a Broadway star by 1917 and was featured in several revues and book musicals before talkies came in (even making a silent movie version of his hit *Kid Boots* in 1926). His other stage hit was *Whoopee* (1928), a daffy affair with Cantor playing the hypochondriac Henry Williams who goes to a rural California retreat for his health. The nervous fellow somehow gets involved helping a ranch owner's daughter, Sally Morgan (Frances Upton), who is being forced to marry the local sheriff. Henry helps her escape but ends up hiding from the law, disguising himself as an Indian on the nearby reservation, and then passing himself off as a black-faced singing waiter. It was foolish fun all designed to show off Cantor's peculiar talents. *Whoopee* also boasted two song hits, "Makin' Whoopee" and "Love Me or Leave Me," the second sung by Ruth Etting.

Cantor made his feature-length talkie debut with the 1930 film version of *Whoopee* and he would go on to make ten more movie musicals, most of them box office successes. Aside from Cantor's vivacious clowning and some terrific new songs by Walter Donaldson and Gus Kahn ("My Baby Just Cares for Me," in particular), the movie *Whoopee* is notable because it marked the beginning of Busby Berkeley's film career. He staged the dance numbers, using a single camera to move in for close-ups of the chorus girls and to photograph their dance patterns from above. In one number, "Stetson," led by Cantor and Ethel Shutta, the chorines popped up one by one from behind a ledge, each one donning a Stetson hat as she rose. It's a clever number typical of a clever film. Because he rarely returned to Broadway, most of Cantor's subsequent movie musicals were not based on his shows but were tailor made by the studios to please his many fans.

A generation after Cantor started on Broadway, three comic actors found some success on both stage and screen, though only rarely in the same vehicle. Jack Haley, Ray Bolger, and Danny Kaye are all remembered now as screen comedians, but each had substantial Broadway credits as well.

Haley made his musical stage debut in 1924 and by the end of the decade was featured as the comic lead in *Follow Thru* (1929). He played the girl-shy department store heir Jack Martin who got caught up in the

shenanigans during a women's golf championship. Haley's innocent be-
fuddlement and rolling eyes as he crooned "Button Up Your Overcoat"
and other songs made him a star, and Paramount signed him for the
1930 film version. He was equally funny on the screen and went on to
make twenty more movie musicals over the next sixteen years, no role
more memorable than his Tin Woodsman in *The Wizard of Oz* (1939).
But Haley also returned to Broadway for four more musicals, one of
which was filmed with him in the cast. *Higher and Higher* (1940) was
one of Rodgers and Hart's lesser efforts, but Haley was applauded as the
butler Zachary Ash who, facing unemployment because of his boss's
bankruptcy, grooms a parlor maid (Marta Eggert) into a lady so that she
can ensnare a rich husband and secure their future. The show had a
modest run. When RKO made the 1944 film version, they threw out
the whole score and much of the libretto and only kept Haley from the
New York cast. In the film *Higher and Higher*, Haley is again a butler,
now called Mike O'Brien, but this time he wins the maid-in-disguise
(Michele Morgan) when she decides to throw off next-door millionaire
Frank Sinatra and follow her heart. Far from a romantic lead, Haley was
personable enough that audiences accepted the movie's conclusion. He
was that kind of performer.

Ray Bolger was an even more nimble version of Jack Haley, and he
also found his greatest screen role in *The Wizard of Oz* (as the Scarecrow). Bolger's two greatest Broadway performances were the vaudevil-
lian-turned-professor Phil "Junior" Dolan in *On Your Toes* (1936) and
the cross-dressing Oxford student Charley Wykeham in *Where's
Charley?* (1948). Bolger was a superb dancer as well as an inventive
comic, and both talents were utilized to the fullest in *On Your Toes*
where he clowned his way though the farcical plot, sang a handful of
memorable Rodgers and Hart songs, and was principal hoofer in two
extended dance sequences, the "Princess Zenobia" ballet and "The
Slaughter on Tenth Avenue." It was a tour de force performance fondly
remembered by audiences for years. But Bolger was not chosen for the
1939 film version, even though he had already been featured in three
movie musicals. The role was given to Eddie Albert, a lightweight
song-and-dance man, and the movie was a travesty of the Broadway
original. All of the wonderful Rodgers and Harts songs were reduced to
background music, and an improbable plot about Russian spies weighed

the whole film down so that it was as ponderous as it was dull. Only Balanchine's choreography for "The Slaughter on Tenth Avenue" was bearable, and even that was done better years later by Gene Kelly and company in *Words and Music* (1948).

But Bolger had better luck with *Where's Charley?* This musical version of the classic farce *Charley's Aunt* was songwriter Frank Loesser's Broadway debut, and the score was filled with tuneful numbers. The showstopper was "Once in Love with Amy," which Bolger delivered in an oldtime vaudeville style, complete with audience participation. Dressing up like his maiden aunt to secure a chaperone for some young ladies visiting his Oxford digs, Bolger turned the old drag routine into a fine art. He was perhaps the most graceful and poetic of the great comics. His performance in the 1952 film version is probably only a pale copy of his stage Charley, but it is impressive all the same. The movie remained fairly faithful to the original, keeping many of the songs and some of the Broadway cast, and adding actual Oxford University locations. But the film lacks sparkle. Bolger shines, but he seems surrounded by dead weight. Maybe *Where's Charley?* needed that audience participation.

Danny Kaye was just starting to make a name for himself on Broadway when he was wooed away by the studios and didn't return to the New York stage for twenty-nine years. His breakthrough role was the effeminate magazine photographer Russell Paxton in *Lady in the Dark* (1941) who rattled off the names of dozens of Russian composers in the song "Tschaikowsky." When the show was filmed in 1944, both Kaye and the song were dropped. His next stage role, the GI Jerry Walker pursued by a housewife in *Let's Face It!* (1941), put his name above the title. But Bob Hope was given the part when the musical was filmed in 1943. The next year Kaye was brought out west by Samuel Goldwyn, who starred him in *Up in Arms*, followed by fourteen musical films built around his quirky but undeniable talents. Like Jolson, Kaye came off best in tailor-made vehicles that allowed him to stop the action for a comic bit or a rapid-fire specialty song. What Jolson had done at the Winter Garden, Kaye did for years on screen, then later on television.

Comedy teams have always flourished on stage and in the movies, yet very few comic duos found success in both media. For one reason or another, most of Broadway's favorite teams failed to make the transition to the movies. Bobby Clark and Paul McCullough, for example, brought down the house in revues and book musicals such as *The Ram-blers* (1926), *Strike Up the Band* (1930) and *Thumbs Up!* (1934) but never appeared on the screen. Clark was one of the broadest of comics, with his painted-on glasses, sawed-off cane, and leering expression. His partner McCullough was the beefy straight man who usually played the stooge to Clark's outrageous schemes. Perhaps they were too big for the movies. When *The Ramblers* was filmed in 1930 as *The Cuckoos*, the comedy team of Bert Wheeler and Robert Woolsey took their place.

The famous vaudeville duo of Ed Gallagher and Al Shean were fea-tured in a handful of Broadway shows, but Hollywood was never much interested in them. The twosome was not very flexible, usually playing themselves in stage shows, but there was something about their rhyth-mic comedy timing that would have filmed well.

One comic team cannot be easily explained away. William Gaxton and Victor Moore were paired for seven Broadway book musicals, and, although each made films, the studios only put them together in one movie, the long-forgotten Mae West vehicle *The Heat's On* (1943). Unlike most comedy teams who began together in vaudeville, Gaxton and Moore were actors who were cast in a play together, and the comic rapport that developed was so entertaining that producers reteamed them in subsequent shows. They were first paired in *Of Thee I Sing* (1931) in which Gaxton played the brash presidential candidate John P. Wintergreen and Moore was the bumbling vice president Alexander Throttlebottom. The pattern worked so well that Gaxton continued to essay slick operators while Moore was the lovable loser in musicals such as *Anything Goes* (1934), *Leave It to Me!* (1938), and *Louisiana Purchase* (1940). The last was filmed in 1941. Moore got to reprise his funny per-formance as the squeaky-clean Senator Loganberry, but Bob Hope was given Gaxton's role of the slippery businessman who outwits him. To see Gaxton and Moore on film together, one must endure the unfunny *The Heat's On* in which they played two crooked theater producers. It is a sad and inaccurate record of one of Broadway's funniest duos.

In the two decades following World War II, the Broadway musical's four favorite female stars were Ethel Merman, Mary Martin, Gwen Ver-don, and Carol Channing. None of them was favored by Hollywood, and very few of their many cherished performances were preserved on film. Is this a coincidence, or is there something in the makeup of these theater giants that the screen doesn't like? Were they so unphotogenic that the studios seemed to go out of their way to give their famous roles to others to play on the screen? Or were they labeled stage stars and considered unbankable in Hollywood? Not easy questions to answer, but yes might be the most accurate reply. All four of these woman were bigger than life, and the stage was obviously the best venue for their talents. But that doesn't always explain the bizarre decisions Tinsel Town made when it came to casting these ladies in the movies. Looking at their stage and film careers side by side is a sobering illustration of the difference between a Broadway and a Hollywood star.

Ethel Merman burst on the Broadway scene in the supporting role of Kate Fothergill in *Girl Crazy* (1930), holding one note for innumerable measures as she led the cast in singing "I Got Rhythm." Here was the very definition of a Broadway belter. But Merman was more than just a loud voice. Her comic instincts were uncanny, her diction in both singing and speaking was impeccable, and she dominated the stage as few performers could. *Girl Crazy* was filmed three times, none of them with Merman, but her ghost seems to haunt each film when "I Got Rhythm" is performed. Actually, Merman made her first film the same year as the stage *Girl Crazy*. She was a last-minute replacement for Ruth Etting in an Ed Wynn vehicle called *Follow the Leader* (1930) and got to sing a number called "Satan's Holiday." Merman would make eight movie musicals in the 1930s, and, though never the leading lady, she managed to shine in featured parts. Only one of those eight gave her a chance to re-create one of her Broadway performances: evangelist-turned-singer Reno Sweeney in the 1936 film of *Anything Goes*. Merman wowed Broadway audiences in the 1934 Cole Porter show, singing such favorites as "Blow, Gabriel, Blow," "I Get a Kick Out of You," "You're the Top," and the title number. She sang the last three in the film, and there was no question that the round-faced, brassy performer had some kind of screen appeal. But the studios must have liked their singing comediennes to be thinner and less forceful because Hollywood would only let Merman reprise one of her other stage performances on screen—and she'd have to wait seventeen years for that one.

The eight Broadway musicals that Merman starred in between 1939 and 1966 were hits, save one. It is a record that has never been equaled.

But she would appear in none of the film versions except for one. Hollywood gave her specialty bits in original film musicals or let her play a mother in *There's No Business Like Show Business* (1954), but her Broadway roles went to others. Merman essayed two roles in the Cole Porter musical *DuBarry Was a Lady* (1939): the sassy nightclub singer May Daly and, in an extended dream sequence, the French courtier Madame DuBarry. She was teamed with Bert Lahr (as a washroom attendant who dreams he is Louis XV), and the chemistry on stage was electric; but the 1943 film version featured Lucille Ball and Red Skelton in the roles. Although both would become comic giants later in television, Skelton and Ball do not impress in this film. It is generally a lackluster movie, with even the few remaining Porter songs failing to ignite any excitement. *DuBarry Was a Lady* definitely needed oversized talents like the stage originals.

On Broadway, *Panama Hattie* (1940) cast Merman as Hattie Maloney, a big-hearted nightclub owner in Panama City who falls for a posh Philadelphia millionaire (James Dunn). But before he'll marry Hattie, she has to win the affections of his bratty eight-year-old daughter (Joan Carroll) by a previous marriage. Merman piled on the comedy and the charm, sang "Let's Be Buddies" and "Make It Another Old-Fashioned, Please," and both Carroll and the audience were in the palm of her hand. *Panama Hattie* was a typical example of Merman turning a routine musical comedy into entertainment gold. Without her there was no show, and the musical has rarely been heard of since.

The same can be said for the 1942 movie version. For reasons that are beyond logic, little Ann Sothern with the funny but underpowered voice was cast as Hattie. She is obviously out of her league carrying the big, star-studded movie, and her career suffered for it; Sothern would only make four subsequent film musicals, never in the leading role. But there are things to enjoy in the *Panama Hattie* film: Lena Horne singing Porter's "Just One of Those Things," the clowning of Rags Ragland, Ben Blue, and Red Skelton (funnier this time around), and Virginia O'Brien's hilarious, deadpan rendition of "Fresh as a Daisy."

Something for the Boys (1943), with a ridiculous libretto by Herbert and Dorothy Fields, was a series of comic adventures for Blossom Hart (Merman), a chorine-turned-defense worker. She inherits a ramshackle Texas ranch located near an army base, falls for a sergeant (Bill Johnson), turns the ranch into a home for soldier's wives, and then is accused of running a bordello by a rival after the sergeant's heart. The musical has a very bizarre plot twist: the carborundum in Blossom's dental fillings somehow pick up radio waves, and she is able to intercept distress signals from a faltering plane and lead the pilot to safety. Cole Porter again provided the songs, but only the jovial "Hey, Good Lookin'" found any popularity afterward. *Something for the Boys* was a pretty feeble show all around (especially in light of *Oklahoma!* which opened two months later), but Merman kept it on the boards for over a year. She was more than a Broadway star; she was an insurance policy. But again Hollywood wouldn't risk her. They cast Carmen Miranda in the 1944 movie version and moved the locale from rural Texas to the backwoods of Kentucky (as if that was a better milieu for the Brazilian bombshell). Miranda was at the peak of her popularity and stole every movie she had previously appeared in, but her funny, outrageous performance as Chiquita Hart (as Blossom was renamed) was starting to look too familiar. Her career started to wane with *Something for the Boys*, and none of her six subsequent movie musicals was a hit.

On Broadway, however, Merman was still going strong, finding her biggest success of all in *Annie Get Your Gun* (1946). Although Herbert and Dorothy Fields wrote the libretto with Merman in mind and Irving Berlin tailored his score to her unique talents, *Annie Get Your Gun* was not merely a star vehicle. The show has remained popular for decades, and, while it needs a star to be revived on Broadway, it doesn't depend solely on Merman. It was the best book and character yet given her, and she made the most of it, moving from the naive, feisty hick Annie Oakley from the sticks to the heartsick Annie in love with fellow sharpshooter Frank Butler (Ray Middleton) to the defiant Annie unable to play second fiddle to his male ego. The range of songs Berlin wrote for her also allowed Merman to stretch herself: the cocky "Doin' What Comes Natur'lly" and "Anything You Can Do," the reflective "I Got Lost in His Arms" and "They Say It's Wonderful," the quiet "Moonshine Lullaby," and the celebratory "I'm an Indian Too" and "I Got the Sun in the Morning." The belting comedienne became a musical comedy actress with *Annie Get Your Gun*. Still, Hollywood was not impressed. MGM spent a record $700,000 for the screen rights and cast Judy Garland in the 1950 movie. After two months of filming, Garland was too sick to continue, so the studio considered Betty Garrett to replace her and then took a chance and hired Betty Hutton. It must have been quite a blow to Merman's considerable ego to be rejected three times for the same part. Hutton was a popular comic actress with many films to her credit, including thirteen musicals. But in the musicals she usually played supporting characters, and her loud and overbearing kind of comedy was best enjoyed in small doses. Hutton managed to tone down her pyrotechnics for Annie Oakley's more tender moments, but she still doesn't seem like a leading lady. Mostly the character is overplayed, and her singing often slips into her trademark air raid siren voice. If Merman was too oversized for the screen, what do you call this?

Actually, the whole movie was overproduced and Hutton wasn't the only bit of overkill. The staging of some of the production numbers seem like desperate attempts to create excitement through large numbers. "There's No Business Like Show Business" is a joyless parade, and "I'm an Indian Too" looks more like an Olympics event than a dance number. But there are elements of the film that work. Howard Keel, in his screen debut, is a personable Frank Butler, ten of Berlin's fifteen stage songs are retained, and screenwriter Sidney Sheldon and director George Sidney knew how to open up the stage piece and use locations effectively. So it might have been worse. And moviegoers didn't seem to mind; *Annie Get Your Gun* was the most popular film of 1950.

That same year Merman and Berlin had another Broadway hit with *Call Me Madam* (1950). It was a vehicle but a well-crafted one that boasted several notable songs. Merman played Washington hostess Sally Adams who is made ambassador to the tiny European nation of Lichtenburg. The Howard Lindsay–Russel Crouse libretto was an obvious bow to the current celebrity Pearl Mesta, whom President Truman had recently appointed to the Luxembourg embassy.

Once in the charming little country, Sally falls for the gentlemanly foreign minister (Paul Lukas) and helps her aide (Russell Nype) win the heart of the local princess. It wasn't the most exciting story, but the characters were likable, and the songs, particularly "You're Just in Love" and "It's a Lovely Day Today," never failed to please. Merman, age forty-two but looking older, was finally limited to matron roles, yet her Sally Adams was as vibrant and funny as her 1930s ingenues.

Maybe it was because it was a matronly character that Tinsel Town finally let Merman play the role on screen. *Call Me Madam* (1953) is the only complete record of a Merman performance and, not inconsequently, her finest movie appearance. It certainly helped that the libretto and most of the score remained the same and that she got winning support from George Sanders as the minister and Donald O'Connor as the aide in love with Vera-Ellen. But most important, the film allowed Merman to do what Merman did best: dominate a story and energize it with her star quality. Although it was close to the stage original, Walter Lang directed the lighthearted piece as a movie. One watches it today with great enjoyment but also with great regret that Merman was not used by Hollywood more often.

Of course, the greatest of those regrets is *Gypsy* (1959), Merman's finest hour on Broadway and one of the highpoints of the postwar theater. A memoir by the burlesque queen Gypsy Rose Lee inspired the musical in which Gypsy's overbearing, indomitable mother Rose became the focal point of the tale. It is a backstager (like several previous musicals), and it is a show business biography (like *Annie Get Your Gun* and others), but neither description is accurate for *Gypsy*, which goes far beyond both genres. Arthur Laurents wrote the expert libretto that was unsentimental and unwavering in its portrayal of the characters and the times. Jule Styne (music) and Stephen Sondheim (lyrics) provided a superior score that was just as uncompromising. But at the center of it all was Merman giving a performance that not even her staunchest fans could have anticipated. How did the comic soubrette of the 1930s become this consummate actress-belter? Maybe being mistreated by Hollywood for years provided Rose's bitterness and stubbornness. Or maybe Merman had been capable of such heights all along, but no one had ever handed her a script that demanded them of her. *Gypsy* was an artistic and commercial hit and continues to enthrall audiences with its humor and heartbreak. For musical theater actresses, it is *Hamlet*, the ultimate test and crowning triumph. But the ghost of Merman is always there.

Regardless, Warner Brothers gave the part to Rosalind Russell. Not casting Merman in the 1962 film is considered the greatest faux pas in the history of movie musicals. It cannot be satisfactorily explained logically, artistically, or even financially. (Russell was a popular movie star but not *that* popular.) So for many it is impossible to judge the resultant movie fairly. But the fact remains that it is a faithful, competent, and effective version of the Broadway hit. Only one song ("Together, Wherever We Go") from the stage score was cut, Leonard Spigelgass's screenplay opens up Laurents's libretto without diminishing it, and the performances throughout are quite good. Natalie Wood's growth from a neglected teen to a celebrated stripper is impressive, Karl Malden is a solid Herbie, and both the kid and adult supporting players are very fine. As for Russell, one can complain about her ineffectual Auntie Mame antics in the role, but she is funny. She never comes close to uncovering the many levels in Rose's character (particularly the monstrous side of her), but Hollywood could have done much worse than cast Russell. (The most popular singing stars in the movies at that time were Doris Day, Shirley Jones, and Ann-Margret; consider those possibilities.) But if one is going to enjoy the movie of *Gypsy*, one has to not mind the ghost of Merman lurking through the whole picture.

To a lesser degree, Mary Martin, Gwen Verdon, and Carol Channing experienced the same kind of Hollywood brush-off. Martin played leading ingenues in ten movie musicals in the 1930s and 1940s and came across in an appealing manner. In one of them, *Love Thy Neighbor* (1940), she even got to re-create her famous comic striptease to "My Heart Belongs to Daddy" that had launched her Broadway career in *Leave It to Me!* (1938). Martin's first starring role in New York was in *One Touch of Venus* (1943). She played a statue of the title goddess who comes to life in modern times and has a yen for a meek little barber (Kenny Baker). Martin had a talent for being coy and innocent while delivering her jokes and songs with aplomb. Her Venus was demure and sexy at the same time. The 1948 film of *One Touch of Venus* eliminated Martin and all of the charming Kurt Weill–Ogden Nash score except "Speak Low" and "The Trouble with Women." With so few songs, so little dancing, and so much uninteresting talk, the picture hardly seems like a musical. Ava Gardner played Venus and, whatever her other acting strengths, being ethereal and magical was not among them.

Martin's two best Broadway roles were also played by others on the screen. Her Navy nurse Nellie Forbush in *South Pacific* (1949) was perhaps her archetypal character: spunky, optimistic, romantic without being too soft, funny without ever being crude. Merman was gutsy and brazen; Martin was more wholesome. Her Nellie was an affirmation of life in the midst of a world war. Mitzi Gaynor, who played Nellie in the 1958 film, was pretty and perky, which is not the same thing. Twentieth Century–Fox had considered Doris Day and even Elizabeth Taylor for the part before going ahead with Gaynor; they never seriously considered Martin, who was forty-five years old and hadn't made a movie musical in years. Yet the next year Martin played the young postulant Maria in *The Sound of Music* on Broadway and got away with it. Of course, there was something maternal about Maria, and Martin's rapport with children on stage was legendary. Also, she was expert in finding the comedy in the character, something Julie Andrews soft-pedaled when she played Maria in the hugely popular 1965 movie. Well, a fifty-two-year-old postulant was beyond even the miracle tricks of Hollywood, so there were few complaints when Martin was passed over for that part. But more than age was the issue. Martin was fine on the screen but effervescent on stage. The television version of her *Peter Pan* (1954) is a glowing testament to her stage presence. That's the kind of magic she will be remembered for.

Gwen Verdon will be remembered as the finest dancer of the great Broadway superstars. She was not the tall, frail ballerina type, and her dancing, usually devised by Bob Fosse, was always more muscular than pretty. Verdon first wowed Broadway in the supporting role of Claudine in *Can-Can* (1953). Having to chose between two suitors, the starving artist Boris (Hans Conreid) and the oversexed art critic Hilaire (Erik Rhodes), Verdon filled the time thrilling audiences with her distinctive moves during the "Garden of Eden" ballet. By the time a movie of *Can-Can* was made in 1960, Verdon had become a bona fide Broadway star with three hits to her name. All the same, the studio considered Barrie Chase and then cast Juliet Prowse as Claudine. The movie mangled the delectable Cole Porter score (the lovely "I Love Paris" was only used under the credits), and superstars such as Frank Sinatra, Shirley MacLaine, Maurice Chevalier, and Louis Jourdan each seemed duller than the next. Ironically, the only bright spot in the film is Prowse.

Verdon was top billed in Broadway's *Damn Yankees* (1955) and her Lola, who works for the devil (Ray Walston), was a show in itself. Although she was no beauty, the red-headed Verdon knew how to be sexy and funny at the same time, always maintaining a little bit of a waiflike quality in her characterizations. She got to reprise her Lola in the 1958 film, and, while it is only an echo of her stage performance, Verdon is a joy to watch. The camera captured her dancing beautifully but was not very kind to her in other ways. She was only thirty-two years old at the time, but she seems older on screen; Hollywood noticed, and Verdon didn't make movies until thirty years later when she played spry senior citizens in nonmusicals.

But on Broadway she continued to play ingenues, such as the kookie but lovable Charity Hope Valentine in *Sweet Charity* (1966). As a taxi dancer who literally wears her heart on her sleeve (Charity has a tattooed heart on her forearm), Verdon knew she had outgrown the sexy bit but still knew how to dazzle as the funny waif. *Sweet Charity* was a dancing show, and the whole production seemed to take its cue from her. Of course, director-choreographer Bob Fosse was behind it, but when he tried to re-create it all on screen in 1969 without Verdon, there was an obvious hole in the middle. Shirley MacLaine played the waif very well, and her Charity has its moments, but the movie doesn't take its energy from her. In fact, MacLaine seems to be trying to keep up with the others, especially when surrounded by superior dancers such as Chita Rivera and Paula Kelly. Verdon doing Charity in the film was out of the question, but the resulting movie made it clear how truly rare a talent like Gwen Verdon was.

Then there is Carol Channing, the Broadway star most imitated and lampooned because her stage persona is so cartoonish. Was she indeed too big for the screen? Channing only appeared in a few movies, but in her one musical, *Thoroughly Modern Millie* (1967), she shone as the wacky millionairess Muzzy. (She even got an Oscar nomination for it.) True, that musical spoof was pretty cartoonish itself, but there is no question Channing delivered the goods. Still, Hollywood wasn't buying, and her two best stage roles were given to others to portray on screen.

Gentlemen Prefer Blondes (1949) seemed like it was custom-made for Channing, but, in truth, she was custom-made to play the obtuse, crafty Lorelei Lee. In a way, Channing became Lorelei for that musical and decided to keep playing her on and offstage for the rest of her career. There is certainly a touch of the Roaring Twenties flapper in her Dolly Levi. Channing was not the first choice for *Hello, Dolly!* (1964)—

legend has it that Ethel Merman turned it down first—but she quickly made it her own.

Both Lorelei and Dolly were fundamentally one-joke comic characters, but when Channing played a cartoon, she made it seem three-dimensional. She was also praised for being an audience star, one who seemed to absorb her energy from a live audience and then gave it back to them tenfold. But movies don't know what to do with that kind of performer, and not only were Lorelei and Dolly given to others but they were purposely cast so that the characters in no way resembled Channing. Marilyn Monroe's gold digger in *Gentlemen Prefer Blondes* (1953) and Barbra Streisand's matchmaker in *Hello, Dolly!* (1969) defy comparisons with Channing. Maybe that is the sign of a true Broadway star: no comparisons.

The list of stage celebrities who were denied the opportunity to recreate their best performances on screen seems endless. Gertrude Lawrence saw Ginger Rogers play her Liza Elliott in *Lady in the Dark* (1944), Alfred Drake lost both his poet Hajj in *Kismet* (1955) and his Petruchio in *Kiss Me, Kate* (1953) to Howard Keel, Barbara Cook had her Marion the librarian given to Shirley Jones in *The Music Man* (1962), Tammy Grimes' Molly Brown went to Debbie Reynolds in *The Unsinkable Molly Brown* (1964), Angela Lansbury musicalized Auntie Mame but saw Lucille Ball play her in *Mame* (1974), Zero Mostel's Teyve was given to Topol in *Fiddler on the Roof* (1971), and Julie Andrews lost her Eliza Doolittle to Audrey Hepburn in *My Fair Lady* (1964) and her Guenevere to Vanessa Redgrave in *Camelot* (1967). And what lesson can be drawn from all this? Broadway stars. Screen stars. They're different.

CHAPTER FIVE

~

Ah, Sweet Operetta!

Imagine a silent film version of a Shakespeare play. No poetry, just a few quotes in the titles and the story. There were many of them, and some weren't half bad. Now imagine a silent film operetta. No music, just the costumes and the story. There were several of those as well. In fact, a 1927 silent version of *The Student Prince* was very popular. But an operetta without music? And with some of the most feeble plots ever seen on a stage? By rights, operetta and film (silent or sound) should make a terrible combination. Operetta is about singing. Plot, characters, dancing are negligible; scenery and costumes are ranked higher. Operettas have their own reality, their own time frame, their own kind of logic. The world stops for an operetta because such a musical entertainment doesn't fit in any real world. They used to be very popular in summer theaters because each operetta is like a three-hour vacation from life. Maybe that is why movie operettas were so favored during the Depression. And they've been welcome on the screen other times as well. They are still big on Broadway, if they are disguised enough. For what else is *Phantom of the Opera* but an operetta?

As a working definition, we shall say an *operetta* is a light form of opera that uses dialogue and tends toward the amusing and romantic rather than the profound or tragic. American operetta grew out of European models and for many years copied Viennese and French forms, as well as the comic operettas from Great Britain, such as the Gilbert and Sullivan musicals. The great age of Broadway operettas was from the 1890s to the stock market crash of 1929. That was the age of Victor Herbert, Rudolf Friml, and Sigmund Romberg—the generally acknowledged masters of the genre in America. But many works by Jerome Kern, Otto Harbach, the Gershwins, and Rodgers and Hammerstein can rightly be described as operettas. All of these celebrate song and the human voice above all, and, while a few have rather intricate and sophisticated plots and characters, most are just about the music.

Just when they were dying out on stage, operettas became popular on screen. One would think that Hollywood would be afraid of them. They are, after all, the most static of theater forms. Only the lavish sets and costumes offer any visual pleasure and film, as they say, is a visual medium. But there were operetta movies from the start. In fact, the first Broadway musical to be adapted for the screen was the 1929 version of the operetta *The Desert Song*. Of course, the studios hated the plots and usually replaced them with new ones (which were often as insipid). This was easy to do because the songs were pliable; one love duet can pretty much work for any set of lovers in operetta. But Tinsel Town loved the sets and costumes, so the locale of the stage piece was almost always retained. The film versions also had to cut down on the number and length of the songs. But there is so much music in a stage operetta that just a sampling of the highlights was satisfying enough. Call it operetta lite, or a lighter form of light opera.

Let's look first at Hollywood and the great triumvirate of American operetta composers. Victor Herbert died in 1924 and never experienced a talkie himself. But that didn't keep three of his many stage hits from being filmed. Perhaps his most enduring work is *Babes in Toyland* (1903) with its meandering plot (by lyricist Glen MacDonough) and tuneful collection of songs. Correctly billed as an "extravaganza," *Babes in Toyland* followed the adventures of two children (Mabel Barrison and William Norris) who escape from their wicked Uncle Barnaby (George W. Denham) and are shipwrecked in the magical Toyland, where various Mother Goose characters come to their aid. There was plenty of spectacle on hand and such notable numbers as "I Can't Do the Sum," "March of the Toys," "Go to Sleep, Slumber Deep," and the haunting "Toyland." The show ran a then-impressive 192 performances and was frequently revived for fifty years. The first movie version came out in 1934 and was charming, even if it bore little resemblance to the original operetta. The comedy team of Stan Laurel and Oliver Hardy were top billed, playing incompetent toy makers in Toyland who, together with the Mother Goose creations, defend the fantastical land from an attack by the Bogeymen. Although the picture was only a swift seventy-nine minutes long, it managed to include most of the song favorites as well as an interpolation of "Who's Afraid of the Big Bad Wolf?" A 1961 version of *Babes in Toyland* put out by the Disney studio (it was its first live-action musical) was closer to the original stage piece but was a colorful bore. The youngsters in peril were now teenagers Annette Funicello and Tommy Sands, with Ray Bolger as their evil uncle; none was very convincing or much fun. Ed Wynn's oversized performance as the Toymaker was more sprightly and there were a few enjoyable production numbers, especially Bolger's "Castle in Spain" dance that involved dancing water fountains. Operetta was pretty much dead by the 1960s, so one can understand the timid approach the film took to the piece. But it didn't have to be this dreary.

Naughty Marietta (1910) is considered Herbert's masterpiece. The score is very demanding (he wrote it for an opera company rather than a theater cast) and quite ingenious, even if today the duet "Ah, Sweet Mystery of Life" is the ultimate operetta cliché. Rida Johnson Young wrote both the lyrics and the libretto, which was set in 1780s New Orleans and focused on the Neapolitan Marietta (Emma Trentini), who flees an unwanted marriage in France and falls under the charms of the lieutenant governor's son Etienne (Edward Martindel). But he turns out to be the dreaded pirate Bras Piqué in disguise, so Marietta ends up in the arms of Captain Dick Warrington (Orville Harrold), who, with his Rangers, captures the scoundrel. The plot was serviceable, but the songs were exceptional, ranging from the rousing "Tramp! Tramp! Tramp!" and the lyrical "'Neath the Southern Moon" to the lively "Italian Street Song" and the rhapsodic "I'm Falling in Love with Someone."

Naughty Marietta was a mainstay of operetta companies for decades but was not filmed until there was a demand for such things in the 1930s. The movie inaugurated the series of eight Jeanette MacDonald–Nelson Eddy musicals, thereby launching Hollywood's favorite singing couple and making operetta films a hot item. The New Orleans setting was kept for the 1935 movie, but the plot shifted a bit: Marietta was now a French aristocrat (disguised as an Italian street singer) fleeing a marriage to a Spanish count. Her ship heading to Louisiana is attacked by pirates, but the mercenary Captain Dick rescues her and spends the rest of the picture wooing her while Marietta is busy hiding her true identity. Highlights of the stage score made it to the screen, and audiences savored every one of them. The movie was also an international success, and Herbert's music finally started to become popular in Europe, a decade after his death.

Herbert's *Sweethearts* (1913) does not have as fine a score as his two previously discussed shows, and it has the kind of plot that gives operettas a bad name. Librettists Harry B. Smith and Fred De Gresac used story ideas that were already considered clichés in 1913. The baby Princess Sylvia of the mythical kingdom of Zilania is abducted by the Prime Minister (Tom McNaughton) and taken to Belgium to escape a revolution at home. She grows up with a family who runs "The White Geese," a laundry in Bruges, no one knowing of her royal ancestry. Back in Zilania, they have given up the missing princess for dead and a distant cousin, Prince Franz (Thomas Conkey), is slated to take the throne. But on his way there he stops at the laundry in Bruges (!), instantly falls in love with the adult Sylvia (Christie MacDonald), and after a handful of complications is cleared up, the two end up ruling Zilania as king and queen. The authors claimed that the tale was based on a real fifteenth-century princess in Italy, but the whole thing smelled of operetta balderdash. Still, the show was a hit at 136 performances and was popular on tour and in revival. (A 1947 Broadway revival rewrote the operetta with the beloved comic Bobby Clark as the Prime Minister, and the production ran twice as long as the original).

MGM must have liked the songs and the Belgian setting because that was all it kept when it made the 1938 movie version. It was another vehicle for MacDonald and Eddy, but the totally new script by Dorothy Parker and Alan Campbell let the two singers loosen up a bit and play contemporary Broadway stars who are performing *Sweethearts* on the stage. It's a bright and satirical screenplay in which the married couple is so hassled by the demands from their producer (Frank Morgan) and predatory relatives that they decide to chuck it all and go to Hollywood.

To stop them, the producer and his cronies make Mrs. think that Mr. is fooling around with his secretary. The two separate, the Hollywood contract falls apart, the ruse is discovered, and all goes back to the way it was before by the time the couple reprises the title song for the fifth time. MacDonald and Eddy were never funnier (if indeed they ever had much opportunity to be funny at all), and they still had those lush Herbert songs to give full voice to, this time usually in the context of the operetta they were performing. (Ken Russell used a variation of this idea decades later when he made a movie of *The Boy Friend*.)

Rudolf Friml had a limited theatrical career (1912 to 1934), but in that time he composed twenty Broadway operettas, and a good number of them were successful. His first effort was *The Firefly* (1912), a Cinderella tale with a bit of sass to it. Impoverished New York street singer Nina (Emma Trentini) escapes from her cruel music teacher and disguises herself as a cabin boy on a dowager's private yacht. The fact that she secretly loves the dowager's handsome son Jack (Craig Campbell) sets Nina to singing. When a music professor (Henry Vogel) hears her, he thinks he has discovered some kind of tenor virtuoso and starts to coach him/her. As the boat sails the Caribbean, the complications pile up, but Nina eventually becomes a prima donna and Jack's wife. Otto Harbach wrote the libretto, and it avoided many of the operetta plot pitfalls. He also penned the lyrics for Friml's music, resulting in such song favorites as "Giannina Mia," "Love Is Like a Firefly," and "Sympathy." Friml's debut show was a hit, and he was much in demand on Broadway until the vogue for operettas passed twenty years later.

The Firefly was filmed in 1937, and not only were the best numbers kept, but an even bigger hit song was added: "The Donkey Serenade" by Herbert Stothart, George Forrest, and Robert Wright. The original libretto might have made for a playful screenplay, but the studio threw it out completely (not even keeping the Caribbean setting) and hired Frances Goodrich and Albert Hackett to start from scratch. What they came up with was rather serious but interesting enough; in fact, it was a lot like an old operetta. During the Napoleonic invasion of Europe, the Spanish singer Nina Maria (Jeanette MacDonald) acts as a spy, flirting with French officers to get information that will protect King Ferdinand II. This Spanish Mata Hari is undone by the counterspy Don Diego (Allen Jones), who, of course, has fallen in love with her. After some passionate duets (and a romantic ride together in a donkey cart), war breaks out, and not until the smoke has cleared are the lovers reunited. The movie is sluggish, but the music is fine, and Jones and MacDonald have a warm screen rapport, something not always found in MacDonald's vehicles with Nelson Eddy.

Two other Friml hits were also filmed—twice each, in fact. *Rose-Marie* (1924) was not only Friml's greatest success but was the most popular Broadway musical until *Oklahoma!* came along nineteen years later. Oscar Hammerstein and Harbach wrote the libretto, and it was a fairly daring one for operetta, creating some complicated characters and dealing with murder and revenge. Set in the Canadian Rockies, the central romance was between singer Rose-Marie La Flamme (Mary Ellis) and fur trapper Jim Kenyon (Dennis King), but she is pursued by the wealthy city slicker Edward Hawley (Frank Greene). Hawley's mistress Wanda (Pearl Regay) is a half-breed Indian, and when she gets into an argument with the local troublemaker Black Eagle (Arthur Ludwig) and stabs him to death, Hawley sets it up so that Jim is the suspected murderer. The Mounties try to track down the innocent trapper, and Rose-Marie is blackmailed into marrying Hawley. But Jim's pal Hard-Boiled Herman (William Kent) gets the truth out of Wanda, the Mounties arrest the real killer, and Jim interrupts the wedding in time to claim Rose-Marie for himself. It was an intricate tale and told well, each of the characters vividly written and the plot developments laid out logically. The score was also first-rate, with such perennial favorites as "Indian Love Call," "The Mounties," and the gushing title song. *Rose-Marie* was not only a hit in New York and on the road, but it packed houses in London, Paris, Berlin, Stockholm, Moscow, and other cities abroad.

The first movie version was made by MGM in 1936 as *Rose Marie* (Hollywood hated hyphens; they looked British), and it starred MacDonald and Eddy, of course. (Opera singer Grace Moore was originally intended to play the title character.) Goodrich and Hackett again worked on the screenplay, and again they made major changes to the libretto. Canadian opera singer Marie de Flor hears that her brother John (James Stewart), a convicted murderer who has escaped from prison, is hiding out in the Rockies, so she disguises herself as "Rose Marie" and sets out to help him. Also looking for John is Sergeant

Bruce (Eddy) of the Mounties. The two fall in love in the rugged but beautiful wilderness, but when they catch up to John, the officer must do his duty. It's not a terrible script, but neither is it as good as the Broadway libretto. Also, only four songs from the stage score were used, the rest of the music consisting of opera arias for Marie and some unimpressive interpolations. Regardless, the movie was very popular, and MGM returned to the property in 1954, giving the tale the full-color Cinemascope treatment. Again, the score suffered, and the screenplay was a mixture of the two earlier versions without being as good as either. Rose Marie (Ann Blyth) still loves a Mountie, here named Mike Malone (Howard Keel), but he is beloved by Wanda (Joan Taylor), now the ravishing daughter of an Indian chief. Rose Marie doesn't end up with her Mountie this time but with the fur trapper Duval (Fernando Lamas). One successful addition to the improbable tale was Bert Lahr as a comic Mountie who sings "I'm a Mountie Who Never Got His Man." This *Rose Marie* is a beautiful-looking movie (filmed on location in the Rockies) but an unsatisfactory one. The public agreed, and it did poor box office.

Friml's swashbuckling operetta *The Three Musketeers* (1928) was never filmed, but similar in its derring-do was *The Vagabond King* (1925), which came to the screen in 1930 and again in 1956. It was based on the popular play *If I Were King* (1901) about the notorious and romantic poet-outlaw Francois Villon (Dennis King) during the time of King Louis XI of France. The dashing ruffian woos the aristocratic Katherine de Vaucelles (Carolyn Thomson), repels the Duke of Burgundy's soldiers by raising an army of vagabonds, rules as King of France for one day, then outwits the gallows so that he can wed his high-class sweetheart. It was rip-roaring fun, and the songs (lyrics by Brian Hooker) were immediately popular: "Only a Rose," "Hugette Waltz," "Song of the Vagabonds," and so on. The first film version was a primitive work (though it boasted two-color Technicolor), with plodding camera work and a heaviness in its presentation that seemed to suck all the life out of the story. King got to reprise his Villon and Jeanette MacDonald was Katherine, but the only performance to come alive was Lillian Roth as the martyr Hugette.

Ronald Colman played Villon in a nonmusical version of *The Vagabond King* in 1938, and then a musical one was made in 1956 by

Paramount. A tenor from Malta named Oreste Kirkop played Villon, Kathryn Grayson was the aristocrat, and Rita Moreno was Hugette. It had excellent production values, but there was something tired about the old tale that late in the game. Both films kept the best of the stage score with some unmemorable songs added each time. Friml lived to 1972 and assisted on both movies by contributing some new music. But he never recovered from the demise of operetta on Broadway and scored no Broadway shows after 1934; operetta was all he knew how to do.

Sigmund Romberg, on the other hand, was the most versatile of the three operetta giants, writing music for Al Jolson vehicles, Ziegfeld revues, and musical comedies, as well as operettas. But of his five stage works that were filmed, all were operettas. One of Romberg's early hits, *Maytime* (1917), had an ambitious libretto by Rida Johnson Young (who also wrote the lyrics) about two lovers divided by class. Ottilie Van Zandt (Peggy Wood), who lives in New York's wealthy Washington Square, loves the struggling self-made man Richard Wayne (Charles Purcell), but she obeys her father and marries a rich man instead. As the years pass, Richard's fortunes rise and Ottilie's fall, so much so that she is left penniless after the death of her husband and must sell her house. But Richard buys it at auction and gives it to her as a gift. The coda for *Maytime* was very moving: Ottilie and Richard's grandchildren (by their respective spouses) are in the same garden where the deceased couple met long ago, and a new love springs up between them. The Romberg score featured two enduring favorites, "Will You Remember?" and "The Road to Paradise." *Maytime* is melodramatic but has a sincerity missing in many operettas. No wonder it was the most popular show of the World War I era.

The 1937 film only kept the title, one song, and the bare bones of the plot, heaping on the melodrama with a trowel. Ottilie was turned into the aging opera star Marcia Moray (Jeanette MacDonald) who gives advice to a young woman to follow her heart. A long flashback follows, about her romance in Paris with the tenor Paul Allison (Nelson Eddy), her decision to think of her career first and forsake him, her unhappy marriage to her manager Nicolai Nazaroff (John Barrymore), and how her jealous husband shot and killed Paul when he came back into her life. Where the original *Maytime* was quietly affecting, the movie is clumsy and blatant. Instead of the touching stage coda, the movie ends with Marie singing a duet version of "Will You Remember?" with Paul's ghost.

One of the most revived operettas of all time is Romberg's *The Student Prince of Heidelberg* (1924), and, although it is set in the typical European setting with royalty and pretty scenery all over the place, it has a better plot than most. Dorothy Donnelly wrote the book and lyrics this time, and she took a few bold steps along the way: there is no girls' chorus, and there is no happy ending. When the German Prince Karl Franz (Howard Marsh) goes to Heidelberg to study, he falls in love with Kathie (Ilse Margenga), the comely waitress at the local Inn of the Three Golden Apples. All of their luscious duets together cannot hide the fact that he is royalty and she is a commoner, so there is a bittersweet parting when the king dies and Karl Franz must return home to be crowned and marry the princess the family has picked out for him. The score for *The Student Prince* (as it is usually titled) remains fresh, and revivals are still done. "Serenade," "Deep in My Heart, Dear," "Golden Days," and the "Drinking Song" are the best numbers in a superb collection of songs.

A silent screen version of the operetta in 1927 with Norma Shearer and Ramon Navarro was quite a hit so it is surprising that a talkie version was not made until 1954. Mario Lanza was slated to play the Prince but, depending on which version you believe, he was deemed too fat or too sick to play the role, or he just walked off the set. (He died five years later of a heart attack at the age of thirty-eight.) But Lanza had already recorded the Prince's singing tract, so his mellifluous voice was used as the singing voice for the unknown but good-looking Edmund Purdom, who played the Prince on screen. Ann Blyth was Kathie and was at her best, so the singing worked. But the acting throughout is pretty stiff (except for such scene stealers as S. Z. Sakall and John Williams), and the screenplay, while mostly faithful to the original, seems to drag on. But there is all that glorious music (most of the score survived), so one learns to be patient.

Two years after *The Student Prince*, Romberg teamed up with Hammerstein and Harbach and came up with *The Desert Song* (1926), which was almost as popular. The libretto, inspired by such recent news events as an uprising of the Riffs in French Morocco and the latest craze for desert romance because of Rudolph Valentino's film *The Sheik*, is a little more far-fetched than a logical viewer might want. A desert outpost is being threatened by the mysterious Red Shadow (Robert Halliday) who is leading the Riff revolt. The Frenchwoman Margot Bonvalet (Vivienne Segal) fantasizes about him, and her fantasies come true when the Shadow abducts her and takes her away to his hiding place in the Sahara. But when surrounded by troops, the outlaw manages to escape. It turns out that the Shadow is the son of the governor, and he has been acting like a sniveling weakling in order to fool everyone. So all is revealed, and Margot gets her Shadow. Only the venerable score holds this sand-filled story together; "One Alone," "Romance," "The Riff Song," and the title number are the standouts.

Hollywood filmed *The Desert Song* three times, and in each case it was the improbable plot that was the problem. The 1929 version featured John Boles and Carlotta King as the lovers, and they got to sing much of the stage score. The screenplay makes few changes and, consequently, the story comes across as a silly, girlish fantasy. The 1943 version was set in the French Morocco of 1937 with the Nazis in control and the Red Shadow (Dennis Morgan) as an American freedom fighter from the Spanish Civil War who leads the oppressed Riffs in underground maneuvers. Irene Manning was his love interest, and, again, the best of the score survived the transition. A third film version of *The Desert Song* was made in communist-conscious 1953, and the studios didn't want the word *Red* used to describe their hero. Gordon MacRae was the Riff leader (now called Paul Hudson) and Kathryn Grayson was a general's daughter who loves him. The storyline seemed to disintegrate with each new version, getting more rather than less preposterous. Even the score was shortchanged in the third effort. It is worth pointing out that none of the three movies was a major box office success.

The New Moon (1928) is considered the last of the great American operettas. Opening the season before the Depression hit, it was a final hurrah of sorts. Hammerstein cowrote the book again and provided the lyrics for Romberg's sweeping melodies, such as "Stouthearted Men," "One Kiss," "Lover, Come Back to Me," "Softly, As in a Morning Sunrise," and "Wanting You." In the days right before the French Revolution, the democratic-thinking aristocrat Robert Misson (Robert Halliday) escapes to French New Orleans, where he falls in love with the high-born Marianne Beaunoir (Evelyn Herbert), she thinking he is a common bondsman. When Robert is captured and put aboard a ship to France, his cohort of stouthearted men act as pirates and attack his vessel (which Marianne happens to be on as well), and they all set up a utopian society on the Isle of Pines. When the French catch up with them, it is to announce that the Bastille has been stormed, and they are all free citizens now. It wasn't any more plausible than *The Desert Song*, but somehow *The New Moon* played better on stage.

An MGM version made in 1930 tossed out the *the* (it was called *New Moon*) as well as the stage libretto and set the story in Russia where the Princess Tanya (Grace Moore) is engaged to a government official (Adolphe Menjou) but loves the dashing Lieutenant Petroff (Lawrence Tibbett). The dynamics were completely different, yet the marvelous songs still made sense, especially when so beautifully sung by the two famous opera singers. MGM remade the film in 1940, and this time the screenplay was surprisingly close to the original. Jeanette MacDonald and Nelson Eddy were the lovers, and most of the score was intact.

Long after the age of Broadway operetta had waned, Romberg composed *Up in Central Park* (1945), which had a musical comedy plot but a score that retained the spirit of operetta. Herbert and Dorothy Fields wrote the libretto about the corrupt Tamany Hall administration in 1870s New York City. A muckraker (Wilbur Evans) tries to expose the graft in the building of the new Central Park, but things get complicated when he is smitten by the daughter of one of Boss Tweed's cronies. It was a beautiful production that captured a Currier and Ives look of the time, and the score (lyrics by Dorothy Fields) was delectable, particularly "Close As Pages in a Book" and "April Snow." But both songs were cut when Universal made a tiresome movie version in 1948. Dick Haymes and Deanna Durbin were the sweethearts in the somewhat rewritten story and both looked as lost as Vincent Price did trying to play Boss Tweed. Only two musical numbers from the Broadway score were used; the new songs were as forgettable as the picture itself.

Two operettas from 1927, not by the renowned triumvirate, were also filmed. *Golden Dawn* was an odd show that had the spirit of a Viennese operetta but was set in Africa during World War I with native and European characters, all played by white actors (some in blackface as needed). The tribal princess Dawn (Louise Hunter) is enamored of the prisoner of war Steve Allen (Paul Gregory) held by the German army. The cruel black overseer Shep Keyes (Robert Chisholm) also loves Dawn, but she spurns him. So when a drought ravages the village, Keyes convinces everyone that Dawn is responsible and the natives revolt. The happy ending: It turns out Dawn is really white, so she and Steve leave Africa together. Hammerstein cowrote the book and lyrics to this truly strange operetta, but much of it impressed audiences and critics, and the flowing music by Herbert Stothart and Emmerich Kalman entertained theatergoers for a profitable 184 performances.

Warner Brothers, anxious to turn out new musicals, bought the rights and filmed *Golden Dawn* in 1930 with Vivienne Segal and Walter Woolf King as the focal couple. The movie is truly absurd and difficult to watch, particularly with Noah Berry in blackface playing the villain. If the whole thing were not in such bad taste, it might have become a camp classic.

Rio Rita (1927) was an obvious copy of the popular *The Desert Song* (1926), but it had its own merits and thrilled audiences for 495 performances. The Guy Bolton–Fred Thompson libretto was set in Texas where a notorious bank robber called the Kinkajou is terrorizing the desert towns. Captain James Stewart (J. Harrold Murray) and his Texas Rangers are in hot pursuit, and when they cross the Rio Grande into a little Mexican town, Jim falls for the local senorita Rita (Ethelind Terry). Their romance is stunted when it looks like Rita's brother is the Kinkajou, but the bandit turns out to be a Mexican general who had been rejected by Rita. Harry Tierney (music) and Joseph McCarthy (lyrics) scored the operetta and came up with such hits as "The Rangers' Song," "The Kinkajou," "If You're in Love You'll Waltz," and the adoring title number.

Rio Rita was first filmed by RKO in 1929 with Bebe Daniels and John Boles as the lovers. Bert Wheeler and Robert Woolsey, the comic relief from the Broadway production, made their screen debuts, and their prankish humor came off well in the new medium. It was a clumsy, stagy movie musical but also lavish, entertaining, and very popular. The 1942 remake turned the operetta into an Abbott and Costello vehicle, the waggish duo taking up much of the screen time in the

Woolsey–Wheeler roles. The lovers this time were Kathryn Grayson and John Carroll, and, with only two songs from the Broadway score left, there wasn't much to sing. This *Rio Rita* greatly disappoints, but, for fans of the comedy team, the movie was a success.

Some of Jerome Kern's Broadway musicals can be classified as operettas; the settings and characters may have been contemporary, but the outstanding scores echoed the old genre. Two of these operetta-like Kern musicals were filmed in the 1930s. *The Cat and the Fiddle* (1931) was about a romance in Brussels between an American jazz composer, Shirley Sheridan (Bettina Hall), and a Rumanian operetta composer, Victor Florescu (Georges Metaxa). Their differing musical styles paralleled the plot's complications until the two lovers and the two types of music were in harmony with each other. Like Harbach's libretto, Kern's score (lyrics also by Harbach) was a mixture of old and new, with such enchanting numbers as "The Night Was Made for Love," "Try to Forget," "She Didn't Say Yes," and "I Watch the Love Parade." The show managed to run 395 performances in the darkest days of the Depression.

In an unusual and surprising move, MGM kept every song from the Broadway score when it filmed *The Cat and the Fiddle* in 1934, and, as sung by Jeanette MacDonald and Ramon Novarro, it sounded lovely. The screenplay, on the other hand, overhauled the libretto poorly, setting many of the scenes in Paris and tacking on a ludicrous ending: the prima donna (Vivienne Segal) of Victor's operetta walks out on opening night, and songwriter MacDonald steps in à la *42nd Street*.

In a similar vein was Kern's Broadway musical *Music in the Air* (1932), which he wrote with Hammerstein. Bavarian sweethearts Sieglinde (Katherine Carrington) and Karl (Water Slezak) hike from their little village to Munich with her music professor father (Al Shean) to interest a big-city publisher in Dad's song "I've Told Ev'ry Little Star." Once there, they get caught up in the machinations of music and theater folk, and Sieglinde is given the lead role in an operetta when the diva abandons the show. But in Hammerstein's refreshing script, she fails to become a star, and the threesome return to the simple life in their native town. The score also included "The Song Is You," "There's a Hill beyond a Hill," and other estimable numbers. *Music in the Air* played a year on Broadway and was made into a well-received 1934 movie. Gloria Swanson as the temperamental operetta star became the main character in the screenplay, and the story centered on her seduction of Karl (Douglass Montgomery) and her jealous lover's promotion of Sieglinde (June Lang). But the film avoided the temptation of turning Sieglinde into a Bavarian Ruby Keeler, and the ending followed the original libretto. Al Shean reprised his stage performance in the movie, but four of the Kern–Hammerstein songs were cut. Still, Kern fared much better in Hollywood than most.

George Gershwin was not so lucky with his operettas on screen. A Gershwin operetta? It sounds like an oxymoron. But what else would you call *Of Thee I Sing* (1931), *Song of the Flame* (1925), and, to a certain extent, *Porgy and Bess* (1935)? The Gilbert and Sullivan–like *Of Thee I Sing* is perhaps Broadway's finest comic operetta; but it was never filmed. Gershwin's atypical *Song of the Fame* was, much to his embarrassment. Hammerstein and Harbach concocted the purple plot about a Russian aristocrat, Aniuta (Tessa Kosta), who disguises herself as a peasant in a flaming red dress and leads the people into revolution. Prince Volodyn (Guy Robertson) loves her, not knowing her double identity, and the two do not get together until they meet in Paris after the fall of the Romanovs. Herbert Stothart and Gershwin wrote the passionate Russian music, but none of the songs found popularity. All the same, the show ran 219 performances and was filmed in 1930 with Bernice Claire and Alexander Gray as the principals. It is an impressive-looking early talkie (Technicolor was used, and for one scene the movie went into wide screen) but musically uninteresting, a bad sign for any operetta.

As for Gershwin's opera *Porgy and Bess*, it failed to become a Broadway hit but has been embraced as a classic since the 1940s. It took Hollywood twenty-four years to finally film it (producer Samuel Goldwyn spent ten years just negotiating the screen rights), and civil rights groups protested it being made at all, feeling that the piece did not accurately portray African Americans. But the 1959 movie has much to recommend it even if it is far from the definitive production of *Porgy and Bess*. Sidney Poitier and Dorothy Dandridge, as the title characters, were dubbed by Robert McFerrin and Adele Addison, so they sound professional enough, but there is a Tinsel Town glossiness to the film's look and performances that is distracting. The opera is not a piece of realism, but it does take place in Catfish Row in Charleston, not the back lot at Columbia. More interesting to watch (and hear) are Brock Peters, Sammy Davis Jr., Pearl Bailey, and other supporting players. As for the score, it was heavily abridged, but that could be said for the original Broadway production as well; Gershwin's vision for *Porgy and Bess* was much grander than any theater or movie screen could encompass. It cries out for the opera house, and today that is where you are most likely to find it. But just the fact that a movie was made that attempted to put this mammoth classic on the screen is a miracle of sorts.

Speaking of operas in the theater, one should include *Carmen Jones* (1943) in this discussion. Hammerstein took Georges Bizet's popular *Carmen* and rewrote the lyrics and libretto, setting the tale in the United States during World War II. Carmen Jones is a sultry African American woman who works in a parachute factory in the South and has a tempestuous affair with Joe, a black army colonel. *Carmen's* Escamillo the bull fighter became Husky Miller the boxer in the Hammerstein version, and events led to the same tragic conclusion as the opera. It was an audacious conceit on Hammerstein's part, but it worked, creating a new piece without destroying one's affection for the original. *Carmen Jones* ran a surprising 502 performances and was filmed in 1954.

Like *Porgy and Bess*, *Carmen Jones* was directed by the overly literal Otto Preminger, and, once again, the central couple (Dorothy Dandridge and Harry Belafonte) had their singing dubbed. But, for some reason, *Carmen Jones* does not work as a film. The highly melodramatic story that is so typical of opera just seems like melodrama on the screen. Dandridge is a convincing temptress, but Belafonte is irritatingly naïve, and the tale becomes less and less convincing as it goes on. But there is still all that exhilarating Bizet music and Hammerstein's lyrics often match it skillfully.

Bizet was not the only classical composer to be heard on Broadway. Selections from the world's great music have often been adapted and squeezed into the song format to create a new-old musical score. *Blossom Time* (1921), which turned Franz Schubert's melodies into a theater score, was one of the early successes (the show toured for decades) and spawned many imitations. *Blossom Time* was not filmed, but two of the better examples of the classical music musicals were. *Song of Norway* (1944) took Edvard Grieg's most familiar orchestral pieces and turned them into songs to illustrate the life of the celebrated Norwegian composer. Robert Wright and George Forrest did the tinkering with the tunes and wrote the lyrics, creating songs such as "Strange Music," "Hill of Dreams," and "Now!" Milton Lazarus's libretto was uninspired claptrap and inaccurate to boot, but when *Song of Norway* sang, it was entrancing. Even though it was a hit, running 860 performances, Hollywood did not film it until 1970—and probably only then because someone in California thought that the Scandinavian fiords would do for *Song of Norway* what the Alps did for *The Sound of Music*. Any Norwegian operetta movie would most likely have failed in the 1970s, but few suspected it would end up as bad as this. The screenplay was embarrassingly sentimental and incompetent, and even the great music was bearable only when used as background to the lovely scenery. Toralv Maurstadt and Florence Henderson were Mr. and Mrs. Grieg, and they had to be the cinema's odd couple of the decade. If operetta films weren't already dead, this one sealed that fate.

Wright and Forrest had another Broadway hit with *Kismet* (1953), fiddling with themes by Alexander Borodin this time. The libretto by Luther Davis and Charles Lederer was much better than the Grieg story, being based on the 1911 play of the same name about a fantastical, romantic Arabian adventure. The poet-beggar Hajj (Alfred Drake) outfoxes the Wazir (Henry Calvin), seduces his beautiful wife (Joan Diener), marries his daughter (Doretta Morrow) off to a handsome caliph (Richard Kiley), and even becomes the emir of Baghdad—all in twenty-four hours. It was a lively, far-fetched tale that played effectively against Borodin's stirring melodies. The show manufactured two hits, "Stranger in Paradise" and "Baubles, Bangles and Beads," and filled out the evening with a remarkable set of songs, climaxing in the intoxicating quartet "And This Is My Beloved."

Kismet was a major hit in New York and London, so MGM bought the rights and lavished a lot on money on the movie version, all for naught. The 1955 film is a gorgeous bore with even the score (greatly abridged) failing to excite. Howard Keel is a broad, full-voiced Hajj, but he irritates rather than amuses. The lovers, Ann Blyth and Vic Damone, seem to disappear in all the marketplace clutter, and Vincente Minnelli's direction seems frantic and pointless. Sebastian Cabot's wily Wazir adds a touch of class to the picture but not enough to save it. The poet Hajj tells us that all that happens is "kismet" (fate), but I tend to blame the studio for this one.

Once in a while a musical opens on Broadway that can be called an operetta without embarrassment (though producers would never bill the show that way). Such a case is A Little Night Music (1973), the adult musical comedy of manners based on Ingrid Bergman's film comedy Smiles of a Summer Night (1955). Stephen Sondheim wrote the flowing, waltzing score, and Hugh Wheeler penned the libretto about romantic triangles and quadrangles under the Swedish summer sun that never quite sets. The lawyer Fredrik (Len Cariou) has a young, virginal wife Anne (Victoria Mallory) who is lusted after by her divinity student stepson Henrik (Mark Lambert). When Fredrik's former flame, the actress Desiree (Glynis Johns), comes to town, the old affair is renewed, much to the jealousy of Desiree's bone-headed lover Count Carl-Magnus (Laurence Guittard) and the concern of his wife, the Countess Charlotte (Patricia Elliott). It was a complicated yet lighthearted musical romp that was superior in all its elements, from the proficient acting-singing performances and the evocative settings by Boris Aronson to the masterful direction of Harold Prince and the scintillating songs.

There was great anticipation for the 1978 film version, especially when it was announced that Prince would direct, Wheeler would do the screenplay, and the cast would include from the stage Cariou, Guittard, and Hermione Gingold (as Desiree's sly mother). But the movie was such a disappointment that it was only given a very limited release and then disappeared altogether. Prince was unquestionably one of Broadway's most gifted talents, but the movie of A Little Night Music demonstrated much too obviously that he was not a movie director. Scenes are presented awkwardly, continuity is confusing, the storytelling is jumbled, and even the camera work is unflattering to the actors, especially Elizabeth Taylor as Desiree. Perhaps to avoid comparisons with Bergman's film, the story was set in Austria, which not only cut out songs about the sun never setting but also took away the Scandinavian milieu that was so magical. The acting is wildly uneven: Taylor looks lost and in pain, especially when she sings. Diana Rigg is a fine Charlotte, and Lesley-Ann Down is also admirable, though obviously too old for the teenager Anne. But even the usual scene stealer Gingold is just plain dull in this oddly dissatisfying film. It has not hurt the reputation of the stage musical, which remains a beloved favorite and is often revived, but the movie didn't do film operetta any good. The genre was long gone, and this one opportunity to revive it quietly passed away with it.

CHAPTER SIX

~

Waiting for the Revues
to Come Out

Near the beginning of the 1941 Universal film *Hellzapoppin'*, a movie
director (Richard Lane) tells the comic team of Olson and Johnson
that this movie cannot be like their 1938 Broadway revue *Hellzapoppin'*: all gags and scattered pieces of entertainment. "This is Hollywood," he tells them. "We change everything here. We've *got* to!" He
might as well told them that there is no such thing as a movie revue.
Not an accurate statement, but one that has been the philosophy in
Tinsel Town over the decades.

A *theater revue* is a collection of songs, dances, and sketches that are
written, scored, and staged to hang together in a plotless entertainment. It is not the same as a vaudeville show in which a bunch of individual acts are created separately and then strung together to fill out
a program.

The first distinctive American revue was *The Passing Show* (1894),
and it was so successful that the Shubert Brothers presented a series of
revues with that name. The idea quickly caught on and soon there were
the *Ziegfeld Follies*, George White's *Scandals*, Earl Carroll's *Vanities*, Irving Berlin's *Music Box Revues*, and others. The heyday of the Broadway
revue was the 1930s in which clever, topical, and well-written shows
raised the form to a high art. *The Little Show* (1929), *The Band Wagon*
(1931), *As Thousands Cheer* (1933), and *Pins and Needles* (1937) were

among the most fondly remembered revues of the era. By World War II, the genre was in decline, and today the only kind of Broadway revues left are the tribute shows to a particular artist or era, such as *Ain't Misbehavin'* (1978) or *Swing!* (1999).

But revues were so popular on the stage when films started talking that every studio made a movie revue in the early days. It made sense artistically and financially. Since the stars were all on contract, you simply gave each one a song or sketch in the movie and ended up with a star-studded extravaganza. MGM was the first to latch onto the idea, presenting its roster of stars in *The Hollywood Revue of 1929*. (The title tells you that the studio hoped this would become an annual money-maker.) It was followed by Warner Brothers' *On with the Show* (1929) and *The Show of Shows* (1929), Universal's *King of Jazz* (1930), Paramount's *Glorifying the American Girl* (1930) and *Paramount on Parade* (1930), and so on.

Some great songs and splendid production numbers came from these early revues, but something was wrong. Audiences felt mildly dissatisfied. Movies meant stories, not vaudeville shows, and the public's interest in film revues quickly faded. By the mid-1930s, they were gone. Or, more accurately, they changed. A string of acts was still palatable on the screen if it was loosely tied together with some kind of story. The operative word here is *loosely* because the excuse for a plot could be pretty feeble; as long as it seemed like a continuous story, the movie was not a pure revue, and the moviegoers bought it. So Hollywood presented *The Big Broadcast* (1932) and its many sequels, a whole series in the likeness of *The Broadway Melody of 1936* (1935), *The Gold Diggers of 1933* and its follow-ups, and other disguised revues. The stage genre known as the revue became a new animal on the screen. As the guy said, "This is Hollywood. We change everything here."

Many Broadway revues were turned into movies, but, with very few exceptions, they were given some kind of plotline to justify their being put on the screen. We will look at some of the famous revue series and at some notable individual revues and see what happened when Hollywood got a hold of them.

Since I started the chapter with *Hellzapoppin'*, we'll consider that 1938 show first. Here was a freak success, a revue that ran 1,404 performances despite poor reviews, lack of Broadway stars, little spectacle, and no memorable songs. What the show had was total comic chaos in the form of comedians Ole Olson and Chic Johnson, two vaudevillians who had perfected their zany antics on the road during the previous fourteen years. The jokes and gimmicks in *Hellzapoppin'* came fast and furiously, firecrackers literally exploded, even sirens and gunshots were heard throughout the show. There were running bits, such as a man who kept going up and down the aisles all evening trying to deliver a potted plant to a lady in the audience; the plant got bigger with each entrance, and by the time the audience exited, he was sitting in the lobby with a full-size tree. It was that kind of humor. Amid the sophomoric comedy was some brassy satire as well, such as a film clip shown at the opening in which Hitler, in a Yiddish accent, praised the revue about to begin. Mussolini, speaking in an American Negro dialect, also sent his compliments. And such nonsense went on all evening. By the time it closed, *Hellzapoppin'* held the record for the longest-running musical in Broadway history.

How could Hollywood ignore such success? But how could they make a film of it? By adding a story, of course. Robert Paige loves singer Jane Frazee, but wealthy Lewis Howard is also after her, so Paige arranges to put on a big revue and make her a star on Broadway and. . . . It really didn't matter. In fact, the whole movie took the format of a surreal pitch by a Hollywood director, telling Olson and Johnson what they could and could not do on screen. The result is a fast-paced, very disjointed, but surprisingly modern comedy; an early, primitive Monty Python flick. The comedy duo repeated some of their stage gags and added others, Martha Raye chased after a rich count (Misha Auer), and specialty acts were thrown in as part of the revue being staged. Some of the comedy bits (mostly visual) worked, but a lot of them didn't. Where the Broadway revue had been audacious and outrageous, the humor in the movie was safe and conventional; spoofing the recent *Citizen Kane* was Hollywood's idea of cutting satire. The stage songs were replaced by new ones by Gene De Paul and Don Raye, and they were a little better, which wasn't saying much. The 1941 movie set off no firecrackers, to say the least, but audiences were curious after hearing about *Hellzapoppin'* in New York all those years. Olson and Johnson would make nine films together, but this was the only one that came close to being a hit.

Although it did not run nearly as long as *Hellzapoppin'*, *The Band Wagon* (1931) was considered by many to be the finest Broadway revue of the 1930s. It boasted a superb score by Arthur Schwartz (music) and Howard Dietz (lyrics), introducing such delectable favorites as "Dancing in the Dark," "I Love Louisa," "High and Low," and "New Sun in the Sky." George S. Kaufman and Dietz wrote the comedy sketches, Albertina Rasch choreographed the production numbers, and Hassard Short directed the whole thing beautifully as the show flowed along on twin turntables. *The Band Wagon* starred Fred and Adele Astaire (her last Broadway show), Frank Morgan, Helen Broderick, and Tilly Losch, and they were never better.

Surprisingly, Hollywood did not jump on the band wagon and turn the revue into a film until twenty-two years had passed. But it was worth the wait because the 1953 movie is a musical classic. Betty Comden and Adolph Green were given the task of writing a screenplay that would utilize the full catalog of songs by Dietz and Schwartz, few of which had been used in the movies since most came from Broadway revues. What they came up with was a nimble-witted script that was sportively autobiographical. Songwriters Nanette Fabray and Oscar Levant (thinly disguised versions of Comden and Green) write the score for a Broadway revue that will serve as a comeback vehicle for a Fred Astaire–like Hollywood hoofer getting on in age. Of course, Astaire played the part. Jack Buchanan was the overly artistic director (patterned after Vincente Minnelli, the film's actual director) who destroys the merry show by turning it into "art": a musical version of *Faust*. Predictably, the stage show is a disaster, so Astaire, Levant, and Fabray quickly rewrite it as a musical revue called *The Band Wagon*. Cyd Charisse and James Mitchell were on hand for their dancing talents, and the movie climaxed with a wry, droll ballet, "The Girl Hunt," that spoofed the current fad for tough-guy books by Mickey Spillane. (Alan Jay Lerner wrote the narration, and it was quietly hilarious.) The film overflows with outstanding songs and first-rate production numbers (choreographed by Michael Kidd): "Triplets," "Dancing in the Dark," "By Myself," "A Shine on Your Shoes," "I Guess I'll Have to Change My Plan," "Something to Remember You By," and several others. Dietz and Schwartz hadn't written songs together in years, but they joined forces again and came up with the new number "That's Entertainment," which would soon become the unofficial anthem of Hollywood musicals. *The Band Wagon* is probably the best example of how a sparkling Broadway revue could become an equally memorable musical film.

There were two popular patriotic revues on Broadway during the 1940s; one near the beginning of the war and the other as the troops were returning home. Irving Berlin had scored a famous patriotic revue in 1918 called *Yip, Yip, Yaphank* that raised money for the war effort. He repeated the idea in 1942 with *This Is the Army*, a revue whose cast was made up of enlisted men, only a few of whom were recognized Broadway names. Although there was a certain amount of flag waving, much of the revue was comic as it poked fun at life in the military. Berlin himself appeared on stage and sang the droll "Oh, How I Hate to Get Up in the Morning," a number he had introduced in the 1918 show. Other songs included the dreamy "I'm Getting Tired So I Can Sleep," the jocular "The Army's Made a Man Out of Me," and the catchy "This Is the Army, Mr. Jones."

The considerable profits from *This Is the Army* went to the Army Emergency Relief Fund, as did the money from the 1943 Warner Brothers film version. Twelve of the show's sixteen songs were kept, as well as much of the cast (including Berlin). But the inevitable plot had to be added and the one devised by the studio was dull and plodding and dragged the picture down whenever the musical numbers stopped. The movie starts during World War I with George Murphy putting on an all-soldier revue called *Yip, Yip, Yaphank*. Then the years passed, and Murphy's son (Ronald Reagan) puts on a similar show as America marches off into World War II. The production numbers (staged by LeRoy Prinz and Robert Sidney) are on a colossal scale and tend to impress by their numbers rather than their ingenuity, but there is much to enjoy in the movie. And for a patriotic musical, you couldn't do better than bring Kate Smith in to sing "God Bless America."

Call Me Mister (1946) was a Broadway revue about enlisted men adjusting to civilian life as they returned from overseas. Like *This Is the Army*, the show had its somber moments but mostly was a humorous look at demobilization. Harold Rome wrote the score and it was filled with variety and skill. The title number waggishly looked at the soldiers' homecoming, the late Franklin D. Roosevelt was saluted in "The

Face on the Dime," and a USO canteen hostess (Betty Garrett), fed up with all the songs from Latin America, complained facetiously with "South America, Take It Away." The most sobering number in the revue was "The Red Ball Express" in which an African American truck driver (Lawrence Winters) who had carried important supplies during the war was denied a job in the postwar employment boom because of his race. As with the earlier revue, the cast of *Call Me Mister* was mostly comprised of the real thing: ex-GIs and USO workers.

The 1951 movie version only kept three of Rome's songs and dismissed the whole premise of enlisted men returning from the war. It was now a romantic comedy set in Japan during the then-current Korean War with USO singer Betty Grable having marital difficulties with her GI husband Dan Dailey. It was a tiresome plot about Dailey putting on a camp show in order to bring Gable back to him, but many of the musical numbers (staged by Busby Berkeley) were enjoyable. Of the new songs added for the film, the best was "Lament to the Pots and Pans," a comic ditty sung by Danny Thomas doing KP duty. Dailey danced to the title number, Grable sang "Japanese Girl Like American Boy," and an oversized finale called "Love Is Back in Business" used the same kind of crowding effect seen in *This Is the Army*.

There was one occasion when Broadway got a jump on Hollywood and gave a revue a plot before it was sold to the movies. *Take a Chance* (1932) started out as a revue called *Humpty Dumpty* with a score by Nacio Herb Brown and Richard A. Whiting and the theme of events from American history. Despite a winning cast featuring Eddie Foy Jr. and newcomer Ethel Merman, and even with such dandy songs as "Eadie Was a Lady" and "You're an Old Smoothie," *Humpty Dumpty* was an unqualified disaster, and it folded in Pittsburgh in one week. But the producers kept Merman and her numbers and hired Vincent Youmans for more songs and turned the revue into a book musical about Harvard grad Kenneth Raleigh (Jack Whiting) who is putting on a revue about American history called *Humpty Dumpty* so that he and his sweetheart Toni (June Knight) can star in it. His two primary backers (Jack Haley and Sid Silvers), friends of Toni's, turn out to be crooks, so Kenneth thinks she is in on the swindle. Of course, everything is straightened out by opening night, and, contrary to then-recent history, *Humpty Dumpty* is a big hit.

Take a Chance was also a hit, opening six months late in New York but running 243 performances in those early days of the Depression. Hollywood bought the rights but not Merman so Lillian Roth got to sing the spirited "Rise 'n' Shine," the interpolated Youmans number that was the highlight of the Broadway show. Paramount added the little-known "It's Only a Paper Moon" to the movie, and it, too, became a hit. The hackneyed backstage story was repeated on film, looking more feeble than before, but the production numbers were fine and there were personable performances by Charles "Buddy" Rogers, James Dunn, Cliff Edwards and, from the Broadway cast, June Knight. The 1933 movie was not a major success yet had its charms.

When Hollywood was buying up Broadway revues, they could not ignore the handful of popular revue series that managed to create not just one hit but a series of moneymakers. So at least one film version was made from each of the celebrated series. *Artists and Models* had half a dozen Broadway editions between 1923 and 1943, and, as the title suggested, one was very likely to see undressed females in artistic poses in every show. Actually, the series began as a revue sponsored by the Illustrator's Society of New York and was a rather classy affair. The Shubert Brothers bought the name and presented a series of less enlightened but provocative-looking shows.

Hollywood liked the title, too, and made three films that kept precious little from Broadway except the name. Paramount's *Artists and Models* (1937) had a story, of course, and it was fairly routine, but the movie is a surprising delight. Advertising agent Mac Brewster (Jack Benny) is hawking a silverware company and stages a beauty contest to find a queen for the Artists and Models Ball. Ida Lupino posed as a socialite to get in on the deal, and she was joined by such prankish talents as Ben Blue, Judy Canova, Richard Arlen, and Martha Raye. Like a true revue, it was the production numbers that shone, especially when they featured Louis Armstrong, Connee Boswell, and others. Even the score (by a variety of tunesmiths) had its merits, including "I Have Eyes," "Whispers in the Dark," and "Public Melody Number One."

The film was so popular that Paramount quickly followed it with *Artists and Models Abroad* (1938) where Benny returned as the manager of an all-girl theatrical troupe stranded in Paris. He woos a Texas millionaire's daughter (Joan Bennett) at first for her money and then for her heart. The predictable tale ended with the predictable Paris fashion show, but there was one unexpected song of quality, "What Have You Got That Gets Me?"

Because the second movie did poor business, Paramount dropped *Artists and Models* until 1955 when they used the title for a Dean Martin–Jerry Lewis musical comedy. The fact that Martin played a struggling artist justified the title, in a way, and the picture ended with a big production number with models wearing splashes of color on a giant palette. The plot revolved around Martin's roommate (Lewis) who is a would-be children's book author but whose pulplike nightmares end up becoming popular comic books. Shirley MacLaine and Dorothy Malone were the next-door neighbors and supplied the love interest. The score by Harry Warren and Jack Brooks was pleasant, and the ballad "Inamorata" became quite popular. *Artists and Models* is a Martin–Lewis film that can be enjoyed even if you aren't one of the team's fans. And it is an interesting example of a movie that is inspired (sort of) by a revue but that isn't about putting on a revue.

The revue series Earl Carroll presented on Broadway between 1923 and 1940 was named the *Vanities*, a double entendre title; the beautiful ladies were perhaps vain, but they were certainly dressed as scantily as a female would be at her vanity table. It was an obvious attempt to cash in on Ziegfeld's celebrated *Follies* girls, but Carroll was more interested in sexy and suggestive gals than American beauty roses. In fact, his shows often put him at odds with the law (which only helped business). Few worthwhile songs or top-ranked singing or dancing stars would be found at the *Vanities*, but some of the best comics in the business appeared in them, from Sophie Tucker and W. C. Fields to Helen Broderick and Milton Berle.

Maybe it was the lascivious reputation the revues had, but no major Hollywood studio would touch it. Yet Republic Pictures released Earl Carroll's *Vanities* in 1945, and it gave audiences a sanitized version of what the Broadway series might have been like. A plot was added, of course, and it asked moviegoers to stretch their credibility somewhat. Princess Drinia of Turania (Constance Moore) travels to New York City with her mother (Mary Forbes) and the Grand Duke (Alan Mowbray) to raise funds for their insolvent little nation. Wouldn't you know it, but the princess ends up starring in one of Mr. Carroll's famous *Van-*

ities revues. It's all harmless fun, and, while the production values don't match the bigger studios, there is Eve Arden for the wisecracks and Woody Herman and his orchestra for the big band sound. Although they may have sounded naughtier than the *Vanities*, George White's *Scandals* were actually a class affair. In fact, artistically speaking, many considered them the most accomplished of the revue series. White was a dancer and choreographer (he had appeared as a hoofer in some of the early *Follies*), and he made sure his girls didn't just hang around and pose. The *Scandals* featured dance and new songs rather than just females and White hired the best dancers and the most promising songwriters of the day. George Gershwin and the team of DeSylva, Brown, and Henderson were among the many tunesmiths who got their first recognition scoring the *Scandals*. Among the songs that White introduced were "Somebody Loves Me," "Life Is Just a Bowl of Cherries," "Black Bottom," "The Birth of the Blues," and "I'll Build a Stairway to Paradise." Ziegfeld may have had the stars, the scenery, and the girls, but White offered some of the best musical numbers in town. There were thirteen editions of the *Scandals* between 1919 and 1939, as well as three film versions and White himself was involved with all three.

George White's *Scandals* (1934) is mostly recalled today because it introduced Alice Faye to movie audiences. It was a routine Fox backstager about a revue star (Rudy Vallee) and whether he and the leading lady will end up in each other's arms (as if we didn't know). The whole movie might have quietly disappeared into the footnotes of film books, but just before shooting began the star Lilian Harvey quit, and Vallee suggested the studio replace her with his band vocalist Faye. (Such background history is actually more interesting than the plot in the film.) While George White's *Scandals* was not a big hit, moviegoers were instantly drawn to Faye as she scolded with the wry song "Oh, You Nasty Man," and she was top-billed from then on. Not that she is the only worthwhile aspect of the film. Vallee crooned the warm "Hold My Hand," Jimmy Durante did his thing (for one number in blackface), and there was a memorable production number with a giant champagne glass with chorus girls diving off the rim and into the bubbly.

White codirected and cowrote the film, and everybody must have been happy because the next year Fox made George White's *1935 Scandals* with Alice Faye again and White himself playing a big-time

Broadway producer named George White. He is scouting acts in Florida and signs up Faye and her sweetheart–singing partner James Dunn. But life on Broadway was not all roses, and their romance got a little rocky until the final production number. It was pretty much the same plot as the previous year's edition. But this one had an admirable score by Jack Yellen, Cliff Friend, Joseph Meyers, and others (including sometime-lyricist White) that included "It's an Old Southern Custom," "You Belong to Me," and "According to the Moonlight," which Faye sang, and her recording was her first disc hit. Just as the first *Scandals* movie introduced a major Hollywood talent, this one introduced the tap-dancing sensation Eleanor Powell in a short but impressive sequence. (Within a year, Powell was the star of her own movie musical, *The Broadway Melody of 1936*.)

Ten years passed before RKO made the final movie in White's series, this one called *George White's Scandals of 1945*. It is easily the least satisfying of the three films. Another backstager with two couples having lovers' spats in the wings, it featured Jack Haley, Joan Davis, Phillip Terry, and Martha Holliday, when it really needed Alice Faye. The only noteworthy songs were old favorites added to the score, such as organist Ethel Smith's lively rendition of the Gershwins' "Liza." Interestingly, one number actually came from a Broadway *Scandals*: Haley and Davis performed a pleasant version of "Life Is Just a Bowl of Cherries" from the 1931 edition.

Although only one film is directly descended from the grand-daddy of all revues, the *Ziegfeld Follies*, the presence of the great impresario could be felt in several movie musicals. Florenz Ziegfeld supervised the early talkie *Glorifying the American Girl* (1930), which, primitive as it was, gives one an idea of what a Ziegfeld stage extravaganza looked like. But Ziegfeld's continual money worries kept him from becoming a major player in Hollywood, and his reputation rests on his illustrious stage career. He produced his first *Follies* at a rooftop theater in 1907, and it was so successful he transferred it to Broadway, where it was followed by twenty more editions before he died in 1932. (His widow Billie Burke sold the Ziegfeld name to producers who used it for a handful of subsequent revues, but none were true Ziegfeld creations.) He hired the biggest stars, the best designers, and the top songwriters for his shows, but each edition eventually came down to beautiful ladies in eye-popping costumes in dazzling settings.

Although the revues were very popular, Ziegfeld spent so much money on each production that he became more famous than rich. Since the name Ziegfeld meant lavish entertainment, Hollywood often conjured up his person in its own musicals, most memorably the biopic *The Great Ziegfeld* (1936) that emulated the showman in its spectacle. The man himself was impersonated by actors in *Sally, The Eddie Cantor Story, Ziegfeld Girl, Funny Girl, Funny Lady,* and others, as well as all those backstagers where there was often a Ziegfeld-like producer. But there was one occasion in which Hollywood attempted to make a true *Follies* on film.

MGM producer Arthur Freed planned the screen *Ziegfeld Follies* for several years and considered dozens of songs and sketches for the project. Filming took place over a period of two years, the final result released in 1946. It was really an old idea, one from the days of the first talkies: take all the talent at MGM and put them in one big show. Freed insisted there be no feeble plot to give the revue a story, but he did settle for a prologue in heaven where Ziegfeld (William Powell) looks down upon MGM and imagines the kind of show he could put on with all those stars, directors, choreographers, designers, and songwriters. The rest of the film is strictly a revue, with musical numbers and comic sketches presented with no recurring theme or narration segues. Some acts look stagy; others are pure cinema. (Several different directors worked on the film.) Most of the musical numbers are top-notch, but too many of the sketches fall flat. This is probably because movie musicals can create song and dance in a studio, but sketches need an audience. Still, the chance to see Fanny Brice (the only cast member who actually appeared in a *Follies* in her career), Victor Moore, Hume Cronyn, Keenan Wynn, Red Skelton, William Frawley, and others deliver well-polished comic routines is fascinating, if not always funny. There are many splendid musical moments, including new songs written for the film (such as Lena Horne singing "Love") and old favorites (like the stunning "Limehouse Blues" with Fred Astaire and Lucille Bremer). Some production numbers are lavish, like the opening "Bring on the Beautiful Girls," followed by the tongue-in-cheek "Bring on Those Wonderful Men." Other numbers are quite simple, such as Judy Garland's sprightly impersonation of Greer Garson with the song "Madame Crematon." There is even a water ballet for Esther Williams, something the real Ziegfeld would have done had he figured out how to flood the New Amsterdam Theater.

But the two highlights of *Ziegfeld Follies* (both featuring Astaire) are "The Babbitt and the Bromide" and "This Heart of Mine." The former is a droll song-and-dance duet the Gershwins originally wrote for Astaire and his sister Adele in Broadway's *Funny Face* (1927). He reprises it (with new choreography) with Gene Kelly, the only screen teaming of the two great Hollywood hoofers, and it is a marvel to behold. "This Heart of Mine" was written for the movie by Harry Warren (music) and Freed (lyric), and the enchanting ballad is turned into a twelve-minute minimusical (choreographed by Robert Alton) about a jewel thief (Astaire) who woos a society lady (Bremer) and subtly steals her bejeweled bracelet while they dance together. Just when it looks like he will escape, it becomes clear that she knows what he has done, and she offers her necklace as well. Their look of mutual understanding is priceless as they dance away into the night. It is one of the greatest of all narrative movie ballets.

Ziegfeld Follies was not a smash hit, and never again would a studio try and re-create a Broadway revue on the screen. Just as Broadway itself turned its back on the revue format in the late 1940s, so, too, would Hollywood give up trying to capture this unique kind of entertainment on film. Plot would continue to drive most movie musicals, and even the idea of a film climaxing with the Big Show would go out of fashion by the end of the 1950s. The revue became a thing of the past, both on Broadway and in the cinema. But what glorious moments passed away with it!

CHAPTER SEVEN

~

Too Hot to Handle

Sex and politics, those two mainstays for censorship in the arts, have given both Broadway and Hollywood trouble over the years. It is hard to remember in the early twenty-first century, when anything can and has been done in movies and on stage, that there was a time when both media had to bend over backward to avoid disapproval by powerful and righteous groups. A play that opened during Lent or a film that was condemned by the Legion of Decency was box office poison, and one could not avoid the consequences. And even if you got past the watchful eye of the censors, there was always the possibility that the public itself would take offense and turn its back on your product.

An added problem was the different periods of censorship that each media experienced: plays were most carefully monitored up to World War I, while Hollywood had its strongest code of behavior enforced between the mid-1930s and the late 1950s. This made for an obvious discrepancy; the freedom allotted Broadway was not enjoyed in Tinsel Town. Thus, many musicals got cleaned up in the transition from stage to screen.

From the earliest days of theater in the colonies, there was an antagonism toward players and plays. After all, the New England ethic was Puritan, and the Philadelphia mentality was largely Catholic or Quaker. As late as the 1890s, some theaters were called concert halls, museums, or atheneums to get past the stigma of a "playhouse." Early works by George Bernard Shaw, Henrik Ibsen, and other "problem play" authors were raided by the police. Actresses were not considered socially acceptable or sufficiently moral until the nineteenth century was nearly over.

And as for stage musicals, their very birth was greeted with moral outrage. *The Black Crook* (1866), considered the first musical play, was denounced from church pulpits for its lewd display of chorines in pink tights; the effect on stage was that of naked legs. But *The Black Crook* flourished because of the controversy, and subsequent musicals quickly learned that a bit of leg never hurt any show. By the end of World War I, Broadway was getting away with a lot more in terms of sex and politics. The second has rarely raised as much commotion in America as the former, but politics is a trickier subject to finesse regarding public taste. Freedom of speech says a play can condone any political belief, but no one ever made any money by going against the popular thinking of the time. When *Of Thee I Sing* (1931) opened, its potent satire on government and politics was considered daring but enjoyable. When the same creative team presented the equally satirical *Let 'Em Eat Cake* (1933), the Depression was at its lowest ebb, and audiences didn't feel like laughing at the system. Public opinion is the harshest censor because you cannot sneak by it.

Early movies were not censored because no one took them seriously. A lewd one-reeler shown at a nickelodeon was on the same level as a freak show attraction or French postcards on sale at a carnival. It is surprising to see how much nudity and sexual suggestion were prevalent in the early flickers. Dialogue was summarized by title cards, so the quoted lines may be in good taste, but the foulness implied in the character's actions or even gestures could be rather colorful. Even some of the early musicals were pushing the boundaries of what you could show on screen.

One musical that perhaps pushed a little too far was *Roman Scandals* (1933). While Ruth Etting sang "No More Love" in a Roman slave market, naked females, barely covered by their long blonde hair, were chained to the walls as a grotesque guard went about lashing his whip at the writhing gals. That scene, and the then-current Mae West single-entendres, are often pointed to as the reason Hollywood developed its own Production Code. While it is easy today to laugh at the ridiculous rules (the length of a kiss, the positioning of limbs during an embrace, and so on), one must remember that the code was rigorously enforced by the studios themselves.

Yet even abiding by the code could lead you into trouble. The Catholic Church condemned *Gone with the Wind* (1939) because of Clark Gable's "I don't give a damn." Yet characters were calling each other "bastards" and swearing "God damn" on Broadway as far back as the war drama *What Price Glory?* (1924). With such a difference in acceptance levels, moving a musical from one medium to the other was not going to be easy.

I don't think it is an exaggeration to say that 90 percent of the Broadway musicals that were filmed between 1935 and 1960 were censored in some way. Often this censorship was minor. Sometimes a prostitute was changed to just a woman who wore too much makeup. Or a couple living in sin were conveniently married in the film version. African American characters who weren't servants usually became white on the screen so as not to offend southern moviegoers. Often it was just a matter of a lyric or two. Cole Porter's scores, filled as they are with subtle and not-so-subtle sexual references, were prime for a celluloid clean up. But even Oscar Hammerstein, far from our most lascivious lyricist, saw some lines and lyrics from *Oklahoma!* changed when it was filmed as late in the game as 1955. One could go through the catalog of movie musicals and list the numerous little alterations made from the stage original. Instead, I have chosen ten films, both old and more recent, that can serve as illustrative examples of properties that, as they had appeared on stage, were too hot for Hollywood to handle.

Strike Up the Band (1930) was a case of a musical being doctored for both the stage and the film. The original libretto by George S. Kaufman was a wicked piece of satire in which industrialist Horace J. Fletcher urges America to go to war against Switzerland over the tariffs on Swiss cheese. Fletcher is even willing to fund the war if it will be named after him. The resulting conflict is so financially successful that, as the play ends, a new war against Russia over caviar is planned. Reflecting this blatant condemnation of capitalism and patriotism was the score by the Gershwins, led by the tongue-in-cheek title song that suggests one can arouse a patriotic fervor over just about anything. *Strike Up the Band* previewed in New Jersey in 1927 and left audiences cold, folding in two weeks and abandoning plans to continue on to Broadway. Perhaps the booming late 1920s was not the time to mock the system.

But three years later a softened, more silly version of *Strike Up the Band* did open in New York and managed a decent run. What was different? Morrie Ryskind rewrote Kaufman's libretto, making the war over Swiss chocolate and putting the whole plot in the context of a dream. Audiences were more willing to accept a cartoonish satire that made no pretense of really happening. The second version also boasted the comic talents of Bobby Clark and Paul McCullough as buffoonish politicians, the presence of veteran vaudeville favorite Blanche Ring, and a revised Gershwin score that included the romantic "I've Got a Crush on You." The title song remained but was presented (and accepted) as a patriotic anthem. Kaufman could not have been too pleased with what Ryskind did to his script, but he was savvy enough to be practical about it. *Strike Up the Band* was a modest hit (190 performances in the early Depression days), and the next year Kaufman and Ryskind collaborated on the classic musical satire *Of Thee I Sing*.

Hollywood showed no interest in filming *Strike Up the Band*, particularly once war broke out in Europe. But Tinsel Town liked a hit song when it heard one, so it used "Strike Up the Band" as the title song of a 1940 movie musical that bore no relation to the stage original. The plot and score were discarded, and a Mickey Rooney–Judy Garland "let's put on a show" musical took their place. All about Rooney's high school jazz band trying to win a contest and perform with Paul Whitman's Orchestra, the tale eschewed any satire whatsoever (unless one considers a spoof of an old-time mellerdramer and the song "Heaven Will Protect the Working Girl" a satire) and just sought wholesome escapism. The movie has it moments (particularly with Busby Berkeley's inventive staging of Arthur Freed and Roger Edens's song "Our Love Affair" and Garland's touching ballad "Nobody"), but its stage origins are obliterated. The title song became a big band salute to the American spirit and winning the Whiteman contest stood for what democracy was all about.

Also politically charged was *Knickerbocker Holiday* (1938). Librettist Maxwell Anderson wanted to make a point about totalitarianism and the evils of too much government. But instead of going for such obvious targets as Hitler and Mussolini, Anderson chose Franklin Roosevelt, showing how the current president's programs and control over various branches of government were dangerous precedents and a threat to true democracy. The musical was a historical allegory, set in New Amsterdam in 1647 with Pieter Stuyvesant (Walter Huston) as the singing-dancing (even with a peg leg) dictatorial Governor. The radical freedom fighter Brom Broeck (Richard Kollmar) opposes Stuyvesant politically and emotionally (he wants to marry the girl selected to wed the Governor) and is sentenced to hang until he helps thwart an Indian attack and becomes a hero. The script is littered with topical references, not the least subtle being a foolish, Dutch comiclike councilman called Roosevelt. Although this was a few years before FDR's strong popularity during the war, there were still many who liked Roosevelt and his recovery programs. And even though *Knickerbocker Holiday* was often as funny and entertaining as it was preachy, the show often flew in the face of popular opinion. It only managed to run its (unprofitable) 168 performances because of Huston. His Stuyvesant was charming, roguish, and even touching, particularly when he sang the unforgettable "September Song." In a way, Huston's performance belied the whole musical's premise; if a man can be this delightful, why worry that he's a dictator?

When the film version was made in 1944, Roosevelt was still in office, but neither he nor anyone else could be offended by the watered-down piece of romantic fluff that shone on the screen. Oddly, movie star Huston was passed over, and character actor Charles Coburn played Stuyvesant as the grumpy business tycoon that he usually played on film. Nelson Eddy was Bram, now a printer who has advanced ideas (such as democracy) and is thrown in jail, giving the peg-legged Governor a chance to flirt with Bram's fiancée (Constance Dowling). It was all rather harmless and enjoyable in an old-fashioned operetta kind of way. (With all the pretty period costumes and sets, it looked like an operetta). Only three songs from the stage score were retained (including "September Song"), and new ones were supplied by Jule Styne, Sammy Cahn, and others. Some numbers are charming, and Coburn somewhat holds the picture together. But as a musical satire, the film of *Knickerbocker Holiday* is toothless and forgettable.

Earlier in the decade, *Gay Divorce* (1932) caused different problems for Hollywood, but not political ones this time. The Broadway libretto by Dwight Taylor was an up-to-the-minute piece that mined the comic possibilities of the current divorce laws. Unhappily married Mimi Pratt (Claire Luce) wants to dump Mr. Pratt, but the law says she must be caught in the act of adultery for a decree to be granted. She hires the rather effeminate Italian Tonetti (Erik Rhodes), a professional correspondent, who will check into a hotel with Mimi to give an official stamp to the adultery. Novelist Guy Holden (Fred Astaire) is secretly smitten by Mimi and follows her to the hotel where he is mistaken by her as the correspondent. Tonetti also shows up, and in the subsequent confusions Mimi falls in love with Guy, marrying him as soon as her divorce comes through. Cole Porter wrote the score, and it was delectable, though only "Night and Day" went on to become justly famous. (The entrancing ballad "After You, Who?" never got the recognition it deserved, being introduced too close to the more celebrated song.) Gay Divorce was Astaire's first and last Broadway appearance without his sister Adele; she married an English lord and retired. But Luce and Astaire made a tantalizing couple, and, unlike his previous shows when the dance highlights were by brother and sister, this time they were romantic duos performed by lovers. Astaire had finally become a true romantic leading man. Worried that he would flop in a musical without his sister, Astaire was relieved when the musical was a hit. All the same, he left the show before the end of its 249-performance run to take up Hollywood's offer.

RKO bought the screen rights for Gay Divorce, but there was trouble right away with the title. It wasn't the word gay; it had not yet gained its homosexual connotation. But "divorce" was the problem. Rarely was it mentioned in the movies, and the idea of a happy divorce was too much of a mockery of the institution of marriage. Yet the Hays Office allowed the title The Gay Divorcee, reasoning that a woman might be happy about such an unwholesome thing as divorce.

The 1934 film was Astaire's first starring role. He had been seen as supporting characters in the earlier musicals Dancing Lady (1933) and Flying Down to Rio (1933), teamed with Ginger Rogers in the second. The twosome had lit up the screen when they danced "The Carioca," so RKO put them in the central roles in The Gay Divorcee. The plot stayed the same, though Guy Holden was now a dancer rather than a novelist and the divorcee was named Mimi Glossop. The details about the necessary adultery were omitted, and if you didn't know better, you would think that Tonetti (Rhodes again) was coming to cook spaghetti for Rogers. The Porter score was dropped except for "Night and Day," but the new songs by Harry Revel, Mack Gordon, Herb Magidson, and Con Conrad were splendid, particularly "The Continental," the Oscar-winning song that provided the dancing team with their famous ballroom duet. Betty Grable and Edward Everett Horton supplied the comedy (and sang the facetious "Let's K-nock K-nees" together), along with Eric Blore, Alice Brady, and William Austin in support. *The Gay Divorcee* remains today a thoroughly delicious movie musical, yet RKO held its breath when it was first released, fretting that the subject matter might offend some moviegoers. But everyone was too busy falling in love with Astaire and Rodgers in their first of many starring movies together. Instead of being too hot to handle, the picture was just hot.

Moving from divorce to marriage, different difficulties presented themselves with *I Married an Angel* (1938). The property began as a proposed Rodgers and Hart film musical but was aborted by the studios early on. The team took the material to Broadway where they wrote the libretto themselves, and it was filled with delightful mischief and sly commentary on marriage, sex, and contemporary mores. The musical is a fantasy set in Budapest where the aristocratic banker Willie Palaffi (Dennis King), a playboy who resists setting a wedding date with his fiancée Anna Murphy (Audrey Christie), gets so fed up with the grasping women all around him that he vows to wed no one but an angel. When a literal angel (Vera Zorina) arrives, Willie marries the innocent and willing creature. She awakens from the wedding night and realizes she has "lost her wings" (lots of suggestive jokes about that), yet the angel remains blessedly naive and truthful, politely telling fat people that they are fat and revealing embarrassing indiscretions that she has overheard. This stress on Palaffi is augmented by Anna's revenge tactics that put the bank in trouble. But Willie's worldly-wise sister, the Countess Palaffi (Vivienne Segal), comes to the rescue by getting firm support for his bank and teaching the celestial bride how to use her feminine powers and play the society game. The adult fairy tale was made more satirical by some lavish, tongue-in-cheek production numbers, such as the irrelevant "At the Roxie Music Hall" which lampooned the overproduced extravaganzas to be found at Radio City Music Hall. George Balanchine choreographed a long and inventive ballet in each act, and there were even sections of the script that were written in rhyme. All of the Rodgers and Hart songs were expert, and two hits came from the score: "Spring Is Here" and the title ballad. *I Married an Angel* was one of the team's biggest hits (338 performances) and ranks as one of their boldest and most exhilarating experiments.

MGM, the same studio that had started the project, bought the screen rights after the show was so successful. But Rodgers and Hart had nothing to do with the 1942 film and it shows. Anita Loos wrote the dreary screenplay that avoided the fantasy elements by making much of the story a bad dream that Willie (Nelson Eddy) has on his birthday. Whenever the tale got a little too surreal, the camera would cut back to Willie tossing and turning in his sleep, as if to apologize for the ridiculous story. All the sexual allusions were cut, and when the angel (Jeanette MacDonald) suddenly finds herself without wings, no one seems much interested—just the usual thing that happens to angels when they stay on earth too long. The character of the Countess was eliminated, so the angel learned how to use "A Twinkle in Her Eye" (a stage song cleaned up by George Forrest and Robert Wright) from (in-explicably) one of Willie's old girlfriends. Most of the Broadway score was dropped and the knowing, reflective "Spring Is Here" was also rewritten by Forrest and Wright into an insipid love duet. With all the wit and sass drained out of the story, the songs, and the characters, *I Married an Angel* is an endless bore about absolutely nothing. It didn't help that both MacDonald and Eddy gave what are arguably the worst acting performances of their careers. Both are annoying to watch and, too often, seemed annoyed with each other. No wonder they never made another movie together.

Rodgers and Hart's most daring Broadway show, *Pal Joey* (1940), suf-fered a similar fate in Hollywood, though it is a much easier film to sit through than *I Married an Angel*. Celebrated author John O'Hara, in his only musical endeavor, wrote the libretto for *Pal Joey*, and there was a wry tone and sense of cynicism in the story and characters that were unique to the Broadway musical. The show has often been described as the first adult musical, which is accurate but only half the story. O'Hara makes no effort to charm or appease his audience and Lorenz Hart's lyrics flow from this hard-as-nails attitude toward entertainment. Based on a series of short stories, the libretto is a well-crafted tale of a heel who makes no apologies to the world and has no intention of changing. Joey Evans (Gene Kelly) is a third-rate nightclub hoofer who borrows money and beds chorus girls with no idea of taking responsibility for either action. We see him in top form early in the musical as he woos the naive stenographer Linda English (Leila Ernst), singing the disarming "I Could Write a Book" with hardly an effort at sounding sincere. But Joey quickly dumps Linda when a bigger fish comes along in the form of the wealthy, bored society dame Vera Simpson (Vivienne Segal), a gal who barely keeps up a respectable front for her husband. Vera and Joey are on the same wavelength, and their torrid affair is without pretense on both their parts. But when Vera tires of Joey and blackmailers make the situation sticky, she dismisses both problems with simple, professional ease. Vera, it turns out, is a smarter version of Joey. In a traditional musical, a changed Joey would crawl back to Linda, ask to be forgiven, and a happy ending might be suggested. But O'Hara has Linda finally wise up, refuse Joey, and the heel moves off into new territory and new, unsatisfying conquests. The Rodgers and Hart score is sometimes abrasive, sometimes sarcastic, never pretty. It is surprising that "Bewitched, Bothered, and Bewildered" ever became popular; it is such a sour lament. Pal Joey is the team's most integrated score and, coming three years before Oklahoma!, an amazingly far-sighted show. Despite complaints from several of the critics about the unpleasant nature of Pal Joey, the musical ran 374 performances. It was even more popular when it was revived on Broadway in 1952, running 540 times and receiving generally complimentary approval from the press this time. In both instances, audiences responded to the cynical honesty of the piece. It would never find the mainstream popularity of, say, the Rodgers and Hammerstein musicals, but Pal Joey remains a classic of sorts. If it were not too tough, it might be done more often today, but then it wouldn't be Pal Joey.

It is not difficult to see why Hollywood avoided the property for years. Columbia bought the screen rights in 1940 but then didn't know what to do with them. Such a cynical musical in the war years was anathema to the moviegoing public. Or at least that's what the studios believed. And how do you take that cynicism out of the story? You could hide Joey and Vera's living together in guilt-free sin, and you could tone down the loose moral tone of the piece, but how do you hide Joey? After the successful 1952 production the musical was considered again, but only in 1957 did a film version get made. It was sanitized far beyond what other movies of the time were getting away with on screen, and the changes made were more of a foolhardy nature than a result of censorship. Joey was changed from a dancer to a singer, Linda became a chorine, and Vera a wealthy widow who (get this) was a stripper before she married money. The illicit affair is turned into a few hard-boiled verbal exchanges, the blackmailers are gone (they have nothing to pin on the dame), and the happy ending has Joey and Linda going off together into the sunset. The screenplay (by Dorothy Kingsley) uses little of O'Hara's crisp, mocking dialogue and replaces it with banal talk that thinks it's coy. Most of the score was tossed out and replaced by some Rodgers and Hart classics that were not only inappropriate but often poorly presented.

For years there was talk of Gene Kelly re-creating his Joey on screen with his cinema partner Rita Hayworth as Linda. But by the time *Pal Joey* was filmed, Hayworth was closer in age to Vera, and Frank Sinatra was cast as Joey (hence the change from hoofer to crooner). Both stars are very fine in the film, sometimes bringing a jaded, world-weary quality to the characters that's not in the dialogue. In fact, Sinatra was ideal for Joey, and it could have been the film role of his career. But the screen Joey didn't do anything but hang around, look like a heel, and sing some of the numbers with a smooth style out of sync with the supposedly seedy surroundings. Kim Novak as Linda is never less than embarrassing; her singing was dubbed, but she still looks like she is in pain. George Sidney directed, and the movie sometimes has the right look, though the location of the tale was changed from urban, rainy Chicago to sunny, picturesque San Francisco. Hermes Pan staged the numbers in the nightclub, and they avoided the Hollywood overkill production values. All in all, this might have been a *Pal Joey* that worked. But it was done in by the screenplay and the studio's desire to make a pleasing movie musical out of a stubbornly brilliant antimusical.

Sex and politics may form the basis for most controversy in movie musicals, but they don't include the question of race. Hollywood was very cautious (fearful even) of how it used African Americans in musicals. Even the most beloved black entertainers, such as Louis Armstrong and Lena Horne, were usually limited to specialty spots that could be edited out when the film was shown in the Deep South. There are some wonderful exceptions of "all-Negro" musicals that were made—the early *Hallelujah* (1929) is still a marvel to behold—but a black Broadway musical being turned into a movie was rare. Innovative stage works such as *Shuffle Along* (1921), *St. Louis Woman* (1946), and *House of Flowers* (1954) were never filmed. But two outstanding stage musicals were, and the results were sometimes exhilarating.

Broadway's *Cabin in the Sky* (1940) was a musical folk parable set in the rural South, part fantasy, part tall tale. Lynn Root's libretto centers on the useless but likable idler Little Joe Jackson (Dooley Wilson) who wastes his life in petty gambling, much to the grief of his wife Petunia (Ethel Waters), who loves him without reservation. When Joe gets wounded in a brawl and is on the point of dying, Petunia prays to heaven so strongly that the "Lawd" sends down his General (Todd Duncan) to look into the situation. He decides to let Joe live for six months to mend his ways, so Joe recovers and pulls himself together until Lucifer Jr. (Rex Ingram) starts tempting him with gambling, booze, and the sexy Georgia Brown (Katherine Dunham). In a tavern melee, Petunia is accidentally shot by Joe, and soon both are standing at the Pearly Gates. But Petunia pleads so fervently for Joe's salvation that both are welcomed into paradise. It was a simple but sincere tale and was given breadth by the sterling performances and the masterful songs by Vernon Duke and John Latouche: "Honey in the Honeycomb," "Love Turned the Light Out," "Taking a Chance on Love," and the title number.

Cabin in the Sky was a modest success on Broadway, and the 1943 film version was a modest miracle of its own. Vincente Minnelli directed (his first movie) and gave the story a warm and stylized look. The screenplay by Joseph Schrank made one major concession to the Hollywood mentality: the entire plot was all a dream by Joe (Eddie Anderson). But this *I Married an Angel*–like compromise didn't damage the musical terribly because it was still a parable, and it was done with care and talent. Waters got to reprise her stage performance as Petunia, and the role is a treasured record of her remarkable singing and acting abilities. Also, Lena Horne is a very alluring Georgia Brown. Only Anderson disappoints at times, drifting from folklore into vaudeville on occasion. Only three of the Broadway songs were kept in the film, but Harold Arlen (music) and E. Y. Harburg (lyrics) added some estimable new ones, including the roguish "Life's Full of Consequence" and the glowing ballad "Happiness Is a Thing Called Joe." The fact that MGM even made *Cabin in the Sky* is a welcome surprise; that it was made as well as it was is even more joyous.

Much different in tone was *Lost in the Stars* (1949), a disturbing musical drama based on Alan Paton's celebrated novel *Cry, the Beloved Country* about the plight of "coloreds" in South Africa. Maxwell Anderson wrote the stage adaptation, and it avoided the preachiness of his earlier *Knickerbocker Holiday*. This is no folk tale but a realistic story of a white and a black family destroyed by apartheid. The minister Stephen Kumalo (Todd Duncan) leaves his rural village and journeys to Johannesburg to find his wayward son Absalom (Julian Mayfield). The white planter James Jarvis (Leslie Banks) also has a son, a liberal who has gone to the big city to help ease the plight of the Coloreds. During an attempted robbery, Absalom shoots James's son dead and is condemned to hang. Yet the two fathers, instead of continuing the country's belief in separatism, are joined in grief. It was a harrowing story, and, heightened by Kurt Weill's haunting music and Anderson's penetrating lyrics, *Lost in the Stars* was one of the most powerful musicals of the decade.

Of course, a movie version was a long shot. Not until 1974 was one made by the adventurous American Film Theater organization and, as faithful as it was to the stage original, it disappoints. The distinguished score survives the transition and provides the movie's only distinction. Brock Peters as Kumalo and Paul Rogers as Jarvis are commendable, but some of the other acting is frightfully melodramatic, as are some of the scenes as directed ploddingly by Daniel Mann. Although it uses some location filming, much of the musical looks achingly stagebound, and the overall effect is one of distanced curiosity rather than potent moviemaking. *Lost in the Stars* is not a case of Hollywood ruining a stage work; it is just an example of incompetence.

If *Cabin in the Sky* is fantasy and *Lost in the Stars* is racial outrage, where does that put *Finian's Rainbow* (1947)? Right in the middle, of course, because the quirky, unique musical is both. E. Y. Harburg and Fred Saidy wrote the Broadway libretto and filled it with whimsy, romance, and plenty of social satire. The whimsical sections concern the Irishman Finian McLonergan (Albert Sharpe) who steals a leprechaun's pot of gold and travels to America to plant it in the ground near Fort Knox, thinking the gold will grow in size and value. But the angry leprechaun Og (David Wayne) follows Finian to Rainbow Valley to retrieve his gold, only to find that without it he is slowing turning into a mortal. The romantic side of *Finian's Rainbow* deals with Finian's daughter Sharon (Ella Logan), who falls for the labor organizer Woody (Donald Richards), even as Og starts having sexual urges for any woman who happens to be near. The social satire is handled by the bigoted Southerner, Senator Billboard Rawkins (Robert Pitkin), who milks the local sharecroppers dry and does his part in keeping segregation alive by passing laws controlling the African Americans in his district. When Sharon, in a fit of anger, wishes the Senator was black in order for him to experience bigotry firsthand, her wish comes true because she was standing close to the buried crock of gold. The Senator turns black, learns a lesson, and is turned back the way he was, just as Sharon and Woody are united and the residents of Rainbow Valley celebrate their victory over oppression. There were probably too many issues stuffed into *Finian's Rainbow* but the musical managed to play wonderfully on stage. The quiet anger of the piece was offset by its prankish sense of humor, and the fantasy was handled lightly and with enchantment. Also, the tuneful score by Burton Lane (music) and Harburg (lyrics) overflows with whimsy ("Something Sort of Grandish"), romance ("Old Devil Moon"), and satire ("When the Idle Poor Become the Idle Rich"). "How Are Things is Glocca Morra?" was the big hit ballad, but also popular were "If This Isn't Love," "When I'm Not Near the Girl I Love," and "Look to the Rainbow." The original *Finian's Rainbow* boasted spirited production numbers choreographed by Michael Kidd and also featured the first truly integrated chorus in Broadway history, the black and white sharecroppers singing and dancing together rather than separated as in, say, *Show Boat*.

Despite its success (725 performances) and the number of hit tunes that came from the show, Hollywood was understandably fearful of making a movie of *Finian's Rainbow*. The whole idea of a white man turning (even temporarily) black and being a better person for the experience would not sell in most of America, not to mention the South.

Several attempts were made to come up with a workable screenplay, only to have production plans scrapped. An animated film version was even prepared, and Frank Sinatra, Ella Fitzgerald, Judy Garland, and Louis Armstrong recorded some songs for the soundtrack; but that project was later dismissed as well. Not until the Civil Rights movement of the 1960s did Warner Brothers feel the climate was right and gave the go-ahead for the 1968 film. Harburg and Saidy wrote the screenplay, and all but one song from the stage were used. Oddly, the director chosen was Francis Ford Coppola, still pretty much an unknown in Hollywood and with no musical experience to speak of. But there were two giants of the musical form recruited for the project: choreographer Hermes Pan and Fred Astaire as Finian in his last film musical. Here were the makings of a classic movie musical, but it was not to be. While there are many exciting things going on in *Finian's Rainbow*, the overall effect is more silly than whimsical, more strident than lightweight.

Although Harburg and Saidy made few changes in their script, the story doesn't play as well as it does on the stage. Woody is changed from a labor organizer to the manager of a co-op of farmers, hoping to make his fellow residents rich by developing, with the Luther Burbank–like black science student Howard (Al Freeman Jr.), a new kind of tobacco that will produce naturally mentholated cigarettes. (Howard tries cross breeding tobacco with mint plants.) It is a funny conceit but not one that helps hold the film together, even when they discover the secret in the last reel. Also part of a new climax is an attempt by the local authorities to burn Sharon and Woody alive in a barn because she is declared a witch. Not only is it preposterous but it kills any attempts to make the establishment into clownish cartoons. The role of Finian is built up to give Astaire more to do and he doesn't disappoint. Neither does Petula Clark as Sharon, even if her interpretation of some of the songs may sound a bit more Carnaby Street than Broadway. Also enjoyable is Keenan Wynn as the Senator, even if his blackface makeup is inconsistent from scene to scene. Don Francks as Woody is earnest and charmless and Tommy Steele as Og overacts enough to make a real leprechaun blush. Coppola is very inventive with his camera, sometimes too inventive. Most musical numbers are chopped up into montage sequences, cutting not only from character to character but from one time and place to another. Sometimes this is clever and effective, as in "The Begat" and "How Are Things in Glocca Morra?" but usually it is just annoying, as in "If This Isn't Love" and "Old Devil Moon." "Look to the Rainbow" is used several times throughout the film, but it only works in a delightful scene in which Astaire turns the song into a community dance-along with the residents of the valley. Astaire was sixty-eight when the film was made and looks it, but when he moves, he is as ageless as any leprechaun. *Finian's Rainbow* is worth cherishing if for no other reason than to see a master make his gentle but still enthralling movie musical exit.

Nothing made Hollywood more nervous in the 1950s than the paranoia about communism infiltrating American life. Any reference to Russia or the Cold War was bound to sink any film musical and heaven forbid if a character (or the actor playing him) was labeled a Red. So the case of *Silk Stockings* (1955) is an interesting one. It started as the brilliant screen comedy *Ninotchka* (1939) written by Billy Wilder, Charles Brackett, and Walter Reisch for Greta Garbo's comic debut. The now-familiar story centers on the title Soviet official (Garbo) who comes to Paris to sell some of the former Russian aristocracy's jewels but ends up being seduced both by the city and by an affable French count (Melvyn Douglas). It was a witty, literate, and totally charming comedy; more significantly, it was made when Russia was America's ally in those confusing dark days leading up to World War II. To make a musical out of *Ninotchka* in the Cold War 1950s might not strike one as a very fruitful idea. True, the original film pokes fun at the dour, humorless Soviets. But jokes about being sent to Siberia were not going to sit well after the discovery of Stalin's atrocities. Still, Broadway producers Cy Feuer and Ernest Martin went ahead, hiring George S. Kaufman to direct and write the libretto and Cole Porter for the songs (his last Broadway show), calling their musicalization *Silk Stockings*.

There was trouble on the road, however, and Kaufman was out, Abe Burrows took over the writing chores, and Feuer himself became the director. What opened on Broadway received mixed notices but was enjoyed by the public for 478 performances. Changes were made from the original movie to make room for the songs. Ninotchka (Hildegarde Neff) now comes to Paris to fetch a Russian composer (Philip Sterling) who has defected and is scoring a movie version of *War and Peace*. His agent is the American Steve Canfield (Don Ameche) who seduces

Ninotchka with such smooth Porter ballads as "Paris Loves Lovers" and "All of You." Despite her growing affection for Steve and the West, she returns to Russia. But after a scene or two showing how dreary the place is, Ninotchka pleases the audience and herself by rejoining her sweetheart in the City of Light. The Soviets were played as silly and ineffectual bureaucrats who all secretly wanted to escape the homeland. (Even Ninotchka's stern supervisor defects at the end of the story.) In questionable taste was a comic number outlining the disadvantages of being sent to "Siberia" and some jokes about composer Prokofiev being arrested by the state. And the agony of living in Soviet Russia was reduced to the jazzy lament "The Red Blues." But audiences on Broadway laughed, and there was enough showmanship on stage to make anyone forget the Cold War.

MGM filmed *Silk Stockings* in 1957 as a vehicle for Fred Astaire and Cyd Charisse, who had been paired so successfully four years earlier in *The Band Wagon*. Leonard Gershe and Leonard Spiegelgass wrote the screenplay, sticking fairly close to the stage libretto but opening up more room for dance. Astaire was now a movie producer rather than an agent, but the rest of the plot continued on, the more stinging Kaufman–Burrows lines dropped for safety's sake. The Russians (Peter Lorre, Jules Munshin, Joseph Buloff, and George Tobias) were played as cuddly incompetents and are so lovable that even Khrushchev might have liked them. The scenes in Russia are Hollywoodized, particularly Ninotchka's crowded rooming house, which looks more like summer camp than Soviet institutional housing. But *Silk Stocking* mostly avoids the Cold War shivers by being so entertaining. The dance duets by Astaire and Charisse are sensational, in particular one choreographed by Hermes Pan and Eugene Loring for "Fated to Be Mated," one of the two new songs Porter wrote for the screen version. Rouben Mamoulian directed with a light touch and a lot of style so that even the book scenes do not lag terribly. What might have been an uncomfortable satire on Soviet philosophy was watered down into a mindless but enjoyable movie musical.

One would think that by the time the radical 1960s had passed, Hollywood would no longer care about cleaning up or softening Broadway musicals for the screen. But two films from the 1980s show that old habits die slowly and the studios continued to fret over the possibility of offending its audience.

The Best Little Whorehouse in Texas (1978) was a ribald but congenial satire on Southern conservatism. Based on the story of an actual Lone Star brothel, the libretto by Larry L. King and Peter Masterson is a modern parable about a celebrated whorehouse that is closed down as a way for politicians to appeal to their righteous constituents. The tone was comic throughout, with the Texas muckrakers portrayed as ignorant but powerful bigots and the whores as wholesome, harmless citizens. The thin premise was directed and choreographed with such style by Tommy Tune and the songs by Carol Hall were often so proficient that *Whorehouse* played like solid gold on Broadway. The unpretentious musical chalked up 1,703 performances and even toured to the Bible Belt with little difficulty.

Universal and RKO copresented the 1982 film version, hedging their bets by putting major stars in the cast and reworking the script into an often somber, sometimes moral country music TV special. The aging madam of the stage was turned into a younger, more wholesome gal (Dolly Parton) who talks about what a great man Jesus was, just to assure moviegoers that the beloved singer hadn't lost her morals. In the Broadway version, the worn-out sheriff who is forced to close the whorehouse feels sorry for the "good old gal," and the musical ends on a wistful note. On screen, the still-beefy Burt Reynolds plays the sheriff as a Texan knight in shining armor who tries but cannot defeat the authorities in power, but he can marry the madam in the end, so everything down in Texas is just fine. Where some of the dancing on the stage bordered on the raunchy, the film's production numbers look like a theme park show guaranteed to culminate in a parade rather than sex. The only redeeming aspect of the movie was Charles Durning as the slippery, two-faced governor of Texas who manages to please both sides of the controversy without losing any votes. It is a broad, cartoonish performance, but when he sings and dances to "Side Step," one gets a glimpse of the kind of musical satire *The Best Little Whorehouse in Texas* might have been.

Little Shop of Horrors (1982) has an interesting pedigree. The low-budget 1960 sci-fi movie of the same name has achieved cult status over the years and is widely enjoyed for its cheesy special effects and amateurish acting. The tale of a man-eating plant who brings a nerdy florist clerk fame then eats him and his girlfriend was high-flying camp and not the easiest genre to musicalize. But librettist-lyricist Howard Ashman found the right combination of spoof and sincerity and staged the clever little musical off-Broadway himself. It quickly caught on, remaining for 2,209 performances and becoming a popular staple in schools and summer stock. Alan Menken wrote the tuneful 1960s music, and the songs were a delightful pastiche of the era as well as pleasing in their own right. True to its offbeat source, the musical ends with the plant devouring all the characters and setting out to take over the world, starting with the audience in the theater. It's a clever and dynamic ending for a very ingenious little show.

Yet the 1986 film version, while remaining faithful to the original, doesn't have the courage of the stage work. The score is pretty much preserved (plus a rhythmic new number by the team called "Mean Green Mother from Outer Space"), and most of the stage dialogue remains, but Ashman's screenplay softens the cataclysmic ending by having the nerd destroy the plant. To maintain the suggestion of an Armageddon-like future, the film concludes with baby offspring of the killer plant grinning at the camera. It is a cute ending. But what made *Little Shop of Horrors* so playfully potent on stage was the fact that is was never cute and it made fun of cuteness.

Still, there is much to recommend in the film, particularly the funny, goofy performances by Rick Moranis and Ellen Greene as the nerd and his girl and by Steve Martin as her merrily sadistic dentist-boyfriend. The score remains as impressive as on stage and Frank Oz directed with a feel for both the musical and pulp sci-fi style. But all the same, there is something disturbing about a 1986 movie musical that needs to play it safe. Is a man-eating plant taking over the world too hot for Hollywood to handle? Evidently so.

CHAPTER EIGHT

~

Why Can't the English?

Here is a common misconception perpetuated by American theatergoers: The British gave us the Gilbert and Sullivan shows and a handful of other English operettas before the turn of the century, then the Americans created musical comedy, and from then on England put on second-rate musicals while waiting for Broadway shows to arrive in the West End. In reality, the English musical was and continues to flourish independently of Broadway. It might be true that the United Kingdom rarely produced a talent on the level with Kern, Gershwin, Hammerstein, or Sondheim, but some of its best songwriters and authors were as familiar to London audiences as Lerner and Loewe and Richard Rodgers were in America. The West End also produced long-run hits that managed to chalk up figures to compete with (and often surpass) Broadway's champions. In the 1920s, *Mr. Cinders* ran 529 performances; in the 1930s, *The Dancing Years* lasted 969 performances; the 1940s saw *Bless the Bride* and *King's Rhapsody* each run over 800 times; and in the 1960s, *Robert and Elizabeth* ran 948 and *Charlie Girl* lasted a staggering 2,202 performances. What do these shows have in common? None of them ever attempted to cross the Atlantic. Both West End and Broadway producers thought them too British to appeal to Americans. And maybe they were right. *Salad Days* (1954) ran 2,283 performances in London; when it played on Broadway, it only lasted 80 performances.

So where does the misconception come from? Because only a dozen or so West End musicals ever found major success in New York, American theatergoers assumed there was not much to send over. And while the presence of several Broadway musicals playing in London has always been a given, English musicals running a long time in New York were rare until the British invasion of the 1970s and 1980s. Yet even in that age of the Webber shows dominating Broadway, American musicals were often comprising half of the offerings in London. (Ironically, at the same time British plays often dominated Broadway's nonmusical fare.) So what conclusion can be drawn? There are Broadway hits and there are West End hits. It is when a musical finds success in both venues that you start to wonder if Bernard Shaw was wrong about how different the two countries are. Let us look at ten British musicals that had an impact on Broadway and then were filmed. In some ways, these ten are abnormalities; how else could they please Broadway, the West End, and Hollywood?

Noel Coward can be viewed as the English George M. Cohan, though no one would ever mistake one's work for the other. Yet each was an actor, producer, director, playwright, librettist, lyricist, and composer and found success in each category. While most of Coward's plays were initially popular in America (and continue to be so), his only musical to find an audience on Broadway was *Bitter Sweet* (1929). He wrote both the book and the score for this nostalgic operetta that was purposely decades behind the times. Coward said he thought it was time to bring back the lush, romantic operettas of the past and he was probably right. The show opened in London three months before the stock market crash and still managed to run 697 performances. When the Broadway version opened a month after the crash, it only ran a modest 157 performances but returned to American stages steadily over the next four decades.

The plot takes the form of a long flashback: An aged Marchioness recalls a youthful romance with her singing teacher and her tragic loss when he is killed in a duel. The story starts in the present but soon leaves the Roaring Twenties to return to the more romanticized 1800s. Coward's score reflects this change, beginning with some jazzy numbers but soon is deep in nostalgia with operatic songs such as "I'll See You Again." "If Love Were All" and "Zigeuner" were the show's other two hits, but more knowing were the sly "Ladies of the Town" and the campy "Green Carnations" sung by an effeminate foursome who explain why the 1890s were indeed gay.

The first film version of *Bitter Sweet* was made in Great Britain in 1933 and featured Anna Neagle as the heroine. The plot was altered somewhat (her true love is killed by a gangster), but enough of the score survived to make the movie popular. When MGM remade the operetta in 1940 as a vehicle for Jeanette MacDonald and Nelson Eddy, the story was somewhat restored, but only the elaborate sets and the remaining Coward music were applauded. (It is said that Coward thought the final cut so awful that he wept upon seeing it.) The two stars, in their sixth screen pairing, seemed equally miscast (both were too old for the youthful characters in the flashbacks), and any evidence of wit or cleverness in the tale (including "Green Carnations," of course) was gone. Coward always had better luck with British film versions of his works; Hollywood and the West End seemed to be at odds with each other. This can be seen in *Bitter Sweet* in which Coward has the two struggling lovers living (and singing) in poverty in a garret—yet MGM's idea of a garret is a penthouse-like loft of palatial proportions. No wonder Coward wept.

One of the biggest West End hits of the 1930s was *Me and My Girl* (1937), a contagiously merry musical comedy about a cockney lad, Bill Snibson, who finds out he is the long-lost heir to the Barony of Hareford. He leaves his Lambeth neighborhood (and his sweetheart Sally) to take his place among the aristocracy where he is pursued by a gold-digging society gal. But true love wins out when Sally appears acting all posh and winning back both Bill and the upper-crust family. L. Arthur Rose and Douglas Furber wrote the delightful libretto that harkened back to the old cliché of bluebloods in disguise and (unknowingly) looked ahead to *My Fair Lady*. Rose and Furber provided the light-hearted lyrics for Noel Gay's music, and the score was loaded with catchy tunes, none more so than the celebrated romp "The Lambeth Walk." The musical ran a whopping 1,646 performances (despite the fact that it was bombed out of two theaters during the Blitz), but attempts to bring it to Broadway never materialized. (How do you explain Cockneys and Lambeth to Americans?)

Yet MGM coproduced the 1939 film version, now titled *The Lambeth Walk*, starring Lupino Lane who had conquered audiences with his sly, silly Bill on stage. Lane was a unique, brilliant physical comedian, and the film is worth seeing just for his sprightly performance. While the stage version was infrequently revived, its memory lived on in Britain. When the show was revived in London in 1985 (with a libretto tweaked here and there by Stephen Fry) with Robert Lindsay as Bill, it was a sensation and ran over four thousand performances. Arguing that so many Englishmen can't be wrong, *Me and My Girl* finally appeared on Broadway in 1986 with Lindsay reprising his West End performance, and the show was a hit. Since then, the old British musical has entered the repertoire of consistently produced works in America. Can *Salad Days* be next?

The Boy Friend, an English musical that spoofs old West End musicals, is also a popular favorite by all kinds of producing groups in America. Sandy Wilson wrote both libretto and score, and he echoed the past with such melodic invention that the musical is enjoyed by audiences who know nothing of the genre being pastiched. The simple-minded plot is about boarding school student Polly Browne and her innocent romance with a handsome young heir whom she thinks is a delivery boy. It is all so familiar but Wilson's tongue-in-cheek dialogue and infectiously charming songs make *The Boy Friend* seem fresh and invigorating. Anne Rogers was Polly in London, where the show opened in 1954, and went on to run 2,084 performances. Ten months later a version opened on Broadway with ex–child prodigy singer Julie Andrews as Polly, and both musical and leading lady were warmly welcomed (though the show ran a less impressive 485 performances). The musical was taken up by amateur groups across the country and Andrews went on to play Eliza Doolittle two years later.

As popular as *The Boy Friend* was in both Britain and America, it was not at all a likely candidate for the screen so no one was surprised when seventeen years went by and no film version was made. But director Ken Russell, known for his offbeat filmmaking, saw a movie in the old pastiche and devised a screenplay in which *The Boy Friend* is performed by a second-rate provincial theater troupe while a film producer watches and reimagines the whole thing as a lavish Hollywood musical. The result in 1971 was a clever and stylish piece of camp that moviegoers either adored or loathed. Former model Twiggy was the backstage assistant who must go on and play Polly when the star

(Glenda Jackson) breaks her foot—an homage to 42nd Street as well as several other cinema musicals. Most of Wilson's score was retained for the screen and two standards, "All I Do Is Dream of You" and "You Are My Lucky Star," were added to the backstage story and were wistfully sung by the sweetly amateurish Twiggy. Also memorable in the cast were Max Adrian as the company's seedy but optimistic manager, Christopher Gable as a smiling, brainless leading man, and long-legged Tommy Tune as a featured dancer in the troupe. With Tony Walton's nearly surreal sets and Russell's odd talent for finding the grotesque in everything, the movie of The Boy Friend is a unique, if sometimes baffling, film experience.

The 1960s saw two London musicals based on British literary classics come to Broadway with success: Oliver! (1963) and Half a Sixpence (1965). Lionel Bart, a one-man dynamo who has written several West End hits, had his only American triumph when he adapted Dickens's novel Oliver Twist into a lively musical that sometimes resembles British music hall but other times strayed into Rodgers and Hammerstein territory. Bart's songs were instantly likable in a sing-along way and became very popular in both the States and his native country. In London, Ron Moody played the thief master Fagin, Keith Hamshere was the young Oliver who falls into his clutches, and Georgia Brown was Nancy, the Cockney gal who saves him. The 1960 production ran 2,618 performances (a London record at the time), and the American version followed in 1963 with Clive Revill as Fagin, Bruce Prochnick as Oliver, and Brown reprising her Nancy. While its 744-performance run may have paled in comparison to the West End tally, it was still the longest-running British musical in Broadway history.

Even more impressive, the 1968 movie version went on to become the most critically and popularly successful film ever made from an English musical. There is much to recommend in the movie, such as Moody's electric re-creation of his stage Fagin with commendable support from Jack Wild as the Artful Dodger, Shani Wallis as Nancy, and Oliver Reed as the deadly villain Bill Sikes. Carol Reed's direction is usually controlled and honest. Some of the settings depicting Victorian London are stunning, and a few of the musical numbers, such as the animated "You've Got to Pick a Pocket or Two," are first-class. But there is much in the film version that comes across as artificial and at cross purposes with Dickens. Most of Onna White's choreography is overblown and self-conscious, such as the endless bouncing about during "Consider Yourself" and the unmotivated parade for "Who Will Buy?" both looking like a parody but aching to be taken seriously. Mark Lester is pretty much a vacuum as the young Oliver so much of the heart of the stage piece is gone. Some of the scenery is obviously painted, and much of the design can't decide whether to show Dickens's London or Hollywood's. For a movie musical that won a bushelful of Oscars, parts of it are rather feeble.

Less ambitious but also likable was *Half a Sixpence* (1963). Written as a vehicle for West End star Tommy Steele, the libretto by Beverly Cross was based on H. G. Wells's novel *Kipps*, a story that was not unlike *Me and My Girl*. Orphan Arthur Kipps works as a draper's apprentice but when he inherits a fortune, he turns his back on his working-class sweetheart Ann and courts a classy aristocrat. Then when Kipps loses all his money in a bad business investment, he returns to Ann, and the two marry and open up a modest bookshop together. *Half a Sixpence* had a nimble music hall–like score by David Heneker, and, boosted by Steele's sprightly performance and growing popularity, the 1963 London production ran 677 performances.

Steele reprised his Kipps on Broadway in 1965 where the show (with minor changes in the score) ran almost as long, and he then made the 1967 film version. It is a faithful screen adaptation in regard to story and score, but it totally missed re-creating the charm of the stage work. The widescreen sets seemed postcard-like and the boisterous dances were more energetic than inspired. As in most of his screen appearances, Steele failed to tone down his performance for the camera, and the result annoyed rather than pleased many moviegoers. Director George Sidney is at his most awkward here; scenes fail to pay off and the expensive production is surprisingly ineffective. Carol Reed had directed a nonmusical movie of the tale as *Kipps* in 1941 with Michael Redgrave as the hero, and it was a restrained but moving film. After Reed's success with *Oliver!* maybe he ought to have been given *Half a Sixpence* to direct as well.

The British musical invasion of Broadway in the 1970s and 1980s began with *Jesus Christ Superstar* (1971) and gained momentum with succeeding Andrew Lloyd Webber shows. Ironically, this musical was seen on Broadway before it played in London, though the original concept album had made the show a household word in both countries before it ever hit a legit stage. Tim Rice's libretto about the last seven days of Christ, viewed from the perspective of Judas, was all lyrics so Webber's music never stopped, and the result was a sung-through pop opera of sorts. Yet the score is much richer than what most thought of as rock music, using hymns, gospel, and even vaudeville turns to tell its story. The New York production, directed as a campy, hyperactive carnival by Tom O'Horgan, didn't seem to trust the material, and the expressionistic sets and outrageous costumes sometimes dwarfed the musical's ideas. But the piece's preopening popularity (and some juicy controversy over the Broadway staging) kept *Jesus Christ Superstar* on the boards for two years. After next being produced in Australia, the musical opened in London in 1972 in a rather subdued, traditional staging by Jim Sharman that let the "popera" speak for itself. Now more than just a trendy curiosity, the musical was widely embraced and continued to run in the West End for 3,358 performances—a new British record. *Jesus Christ Superstar* continues to be produced on professional and amateur stages, on video, in churches, and in concert halls. What was initially thought of as somewhat sacrilegious is now considered traditional and even reverent.

The 1973 movie version, cowritten and directed by Norman Jewison, bent over backwards to find a cinematic way of filming what was essentially a song-filled pageant. Having a bus load of tourists in contemporary Israel act out the New Testament story struck some as theatrical and imaginative, others as cutesy and irritating. But one must admit that the movie is beautifully filmed, the score is faithfully treated, and some of the performances are magnetic (particularly Carl Anderson as Judas). The film met with mixed notices and audiences tended to stay away and return to stage or concert revivals of the musical.

Webber and Rice's *Evita* (1979) is a more mature work, arguably their finest hour. Another sung-through biography with an eclectic mixture of musical styles, the musical about the Argentine heroine Eva Peron was also a concept album before it was first produced on stage, this time in London. *Evita* is unique as a rags-to-riches musical because the central character is both celebrated and derided throughout the show. Eva's calculating, self-centered ways are colorfully illustrated, but, as with many of the people she won over, Webber and Rice seem to be seduced by her as well. The result may be ambiguous politically but as a theater piece it is masterful. The title role is one of the most demanding in the history of musicals (actresses rarely perform it eight times a week), and Elaine Paige (in London) and Patti LuPone (in New York) both triumphed as Eva. Just as Judas presented a tormented, cynical point of view in *Jesus Christ Superstar*, the young revolutionary Che acted as a sarcastic commentator throughout *Evita*, balancing the public and private personas of the powerful lady politician. The songs were even more theatrical than in the team's earlier effort, some becoming hits but all of them effective parts of a vivid musical tapestry. The unseen star of the show was Harold Prince who staged both the West End and London productions. Using Brechtian techniques, multimedia, and even Meyerhold's "biomechanics" in which actors sometimes functioned as machines, the stage *Evita* never looked or felt like a concert. It was possibly the celebrated director's most ingenious and satisfying work in the theater.

It took twenty years for *Evita* to go from concept album to movie musical, during which time various studios, directors, and stars were linked to the project. Finding a bankable singing star was often the stumbling block, and when the controversial sex-symbol singer Madonna was finally chosen, Argentina balked, Hollywood pundits laughed, and the film seemed doomed. But director and cowriter Alan Parker, who had experience filming such unusual musical projects as *Fame*, *Bugsy Malone*, and *The Commitments*, tackled the ambitious project head-on and came up with a surprisingly powerful film. The story was still sung through, but it didn't seem like it because of the kinetic camera movement, the superb photography, and some riveting performances. Some critics deemed Madonna too cold as Eva Peron, though she was no more so than Paige, LuPone, and the infamous lady herself. Madonna even handled the difficult singing chores with aplomb. The fiery Che of the stage version was turned into a quieter, more subtle Everyman played with sly charm by Antonio Banderas who kept popping up in a variety of minor roles, allowing him to comment as on stage. Although his role was greatly abridged from the play, Jonathan Pryce was also splendid as the dictator Juan Peron. The film borrowed little from Prince's stage production, taking a more realistic, painterly approach to the tale than the harsh, documentary one in the theater. Yet the movie was able to sharpen and clarify some of the political complexities of the story and expertly used montage sequences to dramatize the Perons's rise to power and illustrate Eva's various campaigns and travels. The screen *Evita* was not a box office blockbuster, but neither was it a debacle like other recent film musicals had been. It offered one proficient solution to filming a sung-through musical; time will tell whether future movie versions of *Phantom of the Opera* and its ilk will come off any better.

In the meantime, two other Webber hits—*Joseph and the Amazing Technicolor Dreamcoat* and *Cats*—were considered too risky for a feature movie musical but were reimagined and filmed on video. The musical about biblical Joseph began as a fifteen-minute cantata that Webber and Rice wrote in 1968 for a boys' school to perform. Over the years it grew into a record album, a one-act musical, and, finally, a ninety-minute sung-through show that remains a popular favorite with schools, churches, and amateur groups. The first professional production in London in 1972 had a modest run but the piece later became the most successful touring show Great Britain had ever seen. *Joseph* was done by groups across America before the first professional Off-Broadway production in 1981, a colorful, tongue-in-cheek version directed by Tony Tanner that transferred to Broadway with success. Like the best stagings of the musical, it did not take itself very seriously. Just as the score changes styles in order to pastiche everything from Calypso numbers to country hoedowns, the anachronistic script is not afraid to make jokes and poke fun at itself. Along with *By Jeeves*, it is Webber's most lightweight musical. At times it is also his least inventive. In this early work, he and Rice depend on a narrator to give exposition and relay plot rather than dramatizing the events. Some of this was necessary for the fifteen-minute performance, but even the longer versions spend more time telling rather than showing. Since the story is devoid of major female characters, this narrator is usually played by an actress-singer. It ends up being the largest role in the musical, even Joseph himself only taking center stage with the ballads. Yet for all its primitive dramaturgy, *Joseph and the Amazing Technicolor Dreamcoat* remains a joyous frolic when presented well.

The 1999 video version was devised by its original creators, Rice writing the teleplay in which the story is told as a school performance—shadows of the show's birth. The video boasts a fine cast, headed by British musical star Maria Friedman as the narrator and American TV star Donny Osmond as Joseph. The entire score is retained, and most of it sounds terrific, but too often the production takes itself too seriously. The jokes remain, but the musical is sometimes filmed in a misty, "meaningful" way that makes it more interesting than fun. The sets and costumes are still anachronistic but one misses the cartoonish quality that many stage productions possessed. Although the video version was widely broadcast and many cassettes were sold, the musical will always be remembered as a stage piece.

Webber's long-run champ *Cats*, which broke records both in London and New York, is a musical much maligned, and it is easy to make fun of it or dismiss it. Its phenomenal success has never been satisfactorily explained, nor can it be denied. Without a plot, any three-dimensional characters, or an intriguing theme, *Cats* still manages to be theatrical. T. S. Eliot's series of poems make for some estimable lyrics, and there is no question that Webber's music is full of variety and inventiveness. Only "Memory" (with a lyric by director Trevor Nunn based on some poem fragments by Eliot) is in the traditional pop ballad style, but all of the score is accessible, even when it uses tricky classical forms not familiar to audiences outside an opera house or concert hall. The atmospheric environmental setting, the clever choreography, and Nunn's adroit staging all contributed to the show's success, but *Cats* remained a song cycle on stage, and it is the quality of those songs that is, I believe, most responsible for the musical's longevity.

Talks about a movie version of the hit show had been going on for years (and still continue) when a video version was made in 1998. (The renowned British playwright Tom Stoppard has written a screenplay for a projected film, and Steven Spielberg once planned to make an animated movie of *Cats*; neither plan has been totally dismissed.) The video uses the famous junkyard set from the stage, but it is not filmed in a theater before a live audience. Instead, the camera treats the show like some kind of mystic music video, and special effects are added that could not be done on Broadway or the West End. Gillian Lynne's stage choreography sometimes suffers from all the quick cutting, and the feel of the whole musical is often more dizzying than enervating. But the video version does have a gifted cast headed by Elaine Paige, the London originator of the old glamour cat Grizabella, and Ken Page, Broadway's first wise cat Deuteronomy. Perhaps the video's most affecting performance is by veteran actor Sir John Mills who, as the aged theater cat looking back on his career, brings a wistfulness that was not to be found on the stage.

The final British musical to consider may be the most unusual, not because it is the funky rock-and-roll spoof *The Rocky Horror Show* but because it flopped on Broadway and then became a very popular film. Richard O'Brien wrote book and score for this loosely structured show that lampooned Hollywood sci-fi B movies and had fun camping up every kind of sexual proclivity it could think of. An engaged couple seeks refuge in the Gothic mansion of the transvestite Dr. Frank 'n' Furter, and soon they find themselves among the various experiments going on before they realize most of the castle's inhabitants are aliens. There wasn't much story, and the show came off as more a rock concert with jokey dialogue than a musical comedy. It opened in 1973 in a small London theater and stayed for 2,358 performances, followed by frequent English revivals over the years. The Broadway version opened two years later with the same director (Jim Sharman from *Jesus Christ Superstar*) and cast members O'Brien and Tim Curry (as Frank), but the critics were baffled, word of the show never reached its intended public, and it closed in a month.

When the film version (titled *The Rocky Horror Picture Show*) was released five months later that same year, it also was dismissed by the critics and failed to find an audience. It was not until a few years later that the movie developed a cult audience through midnight showings in major cities across America. These madcap ritual screenings involved the audience not just in singing along to the songs but dressing up like the characters, performing scenes in front of the screen, and sporting such necessary props as squirt guns, propane lighters, candles, and pieces of toast. Here was a moviegoing experience even its creators could not have foreseen. But what about the film itself? Without all the off-screen ritual, it comes across as an often funny spoof that may rely on repetition more than inventiveness but never seems to run out of energy. Curry's Frank 'n' Furter is a sort of camp classic, and Barry Bostwick and Susan Sarandon are appropriately naive as the innocent couple caught up in all the erotic and comic shenanigans. Sharman directed the film as well, and most of it is deliberately stage-bound as rooms in the mansion become different stages for various numbers. *The Rocky Horror Picture Show* remains popular, yet the stage version is still little seen in America. Even a highly praised Broadway revival in 2000 could not find an audience for more than 436 performances in a small theater. Here is a London show that still struggles to cross the Atlantic with success. It is part of a long tradition.

CHAPTER NINE

∾

What Were They Thinking?

To make a mediocre film out of a mediocre Broadway musical takes competence. Think of *Gentlemen Prefer Blondes* or *The Unsinkable Molly Brown*. To make an exceptional movie from a superior stage work takes talent. *The King and I* and *The Music Man* come to mind. To make a movie classic out of a routine musical play would take something bordering on genius. I can't think of one example, probably because there aren't any.

But what does it take to turn a certified Broadway hit into a dud film? Lack of talent? Not enough. Thick-headedness? Perhaps. Stubbornness and egotism? Probably. Most of the successful stage musicals that were turned into horrendous movies were a case of ignoring what made the original so special and changing everything for the worse. Terrible casting certainly helps. And a director who has no sense of what makes a film musical work is essential. Mistakes have always been made and risks have often been taken. But to make a celluloid turkey out of a Broadway success is a phenomenon that one cannot watch without some kind of fascination. Call it artistic suicide or just poor taste, but the colossal movie flop is the road accident we just cannot help staring at.

Of course, deciding which films fall into this category is a very subjective process. A beloved Broadway musical that lost much in its transition to the screen may strike one person as a disaster, another as a not-so-fair copy. Also, some movies might not serve the original well but still

135

be very popular. *Grease* is a good example. So I have limited myself to a half dozen solid, successful Broadway musicals that were made into films that were both critical and popular misfires. In some cases, the movie quickly disappeared, and few recall that it was ever made; other examples are colorful embarrassments that, once seen, cannot easily be forgotten. But each case seems to come down to weak direction, ill-advised casting, and foolish decisions regarding changes to the original.

Paint Your Wagon is little known today as a stage piece, and the expensive movie flop in 1969 certainly helped bury it forever. But the 1951 show was quite accomplished and was a modest Broadway hit that held its own while *Call Me Madam*, *The King and I*, and *Guys and Dolls* were packing in the audiences down the street. Alan Jay Lerner wrote the libretto, and it is a very traditional but quite effective tale with a bittersweet flavor to it. In 1853 California territory, prospector Ben Rumson (James Barton) and his daughter Jennifer (Olga San Juan) discover gold near their camp. Word gets out and soon thousands of gold-crazy miners flock to the area, turning it into the prosperous town of Rumson. Widower Ben falls in love with the divorced Mormon wife Elizabeth (Marijane Maricle), but when Jennifer is attracted to the dashing Mexican prospector Julio Valvaras (Tony Bavaar), Dad sends her back east for schooling. Before long, the mother lode is exhausted, the miners leave (and so do Elizabeth and Julio), and Rumson becomes a ghost town with only lone Ben still dreaming of making his fortune. He plans to set out and try elsewhere but, just as Jennifer returns, he quietly dies as he sings of following the "Wand'rin' Star." Julio returns, his illusions about striking it rich shattered, and he and Jennifer settle down together into frontier married bliss. The score by Frederick Loewe (music) and Lerner (lyrics) was a thrilling mixture of robust, choral numbers like "I'm on My Way" and "There's a Coach Comin' In," and lyrical ballads such as "I Talk to the Trees," "Another Autumn," and "They Call the Wind Maria." Agnes De Mille provided the vigorous choreography, and the show was often a celebration of Americana. Although it ran 289 performances, *Paint Your Wagon* just missed making a profit, though it ran nearly twice that long in London, where it was an unqualified success.

Hollywood wasn't too interested in an almost-hit, so the film version was not made until eighteen years later, and only then because Paramount insisted on major box office stars who were recognized for their film westerns. What they didn't insist on were singers, so Lee Marvin and Clint Eastwood were signed up, and Joshua Logan was hired as director (even though his recent helming of *Camelot* had proven he was past his prime). Lerner threw out about half of his stage libretto and, writing the screenplay with Paddy Chayefsky, replaced it with one of the most insipid of all musical plots, trading in raucous fun and wistful charm for raunchy farce and a stillborn romantic triangle. Ben (Marvin) is neither a father nor widower in the film but a crusty old prospector who hates people. Instead of Julio, there is an aimless cowboy named Pardner (Eastwood) who goes into business with Ben and falls in love with Mormon divorcée Elizabeth (Jean Seberg). But Ben kind of likes her too (so we are told but he could have fooled everyone), so Elizabeth suggests they live together as a backwoods menage à trois. While the audience watches on with disbelief, the trio settle into domestic life until the boom town (now called "No Name City") goes bust and Ben gets restless, following the other deserting miners and leaving Elizabeth and Pardner as a traditional married couple.

Half of the score was discarded and five forgettable new songs were written by Lerner and composer André Previn. But rarely did any of the musical numbers take off; usually the story stopped dead while the nonsingers did their best, or the miners just tramped around in the mud in time to the music. Seberg was dubbed, but Eastwood and Marvin did their own vocals. The former got away with the folk song–like "I Still See Elisa" but could not bring "I Talk to the Trees" to life. (The camera focused on the trees rather than the singer.) Marvin talk-sang his numbers, a sort of growlly, grizzly Rex Harrison, and his recording of "Wand'rin' Star" was actually a big seller. But the two macho stars give surprisingly muted performances. Eastwood's usual quiet charisma is just quiet here, and Marvin's cranky Ben is uncomfortably phony. The film was shot in the mountains and forests of Oregon and cost a record $17 million, yet it is not a very impressive-looking movie. Watching No Name City collapse (because Ben and Pardner have dug tunnels under all the buildings to catch the stray gold dust falling between the floor boards) is neither a comic nor thrilling spectacle. Like everything else in this bizarre musical disaster, it is numbing and puzzling.

Paint Your Wagon still shows up on television, which is more than you can say about *The Fantasticks* (1960). The 1995 film was so dreadful that the studio kept it on the shelf for five years before giving it a very limited release and putting it on video, not even wasting money on making many prints for movie houses. Forty years is a long time to wait for a screen version of a stage musical but, in the case of *The Fantasticks*, it was still too soon. The little Off-Broadway show is a timeless fable about young love, parents, and maturing. Tom Jones wrote the charming libretto and lyrics, and Harvey Schmidt composed the tuneful, ageless music. The piece stresses simplicity of character (they are all familiar types), of story (a traditional "boy meets girl" tale), and of staging (a single platform with cardboard props). *The Fantasticks* worked its unpretentious magic in a tiny Greenwich Village venue for decades but was also effective in theater spaces around the world. It is one of the American theater's gentlest triumphs.

But *The Fantasticks* was not indestructible. For example, it did not work when played by stars in bigger theaters. (A tour with Robert Goulet in the early 1990s was a quick failure.) So making a film was going to be problematic, to say the least. Yet in 1964, an abridged television version with John Davidson, Susan Watson, Ricardo Montalban, Stanley Holloway, and Bert Lahr played very well on the small screen. The intimate theater space could translate into an intimate studio. But a movie confined to a studio space would be difficult to sell, and for years different people (including Jones and Schmidt) tinkered with various ways to make a film version work.

Those who said it couldn't be done were justified when the movie was released in 2000; it couldn't be done. But did it have to be this bad? Every decision regarding the film seems to be wrong, most of the performances are sterile, and even the lovely score sounds harsh and annoying. No wonder it sat on the shelf for five years. Jones and Schmidt wrote the screenplay, placing the tale in a prairie setting with a visiting circus in town to provide the lame theatrics. The two neighboring houses are somewhat stylized, somewhat gritty, as are the performances by Joel Grey and Brad Sullivan as the fathers. Joe McIntyre and Jean Louisa Kelly are the fumbling lovers, showing us how charmless naiveté can be and substituting grimaces and doe-eyed stares for sincerity. On stage, the story is conjured up and narrated by the romantic bandit El

Gallo, inviting us to join him with the indelible ballad "Try to Remember." On screen, El Gallo (Jonathon Morris) is an ineffectual bore,
and by the time he finally gets around to singing the famous song, we've
lost interest in him and the whole movie. Michael Ritchie was the hap-
less director, and Francis Ford Coppola was among those who tried to
reedit it to make the final cut bearable. It was a task more daunting
than the entire *Godfather* saga. There is only one detail in *The Fantasticks* that works: Barnard Hughes's quirky performance as the Old Actor. It is very brief and cannot begin to save the movie, but for a few
moments one gets a glimpse of the play's magic and perhaps the film
that might have been.

One only had to wait eight years for the film version of *Mame* to be
made, and it spent no time on the shelf, though a few weeks after it was
released that was where the many prints were put. *Mame* had always
been a lucky property, a seemingly indestructible force. It had been a
best-selling book, a popular play, a very funny film (with Rosalind Russell as the lovable, eccentric Auntie Mame), and then a Broadway musical smash in 1966 with 1,508 performances and many road companies. Jerry Herman wrote one of his most tuneful scores for the episodic
libretto by Jerome Lawrence and Robert E. Lee, and the show solidified
Angela Lansbury's musical stage career when she played the kookie
aunt with humor and panache. Gene Saks directed and Onna White
choreographed, both in top form, and with such supporting players as
Bea Arthur as the sardonic actress Vera and Jane Connell as the naive
nanny Agnes, *Mame* was a delight from top to bottom. So how could
the 1974 movie go so wrong?

Lucille Ball, television's fondly remembered queen of comedy, as
Mame Dennis sounded good on paper. After all, she had been playing
a variation of the wacky character on the tube for years. Arthur and
Connell were rehired, most of the score was retained, and the services
of Saks and White were secured. A fine supporting cast was assembled
and a lot of money was spent on the location sets that ranged from
1920s Manhattan to a southern plantation. This should have been a
hit. But *Mame* fails to work on the screen in such a blatant way that it
continually surprises one by how awful it is. Much of the blame has
been placed on Ball and jokes about her soft focus close-ups have become legendary. True, she was too old for the role, her singing voice was

an uncomfortable groan, and her kind of comic antics were not shown to advantage on the big screen. But more damaging is that Ball comes across as feeble in the picture. An old, croaking, overacted Mame Dennis might work, but a feeble Auntie Mame? It single-handedly killed the movie. There's no getting around it: this musical rides on the shoulders of one actress. Ball's lack of energy and warmth seems to pervade over the whole project, making others look somewhat emaciated as well. Robert Preston as her southern beau seems geriatric (he was only fifty-five at the time), the child and adult Patricks (Kirby Furlong and Bruce Davison) appear wooden and tired, and even Arthur and Connell give their own soft-focus version of their funny stage performances. Saks, a veteran stage director of both comedies and musicals, had never helmed a movie musical before, and it shows. Often scenes appear to be occurring aimlessly, and the camera just happens to past by and film it. The only time *Mame* seems to come to life is during some of White's dance sequences, which managed to work around or ignore Ball as much as possible. It is easy in retrospect to say that Lansbury or one of the many other stage Mames (such as Celeste Holm, Ann Miller, or Janis Paige) would have been much better than Ball in the role. It's obvious now. But who then could foresee what lay ahead? By the time the first rushes made it clear, it was too late.

It didn't take a crystal ball to determine that *The Wiz* was not going to work. When MGM announced that thirty-four-year-old Diana Ross would play youngster Dorothy in the hip, all-black retelling of *The Wizard of Oz*, fans of both the old and the new versions of L. Frank Baum's story started writing "Surrender Dorothy" in the sky. The 1975 Broadway show had not looked very promising, either, encountering lots of difficulties on the road and coming into town with little advance and lots of poor word of mouth. But directors, songs, and scenes were changed before opening night, and *The Wiz* was a surprise hit, delighting audiences for four years. It was a vivacious musical with William F. Brown's libretto filled with sassy, self-mocking dialogue and Charlie Smalls's Motown-sounding pop score overflowing with energy and joy. Much of the credit also goes to replacement director Geoffrey Holder, who gave the show a look (he also did the costumes) and feel that was inventive but consistent. While not trying to eclipse the 1939 film, *The Wiz* created a new and celebratory theater piece that proved to be the most enjoyable (and durable) of the African American musicals of the era.

Diana Ross had scored a hit in the 1972 film *Lady Sings the Blues*, but her few subsequent movies were disappointing. Yet she was one of the few bankable actresses of color in Hollywood, so the studio rewrote the musical to justify Ross playing Dorothy. In Joel Schumacher's cockamamy screenplay, Dorothy became a twenty-four-year-old schoolteacher in Harlem whose self-confidence is so low she runs and hides in her bedroom when company comes to the house. Instead of a tornado, a snow storm sweeps up Dorothy and her dog Toto and deposits them far away in . . . Manhattan. The journey that she took to find the wizard crisscrossed all over the island and in Queens, being sure to use familiar landmarks along the way. Even audience members unfamiliar with New York City geography knew this woman was going in circles. Dorothy's friends were a pretty embarrassing lot: an effeminate scarecrow (Michael Jackson), a corny Tin Man (Nipsey Russell), and an annoying Cowardly Lion (Ted Ross). At least the Wizard, played by a hyped-up Richard Pryor, had sparkle, but his role was reduced to a glorified cameo. Mabel King re-created her stage performance as the bad witch Eviline, and her rousing gospel number "Don't Nobody Bring Me No Bad News" in her sweatshop full of flying monkeys was the best number in the film. Even the luminous Lena Horne, as the good witch Glinda, disappoints as she overacts in close-up and sings the score's weakest song, the derivative "Believe in Yourself." Sidney Lumet, a director known for his hard-hitting television and film dramas, was the unlikely director of *The Wiz* (but he was Horne's son-in-law), and Louis Johnson was credited with the frantic and ineffective dancing that employed large numbers rather than talent. A lot of fuss was made about Tony Walton's anachronistic sets that turned Manhattan buildings into fantastical backdrops for the action. But they are only backdrops, rarely having anything to do with the noisy action taking place in front of them and never inspiring the kind of awe one expects when entering the land of Oz.

Like *Mame*, this musical depends on a strong central character, a winning Dorothy that the audience can identify with and cheer on. Stephanie Mills was terrific on stage, her big voice coming from the heart and warming up the whole theater. But Ross is cold, neurotic, and oddly unattractive in the movie. Besides being a grown adult who cannot find her way around her own hometown, she is a damaged and pathetic creature as well. Some audience members might have felt sorry for Dorothy, but most were more sympathetic to their own plight having to endure her. Not only was *The Wiz* a critical and box office bust, but it has damaged the reputation of the stage play. Had this movie worked even a little, the musical would be produced more often today.

The same year that *The Wiz* opened on Broadway, a relatively small musical began off Broadway that would grow to become one of the American theater's most beloved shows. *A Chorus Line* (1975) has an unusual (and well-documented) history. It began as a series of talk sessions and interviews with Broadway dancers and then developed into a dance piece about dancing in the theater. Michael Bennett was the force behind the project but the actual script was written by James Kirkwood and Nicholas Dante (with uncredited help by Neil Simon) and the score was by Marvin Hamlisch (music) and Edward Kleban (lyrics). Using the format of a "gypsy" audition, seventeen applicants reveal their dancing talents as well as their insecurities and dreams as they vie for the eight chorus line jobs in a new Broadway musical. It was a forced and artificial premise for the gypsies to break into songs and dialogue about themselves, but it worked, and, as directed and choreographed by Bennett, the result was an enthralling show whose appeal went far beyond those with theatrical ambitions. *A Chorus Line* ended up being about everyone who ever had to sell themselves and try to be accepted.

Like *The Fantasticks*, the musical seemed to run forever (6,137 performances, in fact, and many road companies for decades), and like its other Off-Broadway wonder, it seemed unlikely material for a film. The entire action of *A Chorus Line* takes place on the bare stage of a theater, not even the wings or other parts of the building. A movie that tried to open this up would destroy the theatrical image of the applicants literally being "on the line"—that is, the white line painted across the stage floor. Also, the libretto is a series of vignettes and flashbacks rather than a causal plot, and we have seen how Hollywood loves story and despises an indefinite collection of acts.

The Broadway show was such a phenomenon that Universal paid a hefty $5.5 million for the screen rights, and various directors, including

Mike Nichols, Sidney Lumet, James Bridges, Bo Goldman, and Bennett itself, struggled in vain to find a way to film it. Universal then resold the rights for $7.8 million to Polygram, who gave it to Richard Attenborough, the British actor-turned-director who had helmed the big-budget biopics *Young Winston* (1972) and *Gandhi* (1982). His only experience with musicals was as coproducer and director of *Oh What a Lovely War!* (1969), the English film version of a popular antiwar stage revue. Perhaps the studio felt that anyone who could handle the thousands of extras in *Gandhi* could figure out how to make a movie of *A Chorus Line*. The screenplay by Arnold Schulman wisely keeps the action in the Mark Hellinger Theater in New York, only leaving the locale for some unexciting flashbacks showing the past love affair between the director (Michael Douglas) and one of the auditionees (Alyson Reed). Most of the stage score stayed (the added songs were by the original songwriters), and the characters were basically the same as on Broadway.

So what was the problem? The musical was all about dance, but on screen Jeff Hornaday's choreography and the hoofing by the gypsies were overwhelmingly mediocre. The acting when the cast wasn't dancing was strident, humorless, and artificial. Without exhilarating dance and involving characterizations, *A Chorus Line* was the longest, dullest show imaginable, and there it was on film to prove it. The movie was released in 1985 (while the original was still running on Broadway), was lambasted by the press and the public, and then quickly and quietly disappeared. Of course, there were so many passionate fans of the Broadway show that perhaps any film version was bound to displease many. But few were prepared for the lifeless movie musical that Attenborough offered them. Maybe *A Chorus Line* never would have made a very good film. But even an uninspired, stagy piece with vibrant dancing and acting would have had some appeal.

Luckily, the movie did not affect the stage version. It played on Broadway another five years, touring productions lasted into the 1990s, and the musical is still frequently revived.

Even more often performed is *Annie* (1977), which survived its colossal dud movie version in 1982 and remains a favorite in schools, community theaters, and in revival. Opening two years after *A Chorus Line*, the musical won the hearts of theatergoers of all ages and stayed on Broadway for 2,377 performances. *Annie* was a family show back when there were few such offerings in New York, but it is also a well-constructed, solid musical comedy that will never lose its wide appeal. Thomas Meehan wrote the libretto, and he must be credited with much of *Annie's* success. (He would later go on to script such Broadway hits as *The Producers* and *Hairspray*.) Using some of the characters from the famous comic strip of the past, Meehan crafted an old-fashioned but skillful plot about the spunky orphan (Andrea McArdle), the millionaire (Reid Shelton) who is charmed by her, and the crooks (Dorothy Loudon, Robert Fitch, Barbara Erwin) who try to cheat her. It was cartoonish but also bright and funny with lovable villains and a playful heroine. The score by Charles Strouse (music) and Martin Charnin (lyrics) was tuneful and often echoed or pastiched Depression-era songs (even if most of the lyrics were rather weak). Charnin directed a top-notch cast (Loudon as the harried harridan Miss Hannigan was particularly funny), and Peter Gennaro provided the spirited if uninventive choreography. *Annie* played wonderfully on Broadway and everywhere else and practically cried out to be filmed.

And why not? This was a conventional musical comedy with many locations, a variety of characters, and songs that were already familiar to many. Making a movie out of *Annie* would be a picnic compared to turning *The Fantasticks* or *A Chorus Line* into film musicals. So how did they come up with the $52 million turkey that failed to entertain even the most indiscriminating children in the audience? Wrong director, poor casting, and plenty of changes for the worse. Columbia paid a whopping $9.5 million for the screen rights and then turned the project over to Randall Kleiser to direct. But at the last minute, Kleiser was out, and veteran John Huston was at the helm. But with Carol Sobieski's dreadful screenplay, it was probably a losing proposition in any case. Some new characters from the comic strip were added, and some songs were cut, but it was in the plotting that *Annie* failed. The libretto was not so much opened up as exploded. Added was a long sequence at Radio City Music Hall that had nothing to do with anything and a frightfully unexciting climax with Annie (Aileen Quinn) trapped on a drawbridge and rescued by an autogyro. Huston had never directed a musical, and looking at the way many of the scenes were filmed, it seemed like he had never *seen* a musical before. The movie was expensive looking (Daddy Warbucks's mansion looked like a Hollywood version of the *Ziegfeld Follies*), but rarely was it impressive. The acting was surprisingly uneven. The red-headed moppet Quinn had as much sincerity and warmth as a wind-up doll (she cannot even convince us she likes the dog Sandy, and the mutt knows it), and Albert Finney's Warbucks is only concerned with looking and sounding like a cartoon. Carol Burnett, on the other hand, is a buffoonish but still human Miss Hannigan, and Tim Curry and Bernadette Peters as her cronies are splendid (if underused). If the movie musical was on its last leg in 1982, *Annie* was like a kick in the shin.

Going back to our original question asking how one makes a film flop out of a Broadway hit, I can only suggest that there is some kind of pattern. Each of these six movies suffered from a lousy choice of director. Only Joshua Logan had experience with movie musicals but not good ones. The leading players in all six samples were mostly mistakes. Lee Marvin might have been acceptable in a better-written and directed *Paint Your Wagon*, but in the case of Lucille Ball, Diana Ross, Aileen Quinn, and the young leads in *A Chorus Line* and *The Fantasticks*, it was cinema sabotage to cast them. *Annie*, *The Wiz*, and *Paint Your Wagon* suffered from disastrous script changes, yet none of the six had significant score changes. Most were overproduced, yet all were victims of weak production numbers.

So what conclusions can be drawn from these six examples? Like the mysterious extinction of the dinosaurs, the golden age of the movie musical died one bad film at a time. These particular half dozen, coming out between 1969 and 1995, were probably a big part of the meteor or whatever it was that spelled the end of an era.

CHAPTER TEN

~

In for the Long Run

When a Broadway hit becomes a popular movie, everybody is happy. Maybe not thoroughly satisfied, but content enough that the film wasn't included in the previous chapter. And many successful stage shows do make popular movies, despite all those changes and compromises that have filled this book so far.

But something happens when a movie musical is a hit. Very often it eclipses the original stage work, and audiences come to think of the film as the official or authorized version of the property. Many theatergoers flock to revivals of Broadway hits expecting to see what they saw on the screen. No wonder they ask where the puppet show is in the Broadway revival of *The Sound of Music* or what happened to "Hopelessly Devoted to You" in the local stage production of *Grease*.

A Hollywood blockbuster is a mixed blessing for a stage property. It could make the show more popular, as in the case of *West Side Story*, which became a frequently produced musical only *after* the film came out in 1961. Or it could discourage future productions because the movie was able to do things that the stage cannot. What actress can compete with the memory of Barbra Streisand's performance in *Funny Girl*, or what theater production can rival the scenery of *South Pacific* or the period decor of *The Music Man*? Some movie versions were initially popular but did not hold up after the initial release; consequently, audiences have forgotten the film and rely on stage revivals to keep the musical alive. *Brigadoon* is a good example of this happening. In the long run, audiences will remember what they like and musicals in each medium will be affected by the other version.

What follows is a discussion of nineteen musicals that enjoyed some measurable success both on stage and as a movie. Each was a long-running Broadway hit, but each was also changed in some way for the screen. Which version is better is a matter of opinion. Which ones have lasted best in the long run is a little less subjective. We can easily label the following stage musicals as classics. But are they screen classics? That is not so easy to label. The plays can be revised when they are revived, a talented director can find a new approach to the story or the characters, scenic designers are allowed to change the look of the shows, and music arrangers may even reorchestrate a score so that it's more appealing to a modern audience. But the movie version is stuck in time. One can argue that the film of *Carousel* has dated badly but still reason that the musical itself is as potent and pleasing as ever. A stage actor can explore new ways to play Henry Higgins in *My Fair Lady*, but Rex Harrison's performance on screen (love it or leave it) is never going to change. That is perhaps the difference between a Broadway classic and a screen classic: the former is a blueprint for future experiments, the latter a frozen work of art that must be enjoyed in its original form.

Let us start with one of the biggest Broadway hits of the 1910s, the Cinderella musical favorite *Irene* (1919). This simple tale concerns an upholsterer, the bright and talkative Irish gal Irene O'Dare (Edith Day), who goes to a Long Island mansion to sew cushions but, after being passed off as a socialite at a grand party, stays and marries a young millionaire (Walter Regan). James Montgomery wrote the unsurprising but spirited libretto, and Harry Tierney (music) and Joseph McCarthy (lyrics) provided the proficient score, "Alice Blue Gown" and the title song being the most well-known numbers today. *Irene* was embraced by war-weary theatergoers for 670 performance (a new record and one that would hold for years), and it spurred over a dozen road companies. Yes, it is very dated, but that is half of its charm. A 1973 Broadway revised revival ran a year and a half thanks to stars Debbie Reynolds and Jane Powell playing the leading lady at different points in the run. On screen, a silent version of the story was made in 1926 with Colleen Moore, then a talkie in 1940 with Anna Neagle as Irene, and both were popular. RKO had bought the rights and planned on making it a Fred Astaire–Ginger Rogers vehicle in the 1930s, but both stars thought it too old-fashioned, so Neagle and Ray Milland became the central couple, and the movie was a surprise hit. This time it was war-weary moviegoers who embraced *Irene*, and it was one of the studio's top-grossing pictures of 1940.

Astaire and Rogers were right; it is a very old-fashioned piece, and Neagle's singing-dancing talents are not overwhelming. But her spunky performance is very winning, and when Irene makes her grand entrance at the high society gathering, you believe that everyone is charmed by her. Only a half dozen songs were used in the film, but the best of the Tierney–McCarthy score is there, as are some humorous supporting performances by Billie Burke, May Robson, Arthur Treacher, and Roland Young (as a temperamental couturier who gets Irene to show off his clothes). *Irene* as both the play and the movie, are pretty much forgotten now, but to those audiences of a past era it was undoubtedly a classic.

There is certainly no other word to describe *Show Boat* (1927), the musical theater's first masterpiece and arguably still the finest Broadway musical play. Oscar Hammerstein's libretto was more ambitious than any previous one seen on the American stage, its scope being far reaching when it came to plot, characters, and themes. And the score by Jerome Kern (music) and Hammerstein (lyrics) remains as impressive and beloved over seventy years later. The epic tale of people whose lives and fortunes revolve around the show boat *Cotton Blossom* on the Mississippi River is indeed melodramatic, and it gets a little sketchy in the second act, but *Show Boat* never loses its power. The initial production ran 572 performances, followed by road companies and overseas productions. But, more important, the show was the first to be taken so seriously that it was revived on Broadway several times after. The script in these later versions is often tampered with, and songs come and go, but it is still *Show Boat*.

There have been three movie versions of the piece. The first was actually a silent treatment of Edna Ferber's novel that was made in 1927 before the impact of sound movies was accepted by several studios.

Universal quickly added sound, providing dialogue in some scenes and the singing of Negro spirituals in others. Then, right before the movie was to be released, the stage version of *Show Boat* opened and was an immediate hit. The studio then added an eighteen-minute prologue to the film in which members of the Broadway company sang some of the hits from the musical. The result, released in 1929, was an odd and disjointed film, and it did not do very well at the box office. But Universal remade *Show Boat* in 1936, and this time they came up with a film classic. Hammerstein wrote the screenplay, and he and Kern added three new songs, including the flowing ballad "I Have the Room Above Her." Nine of the stage score's sixteen songs were retained, and each one was given a superb rendition by a superior cast. Irene Dunne and Allan Jones were the focal lovers Magnolia and Ravenal; Paul Robeson and Hattie McDaniel were Joe and Queenie, the African American couple who work on the show boat; and Charles Winninger and Helen Westley were Captain Andy and his quarrelsome wife. Most affecting of all was Helen Morgan, re-creating her indelible stage performance as the mulatto Julie and singing "Can't Help Lovin' Dat Man" and "Bill." Robeson's vocal interpretation of "Ol' Man River" is another highlight in a movie that is filled with them. *Show Boat* was directed skillfully by James Whale, who gave it an epic sweep while never losing touch with the intimate character drama at its center. It remains one of the very best of all movie musicals. But it wasn't in color. So MGM bought the rights and gave *Show Boat* the Technicolor treatment in 1951.

Because it does not measure up to the 1936 film, the later version is often dismissed. But there is much to recommend in MGM's lavish, highly romantic movie. Kathryn Grayson does not have the depth of Irene Dunne's portrayal but her singing of the Kern–Hammerstein songs is exciting. Howard Keel is a full-voiced Ravenal, William Warfield gives a striking interpretation of "Ol' Man River," and Ava Gardner is very effective as Julie (even though her singing is dubbed). The movie is stolen on two occasions by Marge and Gower Champion as the show boat's musical comedy couple and Joe E. Brown and Agnes Moorehead are fun as the Captain and Mrs. Hawks. George Sidney directed with an eye on the colorful and showy aspects of the story rather than the characters, and John Lee Mahin's screenplay makes several plot changes, few of them for the better. He sticks to Hammerstein for the first half of the story, then eliminates years from the narrative and makes Julie instrumental in bringing Magnolia and Ravenal together only a few years after they separate. It is a quicker, tidier ending, and some prefer it to the original, but it makes *Show Boat* a tight little melodrama rather than a grand, sweeping epic. All the same, the 1951 movie was popular, and, because it is in color, that was the version that was shown on television for many years. Today most prefer the 1936 film, but both are examples of making a hit movie from a long-running Broadway show.

The Rodgers and Hammerstein musicals are the very model of theater classics, most of them being hugely popular in their initial production and remaining so ever since. The five major shows by the team were each filmed, and, while rarely do they measure up to the stage original, each celluloid version was a box office hit. *Oklahoma!* (1943) was the duo's first Broadway collaboration, and, besides being the most successful show of the decade, it was also the most influential. Few theater pieces have been so well documented and analyzed as *Oklahoma!* I will not go into its plot, characters, or exceptional musical qualities, but I do wish to point out that the history of the American musical divides into two epochs: before and after *Oklahoma!* The first truly integrated musical with song, dialogue, and even dance carefully knit into the plot and characters, the show opened up the possibilities for the art form. We are still exploring those possibilities today. *Show Boat* had been a bold and thrilling experiment, but it little altered the direction the musical would take. *Oklahoma!* did and even the most avant-garde piece of musical theater today owes something to this Rodgers and Hammerstein wonder.

Because of his nightmarish experience in Hollywood with Hart in the 1930s, Richard Rodgers made sure he maintained control over his later properties when they were sold to the movies. He and Hammerstein did not even allow a film of *Oklahoma!* to be made until the original Broadway and touring companies had completed their runs, then insisted on a faithful screen adaptation. Sonya Levien and William Ludwig cowrote the screenplay, which was mostly an opened-up version of Hammerstein's stage libretto. Two songs ("Lonely Room" and "It's a Scandal! It's an Outrage!") were cut, and the climax was changed from a knife fight between cowboy Curly (Gordon MacRae) and the vengeful farmhand Jud (Rod Steiger) to attempted arson (Jud sets fire to a haystack during Curly's wedding celebration), which came from the source material: Lynn Riggs's 1931 play *Green Grow the Lilacs*. Keeping all the plot, characters, and dances (including choreographer Agnes De Mille's famous but lengthy dream ballet), the movie ran 145 minutes, one of the longest musicals on record at the time. This was known as the prestige treatment, and *Oklahoma!* was handled with reverence because it was a confirmed classic.

But was all that fidelity and reverence good for the film? It is an accurate movie version of the stage show, but somehow it misses the excitement and the reckless daring of the original. The acting, singing, dancing, locations, and even the costumes are correct and competent, but watching the film, you'd never guess that this was what started a revolution in musical theater. Instead, *Oklahoma!* on screen is a pleasant, enjoyable, slightly dull piece of entertainment. Fred Zinnemann directed (his first and only musical) and certainly knew what he was doing, but he treats the material too gingerly, with too much respect. Even the funnier, coarser aspects of the show, such as the flirt Ado Annie (Gloria Grahame) or the brooding Jud, seem to be so tamed that we learn they are sexy or dangerous only because the other characters tell us so. There isn't a weak performance in the film, but neither is there an electric one. Some moments in De Mille's ballet get close to exciting; the rest of the time we are asked to sit back and appreciate a theater classic.

Carousel (1945) is arguably Rodgers and Hammerstein's finest work (Rodgers declared it his personal favorite on more than one occasion), yet it is the least produced of their five major works. Based on a dark Hungarian play, *Liliom* (1927) by Ferenc Molnar, the story and characters are much more somber and tragic that anything in *Oklahoma!* *Carousel* doesn't need a Jud or any other villain because Billy Bigelow, the central character, is his own worst enemy. He was the most complex, bewildering, and confused character yet seen on the musical stage, and never were you led to believe everything would come out happy for this frustrated brute and the girl who cannot help falling in love with him. Musically it is also complex, songs and dialogue weaving in and out of each other and bringing the new integrated musical to a new height.

Some feel that Rodgers and Hammerstein reached their peak with *Carousel* and that the rest of their musicals were lesser and more compromising efforts. I don't think I would go that far, but there is something about the dangerous energy in this musical drama that is unique. The show ran an impressive 890 performances on Broadway but, compared to *Oklahoma!*'s tally of 2,212 and looking at the relatively few major revivals of *Carousel*, one might suspect it to be a less accomplished work. But *Carousel* is too disturbing, too demanding to join the popular ranks of the other four blockbusters. When it is revived successfully, it reminds us that not all Rodgers and Hammerstein shows are filled with optimism and warm fellowship. The relationship between Billy and Julie is frightfully honest and almost antiromantic; consequently, it has the power to move us more than any other musical couple.

Making a movie of *Carousel* was going to take much more than fidelity and competence, as in the case of *Oklahoma!* It would take an inspired production team to make this, the most challenging, most operatic of musicals, work on the screen. Unfortunately the 1956 movie was unfaithful, incompetent, and certainly uninspired. Although the original creators oversaw the whole project, it was mangled in the process. Henry and Phoebe Ephron's screenplay sticks mostly to the stage libretto in word and action but not in spirit. The film opens with an embarrassing prologue with Billy (Gordon MacRae) polishing stars in heaven and then narrating his life story. The earthly tale fluctuates from realistic locations in Maine to Hollywood sound stages with artificial flora and fauna, sometimes switching in the middle of scenes to the notice of even the most naive moviegoer. The New England exteriors are all postcard settings with the requisite sailboats swishing by in the background, all of which negates the intimacy and immediacy of the story.

Any production of *Carousel* rests on its Billy, and MacRae gives what has to be the worst performance of his film career. His idea of a romantic tough is a guy who pulls up his trousers every once in a while, and even singing with his full, flowing voice, MacRae looks either uncomfortable or silly. Frank Sinatra was slated to play Billy, but he walked off the set once he found out the movie was to be shot in both 35mm and 55mm. (The business-savvy Sinatra wanted twice the salary.) Would he have been better in the role? I doubt it. Period pieces were not Sinatra's forte, and he was always more believable as a smart ass than as a bully. And with the wooden direction of Henry King, it would have taken a masterful actor to make the screen Billy come alive. But at least MacRae sounded good, and his duets with Shirley Jones are pleasing to the ear. He was also fine in sections of the famous "Soliloquy," set along a shore of crashing waves and one of the film's few visuals that works. De Mille's stage choreography was not retained this time, and Rod Alexander's dances ranged from the poetic (as in Louise's ballet) to the interminable ("June Is Bustin' Out All Over").

Again, only two of the stage songs were cut, but few numbers carried the impact that they had on Broadway. The long and complicated "bench scene" built around "If I Loved You" just seems long in the movie and the cozy, intimate "When the Children Are Asleep" is sung by Robert Rounseville in the middle of a crowded flotilla. The powerful anthem "You'll Never Walk Alone" almost works thanks to the solid, unsentimental performance by Claramae Turner as Nettie, and its reprise at the end of the film is moving, even if we have to watch a long shot of Billy hightailing it back up to heaven. *Carousel* was a box office success across the country and 20th Century-Fox earned a considerable profit on the picture. But the film has dated in a manner than no Rodgers and Hammerstein show should. The fantasy elements seem silly today and the romantic ones schmaltzy. In a best of all possible worlds, it would be remade, for its potential is dazzling.

If *Carousel* is the most unsatisfying film treatment of a Rodgers and Hammerstein musical, the 1956 movie of *The King and I* is easily the most satisfying. Yet it was not an easy task to film the exotic stage piece, with its subtle character interplay and foreign melodrama set against a glittering fairy tale–like setting. The 1951 Broadway production boasted two legendary stage performances: Gertrude Lawrence as the English governess Anna Leonowens and Yul Brynner as the commanding but confused King of Siam. Again, no villain was needed in *The King and I*. The friction between sovereign and subject was all the conflict the story needed. Add to that the clash of East versus West, male versus female, and old ways versus new ways, and you had a tale overflowing with dramatic possibilities.

Hammerstein's libretto improves upon all of the source material, from the original governess's diary to the Margaret Landon novel to the

1946 Rex Harrison–Irene Dunne film. Yes, it has its precious moments with all those adorable Asian children, but for the most part the musical is very adult in its treatment of complicated issues. The score is remarkable in the way that it suggests the Orient but never leaves the realm of traditional Broadway. Jerome Robbins's unforgettable dance sequences were among the show's many highlights, "The Small House of Uncle Thomas" ballet encapsulating all the themes of the script while illustrating the power of both Asian and Western performance techniques. *The King and I* was an immediate hit, ran over three years on Broadway, and has remained a familiar and favorite stage staple ever since.

Gertrude Lawrence had died during the show's run, so 20th Century-Fox cast another English actress, Deborah Kerr, in the film version. Her singing had to be dubbed, but Kerr exhibited that inexplicable combination of cool British pluck and warm maternal sincerity. Fortunately for all concerned (and for posterity), Brynner was hired to reprise his towering performance as the King, and he is as alive and glowing on screen as he was on stage. The secondary couple was edited down in Ernest Lehman's screenplay, but for the most part, it was an expert adaptation, opening up the action enough so that it felt like a film but confining the events to a few spaces so that the drama never got lost in any spectacle. Director Walter Lang handled both the pageantry and the character scenes equally well, and the re-created Robbins choreography was as dynamic on celluloid as in the theater.

The King and I is also the best-looking of the Rodgers and Hammerstein films. Walter M. Scott and Paul S. Fox's sets and Irene Sharaff's costumes are bold and theatrical yet avoid cliché. Also, unlike the breathtaking locations in the later *The Sound of Music*, the decor here never overwhelms the story or characters. *The King and I* was one of the longer film musicals of the time (133 minutes), yet it never lags or disappoints. It is the rare, wonderful marriage of stage and screen.

Although *South Pacific* (1949) opened on Broadway before *The King and I*, its film version was not made until 1958, the fourth of the Rodgers and Hammerstein musicals to reach the screen. The Broadway show was a star vehicle for an unlikely pairing: spirited pseudo-soprano Mary Martin and renowned opera basso Ezio Pinza. It was such a nontraditional combination of voices that Rodgers and Hammerstein made sure the twosome did not have a duet together until much of the evening had lapsed and the audiences had accepted the pair. Martin and Pinza played an unlikely couple: rural American nurse Nellie Forbush and debonair French planter Emile de Becque. There was much else about *South Pacific* that was unlikely. It was a wartime piece (based on a collection of James Michener stories), but the Pacific campaign was far off in the background. It had two pairs of lovers but this time each was separated by inner prejudices rather than outside forces. The score ranged from operatic romance to low comedy, and there was both a big band sound to it as well as an exotic, tropical flavor. Joshua Logan, who knew his way around a stage much better than behind a camera, directed with wonderful little touches, such as staging events with a dissolve-like technique as one scene blended over into another. Logan also contributed so much to the libretto that he was eventually listed as coauthor with Hammerstein. *South Pacific* was a blockbuster with a handful of hit songs, vibrant performances throughout, and a run of 1,925 performances.

Much of the Fox production personnel from *The King and I* were reassembled for *South Pacific*, but the result was not as accomplished. Paul Osborn's screenplay took a few liberties with the libretto, trying to open up a musical that was already rather wide in its scope. Dialogue was added, the complete Broadway score was kept (including a short number called "My Girl Back Home" that had been cut on the road), and the pace was slowed down so the movie ended up running a war-weary 178 minutes.

The cast is adequate at best. Mitzi Gaynor makes a valiant effort at Nellie but it never seems to come together for her. Rossano Brazzi (with his singing dubbed by opera star Giorgio Tozzi) has a striking presence but not much depth. John Kerr (also dubbed) as the tragic Lieutenant Cable is stone-faced, and Ray Walston so underplays the rascally Luther Billis that he looks like he's saving his energy for another take. Only Juanita Hall, reprising her stage performance as the crafty Bloody Mary, captures our undivided attention. Ironically, she was dubbed as well, her singing voice having lost something in the nine years since the play opened.

Much of *South Pacific's* sluggishness comes from the stolid direction by Joshua Logan, the same man who had made the Broadway production sparkle. Maybe something happened to him also during the nine years. Certain dialogue scenes seem to stop the film dead with their lifeless talk, while some musical numbers suffer from the singers wandering aimlessly in front of all that lovely island scenery. One of the film's many mistakes was Logan and cinematographer Leon Shamroy's experiment with color filters. For no apparent reason, the coloring on the actors' faces changes as they are singing, drawing attention away from both the performer and the song. The scenery also goes through a similar color show at times, and it cheapens the natural beauty of the shooting location.

Like the previous Rodgers and Hammerstein films, however, *South Pacific* was very popular at the box office. It was given the prestige treatment, and audiences reacted accordingly. But it remains a movie best enjoyed by those who have never experienced a first-class stage production of the musical.

Which leaves us with *The Sound of Music*, the film many love to hate and others hate to love. The 1959 Broadway musical was the only show by the team that Hammerstein did not have a hand in writing. (He was ill at the time and later died during the play's run.) Veteran playwrights Howard Lindsay and Russel Crouse penned the libretto and in some ways it out-Hammersteined Hammerstein. Children gave charm to *The King and I*, but they are more central in *The Sound of Music*. The battle between governess and employer appears in both musicals, but the life-affirming Maria (Mary Martin) ends up marrying the grumpy Captain (Theodore Bikel) in the later work. With its Alpine setting and romantic scenes, *The Sound of Music* often resembles the old-fashioned operettas that Hammerstein began his career writing.

Fortunately, Lindsey and Crouse provided more than a mountaintop love story. It is still a Rodgers and Hammerstein musical, so it has to be about something worth putting on the stage. The political aspect of the libretto gives the show some bite. The pragmatic Baroness (Marion Marlowe) and the self-serving entrepreneur Max Deteiller (Kurt Kasznar) want to survive the Nazi regime, and the Captain wants to battle it. The sophisticated, manipulative courtship between the Baroness and the Captain falls apart over political reasons and is replaced by the simple, emotional romance with Maria. With Maria, the Captain still cannot conquer the Nazis, but at least he can defy them. It is a strong, thoughtful libretto. As for the famous score, it is carefully varied. Contrasting all the sweet kids' songs and merry sing-alongs are cynical numbers such as "How Can Love Survive?" and "No Way to Stop It." As conceived by its creators and first presented on the New York stage, *The Sound of Music* was a lyrical musical play with brains.

But over the years (and because of the 1965 movie version), the show's reputation has changed, and it is often seen today as a merry romp with kids and a cute parable about how nuns and happy singers can outwit even Hitler. In truth, many stage revivals produce it that way. But mainly that misconception comes from the hugely popular film, still the movie musical that has been seen by more people than any other. Ernest Lehman wrote the screenplay, and, whether intentional or not, he removed the bite from the story, softened the grittier parts of the tale, dropped the only two "adult" songs, and turned it into a first-class but relatively mindless entertainment. The political edge to the story is replaced by a romantic one; the Captain (Christopher Plummer) leaves the Baroness (Eleanor Parker) because he prefers Maria (Julie Andrews), not because of their differing political beliefs. Lehman sticks to the stage libretto's plot but rearranges the songs, sometimes to better advantage. "My Favorite Things" was a ditty Maria taught to the Mother Abbess in the Broadway production, but in the film it becomes a late-night sing-along with the children to ward off their fear of a thunderstorm. The stage song originally in that spot, the yodeling "The Lonely Goatherd," is turned into a puppet show by Maria and her charges. It never would have worked on stage, but it's a real charmer on screen. Because Hammerstein had died in 1960, Rodgers wrote both music and lyrics for the film's two new numbers: the spunky march "I Have Confidence in Me" and the warm duet "Something Good." The second replaced the stage love song "An Ordinary Couple," arguably the dullest song the team ever wrote. "Do-Re-Mi" changed from a single music lesson at home to a summer of adventures all around the town. Lehman's screenplay also included the usual opening up of the libretto; in this case, the Tyrolean Alps and the picture postcard city of Salzburg, which practically become characters in the film. It's all done so professionally (Robert Wise was the proficient director) and with such zest that the film's wide appeal is no mystery.

And the performances certainly helped. Audrey Hepburn, Romy Schneider, and Doris Day were seriously considered for Maria, but Andrews was so impressive as a British governess in the not-yet-released *Mary Poppins* (1964) that 20th Century-Fox cast her as an Austrian one as well. All joking about her wholesomeness and squeaky-clean appearance aside, Andrews allows the movie to work. Imagine this picture with an irritatingly cute Maria or even a childishly simple Maria. Andrews plays naive but does it winningly. Plummer is perhaps too subtle for the rest of the film's energetic approach to character. The Captain is a stiff and humorless fellow, but Plummer manages to make those qualities rather attractive on screen. For all its softness and sentimentality, *The Sound of Music* is a superior piece of musical filmmaking. Try to imagine how it might have turned out in less competent hands, or, better, go see *Song of Norway*.

Lerner and Loewe is the other celebrated Broadway team of the postwar years, and their two best musicals were brought to the screen with some success. Like Hammerstein, Alan Jay Lerner wrote the librettos for all his shows as well as providing the lyrics. He fashioned an original tale for *Brigadoon* (1947) and did a masterful adaptation for *My Fair Lady* (1956). The two musicals are very different—the former about emotions overriding reality, the latter about emotions stifled by cool-headedness. The one has lush, romantic lyrics; the other incisive, literate ones. Both are remarkable achievements, yet both made disappointing films.

Brigadoon is a romantic fairy tale with a contemporary point of view. Vacationers Tommy (David Brooks) and Jeff (George Keane) stumble upon a Scottish town in the Highlands, get caught up in the local doings (a wedding, a rivalry, and a death), and meet up with two comely lasses: the lovely Fiona (Marion Bell) for Tommy and the man-hungry Meg (Pamela Britton) for Jeff. But the two Americans (and the audience) gradually learn that the village of Brigadoon is in a sort of time warp, existing that day but not to appear again for one hundred years. It's a fanciful notion and one that puts pressure on Tommy to make a decision to stay with Fiona and be swept out of his own time or to return to New York and his modern, put-offish fiancée. Lerner's libretto is a satisfying mix of bucolic romanticism and down-to-earth character drama. The score echoes this, with the nature songs like "Heather on the Hill" contrasted with the jazzier Broadway numbers such as "Almost Like

Falling in Love." *Brigadoon* borders on operetta at times, but it can still be produced on stage effectively and has remained in the repertory of revived musicals for over fifty years.

At 581 performances, *Brigadoon* was Lerner and Loewe's first big hit but Hollywood didn't film it until 1954, a wait of seven years that is puzzling because it is a fairly traditional show and would pose few problems on the screen. Maybe the studios were nervous about the fantasy element, yet the musical is quite straightforward and has no leprechauns or sorceresses as in *Finian's Rainbow* or *Camelot*. Being such a rural piece, *Brigadoon* could benefit from location shooting in Scotland or some reasonably similar terrain. But MGM nixed the idea, citing the substantial overseas expenses, and the movie was filmed on the back lot. One can argue that a fantasy didn't need real topography, but what designers Cedric Gibbons and Preston Ames came up with was painterly, flat, and dull, with a color palate that looked more like a display window than a habitable Scottish village. Even the goats, sheep, and oxen littered all over the sets looked awkward and artificial. Despite all the manufactured fog and phony sunrise and sunsets, this town was neither magical nor believable.

The other major decision, to turn *Brigadoon* into a dance film, was a fatal mistake. Agnes De Mille had provided some riveting choreography for the Broadway production (including a thrilling sword dance at the wedding ceremony), but the show was not *about* dance. For the screen, Gene Kelly was choreographer and also played Tommy to dancer Cyd Charisse as Fiona, a character who hardly did a step or two in the original. Kelly had the whole town dancing on occasion and made sure there were plenty of pas de deux for he and Charisse. The folklike steps for "I'll Go Home With Bonnie Jean" were fun but the Kelly–Charisse duet for "Heather on the Hill" through the fake trees (which sometimes served as dance bars and poles) was charmless and uncomfortably modern. Where did this Scottish girl learn to dance like Martha Graham? When the twosome sang they were fine (Charisse was dubbed), but their characterizations in the book scenes were annoying; the restless dreamer Tommy became a strident Hamlet and Fiona behaved more like a Park Avenue model than a country lass. Much more enjoyable was Van Johnson as the scene-stealing Jeff. The secondary couple was just about eliminated in the movie (and Meg's two songs were cut), but Johnson was still more interesting than any of the other characters. With unappealing acting and disappointing dancing, that only left the marvelous Lerner and Loewe score. But half of the stage songs were cut (including Loewe's favorite, "Come to Me, Bend to Me"), and no new ones were added because so much of the screen time was spent on dance. (Yet the sword dance, a highlight of the play, was also cut.) So the movie of Brigadoon offers few rewards to viewers today. A modest hit when it was released, few movie musicals have dated as poorly as this one. In retrospect, it is considered one of the low points for Kelly's career, as well as for director Vincente Minnelli and MGM producer Arthur Freed.

The high point for Lerner and Loewe, on the other hand, was My Fair Lady (1956), considered by many to be the best of all Broadway musicals. It may not have the innovation of Show Boat or Oklahoma! but it is perhaps the best example of what those two shows pioneered: a perfect blending of song, story, and character. Lerner's reworking of George Bernard Shaw's Pygmalion is one of the most outstanding of all Broadway librettos, the language of Shaw flowing seamlessly into Lerner's dialogue and lyrics. My Fair Lady didn't just produce hit songs; the entire score was sensational, and everybody knew and loved all the numbers. They still do. Time has only proven the musical more brilliant with each viewing. But this does not mean it was going to be easy to film. First, there was nothing American about the setting or characters. Neither was it set in an exotic, foreign locale with scenery and colorful inhabitants. The musical takes place mostly in period rooms and consists mostly of intelligent talk. There is relatively little dancing, and, more dangerous, it has only the most subdued of love stories. The fact that My Fair Lady was such a huge stage hit is more amazing when one considers everything working against it. But it charmed and captivated audiences from the start, and the musical went on to break all Broadway records. Rex Harrison as Henry Higgins and Julie Andrews as Eliza Doolittle became the standards by which musical comedy performances were judged, even though he could hardly sing and she was a novice actress. Moss Hart directed with a sure hand and the supporting players, scenery, and costumes were exemplary all around. My Fair Lady was the dream Broadway smash.

Of course, Hollywood was eager. Warner Brothers outbid everyone else for the screen rights ($5.5 million plus all kinds of conditions) and gave the picture the prestige treatment of all time. Every song, character, and scene was retained (Lerner wrote the screenplay), as well as Harrison, Stanley Holloway (as Eliza's father Alfred), and designer Cecil Beaton, who had done the stage costumes but now oversaw the entire production. Andrews was not seriously considered (she had never made a movie before), and Hollywood mogul Jack Warner even asked Cary Grant to play Higgins; wisely, he refused. Warner also wanted James Cagney as Alfred Doolittle; he wisely refused as well. But Warner got Audrey Hepburn for Eliza as a box office guarantee and Hollywood veteran George Cukor was hired to direct. To say that anticipations were high would be understatement. No movie musical was ever more eagerly awaited than *My Fair Lady* and probably no movie could have lived up to everyone's expectations.

Was it all that bad? Not at all. But neither was it all that good. It is a polished, elegant movie, but there is something tired and routine about much of it. Harrison's performance shines in spots but often seems like a recorded document of a characterization that had seen better days. Hepburn makes a dazzling lady but a suspect flower girl. Beaton's sets are classy, but the costumes often fall into the realm of fashion show rather than period decor. Some sections of the film work beautifully, such as Alfred's scenes and his two musical numbers, while others fall flat, as in the race at Ascot. Cukor directed with style and ease, but one wishes there was more immediacy and intrigue to the events instead of a very civilized pageant. Still, the film was very popular, won a lot of awards, and remains a favorite on television and video. But almost any professional stage production of *My Fair Lady* can surpass it.

Cole Porter's musicals have popped up throughout this book but we've yet to discuss his most popular stage and screen success, *Kiss Me, Kate*. Perhaps more than any of the major songwriters, Porter had been saddled with mediocre or inferior librettos for decades. But the double-plotted musical comedy that Samuel and Bella Spewack wrote for *Kiss Me, Kate* brought out the best in Porter, and he wrote his greatest score. Two scores, actually. The Shakespearian songs are anachronistically sprightly as they jump right out of the Elizabethan text. The backstage songs have a sly, contemporary flavor and keep the musical sharp and modern. The ingenious libretto manages to tell both the onstage and backstage stories equally well, even though we only see selected scenes from *The Taming of the Shrew*. The 1948 Broadway cast featured Alfred Drake and Patricia Morison as the battling spouses (and the battling Petruchio and Kate), with Lisa Kirk and Harold Lang as the supporting couple both on stage and backstage. All were top-notch, as were the production values and Hanya Holm's splendid choreography. *Kiss Me, Kate* ran 1,070 performances (nearly twice as long as any of Porter's previous shows) and showed that the veteran songwriter could write a superb Broadway score in the post-*Oklahoma!* style.

The 1953 film version matched the stage musical in spirit but some minor distractions keep the movie from reaching the heights of the original. Dorothy Kingsley's screenplay tries to open up the story a bit and each attempt to leave the theater setting is a mistake. On Broadway, the events of the musical take place from 5 P.M. to curtain call during a tryout performance in Baltimore. The film opens months earlier in the apartment of actor-director Fred Graham (Howard Keel), where he and Cole Porter (played by Ron Randell who looks nothing like the real man) are trying to convince Fred's ex-wife Lili (Kathryn Grayson) to be in the show. Ann Miller shows up to dance all over the furniture as she sings and taps to "Too Darn Hot," giving the movie an odd and disjointed start. But once the tale moves to the theater, the screenplay more closely adheres to the stage libretto.

The movie also looks terrific. The backstage locales look real enough, while the *Taming of the Shrew* scenes are colorful and theatrical. The costumes are likewise contrasting, the elegant 1950s clothes set against the garish pseudo-Elizabethan duds. The complete Broadway score (minus a few verses and some censored Porter lyrics) made it to the screen, and everyone sounds great. (No one in the cast is dubbed.) Grayson had spent her Hollywood career playing sweet ingenues, so it was refreshing to see her break out as the shrew and use her trilling voice in such a roguish way. Keel chews the scenery at times, but the script continually reminds us that Fred is a ham, and Petruchio an oversized buffoon. *Kiss Me, Kate* also afforded Miller one of her best roles, and she teams effectively with Tommy Rall in their songs and dances together. A special bonus in the film is "From This

Moment On," an interpolated Porter song that is sung by Miller, Rall, Bobby Van, and Bob Fosse, the last one staging the number and making his (uncredited) choreography debut.

Unfortunately *Kiss Me, Kate* was filmed as a 3-D feature, and too often one has to watch objects or people flung out toward the camera to show off the newfangled effect. (Petruchio's famous soliloquy "Where Is the Life That Late I Led?" is weakened by having him deliver it on a runway that sticks out into both the theater and the moviehouse audience.) MGM soon rereleased it on a normal print, but viewers are still stuck watching all the unmotivated tossing about.

Also capturing the spirit of the original, if not actually surpassing it, is *The Music Man*. Meredith Willson wrote the libretto, music, and lyrics for the 1957 Broadway hit, filling it with nostalgia and humor about his growing up in a small Iowa town early in the century. It is a unique show in many ways. The rural sense of Americana is both celebrated and mocked in Willson's extraordinary libretto. The characters are types, but they are vibrant folk who are portrayed with both sarcasm and affection. The con man Harold Hill (Robert Preston) is a Broadway original: part city slicker, part dreamer, part hero. Marian (Barbara Cook), the librarian who fights him and then falls for him, is one of musical theater's feistier and more intelligent heroines. The supporting characters have much more substance than in most musical comedies, and the changing attitudes of the townfolk throughout the plot is something rarely seen in such shows. Willson's score is also unique, utilizing marches, barbershop quartets, cakewalks, rhythm numbers, and contrapuntal duets in addition to the traditional ballads and character songs. Like *My Fair Lady*, this show shouldn't have worked on Broadway, but it did and it has never stopped pleasing audiences.

The Music Man was very lucky in its transition to the screen in 1962; it could have been dreadful. Warner Brothers wanted Cary Grant to play Hill even though it was obvious that Preston's stage performance was already the stuff of legend. Actually, Phil Harris, Gene Kelly, Danny Kaye, and others were offered the Broadway role but had all turned it down. The producers then decided to take a chance on Preston, a second-ranked movie actor with no singing experience. His screen performance is as magnetic as it was on stage, and it took decades before other name actors would agree to play the part in major revivals, fearful for being compared to Preston. Shirley Jones, a veteran of the Rodgers and Hammerstein movie musicals, was cast as Marian, and as fine as she is, one keeps wondering what the angelic-voiced Barbara Cook would have done with it on screen. The supporting cast was filled with some of the best character actors from Hollywood and Broadway, and original director Morton Da Costa and stage choreographer Onna White repeated their excellent work for the film. Marion Hargrove's screenplay was faithful to the original script but was not afraid to move the action around a bit, add a few short character scenes, and rearrange the order of the songs. The only major change from the libretto is the fantasy ending with Harold Hill's pipe dream materializing into a big brass band with (literally) seventy-six trombones. It's a Hollywood kind of ending yet is so much in keeping with the theme of the musical that one accepts it graciously.

Only one song from Willson's score was dropped, and he rewrote the ballad "My White Knight" into the equally pleasing "Being in Love." Some of the musical numbers play even better in the film, such as "Wells Fargo Wagon," a chorus number that was turned into a series of pungent solos, or "Seventy-Six Trombones" which bursts out of the school gymnasium and onto the streets as only a movie can do. *The Music Man* is a case of a Broadway musical getting the prestige treatment by Hollywood, but, in this case, fidelity to the original does not turn the movie into a reverent, respectfully somber documentation of a stage hit.

West Side Story (1957) opened the same season as *The Music Man* and the urban musical was somewhat overshadowed by the rural one. (*The Music Man* won all the awards and ran twice as long.) This is not to say that *West Side Story* wasn't a commercial and critical hit. It was also one of the most innovative musicals of the decade, particularly in its unconventional use of dance. The production was the product of Broadway giants—producer Harold Prince, composer Leonard Bernstein, and director-choreographer Jerome Robbins—and up-and-coming talents: librettist Arthur Laurents and lyricist Stephen Sondheim. The premise of turning *Romeo and Juliet* into a contemporary musical drama about gang warfare was audacious and more than a little pretentious. But *West Side Story* went where few Broadway shows had dared to venture, and the result was electrifying. The original cast boasted no-name talents, though Carol Lawrence (Maria), Larry Kert (Tony), and Chita Rivera (Anita) would go on to notable stage careers. The real stars were the creators, and the riveting choreography and dazzling score have always remained the backbone of the musical's success. Yet it was not until the very popular 1961 movie version that *West Side Story* entered the mainstream consciousness of American culture, and its many subsequent stage productions over the years were inspired by and relied on the public's memory of the film.

Hollywood gave *West Side Story* the prestige treatment and the entire score, all the characters, and just about the whole libretto were retained for the screen version. Just as important, Robbins was hired as choreographer and codirector (with Robert Wise), so the best elements of the stage original survive the transition. Ernest Lehman's screenplay rearranged a few of the songs, but very little opening up was called for. The comic "Gee, Officer Krupke!" was moved to an earlier spot in the story and the tense number "Cool" was pushed to a later point; fans of the show have long argued over which positioning works best. The sarcastic "America" was enlarged from a comic ditty sung by Anita and some of her girlfriends to a production number (with a memorable dance section) for the Sharks and their girls. Apart from those changes, the movie was a very close copy.

The screen cast is uneven, however, and audiences tend to recall the supporting players more vividly than the leads. Natalie Wood had the right idea for Maria, but she is obviously not Hispanic and looks much older than we suspect the naive immigrant should be. Richard Beymer is a weak Tony, but his blond all-American looks help make the character somewhat believable. Both were dubbed for the singing vocals and their dancing talents were negligible, so it is puzzling why they were even given the roles. Wood had made only a few films and Beymer was a newcomer, so neither carried any box office clout. Perhaps Wise and Robbins wanted to keep *West Side Story* from becoming a performer's showcase. If so, they could not hide the fiery talents of Rita Moreno as the seething Anita, George Chakiris as her boyfriend Bernardo, and Russ Tamblyn as the Jet leader Riff. And individual gang members were so impressive during some of the scenes that they, too, started to glow a little more than the directors might have wished. This was a case in which a strong ensemble was able to carry a movie when the leads let it falter.

As beloved as the film is by many, some aspects of *West Side Story* bother other viewers. The juxtaposition of a modern tenement background and street toughs springing into ballet moves is something more easily accepted on the stage than the screen. Wise begins the film with the camera diving down from an aerial shot of Manhattan to a close-up of the Jets in a concrete playground (foreshadowing his similar opening in *The Sound of Music* four years later), and before you know it, the guys are leaping about in delicate unison. It is an opening that either fascinates one or causes groans and giggles. The realism of the streets (part of the movie was shot on location) and the artistry of the characters' movement do not sit well with many spectators. But there are other times when the dance seems to grow out of the situation so strongly that one accepts just about anything. The highly charged number "Cool," for example, builds powerfully from a bitter, frustrated dialogue scene into a dance of desperation and, ultimately, a release of tension. To love *West Side Story*, one has to suspend belief and give in to Robbins and Wise's vision of human conflict as artistic explosions. And what extraordinary explosions they are!

Bye Bye Birdie is also about the problems of America's youth, but two musicals could not be more different. The 1960 rock-and-roll show started as a silly high school musical meant for amateur groups. But somewhere along the way it ended up on Broadway where it provided a launching pad for some bright new theater talents: director-choreographer Gower Champion, librettist Michael Stewart, and songwriters Charles Strouse (music) and Lee Adams (lyrics). *Bye Bye Birdie* was a sleeper of sorts, running 607 performances when some thought it would close in a week. But the musical comedy has its charms and is still very popular in schools and community theaters. The farcical script is filled with lovable, daffy characters in both the younger and older generations, and the tuneful score has its touches of rock mixed within a set of traditional Broadway songs. Champion's staging also had much to do with the original production's colorful, carefree abandon. Dick Van Dyke and Chita Rivera shone as the adult couple while Susan Watson and Dick Gautier were delightful as the teenager Kim and her Elvis Presley–like idol Conrad Birdie. There were also scene-stealing performances by Paul Lynde as a harried father and Kay Medford as an unbearable mother-in-law-to-be.

Bye Bye Birdie remains a show that is impossible to take seriously but just as difficult not to like.

The 1963 movie version is just as lightweight but not nearly as lovable. While the stage musical spoofed the Elvis hysteria and gently mocked kids and their parents, the movie seems to wallow in its own commercialism. Sweet teenager Kim becomes red-hot *femme fatale* Ann-Margret and the movie takes her at face value. On stage, the efforts to get Birdie on the popular *Ed Sullivan Show* was a joke on America's fascination with celebrity. In the film, getting on the tube is an expected, acceptable move so the comedy has to come from the farcical antics involved in squeezing Birdie into the live telecast. Only half of the Broadway score made it to the screen, but Strouse and Lee wrote a zippy title song that Ann-Margret sang over the credits because it really didn't belong anywhere in the plot. Van Dyke and Lynde got to reprise their stage performances, and they are both dandy, as is Maureen Stapleton as Van Dyke's obnoxious mother. But Janet Leigh disappoints as his romantic partner Rose, and Jesse Pearson's Birdie is unimaginative and flat. Onna White choreographed the film, but none of the numbers match the ingenuity of Champion's stage work. Only the "Shriner's Ballet" comes close, but it needs a dancer as accomplished as Rivera to make it soar. All the same, *Bye Bye Birdie* was a big hit across the country, and, being turned somewhat into a showcase for Ann-Margret, it certainly established her screen career.

The 1960s was filled with eye-popping Broadway shows that were big on stars, hit songs, and spectacle. That is why the success of *Fiddler on the Roof* (1964) is so surprising and refreshing. It was a megahit with a small-scale mentality and eschewed glitz and glamour for intimate musical drama. Not that *Fiddler on the Roof* wasn't overflowing with theatricality and ingenious staging; but the musical was relatively quiet and gentle in its story, characters, and score. Joseph Stein adapted a handful of short stories by Sholom Aleichem into a cohesive stage libretto that centered on one family but was really about a community: the little Russian village of Anatevka soon after the turn of the century. Jerry Bock (music) and Sheldon Harnick (lyrics) wrote the distinguished score that was not afraid to include a Hebrew hymn and a folklike drinking song among its ballads, character numbers, and charm songs. Zero Mostel was the name star, and his philosophical dairyman

Tevye held the show together with his narration, speeches to God, and interaction with most of the other characters. But Tevye's family was really a microcosm for a whole generation of displaced Jews in the Old World who ended up breaking with tradition and seeking a different life in the new one.

As with *West Side Story*, it was director-choreographer Jerome Robbins who made it all work so beautifully. He captured the Old World culture in such numbers as the opening "Tradition" and the ritual bottle dance at the wedding, but he also explored expressionistic storytelling, as in his celebrated staging of "Tevye's Dream." Robbins's mark on every subsequent production of *Fiddler on the Roof* is as evident as the creators of the book and score. What was initially labeled a "Jewish show" soon became an international sensation as different cultures around the world identified with the musical and embraced it as if it was their story as well.

But making a film out of such a fragile, introspective piece of musical theater was not going to be easy. The stage production had stylized scenery by Boris Aronson that suggested a vibrant Marc Chagall painting. The village was presented allegorically, the townspeople joining in a circle to represent the workings of the small community. Even the title image of a fiddler sitting on Tevye's roof was a theatrical one not to be taken literally. But producer-director Norman Jewison solved many of the inherent problems and came up with a movie in 1971 that was both faithful and effective. Filmed on location in rural Yugoslavia and in studios in London, the movie has a realistic look but is rendered softer and more painterly by the beautiful cinematography by Oswald Morris that sometimes suggested Chagall but more often an old sepia photograph or a rural painting by Millet. Stein wrote the screenplay, and it was practically a literal copy of his stage work, even the soliloquies and the remarks addressed to God intact. Only two songs from the Broadway score were cut and, interestingly, the other numbers were not abridged or rewritten. This made for a very long movie (180 minutes) that, because of its leisurely pace, seemed even longer to some viewers. But *Fiddler on the Roof* on screen has the feel of an atmospheric foreign movie rather than a Hollywood musical, and if one surrenders to its episodic narrative and tenderhearted storytelling, it is more absorbing than tiring. (In 1979 United Artists released a 148-minute version, which many preferred.)

One of the reasons the film meanders so is the underplayed acting. Mostel was not seriously considered for Tevye probably because his stage performance was too big, too robust for the screen. His handful of film appearances revealed an oversized actor whose smallest gesture or expression was hilarious but also overpowering. So the studio went with the Israeli actor Topol who had played Tevye on the London stage. It is certainly not an overpowering performance; Topol's Tevye is quietly resigned to his lot, and his sense of humor is subtle and self-effacing. One misses the vitality of Mostel even as it's clear that Topol better fits into this low-key approach to the musical.

The same could be said for the whole cast. Yet Norma Crane underplays the wife Golde so much that she seems to disappear from the picture at times, and even scene-stealing comic Molly Picon plays the matchmaker Yente at half throttle. In keeping his movie unobtrusive and close to the earth, Jewison created a consistent and self-contained vision, but he did end up with some rather muted performances. Robbins's Broadway choreography was re-created by Tom Abbott and Sammy Bayes and there is nothing muted about any of it. The tavern dance and the wedding celebration are just as exciting on the screen, and the surreal dream number uses cinema techniques effectively, remaining a highlight of the show. *Fiddler on the Roof* may be some kind of movie classic, and its shortcomings cannot hinder its prominent place in the movies.

Funny Girl and *Hello, Dolly!* were more typical of the 1960s Broadway smash musical. Both are one-woman showcases surrounded by bright period settings, tuneful songs, and thrilling production numbers. And although the title heroines in each are very different, Barbra Streisand played both on the screen; these were star vehicles, and Streisand was the only female star that Hollywood would bank on. Her stage performance as comedienne Fanny Brice in *Funny Girl* (1964) was a revelation of sorts. We are so used to Streisand now that we sometimes forget how different and how thrilling she was when she first wowed audiences early in her career. Although *Funny Girl* was not written with her in mind (the producers tried to get Carol Burnett, Mary Martin, and Anne Bancroft for the role), Streisand quickly owned the part as few Broadway parts have been owned. In fact, when the film was made in 1968, the show was changed from a Broadway musical with a new star into a movie star vehicle, even though it was her first film. Practically all of the songs not sung by Fanny were cut, and others were added that were tailored to Streisand's particular and considerable talents. Yet *Funny Girl* works fine as a star vehicle, and the movie is very satisfying, one of the few show biz biopics that captures an era and reveals what made the star so special. It may not have been much more accurate than previous biopics, but it felt genuine.

William Wyler directed Isobel Lennart's screenplay (expertly adapted from her own libretto) with one eye on the story and another on Streisand's magnetic screen presence. Omar Sharif as her gambler-husband Nick oozed class and sophistication and was a perfect contrast to the fumbling, self-conscious Fanny. Herbert Ross choreographed the musical numbers, and they were excellent, from the lavish *Ziegfeld Follies* songs to the more intimate numbers like "You Are Woman." The stage score by Jule Styne (music) and Bob Merrill (lyrics) is exemplary ("People" was the standout hit), but the film's use of actual Brice songs, such as "Second Hand Rose" and "My Man," fills out the score and sets the period effectively. *Funny Girl* ranks with *Yankee Doodle Dandy* as one of the most durable biopics about an entertainer and remains a first-class piece of screen entertainment.

Hello, Dolly! opened on Broadway three months before *Funny Girl* but outran it by over a thousand performances, going on to break the record for the longest-running musical (later to be broken by *Fiddler on the Roof, Grease*, and other shows). *Hello, Dolly!* is the happiest show of the decade, with its nostalgic re-creation of turn-of-the-century New York, Jerry Herman's catchy, hummable songs, and a tight-knit libretto by Michael Stewart that is filled with optimism and romantic adventure. Gower Champion directed and choreographed with the pace and pomp of a parade and Carol Channing's matchmaker Dolly Levi was a big cartoonish valentine. *Hello, Dolly!* hasn't dated at all since it has always been more a depiction of musical comedy heaven than any one time period. It, too, is a star vehicle, but it wasn't written with Channing in mind. (Ethel Merman was producer David Merrick's first choice, and she eventually played it late in the run.) Like Streisand, Channing quickly made the role her own and went on to play it on tour and in revivals on and off for thirty years. The only place Channing didn't get to reprise her Dolly was on screen. The 1969 movie is also a parade—a very expensive parade costing $24 million with just about every penny up there on the screen. Gene Kelly directed but, oddly, left the choreography chores to Michael Kidd. The two of them visualized everything in the story on a big scale, so the movie always seems to be in an epic and panoramic frame of mind. *Hello, Dolly!* was not an intimate musical, to say the least, but the movie's mantra seemed to be "big is beautiful."

Well, sometimes it was, as in the joyous "Put on Your Sunday Clothes" number that starts as a duet and ends up with one of Hollywood's best train sequences, or with the song "Dancing" that begins quietly in a hat shop but soon comprises dozens of couples frolicking in the park. But other times big was just big, as in the overstuffed Harmonia Gardens restaurant or a Manhattan parade with thousands of extras but not a lot of excitement to go with it.

Several of the performances were also a bit oversized: Michael Crawford's gangly, gawking clerk Cornelius, Danny Lockin's hyperactive Barnaby, E. J. Peaker's wind-up doll Minnie, and Tommy Tune's artist Ambrose whose height alone qualified for overacting. Walter Matthau was rather subdued in his one-note grumpy performance as Horace Vandergelder, while Marianne McAndrew's Irene Malloy was a pleasing mixture of elegance and sly determination.

Then there was Streisand, miscast and working like hell to overcome it. Her Dolly Levi had to be younger than the many previous ones (she was only twenty-six when filming began) so the character's philosophical chatter and Yente-like meddling would have to be rethought. Streisand's Dolly was more Jewish, an undeniable aspect of the woman that most actresses in *The Matchmaker* and the stage *Hello, Dolly!* usually omit. But Streisand also gave Dolly a touch of class. When Channing arrived at the Harmonia Gardens and joined in singing the title song, she was a brazen old broad whom everybody loved. When Streisand arrived, it was like the entrance of the queen. Her Dolly was closer to a movie star than a turn-of-the-century party gal; in fact, she seemed much too young and desirable to end up stuck with grouchy old Horace.

Whether one accepts the new interpretation of Dolly or not, it was clear early in the film that Streisand was going to save the whole noisy circus. She's a dynamo whose energy and unbridled talent keep the movie afloat. Whether she is kvetching with Horace or addressing her dead husband, Streisand makes her book scenes work like gold. As for her singing, the film allowed her a wide range of emotions, from the quiet soliloquy section of "Before the Parade Passes By" to the raucous "So Long, Dearie" in which she mocks her own belting style. Her finest moment is in the movie's most unforgettable sequence: the sassy "Hello, Dolly!" duet with Louis Armstrong in which she scat sings with the master, and the two set off the kind of sparks found only rarely in movie musicals. *Hello, Dolly!* was one of the top-grossing films of the year but still failed to make a profit because of its inflated production costs. 20th Century-Fox took a loss, but the rest of us have benefited from this, the last of the big-budget Hollywood musicals.

An atypical Broadway hit from the 1960s was *Man of La Mancha* (1965), the musicalization of Cervantes's classic *Don Quixote*. Librettist Dale Wasserman took the epic novel's big scenes and capsulized them into a play within a play, as performed by Cervantes for his fellow prisoners of the Spanish Inquisition. Richard Kiley played both Cervantes and the crazy knight errant, and all the prisoners doubled as the characters Quixote met on his adventures. It is a tight, efficient libretto that works well enough, creating more a sketch rather than a full portrait of either man. But Kiley was exhilarating in the roles and the songs that Mitch Leigh (music) and Joe Darion (lyrics) gave him to sing were bombastic and meaty. "The Impossible Dream" is a cliché today, but one must try to recall the impact it made when first heard in the context of *Man of La Mancha*. Even more moving were the ballads "Dulcinea," "What Does He Want of Me?" and "To Each His Dulcinea." The comic songs were less interesting, mistaking triteness for folk comedy. But if one accepted the melodramatic tone of the musical and relished its lofty ideas, it was one of the most stirring shows of the decade. The 1972 movie version belabored those ideas and sabotaged the score by casting actors over singers and not dubbing any of them. It is an oddly dissatisfying movie to watch, yet it does get some things right. Peter O'Toole practically sings the knight's sentiments when he speaks in his Shakespearean-like voice, but when he sings, O'Toole sounds tentative and weak willed. It is a valiant performance, one to admire if not totally believe or warm up to.

Sophia Loren, as the sluttish Aldonza whom Quixote imagines to be a high-born lady of virtue, has the appropriate fire in her eyes and her famous sensuality is put to good use. But when she sings, Loren appears amateurish and lost. American comic James Coco plays Quixote's squire with vaudevillian ease, but the rest of the supporting cast are distinguished British actors (Harry Andrews, Brian Blessed, John Castle, Ian Richardson) who seem to have wandered in from one of Richard Attenborough's epic films, pronouncing their lines with gusto and pluck.

The look of the movie is also disconcerting. Director Arthur Hiller concentrates on the gritty realism of the piece, both in the prison scenes and in the acted-out adventures. The stage musical never quite left the prison setting, leaving the other locales to the audience's imagination. But when we see those places in the film, one is struck by how ordinary or dreary they are. The color palette for the movie is all earth tones, which might accurately reflect the countryside of La Mancha, but it gets boring very quickly on screen. *Man of La Mancha* failed to have a wide appeal for moviegoers and was quickly withdrawn. But it has found new audiences on video and offers them a few glimpses at what made the Broadway musical so popular.

Grease, on the other hand, was immediately popular both on stage and screen and remains so in both media. Neither version has much to offer in terms of quality songs or cohesive story and characters, but *Grease* succeeds as a celebration of an era (that was never quite like that) for those who were never there. It is a nostalgia piece but appeals most to younger audiences who want to believe in the clichés and stereotypes it presents. Jim Jacobs and Warren Casey wrote the book, music, and lyrics, and none have anything approaching wit or genuine ideas. The songs try to pastiche the music and words of the late 1950s, but the results are not accurate enough to be copies nor clever enough to be parody. Yet the sounds of the musical were familiar enough that *Grease* became the real McCoy for millions of playgoers and moviegoers. The 1972 Broadway production ran eight years and the 1978 movie became the biggest-grossing movie musical of all time, surpassing *The Sound of Music* in money if not in attendance.

Is the movie an improvement over the play? If it is it's only because the film sandwiched in a few genuine pop songs of the era. Also, the added new numbers by Barry Gibb, John Farrar, and others are better than those in the original score. So when the play is revived (and it remains one of the most produced musicals by schools), audience miss

"Hopelessly Devoted to You," "You're the One That I Want," and the rhythmic title song. The movie cast is mostly pleasing: John Travolta and Olivia Newton-John as the main couple and fine support by Stockard Channing and Didi Conn. For those moviegoers with longer memories, one gets to see celebrities from the real 1950s such as Alice Ghostley, Joan Blondell, Eve Arden, Dody Goodman, and Sid Caesar, though they all suffer from weak material. Only Frankie Avalon as Teen Angel in the risible "Beauty School Dropout" number gets a juicy scene. The success of *Grease* suggested to Hollywood that a Broadway musical has to be youth oriented to become a smash hit movie. The studios quickly produced some original film musicals that marketed a similar appeal: *Fame, Flashdance, Footloose, Dirty Dancing*, and others. But this was not a new discovery. The age of the average moviegoer had been dropping since the 1960s. *Grease* just happened to fall into the right demographic.

By the late 1970s, the screen door was opening less frequently. So many big-budget films based on Broadway musicals had lost money (big money) that there was an unofficial moratorium on doing any more screen versions of stage shows. By the 1990s, the screen door was virtually locked. But in 2002 Miramax released a movie version of *Chicago*, and it was so successful that suddenly everyone was thinking about Broadway and the movies again. As I write this, there is much discussion and conjecture going on over whether *Chicago* will launch a new era in movie musicals. Time will tell, but one thing is clear: *Chicago* is a terrific film adaptation of a Broadway hit.

The 1975 stage show was labeled "a musical vaudeville" and librettists Fred Ebb and Bob Fosse told their tale of scandal and purple journalism in the form of a series of variety acts that pastiched 1920s songs. No attempt was made to integrate the numbers and the dialogue in a realistic manner. Instead, the story stopped, the song was announced, and the vaudeville show continued. Yet Kander and Ebb's score for *Chicago* is more than parody. There are expert rhythm numbers, musical soliloquies, comic duets, and soft-shoe turns. And with Fosse as director and choreographer, the show moved like one extended dance piece, even the press conferences and trial scene turned into a gyrating Roaring Twenties ballet.

The original production featured Gwen Verdon and Chita Rivera as the two tabloid murderesses Roxie and Velma and Jerry Orbach as the silky lawyer Billy who gets them off. All three were too old for the parts so Fosse played off that, making them tawdry, world-weary vaudevillians filled with sarcasm and polish. Just to see Verdon and Rivera, two of Broadway's most cherished hoofers, on stage together made *Chicago* special. The show ran 898 performances and then gradually faded out of the limelight until a 1996 concert version with a young cast, and the re-created Fosse choreography, was the talk of the town. The bare-bones production moved to Broadway the next season and has stayed for over seven years. It was a far less satisfying version than the original, but the revival came to life whenever it sang and danced.

It was the surprising popularity of this revival (and its many tours) that prompted Hollywood to finally film the musical. But it was easier said than done. *Chicago* was all theatricality and "razzle dazzle" with a very thin plot and even thinner characterization. We have seen how the studios disapproved of vaudeville shows as movies and they were equally suspicious of a musical in which songs were not logically presented. But what screenwriter Bill Condon came up with solved the problem and actually improved the structure of the musical. The songs remained as vaudeville turns in the film, but each one took place in the imagination of wanna-be star Roxie Hart (Renée Zellweger). It was a tired old cinema device, but when Roxie saw the numbers in her mind they were true vaudeville acts, not Hollywood fantasies. Director-choreographer Rob Marshall staged most of them in a theater setting and then cleverly cut back and forth from the production number to the book scenes, the songs commenting on the story and often revealing the thoughts of the characters. Marshall devised his own dance routines, eschewing the familiar Fosse moves, and let the camera and the editing create tension and build excitement. It was closer to Fosse's techniques in the film *Cabaret* (particularly the opening "All That Jazz" which was used like "Wilkommen") than to his stage *Chicago*, yet it was thrilling to watch. Some complained about all the quick cutting and its similarity to MTV videos and the recent movie success *Moulin Rouge*. But those flashy, empty shows just disguised the lack of plot and character while *Chicago* illuminated them.

It also helped that the movie boasted an uncommonly talented cast who did their own singing. Catherine Zeta-Jones as Velma was as cool and sensuous as Zellweger's Roxie was overeager and unpolished.

Richard Gere was an appropriately slippery lawyer, Queen Latifah a ribald prison matron, and John C. Reilly a heartbreakingly transparent chump of a husband. Only two songs from the Kander and Ebb score were cut, and all of the dance numbers remained, so *Chicago* was filled with the kind of entertainment that makes musicals so special. It was a good old-fashioned song-and-dance show but in the guise of a contemporary, on-the-edge kind of film. *Chicago* was also the best piece of evidence found in years that the Hollywood musical was not dead and gone.

CHAPTER ELEVEN

∼

Reverse Order

The Golden Age of the movie musical was over by the 1960s. Some said the same was true for the Broadway musical. Yet there were several adventurous musical films and Broadway shows in the 1970s and 1980s. The number of products was certainly down, but individual works stood out and reminded audiences that there was still something unique and provocative about the musical form. With the Stephen Sondheim musicals on Broadway and the occasional flashes of brilliance like *Cabaret* on the screen, it was clear that the musical was still with us and that it could, once in a while, still be exhilarating.

But the genre was changing. On Broadway, big spectaculars (mostly from Great Britain) were so popular and ran so long that they gave the illusion that the musical form was flourishing. *Phantom of the Opera* and *Les Misérables* were more than just Broadway shows; they were each an industry: tours, recordings, coffee table books, television specials, and merchandise. They also appealed to people who had never experienced a professional musical production. It was theater as mass media.

In Hollywood, the genre was also changing. The definition of just what a movie musical was altered and films with plenty of dance or lots of singing in the background were included in the category. None of the characters sang in *Saturday Night Fever* or *Flashdance*, but there was

plenty of music and dance, and the pictures *felt* like musicals. On television a new phenomenon called the music video was getting popular,
and it was obvious that movie musicals were going to be affected by it.

But there was a particular change in musicals that was unique in the
history of stage and screen. It was the reversed swing of the screen door.
The last three decades of the century saw original movie musicals re-
fashioned into stage vehicles on Broadway. Screen favorites were scaled
down, had their scores augmented, and were re-created in theaters. It
was an odd conceit, when you think about it. Going from screen to
stage was more than just a reverse move. No matter how popular a
Broadway musical had been, most moviegoers never saw it or, if they
had, did not see the original New York production. The movie version
would be the mass-produced product that everyone could see. But what
happens when you go the other way? You start with a widely familiar
product and then redo it and sell it to a smaller market. Because the
films chosen were usually blockbusters, it was even assumed that audiences would walk into the Broadway theater already knowing the product well. This often led to disappointment. The reason the movie was
such a hit in the first place was in large part due to its skillful use of cinema techniques and memorable performances. But the stage version
could offer neither of these. Theater scenery cannot compete with the
places movies can go, and, no matter how proficient the stage actors,
they have to fight against the audience's memory of Gene Kelly or
Maurice Chevalier in the screen version.

Despite these difficulties, several film-to-stage musicals were produced on Broadway. Some were disastrous misfires, others were enjoyable enough, and a few were ingenious accomplishments. Most lost
money, but the ones that showed a profit were (and still are) major
blockbusters of their own. It was a risky proposition to go through the
screen door backward, but sometimes it paid off in terms of big money
and even high artistic achievement.

We will look briefly at fifteen Broadway shows that were based on
movie musicals. There are, of course, dozens of stage musicals based
on nonmusical movies (see the appendixes), but these fifteen are
based on original film musicals.

The earliest example, *Lili* (1953), is a tentative first step in experi-
menting with the reverse order. The movie just barely qualifies as a mu-

sical and its stage adaptation, *Carnival* (1961), only uses the film's plot and characters, not the music. Lili (Leslie Caron) is a sixteen-year-old French orphan who ends up working with a traveling carnival where she falls for the magician Marcus the Magnificent (Jean-Pierre Aumont) but is beloved by the bitter cripple Paul (Mel Ferrer) who operates the side show puppets. Lili is frightened by the cynical Paul, but when he speaks to her through his puppets, she is enchanted.

It is a charming movie that has the look and feel of a foreign film. Helen Deutsch wrote the screenplay (based on a Paul Gallico short story), and Charles Walters directed with a light touch. Caron may get a little cloying as Lili (her naiveté is sometimes more annoying than touching), but Ferrer and Aumont are superb, as are Kurt Kasznar and Zsa Zsa Gabor in supporting roles. The movie only has one song, the childlike ditty "Hi-Lili, Hi-Lo" by Bronislau Kaper (music) and Deutsch (lyrics), but Walters choreographed two long dream ballets, and Kaper scored the whole film with various musical motifs that add to its magical atmosphere. *Lili* certainly feels like a musical.

Carnival expanded the story somewhat (there is very little plot in the film), kept the main characters, and added a full theater score by Bob Merrill. The catchy movie song was replaced by an equally contagious ditty called "Love Makes the World Go Round" that was sung by Lili (Anna Maria Alberghetti) and the puppets but also served as the show's theme song, played by a concertina at times to marvelous effect. Michael Stewart wrote the libretto, and he managed to turn the tale into a colorful Broadway musical without sacrificing the charm. Jerry Orbach was Paul, the magician (now called Marco) was played by James Mitchell, and Kaye Ballard was very amusing in the Gabor role. Although *Carnival* was a hit (719 performances), it is not often revised because it is a very difficult show to present.

Gower Champion directed and choreographed the original like one continuously flowing circus, the show starting with a sunrise and the carnival workers setting up their tents as the music and the sunlight built in intensity. *Carnival* is quieter and more winsome than most 1960s musicals, but when given a competent production, it still glows with enchantment. The theme song became very popular, but all of Merrill's score is splendid. Some songs, such as "Always Always You" and "Yes, My Heart," have a definite French flavor; others, such as

"Humming" and "Sword, Rose and Cape," are pure Broadway. As in the movie, the puppets play an important role in the stage story but one misses the intimacy of the film's close-ups and the detailed expressions that are often lost in a large theater.

Carnival was never filmed, probably because *Lili* was so memorable that Hollywood feared unflattering comparisons. But it ought to be made into a movie musical; its merits are considerable, and the original movie is now far enough removed.

Another movie musical set in France with Leslie Caron was adapted for the stage twelve years after *Carnival*. The beloved classic *Gigi* (1958) reached Broadway in 1973, but the result was very unsatisfying, and the run of 103 performances was a financial bust. The movie is considered Hollywood's equivalent to Broadway's *My Fair Lady*. Both are Lerner and Loewe shows with plots unlikely to work as a musical and characters that are often antiromantic. The grooming of a teenage girl to become a high-class Parisian courtesan is not your typical musical material, but Alan Jay Lerner's screenplay handles the Colette story with finesse and the songs written with Frederick Loewe are outstanding. From the wry "Thank Heaven for Little Girls" and the celebratory "The Night They Invented Champagne" to the sly character duet "I Remember It Well" and the rhapsodic title song, the *Gigi* score is one of the finest ever written for Hollywood.

The performances throughout are equally auspicious. Caron is much more winning as Gigi than as Lili, and her tomboy charm and blossoming womanhood are fascinating to watch. Louis Jourdan's Gaston is perhaps a French version of Henry Higgins, all bluster and not seeing the beauty before him, but the character is also funny and likable in a very Gallic manner. Maurice Chevalier gives one of his best screen performances as the roguish ladies man Honoré, and Hermione Gingold tones down her usual high jinks and makes Inez warm and affectionate with a twinkle in her eye. Vincente Minnelli directed, and he was never in better form. *Gigi* was a big winner at the box office, at the Oscars, and in the memory of anyone who ever saw it.

Colette's story had been seen on Broadway in 1954 as a nonmusical play featuring Audrey Hepburn as Gigi. It was an intimate production and well received. Even the lavish movie is rather intimate, relying mostly on two character-scenes set against the background of fin-de-siècle Paris. But the 1973 stage version was huge, its re-creations of Maxim's Restaurant, the Tuilleries, and the French Riviera filling the stage of the Uris Theater, Broadway's largest venue. Lerner adapted his own screenplay and, during a less-than-smooth tryout tour, took over as director. It is a surprisingly pedestrian libretto with even beloved scenes from the film failing to work on stage. The glorious movie score was used, as well as five new numbers by the team, but none seemed to catch fire as they had on the screen. Many blamed Karin Wolfe's bland performance as Gigi. She was too old for the part (twenty-eight years and looking very much like it even on the cavernous Uris stage), and her singing lacked excitement. (Actually, she was standby for a younger actress who was dropped on the road.) Yet the rest of the cast were very proficient, but even their scenes and songs were disappointing. Alfred Drake was a debonair Honoré, and his familiar theater voice was warmly welcomed back to Broadway even as this renowned stage star failed to save the show. Daniel Massey was a commendable Gaston, and Agnes Moorehead and Maria Karnilova were fine as Gigi's manipulating relatives.

Gigi on stage came across as lifeless and amateurish despite all the talent and money behind it. Perhaps the movie was too famous and fondly remembered. Perhaps audiences were disappointed that what they saw on stage was not the Gigi they expected. But, frankly, this was not a production to be enjoyed even by those unfamiliar with the screen version. If a Broadway hit can be turned into a dud movie, it's just as true that a movie classic can become a stage turkey.

Yet 42nd Street was a film classic and made a very popular Broadway musical. If Gigi is Hollywood's My Fair Lady, then 42nd Street (1933) might be considered Tinsel Town's Oklahoma! because of its innovations and landmark status. The tough-talking screenplay by James Seymour and Rian James, the brassy performances by a first-rate cast, and Busby Berkeley's cinematic production numbers make the movie look and sound unique. And it was unique, presenting a musical not as it might appear on Broadway but instead using angles, dissolves, and camera tricks to do what only a movie can do. Because 42nd Street is the quintessential backstage musical, its plot about a chorine (Ruby Keeler) who becomes a star when she takes over the leading role in a show is the musical cinema's greatest cliché and the stuff of parody. But

Lloyd Bacon directed the film in that gritty, fast-talking style that was pure 1930s Warner Brothers, and the musical still packs a punch. It helps that the score is superior. Harry Warren (music) and Al Dubin (lyrics) became the preeminent Hollywood songwriters with this film, and unforgettable numbers such as "Shuffle Off to Buffalo," "You're Getting to Be a Habit With Me," and the jazzy title song introduced a sound and attitude that would flourish throughout the Depression years. But the most distinctive thing about 42nd Street was the effect it had on the industry, reinventing the movie musical and opening the door for three decades of adventurous filmmaking in the genre.

The 1980 Broadway production of 42nd Street utilized the plot and added nine Warren songs from other movies to augment the film's four songs into a full stage score. Michael Stewart and Mark Bramble wrote the libretto that stuck fairly close to the film, keeping the book scenes short (perhaps too short) so that there was plenty of room for the songs and production numbers. The only substantial change they made was hinting at a possible romance between the chorine Peggy Sawyer (Wanda Richert) and the hard-boiled producer Julian Marsh (Jerry Orbach). The relationship between Peggy and hoofer Billy Lawlor (Lee Roy Reams), who were the romantic duo of the movie, was downplayed, and audiences were sometimes confused as to which one she really liked. (The writers begged the question by ending the show without Peggy committed to either man.) But plot was secondary to the stage 42nd Street even though it was what drove the film. Consequently, the Broadway show was a dazzling, tuneful entertainment but totally missing that smart-aleck flavor of the Depression musical.

Where the stage show excelled was in its production numbers. Director-choreographer Gower Champion did not try to copy Berkeley's famous stunts when he choreographed the numbers, but he brought his own ingenuity to the task and found theatrical ways to create glamour and spectacle. "Lullaby of Broadway" was staged on a double staircase at the Philadelphia train station, "Shuffle Off to Buffalo" used a compartmentalized set to suggest a train interior, and "Shadow Waltz" eschewed scenery altogether and relied on dancing silhouettes and long shadows on a cyclorama to make bold patterns. Producer David Merrick gave the show a classy mounting with eye-popping sets and costumes and a venerable cast backed by a bigger-than-usual chorus of dancers. *42nd Street* ran over eight years and then was a hit all over again when it was revived on Broadway in 2001.

The success of *42nd Street* prompted theatrical producers to bring three other film classics to the stage in the 1980s, but each one was a major flop and Broadway quickly cooled on reversing the swing of the screen door. The frontier musical *Seven Brides for Seven Brothers* (1954) was turned into a stage musical in 1982, and the result was so dismal that it closed in three days. The raucous story told of seven backwoods brothers who, inspired by the ancient tale of the rape of the Sabine women, kidnap some unmarried girls from the town and steal them away to their mountain cabin. It was an unlikely plot for a movie musical, but under Stanley Donan's expert direction and aided by Michael Kidd's vigorous choreography, the film was a delightful musical tall tale.

The Broadway version was hopelessly incompetent, with the mediocre cast matched by the unimaginative dancing and clumsy staging and shoddy production values. Four of the film songs by Gene de Paul (music) and Johnny Mercer (lyrics) were dropped, and six new ones by other songwriters were added, each one more forgettable than the last. The plot was left intact for the most part, but some things, such as the avalanche that keeps the girls with the boys until the spring thaw, just couldn't and didn't work on stage.

Four years later *Singin' in the Rain* (1952) was turned into a Broadway show, and it wasn't much better (though it lasted an unprofitable 367 performances). Generally considered one of the best movie musicals Hollywood ever produced, *Singin' in the Rain* is also one of the funniest. The screenplay by Betty Comden and Adolph Green about the early days of the talkies is a backstager but, instead of being about Broadway, the movie business is the milieu. Given only the catalog of Nacio Herb Brown (music) and Arthur Freed (lyrics) songs as their inspiration, Comden and Green devised a clever script that spoofed Hollywood, celebrity, and the musical genre itself. But as strong as the dialogue and songs are, *Singin' in the Rain* is a classic because of its incisive direction, witty choreography (both by Gene Kelly and Stanley Donan), and sprightly performers (Kelly, Debbie Reynolds, Donald O'-Connor, and Jean Hagen).

The Broadway version had none of these, and the stage libretto (by Comden and Green) and the celebrated songs could not salvage the show. O'Connor's prankish "Make 'Em Laugh" is one of the most extraordinary few minutes in musical cinema history, yet the song itself (the only one written by Brown and Freed for the film) is not very accomplished; it is O'Connor and the staging that make it fly. On stage it was a hyperactive embarrassment. Don Correia had the unenviable task of playing the Kelly role on stage, and, as was personable as he was, it was a losing proposition. The screen characters are rather stereotypic and not terribly interesting; it was Kelly and company that made them shine. No major star would dare try to play them on stage, so the Broadway version used unknowns who remained unknown. Great effort and expense went into re-creating the famous title number, complete with rain on stage. It was a joyless curiosity and only pointed out how unnecessary the whole Broadway production was.

Only slightly more successful (but still losing money) was the 1989 stage adaptation of Meet Me in St. Louis (1944). The film is one of Hollywood's most nostalgic musicals, capturing an idealized America at the turn of the century and filled with domestic charm. It was one of director Vincente Minnelli's crowning achievements, and everything about the movie was superior, from the renowned score by Hugh Martin and Ralph Blane (with a few actual period tunes thrown in) and the warm and endearing performances to the outstanding sets and costumes. While Judy Garland's performance as the teenage Esther Smith was central, this was basically a family story and one that might translate to the stage. But Irving Brecher and Fred Finklehoffe's screenplay was mangled in the Broadway version, some lackluster new songs were added, and the whole production was wooden and dull. Unknown Donna Kane was cast in the Garland role and proved that this was indeed a part that needs a star. Some well-known actors (George Hearn, Betty Garrett, Milo O'Shea) were hired for the supporting roles, but their valiant efforts were in vain. Meet Me in St. Louis struggled on for 253 performances, never capturing the public's fancy like the old movie continues to do. (A later stage version that stuck closer to the original screenplay was more successful outside New York.)

The first Broadway hit to come from the movies after 42nd Street was the 1994 stage version of Beauty and the Beast. In the 1990s, the Disney studios gave movie musicals a shot in the arm with a series of fully scored animated films that were as popular as they were accomplished.

This little renaissance started with *The Little Mermaid* (1989) and continued with *Beauty and the Beast* (1991), *Aladdin* (1992), *The Lion King* (1994), and other significant pictures. They were mostly scored by Broadway veterans and were decidedly traditional in the choice of song styles. Yet each film was very innovative in how music was used, and the animation techniques matched those of the studio's glory days of the past.

Perhaps the finest of the group was *Beauty and the Beast*, a movie musical that had depth of character and a visual look that rivaled the most romantic of live-action films. Bringing such a fantastical piece to the stage was fraught with difficulties, but the Disney corporation, with its deep pockets and talent for marketing, manufactured a Broadway hit. It was scoffed at by many in the theater profession, labeled a "theme park show" by some, and given the snob treatment at the Tony Awards that season. But the public adored it, and it continues to run a decade later.

While the stage version may not be as inspired as the film, it is a very professional and highly proficient Broadway show. The look of the movie is duplicated, but the story is fleshed out a bit as new songs by Alan Menken (music) and Tim Rice (lyrics) were added to the original Menken–Howard Ashman score. The animated wizardly of the screen version was nearly matched by the ingenious stage effects devised for Broadway, many of the film's most magical moments coming across just as potently in the theater. Hollywood's *Beauty and the Beast* is a wondrous masterpiece; on Broadway, it is a top-flight musical that, as enjoyable as it is, often reminds one of the film's greatness.

Far from a classic by any set of standards, the movie musical *Victor/Victoria* (1982) nevertheless was popular, and it gave Julie Andrews one of the better roles of her later career. In director Blake Edwards's cockeyed screenplay, down-on-her-luck singer Vicki Adams is transformed into a star by the gay nightclub singer Toddy (Robert Preston) who passes her off as a Polish count named Victor who is (supposedly) a female impersonator. Complications set in when an American gangster (James Garner) falls for her/him, and there are a lot of slamming doors and other farcical business to keep the film afloat until the happy ending. Edwards's direction and script wavered between broad farce (he had made all the *Pink Panther* movies) and traditional musical comedy, never getting carefree enough to be truly lighthearted and the serious scenes usually falling flat. A surprisingly bland score by veterans Henry Mancini (music) and Leslie Bricusse (lyrics) didn't help, but Andrews and Preston certainly did, and their one number together, the derivative "You and Me," was one of the movie's few musical bright spots.

Edwards struggled for over a decade to get his musical on Broadway, and it only got there in 1995 because Andrews (his wife) agreed to return to the Great White Way for the first time since *Camelot* (1960). It was a triumphal star return, though the production itself was roundly panned, and even its forced run of 734 performances lost a bundle. As inadequate as the show was, the stage version was a slight improvement over the film. Edwards's libretto was tighter, the farcical pratfalls were minimized, and the story played more like a traditional musical comedy. Mancini had died, so Frank Wildhorn composed some new tunes for Broadway, and they were even worse than the original ones. Tony Roberts was an affable Toddy but paled next to Preston's screen portrayal. (Preston was slated to do the play as well but died before Edwards raised the funds to go to Broadway.) *Victor/Victoria* was a case of a mediocre movie musical making a faithful mediocre stage musical.

In 1996, thirty-six years after the death of Oscar Hammerstein and seventeen years after Richard Rodgers died, Broadway finally got what it hadn't had in nearly four decades: a "new Rodgers and Hammerstein musical." That's how the stage version of *State Fair* was billed, and the words looked magical on a marquee. But the show was hardly new, the movie musical going back to 1945 and even the various stage adaptations kicking around the country for two decades. The famous Theater Guild, the prestigious organization that had first produced the team's *Oklahoma!* and *Carousel* but was now on its last leg, toured the production for several months before bringing it to Broadway. Even the ailing producer David Merrick threw in some money, making it his last Broadway venture before he died in 2000. *State Fair* was marketed as a family show, and indeed it was squeaky clean with such wholesome stars such as John Davidson, Kathryn Crosby, and the original *Annie*, Andrea McArdle. Some lesser-known songs from lesser-known Rodgers and Hammerstein musicals were added to fill out the score, and musically it was a feast. But nothing could hide the weak script, lifeless direction and choreography, and second-rate production values. *State Fair* hung on for a very unprofitable 102 performances but found life in schools and community theaters who were also anxious for a "new" Rodgers and Hammerstein musical.

Yet *State Fair* should have made a very enjoyable show. The 1945 film was the team's only original movie musical, and it was filled with excellent songs, a serviceable story, and some engaging performances. The adventures of the Frake family at the Iowa state fair were certainly homespun and domestically unexciting, as was to be expected in a film appealing to war-weary moviegoers. It was, in some ways, a hayseed version of the previous year's *Meet Me in St. Louis.* Charles Winninger and Fay Bainter were the parents, Jeanne Crain and Dick Haymes their teenage children, and Dana Andrews and Vivian Blaine the more sophisticated sweethearts they encounter at the fairgrounds. It had its share of corn but there were sly touches along the way and songs like "Isn't It Kinda Fun?" "That's for Me," and "It's A Grand Night for Singing" swept the two romances along nicely. The film also featured the beloved ballad "It Might as Well Be Spring," which won that year's Oscar for best song.

Fox remade the musical in 1962 and foolishly tried to update it in tone as well as time. To get rid of the corn, Fox moved the locale to the Texas state fair in Dallas (supposedly rural folk in Texas were not so homespun) and jazzed up the score by rearranging five of the old numbers into pop versions and adding five new ones by Rodgers (including a love song to a hog). Tom Ewell and Alice Faye were pleasantly agreeable as the parents, but the kids (Pamela Tiffin and Pat Boone) were lifeless and annoying. Bobby Darin and Ann-Margret were their love interests, the first crooning and the second sashaying their way through the film, trying to make the picture feel "modern." But *State Fair* is a nostalgic family piece, not a Texan *Bye Bye Birdie*. As popular as the movie was then, it is painful to view today. At least the failed 1996 Broadway production eliminated most of the "improvements" made by the 1962 film and put the musical back in time and back in Iowa. But it wasn't enough.

The most successful (critically and financially) Broadway show to be made from a film musical is *The Lion King*. It is also the most daring and creative transition from screen to stage, using what is best in the movie and reinterpreting it to use what is best about live theater. The 1994 animated film was a blockbuster hit for Disney—in fact, its highest-grossing picture of all time. This was surprising since, unlike the studio's other megahits, *The Lion King* was not based on a familiar fairy tale or widely recognized story. Irene Mecchi, Jonathan Roberts, and Linda Woolverton wrote the original screenplay that employed no human characters but borrowed liberally from *Hamlet* and even Disney's own *Bambi*. It is an efficient script, nicely mixing humor, pathos, and an awe of nature. The songs by Elton John (music) and Tim Rice (lyrics) were also serviceable, though far from extraordinary.

But the animators turned the script and score into something special. *The Lion King* certainly has its thrills and emotional tugs, but it also has something few animated films have captured: a genuine sense of wonder at life's more puzzling questions. The romance between the lion "prince" Simba and lioness Nala is secondary in the plot. The tale is more about Simba's personal journey to self-awareness and self-worth. Without getting preachy, the movie manages to explore the ideas of responsibility, loyalty, and even justice.

This doesn't mean *The Lion King* wasn't much fun. Its humor was sometimes sarcastic, sometimes Borscht Belt, always on the money. The voices of Nathan Lane, Whoopie Goldberg, Jeremy Irons, Rowan Atkinson, and others were hilarious. And these were effectively balanced by the richness of voices like Robert Guillaume and James Earl Jones, bringing a dignity to the animals that few human characters get to play. The African flavor of the movie also helped make it unique and memorable. The animators rendered the landscape with striking artistry, and Hans Zimmer's evocative musical score seemed to encapsulate the tribal spirit of an entire continent. The power of animated filmmaking has rarely been better realized.

News that Disney would follow its successful stage *Beauty and the Beast* with a Broadway version of *The Lion King* was greeted with more than a little skepticism. With no human characters in the story, the necessity of animal costumes and the prospect of a furry cast prancing about the stage conjured up visions of a jungle version of *Cats*. But before long, word started filtering in from the out-of-town tryouts that something sensational was happening. By the time *The Lion King* arrived on Broadway in 1997, it was already a bona fide hit.

What had happened? Julie Taymor, for one thing. The little-known director-puppeteer from regional theater had reimagined and rethought the movie in terms of ritual theater performance. The plot, characters, and score stayed the same (though John and Rice wrote a few new numbers and some of Zimmer's film music was turned into vocals), but the show was now a tribal, almost primitive, celebration of the magic of theater. Although the production utilized all kinds of puppetry, from Indonesian shadow puppets and circuslike stilt figures to African headdresses and kinetic sculptures, the human actors were central. Without smoke and special effects (which had been used so often in *Beauty and the Beast*), Taymor's production allowed audiences to view both the characters and the process of manipulating and enacting those characters. The magic here was the magic of the human imagination. Like the puppets, the scenery and costumes all suggested rather than spelled out the look of the musical. This is not to say that *The Lion King* was simple or barebones. With its hydraulic lifting turntable, flying actors, and moving scenery, it was a very complicated production. Yet, because everything is exposed and forthright, it all seemed so basic. Like the stirring choral chanting by the cast and the intricate masks and costumes, the show was both simply and elaborately overwhelming. It was also pure theater. Had *The Lion King* been a Broadway musical first and someone suggested making a movie out of it, the idea would seem ridiculous. How do you film a theatrical celebration of live performance?

Near the end of the 1990s, two "youth" film musicals were turned into Broadway shows and met with little success. The movie hit *Saturday Night Fever* (1977) qualified as a musical only because of the many scenes at the local dance club and the disco soundtrack score by the Bee Gees that pounded its way through the whole movie. It was a tawdry story about restless youths with dead-end lives who find a bit of heaven dancing their Saturday nights away. Norman Wexler's screenplay was a humorless exposé (it was based on a magazine article about an actual Brooklyn disco) and did not romanticize the characters or their sordid doings. John Travolta, as the central character of Tony Manero, was magnetic both on and off the dance floor and the picture made him a star. When the tale was turned into a Broadway musical in 1999, librettist Nan Knighton vainly tried to turn the background music into theater songs for the characters. The result was as phony as it was incongruous. The documentary-like story did not play well on stage, and only the disco dancing kept audiences in their seats. *Saturday Night Fever* needed either a star or someone who could use the part to become a star. The Broadway version had neither and struggled along for 507 performances before calling it quits.

Footloose lasted 708 performances in New York but also lost a bundle. The 1984 movie was another musical only by nature of its soundtrack score. In fact, all of the songs (save the title number) were written after the filming was completed. Dean Pitchford's screenplay was an implausible tale about a midwestern town that has outlawed dancing and the newcomer (Kevin Bacon) who leads the young citizens in revolt against the local ordinance. Audiences may not have taken the situation or characters seriously, but the best-selling soundtrack (by various songwriters) sold the picture to young moviegoers, and *Footloose* was a hit. The modern fable looked even more far-fetched in its 1998 Broadway version. Again the background soundtrack was turned into theater songs for the characters, and some at least made a little sense. But just as Bacon had the charisma to hold the film together, the stage version lacked star power, and the young, energetic cast protested and danced in vain.

Much more conservative, but equally unsuccessful, was the 1998 stage version of *High Society*, the 1956 film musical based on the stage and screen comedy *The Philadelphia Story*. Philip Barry's play is one of the wittiest comedies of manners in the American theater. The tale of a wealthy Philadelphia Main Liner and her planned second marriage was written for Katharine Hepburn, and she triumphed with it on stage in 1939 and on screen in 1940. When Hollywood musicalized it sixteen years later, comparisons with the earlier movie were deflected by making major changes. The locale was moved from Philadelphia to Newport where a jazz festival is going on; it was a perfect excuse for Louis Armstrong to make an appearance and sing "Now You Has Jazz," one of the handful of sparkling songs Cole Porter wrote for the film. Grace Kelly, who had been a real Main Liner, played the socialite Tracy Lord with such elegant conviction that one could momentarily forget Hepburn. And with Bing Crosby and Frank Sinatra as her admirers who handled most of the songs, *High Society* created its own kind of magic.

The movie was enormously popular, and Porter's atypically sentimental ballad "True Love" became one of his top sellers. Much of the play's literate dialogue was cut for the film, and several characters were practically written out of the story, but screenwriter John Patrick pruned efficiently, and, as directed and choreographed by Charles Walters, the movie musical maintained its own high level of sophistication.

A stage version of *High Society* was seen in London in 1987, but it wasn't until a decade later that an American team put together their own effort, and it played successfully in regional theater before arriving on Broadway in 1998. Absurdist playwright Arthur Kopit was the unlikely author of the book, but there was nothing innovative in his handling of the material. The mansion's domestic staff acted as a kind of chorus, and their opening number and subsequent appearances gave the musical a very contrived and outdated feeling. Kopit restored some of the Barry dialogue and built up the supporting role of the boozing Uncle Willie, probably because John McMartin was so charming in the part. With no Louis Armstrong, the show wisely cut "Now You Has Jazz" but kept the rest of the film score and augmented it with other Porter songs. Some of these had new or added lyrics by Susan Birkenhead to fit them into the *High Society* plot. The result was often cloying as Porter wit and Birkenhead jokes made unhappy partners. Did anyone really want to hear the delectable "Let's Misbehave" rewritten so that it sort of made sense in a new context?

Yet much about the stage *High Society* was highly professional. The producers decided to go with relative unknowns in the cast rather than try and compete with the memory of Kelly, Crosby, and Sinatra. (Or did name stars wisely turn them down?) Melissa Errico has more talent than many stars, but she isn't a star, so her valiant work as Tracy went unrecognized. It didn't help that she wasn't given very much to sing; Kelly couldn't carry a song, but Errico sure could, so why not a singing Tracy? Daniel McDonald and Stephen Bogardus also impressed as her two admirers, but audiences kept waiting for Uncle Willie to come back on. It was that kind of show. Far more accomplished than *State Fair, Footloose, Saturday Night Fever* and the rest, *High Society* still only managed to hang on for 144 performances.

The next case of the screen door swinging in a reverse direction turned out much better. *Thoroughly Modern Millie* was a movie vehicle for Julie Andrews in 1967 when she was still a top box office attraction. It was a silly but likable musical set in the Roaring Twenties that took a very tongue-in-cheek approach to telling its story, complete with silent screen title cards to reveal the characters' thoughts, old-fashioned film techniques like wipes and iris close-ins, and physical comedy reminiscent of Mack Sennett shorts. Andrews played Millie, a "modern" out to find a job as a "stenog" so she can marry her rich boss. Mary Tyler Moore was amusing as the naive Miss Dorothy who is really an heiress in disguise, John Gavin and Edward Fox were the love interests, and Beatrice Lillie shone as the landlady who is selling her young tenants into white slavery. An added bonus was a rare film appearance by Carol Channing as the dizzy millionairess Muzzy who sings a few songs and gets shot out of a cannon. Richard Morris wrote the agreeable mess of a screenplay, and George Roy Hill directed waggishly. Jimmy Van Heusen (music) and Sammy Cahn (lyrics) wrote four songs for the film, most memorably the catchy title number, and old standards from the period were added to fill out the score.

Thoroughly Modern Millie is uneven, some of its comedy bits going on far too long and certain jokes repeated with diminishing payoffs, but often it is thoroughly enjoyable. Morris coauthored the libretto (with Dick Scanlan) for the 2002 Broadway version, and it is much better structured. The basic plot remains the same, but the characters are more fully developed and less time is spent on slapstick and more on singing and dancing. Only a few numbers from the film were retained, and Jeanine Tesori (music) and Scanlan (lyrics) wrote several new songs that were both clever pastiches of the 1920s and delightful in their own right. Michael Mayer was the resourceful director, and Rob Ashford choreographed with such amusing touches as a drunk ballet set to the *Nutcracker Suite* and typists tapping away with both fingers and feet. The bright and spirited production boasted no stars, but newcomer Sutton Foster (as Millie) carried herself like one, and by the end of the season she was proclaimed Broadway's happiest new discovery.

The only part of the musical that failed to live up to the film was Muzzy. Instead of a scatter-brained but philosophical blonde, the character was played by African American Sheryl Lee Ralph as a sleek and classy chanteuse who delivered her two songs in a mellow, nightclub-bish manner that didn't seem to fit with the rest of the show. But so much of *Thoroughly Modern Millie* was so delicious that it felt like a classic 1920s hit that had been revived with panache.

The most recent screen-to-stage musical effort is *Never Gonna Dance* (2003), based on the Astaire–Rogers film *Swing Time* (1936). Considered by many as the team's finest vehicle, the movie has a forced plot about two nightclub hoofers who quarrel in song and dance until he finally wins her over. But along the way are such unforgettable moments such as Astaire pretending he can't dance very well so that he can take lessons from Rogers, the team's luminous "Waltz in Swing Time," the comic support of Victor Moore and Helen Broderick, and a superb score by Jerome Kern (music) and Dorothy Fields (lyrics). "Bojangles of Harlem," the tribute to Bill Robinson, allowed Astaire to do a unique blackface number and "A Fine Romance" was a musicalized scene that predated the Rodgers and Hammerstein model by seven years. George Stevens directed in such a way that any sluggishness in the Howard Lindsay–Allan Scott script was disguised with art deco ease. Even the film's hit song, "The Way You Look Tonight," was presented wryly, with Astaire crooning while Rogers lathered her head in shampoo—antiromantic and still highly romantic. *Swing Time* remains one of the exuberant joys of the movie musical.

The film was called *Never Gonna Dance* until studio heads worried that audiences might take the title at face value think that Astaire and Rogers would not dance in the film. But *Never Gonna Dance* is an appropriate title and the one used by producers when the stage version of *Swing Time* opened in 2003. The unsolvable problem of trying to erase the memory of Astaire and Rogers was somewhat softened by casting two unknown but highly talented performers as the dancing couple. Noah Racey was particularly fine at juggling the dancing and the comedy, while the red-headed Nancy Lemanger was no less proficient, portraying a softer but likable version of Rogers's sarcastic blonde. But as fine as they were, they weren't the cinema icons, and it was difficult to forget that even as one enjoyed their performances.

Much of the rest of the production was highly competent and sometimes even inspired, such as a glorious production number in Grand Central Station. Racey arrives in New York with the intention of giving up hoofing, arguing "I Won't Dance," but the sounds of Manhattan are too much for him, and he succumbs. Librettist Jeffrey Hatcher filled out the screenplay somewhat, adding a nice plot twist in which the Racey character, Lucky Garnett, tries not to become a financial success so that he can drop his upper-class fiancée and link up with Lemanger. The score was augmented by other Kern songs, from the familiar "I'm Old Fashioned" to the obscure "Shimmy with Me." (Only the politically incorrect "Bojangles of Harlem" was cut from the film score.) Also, the Broadway production wisely emphasized dance, and much of Jerry Mitchell's choreography was first-class. But *Never Gonna Dance* only occasionally set off the sparks that one hoped for. This was no embarrassment like *Seven Brides for Seven Brothers*, but neither was it the stage *42nd Street*. The musical only managed to run 84 performances.

As this is written, several other Hollywood-to-Broadway projects are in various states of preparation. *Mary Poppins*, *A Star Is Born*, *The Little Mermaid*, *The Night They Raided Minsky's*, *The Hunchback of Notre Dame*, *White Christmas*, and other movie musicals are planned for the Great White Way. So it looks like the screen door will continue to swing both ways. Which is all for the best because it becomes more and more evident that Broadway and Hollywood need each other. That crazy, marvelous American invention called the musical will continue to change, reach peaks and lows, and reinvent itself as it always has. And both media will somehow continue to produce new musicals that will, on occasion, cross over to the other venue. Those results will continue to please, annoy, or astonish audiences. It's the nature of the screen door.

~

Musicals Directory

The following listing provides the major credits for 176 stage musicals and their movie versions. Section A presents, in alphabetical order, the stage shows' credits followed by information about the films made from them. Section B lists film musicals that were later turned into Broadway shows. If no director or choreographer was credited in the original play or movie, that item is omitted. The songs listed are a sampling of the main musical numbers and not meant to be a complete listing of the score.

Stage to Screen

Animal Crackers
44th Street Theatre, 23 October 1928 (191 performances). *Book:* George S. Kaufman, Morrie Ryskind. *Score:* Bert Kalmar, Harry Ruby. *Director:* Oscar Eagle. *Choreographer:* Russell E. Markert. *Cast:* Marx Brothers, Margaret Dumont, Bobby Perkins, Milton Watson, Bernice Ackerman, Alice Wood. *Songs:* Hooray for Captain Spaulding; Who's Been Listening to My Heart?; Long Island Low-Down; When Things Are Bright and Rosy; Musketeers.
    Paramount (1930). *Screenplay:* George S. Kaufman, Morrie Ryskind. *Score:* Bert Kalmar, Harry Ruby, Mo Jaffe, Nat Bonx, Shelton Brooks.

Director: Victor Heerman. *Cast:* Marx Brothers, Margaret Dumont, Lillian Roth, Hal Thompson, Louis Sorin. *Songs:* Hooray for Captain Spaulding; Why Am I So Romantic?; Collegiate; Some of These Days.

Annie

Alvin Theatre, 21 April 1977 (2,377 performances). *Book:* Thomas Meehan. *Score:* Charles Strouse, Martin Charnin. *Director:* Martin Charnin. *Choreographer:* Peter Gennaro. *Cast:* Andrea McArdle, Dorothy Loudon, Reid Shelton, Sandy Faison, Robert Fitch, Barbara Erwin, Raymond Thorne. *Songs:* Tomorrow; You're Never Fully Dressed without a Smile; It's a Hard-Knock Life; Maybe; Little Girls; Easy Street.

Columbia (1982). *Screenplay:* Carol Sobieski. *Score:* Charles Strouse, Martin Charnin. *Director:* John Huston. *Choreographer:* Arlene Phillips. *Cast:* Aileen Quinn, Albert Finney, Carol Burnett, Tim Curry, Bernadette Peters, Ann Reinking, Edward Herrmann. *Songs:* Tomorrow; You're Never Fully Dressed without a Smile; It's a Hard-Knock Life; Maybe; Little Girls; Easy Street; Let's Go to the Movies.

Annie Get Your Gun

Imperial Theatre, 16 May 1946 (1,147 performances). *Book:* Herbert and Dorothy Fields. *Score:* Irving Berlin. *Director:* Joshua Logan. *Choreographer:* Helen Tamiris. *Cast:* Ethel Merman, Ray Middleton, Marty May, William O'Neal, Kenny Bowers, Lea Penman, Harry Belaver, Lubov Roudenko. *Songs:* They Say It's Wonderful; You Can't Get a Man with a Gun; There's No Business Like Show Business; I Got Lost in His Arms; Doin' What Comes Natur'lly; I Got the Sun in the Morning; My Defenses Are Down; Anything You Can Do; Moonshine Lullaby; The Girl That I Marry.

MGM (1950). *Screenplay:* Sidney Sheldon. *Score:* Irving Berlin. *Director:* George Sidney. *Choreographer:* Robert Alton. *Cast:* Betty Hutton, Howard Keel, Louis Calhern, J. Carroll Naish, Edward Arnold, Benay Venuta, Keenan Wynn, Chief Yowlachie. *Songs:* They Say It's Wonderful; You Can't Get a Man with a Gun; There's No Business Like Show Business; Doin' What Comes Natur'lly; I Got the Sun in the Morning; My Defenses Are Down; The Girl That I Marry; Anything You Can Do.

Anything Goes
Alvin Theatre, 21 November 1934 (420 performances). *Book:* Guy Bolton, P. G. Wodehouse, Howard Lindsay, Russel Crouse. *Score:* Cole Porter. *Director:* Howard Lindsay. *Choreographer:* Robert Alton. *Cast:* William Gaxton, Ethel Merman, Victor Moore, Bettina Hall, Vera Dunn, Leslie Barrie, Vivian Vance. *Songs:* I Get a Kick Out of You; Anything Goes; All Through the Night; You're the Top; Blow, Gabriel, Blow; Be Like the Bluebird; The Gypsy in Me.

Paramount (1936). *Screenplay:* Guy Bolton, Howard Lindsay, Russel Crouse. *Score:* Cole Porter, etc. *Director:* Lewis Milestone. *Cast:* Bing Crosby, Ethel Merman, Ida Lupino, Charles Ruggles, Arthur Treacher, Grace Bradley, Richard Carle, Margaret Dumont, Keye Luke. *Songs:* I Get a Kick Out of You; Anything Goes; Moonburn; My Heart and I; You're the Top; Blow, Gabriel, Blow; Sailor Beware.

Paramount (1956). *Screenplay:* Sidney Sheldon. *Score:* Cole Porter, Jimmy Van Heusen, Sammy Cahn. *Director:* Robert Lewis. *Choreographers:* Nick Castle, Erie Flatt, Roland Petit. *Cast:* Bing Crosby, Donald O'Connor, Mitzi Gaynor, Jeanmaire, Phil Harris, Kurt Kasznar, Richard Erdman, Walter Sande. *Songs:* I Get a Kick Out of You; All through the Night; You're the Top; Blow, Gabriel, Blow; It's De-Lovely; You Gotta Give the People Hoke; A Second-Hand Turban and a Crystal Ball.

Artists and Models Series
The Illustrators' Society of New York staged a popular revue called *Artists and Models* at the Century Roof Theatre in 1923. The producing Shubert Brothers bought the title and presented a half dozen Broadway revues between 1923 and 1943 that tried to compete with the Ziegfeld Follies in showcasing beautiful girls in lavish settings. Ted Lewis, Frank Fay, Charlotte Greenwood, Jane Froman, and Jackie Gleason were among the stars to appear in the *Artists and Models* revues.

Artists and Models, Paramount (1937). *Screenplay:* Walter DeLeon, Francis Martin. *Score:* Harold Arlen, Ted Koehler, Burton Lane, etc. *Director:* Raoul Walsh. *Choreographer:* LeRoy Prinz. *Cast:* Jack Benny, Ida Lupino, Richard Arlen, Gail Patrick, Ben Blue, Judy Canova, Louis Armstrong, Martha Raye. *Songs:* Stop, You're Breaking My Heart; Public Melody Number One; Whispers in the Dark; I Have Eyes; Mr. Esquire.

Artists and Models Abroad, Paramount (1938). *Screenplay:* Howard Lindsay, Russel Crouse. *Score:* Ralph Rainger, Leo Robin, etc. *Director:* Mitchell Leisen. *Choreographer:* LeRoy Prinz. *Cast:* Jack Benny, Joan Bennett, Mary Boland, Charles Grapewin, Fritz Feld, Joyce Compton. *Songs:* What Have You Got That Gets Me?; You're Broke, You Dope; You're Lovely, Madame; Do the Buckaroo.

Artists and Models, Paramount (1955). *Screenplay:* Frank Taslin, Hal Kanter, Herbert Baker. *Score:* Harry Warren, Jack Brooks. *Director:* Frank Tashlin. *Choreographer:* Chareles O'Curran. *Cast:* Dean Martin, Jerry Lewis, Shirley MacLaine, Dorothy Malone, Eva Gabor, Anita Ekberg. *Songs:* Inamorata; When You Pretend; Artists and Models; You Look So Familiar; Lucky Song.

Babes in Arms
Shubert Theatre, 14 April 1937 (289 performances). *Book:* Richard Rodgers, Lorenz Hart. *Score:* Richard Rodgers, Lorenz Hart. *Director:* Robert Sinclair. *Choreographer:* George Balanchine. *Cast:* Mitzi Green, Wynn Murray, Ray Heatherton, Alfred Drake, Nicholas Brothers, Duke McHale, Ray McDonald, Grace McDonald, Dan Dailey. *Songs:* My Funny Valentine; The Lady Is a Tramp; Where or When; All at Once; Way Out West; Johnny One Note; Babes in Arms; I Wish I Were in Love Again.

MGM (1939). *Screenplay:* Jack McGowan, Kay Van Riper. *Score:* Richard Rodgers, Lorenz Hart, Nacio Herb Brown, Arthur Freed, etc. *Director-choreographer:* Busby Berkeley. *Cast:* Mickey Rooney, Judy Garland, June Preisser, Charles Winninger, Guy Kibbee, Betty Jaynes, Grace Hayes, Douglas McPhail, Margaret Hamilton, Henry Hull, John Sheffield, Rand Brooks. *Songs:* Babes in Arms; Where or When; God's Country; You Are My Lucky Star; Good Morning; I Cried for You; I'm Just Wild about Harry.

Babes in Toyland
Majestic Theatre, 13 October 1903 (192 performances). *Book:* Glen MacDonough. *Score:* Victor Herbert, Glen MacDonough. *Director-choreographer:* Julian Mitchell. *Cast:* William Norris, Mabel Barrison, George W. Denham, Bessie Wynn. *Songs:* Toyland; I Can't Do the Sum; Go to Sleep, Slumber Deep; March of the Toys.

MGM (1934). *Screenplay:* Nick Grinde, Frank Butler. *Score:* Victor Herbert, Glen MacDonough, etc. *Directors:* Charles Rogers, Gus Meins. *Cast:* Stan Laurel, Oliver Hardy, Charlotte Henry, Felix Knight, Johnny Downs, Jean Darling. *Songs:* Toyland; I Can't Do the Sum; Go to Sleep, Slumber Deep; March of the Toys; Who's Afraid of the Big Bad Wolf? Disney (1961). *Screenplay:* Joe Rinaldi, Ward Kimball, Lowell S. Hawley. *Score:* Victor Herbert, Glen MacDonough, etc. *Director:* Jack Donohue. *Choreographer:* Tommy Mahoney. *Cast:* Ray Bolger, Tommy Sands, Annette Funicello, Ed Wynn, Henry Calvin, Gene Sheldon, Mary McCarty, Tommy Kirk. *Songs:* I Can't Do the Sum; Castle in Spain; Toyland; The Forest of No Return; March of the Toys; The Workshop Song.

The Band Wagon
New Amsterdam Theatre, 3 June 1931 (260 performances). *Sketches:* George S. Kaufman, Howard Dietz. *Score:* Arthur Schwartz, Howard Dietz. *Director:* Hassard Short. *Choreographer:* Albertina Rasch. *Cast:* Adele and Fred Astaire, Frank Morgan, Helen Broderick, Tilly Losch, Philip Loeb, John Barker. *Songs:* Dancing in the Dark; I Love Louisa; New Sun in the Sky; Hoops; High and Low; Sweet Music.
MGM (1953). *Screenplay:* Betty Comden, Adolph Green. *Score:* Howard Dietz, Arthur Schwartz. *Director:* Vincente Minnelli. *Choreographer:* Michael Kidd. *Cast:* Fred Astaire, Cyd Charisse, Oscar Levant, Nanette Fabray, Jack Buchanan, James Mitchell, Thurston Hall. *Songs:* That's Entertainment; By Myself; Dancing in the Dark; I Love Louisa; New Sun in the Sky; Triplets; I'll Guess I'll Have to Change My Plan; High and Low; Something to Remember You By; A Shine on Your Shoes.

The Belle of New York
Casino Theatre, 28 September 1897 (64 performances). *Book:* Hugh Morton (aka C. M. S. McLellan). *Score:* Gustave Kerker, Hugh Morton. *Director:* George W. Lederer. *Choreographer:* Signor Francioli. *Cast:* Edna May, Harry Davenport, Dan Daly, Helen Dupont, Mabel Howe, Phyllis Rankin, J. E. Sullivan, David Warfield. *Songs:* At Ze Naughty Folies Bergere; Teach Me How to Kiss, Dear; They All Follow

Me; The Anti-Cigarette League; She Is the Belle of New York; The Purity Brigade.

MGM (1952). *Screenplay:* Robert O'Brien, Irving Ellinson. *Score:* Harry Warren, Johnny Mercer. *Director:* Charles Walters. *Choreographer:* Robert Alton. *Cast:* Fred Astaire, Vera-Ellen, Marjorie Main, Keenan Wynn, Alice Pearce, Clinton Sundberg. *Songs:* Baby Doll; Seeing's Believing; Thank You, Mr. Currier, Thank You, Mr. Ives; When I'm Out with the Belle of New York; I Wanna Be a Dancin' Man; Let a Little Love Come In.

Bells Are Ringing
Shubert Theatre, 29 November 1956 (924 performances). *Book:* Betty Comden, Adolph Green. *Score:* Jule Styne, Betty Comden, Adolph Green. *Director:* Jerome Robbins. *Choreographers:* Jerome Robbins, Bob Fosse. *Cast:* Judy Holliday, Sydney Chaplin, Jean Stapleton, Eddie Lawrence, Dort Clark, George S. Irving, Peter Gennaro. *Songs:* Just in Time; The Party's Over; Long before I Knew You; It's a Perfect Relationship; I'm Going Back; I Met a Girl; Hello, Hello There.

MGM (1960). *Screenplay:* Betty Comden, Adolph Green. *Score:* Jule Styne, Betty Comden, Adolph Green. *Director:* Vincente Minnelli. *Choreographer:* Charles O'Curran. *Cast:* Judy Holliday, Dean Martin, Jean Stapleton, Eddie Foy Jr., Dort Clark, Frank Gorshin, Fred Clark. *Songs:* Just in Time; The Party's Over; It's a Perfect Relationship; I'm Going Back; I Met a Girl; Better Than a Dream.

Best Foot Forward
Ethel Barrymore Theatre, 1 October 1941 (326 performances). *Book:* John Cecil Holm. *Score:* Hugh Martin, Ralph Blane. *Director:* George Abbott. *Choreographer:* Gene Kelly. *Cast:* Rosemary Lane, Gil Stratton, Marty May, Nancy Walker, Maureen Cannon, June Allyson, Kenny Bowers, Jack Jordan, Tommy Dix. *Songs:* Buckle Down, Winsocki; Just a Little Joint with a Jukebox; The Three B's; What Do You Think I Am?; Ev'ry Time.

MGM (1943). *Screenplay:* Irving Brecher, Fred Finklehoffe. *Score:* Hugh Martin, Ralph Blane. *Director:* Edward Buzzell. *Choreographer:* Charles Walters. *Cast:* Lucille Ball, Tommy Dix, William Gaxton, Nancy Walker, Virgina Weidler, June Allyson, Kenny Bowers, Gloria

DeHaven, Jack Jordan. *Songs:* Buckle Down, Winsocki; The Three B's; Alive and Kicking; Wish I May Wish I Might; Ev'ry Time; Three Men on a Date; You're Lucky.

The Best Little Whorehouse in Texas
Entermedia Theatre, 17 April 1978 (1,703 performances). *Book:* Larry L. King, Peter Masterson. *Score:* Carol Hall. *Directors:* Peter Masterson, Tommy Tune. *Choreographer:* Tommy Tune. *Cast:* Carlin Glynn, Henderson Forsythe, Pamela Blair, Delores Hall, Jay Garner. *Songs:* Twenty Fans; A Li'l Ole Bitty Pissant Country Place; Hard Candy Christmas; Girl, You're a Woman; Side Step; Bus from Amarillo; Good Old Girl; Twenty-Four Hours of Lovin'; The Aggie Song.
Universal/RKO (1982). *Screenplay:* Larry L. King, Peter Masterson, Colin Higgins. *Score:* Carol Hall, etc. *Director:* Colin Higgins. *Choreographer:* Tony Stevens. *Cast:* Burt Reynolds, Dolly Parton, Dom DeLuise, Charles Durning, Jim Nabors, Lois Nettleton, Theresa Merritt, Robert Mandan, Barry Corbin, Noah Berry. *Songs:* Twenty Fans; I Will Always Love You; A Li'l Ole Bitty Pissant Country Place; Hard Candy Christmas; Side Step; The Aggie Song; Sneakin' Around.

Big Boy
Winter Garden Theatre, 7 January 1925 (56 performances). *Book:* Harold Atteridge. *Score:* James Hanley, Joseph Meyer, B. G. DeSylva. *Directors:* J. C. Huffman, Alexander Leftwich. *Choreographers:* Larry Ceballos, Seymour Felix. *Cast:* Al Jolson, Hugh Banks, Flo Lewis, Edythe Baker, Patti Harrold. *Songs:* If You Knew Susie; Keep Smiling at Trouble, Born and Bred in Old Kentucky; It All Depends on You; Something for Nothing; One O'Clock Baby.
Warner (1930). *Screenplay:* William K. Wells, Perry Vekroff, Rex Taylor. *Score:* various. *Director:* Alan Crosland. *Cast:* Al Jolson, Claudia Dale, Louise Closser Hale, Lloyd Hughes, Eddie Phillips, Noah Berry. *Songs:* Down South; Sonny Boy; What Will I Do without You?; Tomorrow Is Another Day; Liza Lee.

Bitter Sweet
Ziegfeld Theatre, 5 November 1929 (157 performances). *Book and score:* Noel Coward. *Director:* Noel Coward. *Cast:* Evelyn Laye, Gerald

Nodin, Mireille, Tracey Holmes, Sylvia Leslie, John Evelyn. *Songs:* I'll See You Again; If Love Were All; Zigeuner; Green Carnations; Ladies of the Town.

MGM (1940). *Screenplay:* Lesser Samuels. *Score:* Noel Coward, etc. *Director:* W. S. Van Dyke. *Cast:* Jeanette MacDonald, Nelson Eddy, George Sanders, Ian Hunter, Felix Bressart, Curt Bois, Fay Holden. *Songs:* I'll See You Again; Love in Any Language; Dear Little Cafe; Ladies of the Town; Zigeuner.

The Boy Friend

Royale Theatre, 30 September 1954 (485 performances). *Book and score:* Sandy Wilson. *Director:* Vida Hope. *Choreographer:* John Heawood. *Cast:* Julie Andrews, Eric Berry, John Hewer, Ann Wakefield, Ruth Altman, Bob Scheerer, Geoffrey Hibbert, Millicent Martin. *Songs:* I Could Be Happy with You; A Room in Bloomsbury; It's Never Too Late to Fall in Love; Fancy Forgetting; Safety in Numbers; Won't You Charleston with Me?

MGM (1971). *Screenplay:* Ken Russell. *Score:* Sandy Wilson, etc. *Director:* Ken Russell. *Choreographer:* Christopher Gable. *Cast:* Twiggy, Christopher Gable, Max Adrian, Tommy Tune, Murray Melvin, Vladek Sheybal, Miyra Fraser, Glenda Jackson. *Songs:* I Could Be Happy with You; A Room in Bloomsbury; It's Never Too Late to Fall in Love; Fancy Forgetting; Safety in Numbers; You Are My Lucky Star; All I Do Is Dream of You; Won't You Charleston with Me?

The Boys from Syracuse

Alvin Theatre, 23 November 1938 (235 performances). *Book:* George Abbott. *Score:* Richard Rodgers, Lorenz Hart. *Director:* George Abbott. *Choreographer:* George Balanchine. *Cast:* Eddie Albert, Jimmy Savo, Wynn Murray, Teddy Hart, Ronald Graham, Muriel Angelus, Marcy Wescott, Betty Bruce, Burl Ives. *Songs:* Dear Old Syracuse; Falling in Love with Love; This Can't Be Love; Sing for Your Supper; Oh, Diogenes!; He and She; What Can You Do with a Man?; The Shortest Day of the Year.

Universal (1940). *Screenplay:* Leonard Spigelgass, Charles Grayson. *Score:* Richard Rodgers, Lorenz Hart. *Director:* Edward Sutherland. *Choreographer:* Dave Gould. *Cast:* Allan Jones, Joe Penner, Martha

Raye, Rosemary Lane, Charles Butterworth, Alan Mowbray, Eric Blore. *Songs:* Falling in Love with Love; This Can't Be Love; Sing for Your Supper; He and She; Who Are You?

Brigadoon

Ziegfeld Theatre, 13 March 1947 (581 performances). *Book:* Alan Jay Lerner. *Score:* Frederick Loewe, Alan Jay Lerner. *Director:* Robert Lewis. *Choreographer:* Agnes de Mille. *Cast:* David Brooks, Marion Bell, Pamela Britten, Lee Sullivan, James Mitchell, George Keane, William Hansen. *Songs:* The Heather on the Hill; Almost Like Being in Love; I'll Go Home with Bonnie Jean; Come to Me, Bend to Me; There But for You Go I; Brigadoon; Waiting for My Dearie; My Mother's Wedding Day.

MGM (1954). *Screenplay:* Alan Jay Lerner. *Score:* Frederick Loewe, Alan Jay Lerner. *Director:* Vincente Minnelli. *Choreographer:* Gene Kelly. *Cast:* Gene Kelly, Cyd Charisse, Van Johnson, Elaine Stewart, Barry Jones, Hugh Laing, Virginia Bosler, Albert Sharpe. *Songs:* The Heather on the Hill; Almost Like Being in Love; I'll Go Home with Bonnie Jean; Brigadoon; Waiting for My Dearie.

Broadway

Broadhurst Theatre, 16 September 1929 (603 performances). *Authors and Directors:* Philip Dunning, George Abbott. *Score:* various. *Cast:* Robert Glecker, Sylvia Field, Lee Tracy, Paul Porcasi, John Wray. *Songs:* unidentified numbers heard from offstage.

Universal (1929). *Screenplay:* Edward T. Lower Jr., Charles Furthman. *Score:* Con Conrad, Sidney Mitchell, Archie Gottler. *Director:* Paul Fejos. *Choreographer:* Maurice L. Kusell. *Cast:* Glenn Tryon, Merna Kennedy, Thomas E. Jackson, Paul Porcasi, Robert Ellis, Evelyn Brent. *Songs:* Broadway; Hittin' the Ceiling; The Chicken or the Egg; A Little Love Song; Hot Footin' It.

Universal (1942). *Screenplay:* Felix Jackson, Don Bright. *Score:* Joe Young, Sam Lewis, Harry Akst, etc. *Director:* William A. Seiter. *Cast:* George Raft, Janet Blair, Pat O'Brien, Broderick Crawford, Marjorie Rambeau, S. Z. Sakall, Edward Brophy. *Songs:* Dinah; I'm Just Wild about Harry; Sweet Georgia Brown; The Darktown Strutters Ball; Alabamy Bound; Some of These Days.

Bye Bye Birdie

Martin Beck Theatre, 14 April 1960 (607 performances). *Book:* Michael Stewart. *Score:* Charles Strouse, Lee Adams. *Director-choreographer:* Gower Champion. *Cast:* Dick Van Dyke, Chita Rivera, Susan Watson, Paul Lynde, Kay Medford, Dick Gautier, Michael J. Pollard. *Songs:* Put on a Happy Face; Kids; Got a Lot of Livin' to Do; One Boy; Baby, Talk to Me; One Last Kiss; How Lovely to Be a Woman; Rosie; The Telephone Hour.

Columbia (1963). *Screenplay:* Irving Brecher. *Score:* Charles Strouse, Lee Adams. *Director:* George Sidney. *Choreographer:* Onna White. *Cast:* Ann-Margret, Dick Van Dyke, Janet Leigh, Paul Lynde, Jesse Pearson, Maureen Stapleton, Bobby Rydell. *Songs:* Put on a Happy Face; Kids; Got a Lot of Livin' to Do; One Boy; Bye Bye Birdie; One Last Kiss; How Lovely to Be a Woman; Rosie; The Telephone Hour.

Cabaret

Broadhurst Theatre, 20 November 1966 (1,165 performances). *Book:* Joe Masteroff. *Score:* John Kander, Fred Ebb. *Director:* Harold Prince. *Choreographer:* Ron Field. Cast: Jill Haworth, Joel Grey, Bert Convy, Jack Gilford, Lotte Lenya, Peg Murray, Edward Winter. *Songs:* Cabaret; Wilkommen; Two Ladies; Don't Tell Mama; If You Could See Her through My Eyes; Tomorrow Belongs to Me; Married; Meeskite; It Couldn't Please Me More; Perfectly Marvelous; The Money Song.

Allied Artists/ABC (1972). *Screenplay:* Jay Presson Allen. *Score:* John Kander, Fred Ebb, *Director-choreographer:* Bob Fosse. *Cast:* Liza Minnelli, Michael York, Joel Grey, Marisa Berenson, Helmut Griem, Fritz Wepper. *Songs:* Cabaret; Wilkommen; Two Ladies; Mein Herr; If You Could See Her through My Eyes; Tomorrow Belongs to Me; Money, Money; Maybe This Time.

Cabin in the Sky

Martin Beck Theatre, 25 October 1940 (156 performances). *Book:* Lynn Root. *Score:* Vernon Duke, John Latouche. *Directors:* George Balanchine, Albert Lewis. *Choreographer:* George Balanchine. *Cast:* Ethel Waters, Todd Duncan, Dooley Wilson, Katherine Dunham, Rex Ingram, J. Rosamond Johnson. *Songs:* Cabin in the Sky; Taking a Chance on Love; Honey in the Honeycomb; Love Turned the Light Out; Do What You Wanna Do. MGM (1943). *Screenplay:* Joseph Schrank. *Score:* Vernon Duke, John Latouche, Harold Arlen, E. Y. Harburg. *Director:* Vincente Minnelli. *Choreographer:* Busby Berkeley. *Cast:* Ethel Waters, Eddie Anderson, Lena Horne, Rex Ingram, John Bubbles, Louis Armstrong, Ford Buck. *Songs:* Cabin in the Sky; Taking a Chance on Love; Honey in the Honeycomb; Happiness Is a Thing Called Joe; Life's Full of Consequence.

Call Me Madam

Imperial Theatre, 12 October 1950 (644 performances). *Book:* Howard Lindsay, Russel Crouse. *Score:* Irving Berlin. *Director:* George Abbott. *Choreographer:* Jerome Robbins. *Cast:* Ethel Merman, Paul Lukas, Russell Nype, Galina Talva, Pat Harrington, Nathaniel Frey, Alan Hewitt, Tommy Rall. *Songs:* You're Just in Love; The Hostess with the Mostes' on the Ball; They Like Ike; Marrying for Love; It's a Lovely Day Today; The Best Thing for You; Can You Use Any Money Today?

Fox (1953). *Screenplay:* Arthur Sheekman. *Score:* Irving Berlin. *Director:* Walter Lang. *Choreographer:* Robert Alton. *Cast:* Ethel Merman, George Sanders, Donald O'Connor, Vera-Ellen, Billy DeWolfe, Walter Slezak. *Songs:* You're Just in Love; The Hostess with the Mostes' on the Ball; What Chance Have I with Love?; Marrying for Love; It's a Lovely Day Today; The Best Thing for You; Can You Use Any Money Today?

Call Me Mister

National Theatre, 18 April 1946 (734 performances). *Sketches:* Arnold Auerbach, Arnold B. Horwitt. *Score:* Harold Rome. *Director:* Robert H. Gordon. *Choreographer:* John Wray. *Cast:* Betty Garrett, Jules Munshin, Bill Callahan, Lawrence Winters, Paula Bane, Maria Karnilova, George S. Irving. *Songs:* The Face on the Dime; Call Me Mister; South America, Take It Away; Goin' Home Train; The Red Ball Express.

Fox (1951). *Screenplay:* Albert E. Lewin, Burt Styler. *Score:* Harold Rome, Sammy Fain, Mack Gordon, etc. *Director:* Lloyd Bacon. *Choreographer:* Busby Berkeley. *Cast:* Betty Grable, Dan Dailey, Danny Thomas, Dale Robertson, Benay Venuta, Richard Boone, Jeffrey Hunter. *Songs:* Call Me Mister; Goin' Home Train; Japanese Girl Like

American Boy; Lament to the Pots and Pans; Love Is Back in Business; I'm Gonna Love That Guy.

Camelot

Majestic, 3 December 1960 (873 performances). *Book:* Alan Jay Lerner. *Score:* Frederick Loewe, Alan Jay Lerner. *Director:* Moss Hart. *Choreographer:* Hanya Holm. *Cast:* Richard Burton, Julie Andrews, Robert Goulet, Roddy McDowell, Robert Coote, Mel Dowd. *Songs:* If Ever I Would Leave You; Camelot; How to Handle a Woman; Before I Gaze at You Again; The Lusty Month of May; I Loved You Once in Silence; I Wonder What the King Is Doing Tonight; The Simple Joys of Maidenhood; What Do the Simple Folks Do?

Warner (1967). *Screenplay:* Alan Jay Lerner. *Score:* Frederick Loewe, Alan Jay Lerner. *Director:* Joshua Logan. *Cast:* Richard Harris, Vanessa Redgrave, Franco Nero, David Hemmings, Lionel Jeffries, Laurence Naismith. *Songs:* If Ever I Would Leave You; Camelot; How to Handle a Woman; The Lusty Month of May; I Loved You Once in Silence; I Wonder What the King Is Doing Tonight; The Simple Joys of Maidenhood; What Do the Simple Folks Do?; Then You May Take Me to the Fair.

Can-Can

Shubert Theatre, 7 May 1953 (892 performances). *Book:* Abe Burrows. *Score:* Cole Porter. *Director:* Abe Burrows. *Choreographer:* Michael Kidd. *Cast:* Lilo, Gwen Verdon, Peter Cookson, Hans Conreid, Erik Rhodes. *Songs:* I Love Paris; It's All Right with Me; Come Along with Me; C'est Magnifique; Never Give Anything Away; Can-Can.

Fox (1960). *Screenplay:* Dorothy Kingsley, Charles Lederer. *Score:* Cole Porter. *Director:* Walter Lang. *Choreographer:* Hermes Pan. *Cast:* Frank Sinatra, Shirley MacLaine, Maurice Chevalier, Louis Jourdan, Juliet Prowse. *Songs:* I Love Paris; It's All Right with Me; Come Along with Me; C'est Magnifique; Let's Do It; Just One of Those Things; You Do Something to Me; Can-Can.

Carmen Jones

Broadway Theatre, 2 December 1943 (502 performances). *Book:* Oscar Hammerstein. *Score:* Georges Bizet, Oscar Hammerstein. *Directors:* Hassard Short, Charles Friedman. *Choreographer:* Eugene Loring. *Cast:*

Muriel Smith, Luther Saxon, June Hawkins, Carlotta Franzell, Glenn Bryant, Cosy Cole. *Songs:* Dat's Love; Beat Out Dat Rhythm on a Drum; Stan' Up and Fight; Dere's a Café on de Corner; My Joe. Fox (1954). *Screenplay:* Harry Kleiner. *Score:* Georges Bizet, Oscar Hammerstein. *Director:* Otto Preminger. *Choreographer:* Herbert Ross. *Cast:* Dorothy Dandridge, Harry Belafonte, Olga James, Pearl Bailey, Diahann Carroll, Joe Adams, Brock Peters. *Songs:* Dat's Love; Beat Out Dat Rhythm on a Drum; Stan' Up and Fight; Dere's a Café on de Corner; My Joe.

Carousel
Majestic Theatre, 19 April 1945 (890 performances). *Book:* Oscar Hammerstein. *Score:* Richard Rodgers, Oscar Hammerstein. *Director:* Rouben Mamoulian. *Choreographer:* Agnes de Mille. *Cast:* John Raitt, Jan Clayton, Jean Darling, Eric Mattson, Christine Johnson, Mervyn Vye, Bambi Linn. *Songs:* If I Loved You; June Is Bustin' Out All Over; You'll Never Walk Alone; Soliloquy; What's the Use of Wond'rin?; A Real Nice Clambake; When the Children Are Asleep; Blow High, Blow Low.
    Fox (1956). *Screenplay:* Henry and Phoebe Ephron. *Score:* Richard Rodgers, Oscar Hammerstein. *Director:* Henry King. *Choreographers:* Rod Alexander, Agnes de Mille. *Cast:* Gordon MacRae, Shirley Jones, Cameron Mitchell, Barbara Ruick, Claramae Turner, Robert Rounseville, Gene Lockhart, Susan Luckey, Audrey Christie. *Songs:* If I Loved You; June Is Bustin' Out All Over; You'll Never Walk Alone; Soliloquy; What's the Use of Wond'rin?; When the Children Are Asleep; A Real Nice Clambake.

The Cat and the Fiddle
Globe Theatre, 15 October 1931 (395 performances). *Book:* Otto Harbach. *Score:* Jerome Kern, Otto Harbach. *Director:* José Ruben. *Choreographer:* Albertina Rasch. *Cast:* Georges Metaxa, Bettina Hall, Odette Myrtil, Eddie Foy Jr., José Ruben, Doris Carson, Lawrence Grossmith. *Songs:*Try to Forget; The Night Was Made for Love; She Didn't Say Yes; I Watch the Love Parade; Poor Pierrot; One Moment Alone.
    MGM (1934). *Screenplay:* Bella and Samuel Spewack. *Score:* Jerome Kern, Otto Harbach. *Director:* William K. Howard. *Choreographer:* Albertina Rasch. *Cast:* Jeanette MacDonald, Ramon Novarro, Frank

Morgan, Charles Butterworth, Jean Hersholt, Vivienne Segal, Joseph Cawthorn, Frank Conroy, Sterling Holloway. *Songs:* Try to Forget; The Night Was Made for Love; She Didn't Say Yes; I Watch the Love Parade; Don't Ask Us Not to Sing; One Moment Alone.

Cats

Winter Garden Theatre, 7 October 1982 (7,485 performances). *Score:* Andrew Lloyd Webber, T. S. Eliot. *Directors:* Trevor Nunn, Gillian Lynne. *Choreographer:* Gillian Lynne. *Cast:* Betty Buckley, Ken Page, Terrence Mann, Stephen Hanan, Timothy Scott, Reed Jones, Harry Groener, Anna McNeely, Bonnie Simmons. *Songs:* Memory, Jellicle Songs for Jellicle Cats; Old Deuteronomy; Mr. Mistoffelees; Macavity.

　　TV (1998). *Score:* Andrew Lloyd Webber, T. S. Eliot. *Director:* David Mallet. *Choreographer:* Gillian Lynne. *Cast:* Elaine Paige, John Mills, Ken Page, Rosemarie Ford, Michael Gruber, John Partridge. *Songs:* Memory, Jellicle Songs for Jellicle Cats; Old Deuteronomy; Mr. Mistoffelees; Macavity.

Chicago

46th Street Theatre, 3 June 1975 (898 performances). *Book:* Fred Ebb, Bob Fosse. *Score:* John Kander, Fred Ebb. *Director-choreographer:* Bob Fosse. *Cast:* Gwen Verdon, Chita Rivera, Jerry Orbach, Mary McCarty, Barney Martin. *Songs:* All That Jazz; Nowadays; Razzle Dazzle; Class; All I Care About; The Cell Block Tango; Roxie; My Own Best Friend; Mr. Cellophane.

　　Miramax (2002). *Screenplay:* Bill Condon. *Score:* John Kander, Fred Ebb. *Director-choreographer:* Rob Marshall. *Cast:* Catherine Zeta-Jones, Renée Zellweger, Richard Gere, John C. Reilly, Queen Latifah, Christinne Baranski, Taye Diggs, Colm Feore. *Songs:* All That Jazz; Nowadays; Class; All I Care About; Roxie; My Own Best Friend; Mr. Cellophane; I Move On.

A Chorus Line

Public Theatre, 15 April 1975 (6,137 performances). *Book:* James Kirkwood, Nicholas Dante. *Score:* Marvin Hamlisch, Edward Kleban. *Director-choreographer:* Michael Bennett. *Cast:* Donna McKechnie, Priscilla Lopez, Kelly Bishop, Robert LuPone, Sammy Williams,

Pamela Blair, Wayne Cilento. *Songs:* What I Did for Love; I Can Do That; At the Ballet; I Hope I Get It; The Music and the Mirror; Nothing; Dance: Ten—Looks: Three; One. Embassy/Polygram (1985). *Screenplay:* Arnold Schulman. *Score:* Marvin Hamlisch, Edward Kleban. *Director:* Richard Attenborough. *Choreographer:* Jeffrey Hornaday. *Cast:* Michael Douglas, Terrence Mann, Alyson Reed, Cameron English, Vicki Frederick, Audrey Landers, Gregg Burge, Nicole Fosse, Janet Jones, Matt West, Justin Reed, Pam Klinger, Michelle Johnston. *Songs:* What I Did for Love; I Can Do That; At the Ballet; Dance: Ten—Looks: Three; One; Let Me Dance for You; Surprise, Surprise.

The Cocoanuts
Lyric Theatre, 8 December 1925 (276 performances). *Book:* George S. Kaufman, Morrie Ryskind. *Score:* Irving Berlin. *Director:* Oscar Eagle. *Choreographer:* Sammy Lee. *Cast:* Marx Brothers, Margaret Dumont, Jack Barker, Frances Williams, Mabel Withee, Broz Sisters. *Songs:* Florida by the Sea; A Little Bungalow; Lucky Boy; The Monkey Doodle-Doo.
   Paramount (1929). *Screenplay:* Morrie Ryskind. *Score:* Irving Berlin. *Directors:* Joseph Santley, Robert Florey. *Choreographer:* Sammy Lee. *Cast:* Marx Brothers, Margaret Dumont, Oscar Shaw, Mary Eaton, Kay Frances, Cyril Ring, Basil Ruysdael, Sylvan Lee. *Songs:* When My Dreams Come True; Florida by the Sea; The Tale of a Shirt; The Monkey Doodle-Doo.

Damn Yankees
46th Street Theatre, 5 May 1955 (1,019 performances). *Book:* George Abbott, Douglas Wallop. *Score:* Richard Adler, Jerry Ross. *Director:* George Abbott. *Choreographer:* Bob Fosse. *Cast:* Ray Walston, Gwen Verdon, Stephen Douglass, Shannon Bolin, Russ Brown, Rae Allen, Jean Stapleton, Robert Shafer, Nathaniel Frey. *Songs:* Whatever Lola Wants; (You Gotta Have) Heart; Shoeless Joe fom Hannibal, Mo.; Two Lost Souls; Near to You; A Little Brains—Little Talent; Who's Got the Pain?
   Warner (1958). *Screenplay:* George Abbott. *Score:* Richard Adler, Jerry Ross. *Directors:* George Abbott, Stanley Donan. *Choreographer:* Bob Fosse. *Cast:* Ray Walston, Gwen Verdon, Tab Hunter, Shannon

Bolin, Russ Brown, Rae Allen, Jean Stapleton, Robert Shafer, Nathaniel Frey, Bob Fosse. *Songs:* Whatever Lola Wants; Heart; Shoeless Joe from Hannibal, Mo.; Two Lost Souls; A Little Brains—Little Talent; Who's Got the Pain?

Desert Song

Casino Theatre, 30 November 1926 (471 performances). *Book:* Otto Harbach, Oscar Hammerstein, Frank Mandel. *Score:* Sigmund Romberg, Otto Harbach, Oscar Hammerstein. *Director:* Arthur Hurley. *Choreographer:* Bobby Connolly. *Cast:* Vivienne Segal, Robert Halliday, Eddie Buzzell, Pearl Regay, William O'Neal. *Songs:* The Desert Song; One Alone; The Riff Song; Romance; It; Let Love Go; French Military Marching Song; I Want a Kiss.

Warner (1929). *Screenplay:* Harvey Gates. *Score:* Sigmund Romberg, Otto Harbach, Oscar Hammerstein. *Director:* Roy Del Ruth. *Cast:* John Boles, Carlotta King, Louise Fazenda, John Miljan, Marie Wells, Johnny Arthur, Mynra Loy, Edward Martindel, Jack Pratt. *Songs:* The Desert Song; One Alone; The Riff Song; Romance; Sabre Song; French Military Marching Song; Then You Will Know.

Warner (1943). *Screenplay:* Robet Buckner. *Score:* Sigmund Romberg, Otto Harbach, Oscar Hammerstein, etc. *Director:* Robert Florey. *Choreographer:* LeRoy Prinz. *Cast:* Dennis Morgan, Irene Manning, Bruce Cabot, Gene Lockhart, Lynne Overman, Faye Emerson. *Songs:* The Desert Song; One Alone; The Riff Song; Romance; Sabre Song; French Military Marching Song; Long Live the Night; Fifi's Song.

Warner (1953). *Screenplay:* Roland Kibbee. *Score:* Sigmund Romberg, Otto Harbach, Oscar Hammerstein, etc. *Director:* Bruce Humberstone. *Choreographer:* LeRoy Prinz. *Cast:* Gordon MacRae, Kathryn Grayson, Raymond Massey, Steve Cochran, Ray Collins, Dick Wesson, Allyn McLerie. *Songs:* The Desert Song; One Alone; The Riff Song; Romance; French Military Marching Song; Gay Parisienne; Long Live the Night.

DuBarry Was a Lady

46th Street Theatre, 6 December 1939 (408 performances). *Book:* Herbert Fields, B. G. DeSylva. *Score:* Cole Porter. *Director:* Edgar MacGregor. *Choreographer:* Robert Alton. *Cast:* Bert Lahr, Ethel Merman,

Betty Grable, Benny Baker, Charles Walters, Ronald Graham, Kay Sutton. *Songs:* Friendship; Well, Did You Evah?; Katie Went to Haiti; Do I Love You?; But in the Morning, No.

MGM (1943). *Screenplay:* Irving Brecher. *Score:* Cole Porter, Ralph Freed, Burton Lane, E. Y. Harburg, Roger Edens, etc. *Director:* Roy Del Ruth. *Choreographer:* Charles Walters. *Cast:* Red Skelton, Lucille Ball, Gene Kelly, Virginia O'Brien, Rags Ragland, Zero Mostel, Tommy Dorsey, Dick Haymes, Jo Stafford. *Songs:* Friendship; Katie Went to Haiti; Do I Love You?; No Matter How You Slice It, It's Still Salome; I Love an Esquire Girl; Madame, I Love Your Crepes Suzettes.

Earl Carroll's *Vanities* Series
Producer-writer-director Earl Carroll presented a series of eleven revues between 1923 and 1940 called the *Vanities* that emphasized comedy and risqué tableaus rather than the songs, dances, and lavish production numbers of the Ziegfeld Follies and *George White's Scandals.* Among the comics to be featured in the Vanities were W. C. Fields, Jimmy Savo, Joe Cook, Helen Broderick, Sophie Tucker, Jack Benny, and Milton Berle.

Earl Carroll Vanities, Republic (1945). *Screenplay:* Frank Gill Jr. *Score:* various. *Director:* Joseph Santley. *Choreographer:* Sammy Lee. *Cast:* Constance Moore, Dennis O'Keefe, Mary Forbes, Alan Mowbray, Eve Arden, Pinky Lee, Otto Kruger. *Songs:* Endlessly; Apple Honey; Who Dat Up Dere?; You Beautiful Thing, You; Rockabye Boogie; Riverside Jive.

Evita
Broadway Theatre, 25 September 1979 (1,568 performances). *Book:* Tim Rice. *Score:* Andrew Llyd Webber, Tim Rice. *Director:* Harold Prince. *Choreographer:* Larry Fuller. *Cast:* Patti LuPone, Bob Gunton, Mandy Patinkin, Mark Syers, Jan Ohringer. *Songs:* Don't Cry for Me, Argentina; Another Suitcase in Another Hall; A New Argentina; On This Night of a Thousand Stars; High Flying Adored.

Warner (1996). *Screenplay:* Alan Parker, Oliver Stone. *Director:* Alan Parker. *Choreographer:* Vincent Paterson. *Cast:* Madonna, Antonio Banderas, Jonathan Pryce, Jimmy Nail, Victoria Sus. *Songs:* Don't Cry for Me, Argentina; Another Suitcase in Another Hall; A New Argentina; On This Night of a Thousand Stars; High Flying Adored; You Must Love Me.

Fanny

Majestic Theatre, 4 November 1954 (888 performances). *Book:* S. N. Behrman, Josuha Logan. *Score:* Harold Rome. *Director:* Joshua Logan. *Choreographer:* Helen Tamiris. *Cast:* Ezio Pinza, Florence Henderson, William Tabbert, Walter Slezak. *Songs:* Fanny; Be Kind to Your Parents; Restless Heart; Why Be Afraid to Dance?; Welcome Home; Love Is a Very Light Thing.

Warner (1961). *Screenplay:* Julius Epstein. *Director:* Joshua Logan. *Cast:* Leslie Caron, Horst Buchholz, Maurice Chevalier, Charles Boyer, Georgette Anys, Lionel Jeffries, Baccaloni.

The Fantasticks

Sullivan Street Theatre, 3 May 1960 (17,162 performances). *Book:* Tom Jones. *Score:* Harvey Schmidt, Tom Jones. *Director:* Word Baker. *Cast:* Jerry Orbach, Kenneth Nelson, Rita Gardner, William Larson, Hugh Thomas. *Songs:* Try to Remember; I Can See It; Soon It's Gonna Rain; Much More; They Were You; Never Say No; It Depends on What You Pay; Round and Round.

United Artists (1995/2000). *Screenplay:* Tom Jones, Harvey Schmidt. *Score:* Harvey Schmidt, Tom Jones. *Director:* Michael Ritchie. *Choreographer:* Michael Smuin. *Cast:* Jean Louisa Kelly, Joseph McIntyre, Joel Grey, Brad Sullivan, Jonathon Morris, Barnard Hughes, Teller. *Songs:* Try to Remember; I Can See It; Soon It's Gonna Rain; Much More; They Were You; Never Say No; It Depends on What You Pay; Round and Round.

Fiddler on the Roof

Imperial Theatre, 22 September 1964 (3,242 performances). *Book:* Joseph Stein. *Score:* Jerry Bock, Sheldon Harnick. *Director-choreographer:* Jerome Robbins. *Cast:* Zero Mostel, Maria Karnilova, Bert Convy, Austin Pendleton, Beatrice Arthur, Joanna Merlin, Julia Migenes, Michael Granger. *Songs:* Matchmaker, Matchmaker; Sunrise, Sunset; If I Were a Rich Man; Far from the Home I Love; Tradition; Do You Love Me?; Now I Have Everything; To Life; Sabbath Prayer; Tevye's Dream.

Mirisch/United Artists (1971). *Screenplay:* Joseph Stein. *Score:* Jerry Bock, Sheldon Harnick. *Director:* Norman Jewison. *Choreographer:* Tom Abbott, Jerome Robbins. *Cast:* Topol, Norma Crane, Leonard Frey, Molly Picon, Paul Mann, Rosalind Harris, Michele Marsh, Neva

Small, Michael Glaser. *Songs:* Matchmaker, Matchmaker; Sunrise, Sunset; If I Were a Rich Man; Far from the Home I Love; Tradition; Do You Love Me?; To Life; Sabbath Prayer; Tevye's Dream.

Fifty Million Frenchmen
Lyric Theatre, 27 November 1929 (254 performances). *Book:* Herbert Fields. *Score:* Cole Porter. *Director:* Monte Woolley. *Choreographer:* Larry Ceballos. *Cast:* William Gaxton, Genevieve Tobin, Helen Broderick, Evelyn Hoey, Betty Compton, Jack Thompson, Thurston Hall. *Songs:* You Do Something to Me; Find Me a Primitive Man; You've Got That Thing; Paree, What Did You Do to Me?; You Don't Know Paree.
    Warner (1931). *Screenplay:* Al Boasberg, Joseph Jackson, Eddie Welch. *Score:* Cole Porter. *Director:* Lloyd Bacon. *Cast:* William Gaxton, Claudia Dell, Ole Olsen, Chic Johnson, Helen Broderick, John Halliday, Lester Crawford, Evelyn Knapp.

Finian's Rainbow
46th Street Theatre, 10 January 1947 (725 performances). *Book:* E. Y. Harburg, Fred Saidy. *Score:* Burton Lane, E. Y. Harburg. *Director:* Bretaigne Windust. *Choreographer:* Michael Kidd. *Cast:* David Wayne, Ella Logan, Albert Sharpe, Donald Richards, Anita Alverez, Robert Pitkin. *Songs:*How Are Things in Glocca Morra?; Old Devil Moon; Look to the Rainbow; If This Isn't Love; Something Sort of Grandish; When I'm Not Near the Girl I Love; Necessity; When the Idle Poor Become the Idle Rich; The Begat.
    Warner/Seven Arts (1968). *Screenplay:* E. Y. Harburg, Fred Saidy. *Score:* Burton Lane, E. Y. Harburg. *Director:* Francis Ford Coppola. *Choreographer:* Hermes Pan, Fred Astaire. *Cast:* Fred Astaire, Petula Clark, Tommy Steele, Don Francks, Keenan Wynn, Al Freedman Jr., Avon Long, Barbara Hancock. *Songs:* How Are Things in Glocca Morra?; Old Devil Moon; Look to the Rainbow; If This Isn't Love; Something Sort of Grandish; When I'm Not Near the Girl I Love; When the Idle Poor Become the Idle Rich; The Begat.

The Firefly
Lyric Theatre, 2 December 1912 (120 performances). *Book:* Otto Harbach. *Score:* Rudolf Friml, Otto Harbach. *Director:* Fred Latham.

Choreographers: Signor Albertieri, Sammy Lee. *Cast:* Emma Trentini, Roy Atwell, Craig Campbell, Henry Vogel, Sammy Lee, Audrey Maple, Melville Stewart. *Songs:* Giannina Mia; Love Is Like a Firefly; Sympathy; When a Maid Comes Knocking at Your Heart.

MGM (1937). *Screenplay:* Frances Goodrich, Albert Hackett. *Score:* Rudolf Friml, Herbert Stothart, Otto Harbach, Robert Wright, George Forrest. *Director:* Robert Z. Leonard. *Choreographer:* Albertina Rasch. *Cast:* Jeanete MacDonald, Allen Jones, Douglass Dumbrille, Warren William, Billy Gilbert, Henry Daniell, George Zucco. *Songs:* Giannina Mia; The Donkey Serenade; Love Is Like a Firefly; Sympathy; When a Maid Comes Knocking at Your Heart.

Flower Drum Song

St. James Theatre, 1 December 1958 (600 performances). *Book:* Joseph Fields, Oscar Hammerstein. *Score:* Richard Rodgers, Oscar Hammerstein. *Director:* Gene Kelly. *Choreographer:* Carol Haney. *Cast:* Miyoshi Umeki, Larry Blyden, Juanita Hall, Pat Suzuki, Keye Luke, Ed Kenny, Arabella Hong, Jack Soo. *Songs:* I Enjoy Being a Girl; Love, Look Away; You Are Beautiful; Don't Marry Me; A Hundred Million Miracles; I Am Going to Like It Here; Chop Suey; Grant Avenue; Sunday.

Universal (1961). *Screenplay:* Joseph Fields. *Score:* Richard Rodgers, Oscar Hammerstein. *Director:* Henry Koster. *Choreographer:* Hermes Pan. *Cast:* Miyoshi Umeki, Juanita Hall, Nancy Kwan, Jack Soo, James Shigeta, Benson Fong. *Songs:* I Enjoy Being a Girl; Love, Look Away; You Are Beautiful; Don't Marry Me; A Hundred Million Miracles; I Am Going to Like It Here; Chop Suey; Grant Avenue; Sunday.

Flying High

Apollo Theatre, 3 March 1930 (357 performances). *Book:* John Mc-Gowan, B. G. DeSylva, Lew Brown. *Score:* Ray Henderson, B. G. De-Sylva, Lew Brown. *Directors:* George White, Edward Clark Lilley. *Choreographer:* Bobby Connolly. *Cast:* Oscar Shaw, Bert Lahr, Kate Smith, Grace Brinkley, Russ Brown, Pearl Osgood. *Songs:* Thank Your Father; Red Hot Chicago; I'll Know Him; Good for You—Bad for Me; Without Love.

MGM (1931). *Screenplay:* A. P. Younger. *Score:* Jimmy McHugh, Dorothy Fields, etc. *Director:* Charles F. Riesner. *Choreographer:* Busby

Berkeley. *Cast:* Bert Lahr, Charlotte Greenwood, Pat O'Brien, Kathryn Crawford, Charles Winninger, Hedda Hopper, Guy Kibbee. *Songs:* Happy Landing; We'll Dance till Dawn; Flying High.

Follow Thru
46th Street Theatre, 9 January 1929 (403 performances). *Book:* B. G. DeSylva, Laurence Schwab. *Score:* Ray Henderson, B. D. DeSylva, Lew Brown. *Director:* Edgar MacGregor. *Choreographer:* Bobby Connolly. *Cast:* Jack Haley, Zelma O'Neal, Irene Delroy, Eleanor Powell, Madeline Cameron, John Barker. *Songs:* Button Up Your Overcoat; My Lucky Star; You Wouldn't Fool Me, Would You?; I Want to Be Bad.
    Paramount (1930). *Screenplay:* Laurence Schwab, Lloyd Corrigan. *Score:* Ray Henderson, B. G. DeSylva, Lew Brown, etc. *Directors:* Laurence Schwab, Lloyd Corrigan. *Cast:* Nancy Carroll, Jack Haley, Charles "Buddy" Rogers, Zelma O'Neal, Eugene Pallette, Thelma Todd. *Songs:* Button Up Your Overcoat; It Must Be You; A Peach of a Pair; I Want to Be Bad; Then I'll Have Time for You.

Funny Face
Alvin Theatre, 22 November 1927 (244 performances). *Book:* Paul Gerard Smith, Fred Thompson. *Score:* George and Ira Gershwin. *Director:* Edgar MacGregor. *Choreographer:* Bobby Connolly. *Cast:* Adele and Fred Astaire, Victor Moore, William Kent, Allen Kearns, Betty Compton, Dorothy Jordan. *Songs:* Funny Face; 'S Wonderful; He Loves and She Loves; High Hat; My One and Only; The Babbitt and the Bromide; Let's Kiss and Make Up.
    Paramount (1957). *Screenplay:* Leonard Gershe. *Score:* George and Ira Gershwin, Roger Edens. *Director:* Stanley Donen. *Choreographers:* Eugene Loring, Fred Astaire. *Cast:* Fred Astaire, Audrey Hepburn, Kay Thompson. Michel Auclair, Robert Flemyng, Virginia Gibson. *Songs:* Funny Face; 'S Wonderful; How Long Has This Been Going On?; He Loves and She Loves; Think Pink; Bonjour, Paris!; Clap Yo' Hands; On How to Be Lovely; Let's Kiss and Make Up.

Funny Girl
Winter Garden Theatre, 26 March 1964 (1,348 performances). *Book:* Isobel Lennart. *Score:* Jule Styne, Bob Merrill. *Directors:* Garson Kanin,

Jerome Robbins. *Choreographer:* Carol Haney. *Cast:* Barbra Streisand, Sydney Chaplin, Danny Meehan, Kay Medford. *Songs:* People; Don't Rain on My Parade; The Music That Makes Me Dance; I'm the Greatest Star; You Are Woman; His Love Makes Me Beautiful; I Want to Be Seen with You Tonight; Who Are You Now?; Sadie, Sadie.

Columbia/Rastar (1968). *Screenplay:* Isobel Lennart. *Score:* Jule Styne, Bob Merrill, etc. *Director:* William Wyler. *Choreographer:* Herbert Ross. *Cast:* Barbra Streisand, Omar Sharif, Kay Medford, Walter Pidgeon, Tommy Rall. *Songs:* People; Second Hand Rose; Don't Rain on My Parade; My Man; I'm the Greatest Star; You Are Woman; His Love Makes Me Beautiful; I'd Rather Be Blue Over You; Sadie, Sadie; Funny Girl.

A Funny Thing Happened on the Way to the Forum
Alvin Theatre, 8 May 1962 (964 performances). *Book:* Burt Shevelove, Larry Gelbart. *Score:* Stephen Sondheim. *Director:* George Abbott. *Choreographer:* Jack Cole. *Cast:* Zero Mostel, Jack Gilford, Brian Davies, David Burns, John Carradine, Preshy Marker, Ronald Holgate, Ruth Kobart. *Songs:* Comedy Tonight; Everybody Ought to Have a Maid; Lovely; I'm Calm; Pretty Little Picture; Love I Hear; Free; Bring Me My Bride; Impossible; That'll Show Him.

United Artists (1966). *Screenplay:* Melvin Frank, Michael Pertwee. *Score:* Stephen Sondheim. *Director:* Richard Lester. *Choreographers:* Ethel and George Martin. *Cast:* Zero Mostel, Phil Silvers, Jack Gilford, Michael Crawford, Michael Hordern, Annette Andre, Buster Keaton, Leon Greene. *Songs:* Comedy Tonight; Everybody Ought to Have a Maid; Lovely; Bring Me My Bride.

Gay Divorce
Ethel Barrymore Theatre, 29 November 1932 (248 performances). *Book:* Dwight Taylor. *Score:* Cole Porter. *Director:* Howard Lindsay. *Choreographers:* Carl Randall, Barbara Newberry. *Cast:* Fred Astaire, Claire Luce, Luella Gear, Erik Rhodes, Betty Starbuck, Eric Blore. *Songs:* Night and Day; After You, Who?; I've Got You on My Mind; How's Your Romance?; Mister and Missus Fitch.

The Gay Divorcee, RKO (1934). *Screenplay:* George Marion Jr., Dorothy Yost, Edward Kaufman. *Score:* Cole Porter, Harry Revel, Mack Gordon, etc. *Director:* Mark Sandrich. *Choreographers:* Dave Gould,

Hermes Pan, Fred Astaire. *Cast:* Fred Astaire, Ginger Rogers, Alice Brady, Edward Everett Horton, Erik Rhodes, Betty Grable, Eric Blore, Lillian Miles. *Songs:* Night and Day; The Continental; Don't Let It Bother You; Let's K-nock K-nees; A Needle in a Haystack.

Gentlemen Prefer Blondes

Ziegfeld Theatre, 8 December 1949 (740 performances). *Book:* Joseph Stein, Anita Loos. *Score:* Jule Styne, Leo Robin. *Director:* John C. Wilson. *Choreographer:* Agnes de Mille. *Cast:* Carol Channing, Yvonne Adair, Jack McCauley, Eric Brotherson, Alice Pearce, Rex Evans, Anita Alverez, George S. Irving. *Songs:* Diamonds Are a Girl's Best Friend; A Little Girl from Little Rock; Bye Bye Baby; Just a Kiss Apart; It's Delightful Down in Chile.

Fox (1953). *Screenplay:* Charles Lederer. *Score:* Jule Styne, Leo Robin, Hoagy Carmichael, Harold Adamson. *Director:* Howard Hawks. *Choreographer:* Jack Cole. *Cast:* Marilyn Monroe, Jane Russell, Charles Coburn, Elliot Reed, Tommy Noonan, Taylor Holmes. *Songs:* Diamonds Are a Girl's Best Friend; A Little Girl from Little Rock; Ain't There Anyone Here for Love?; Bye Bye Baby; When Love Goes Wrong.

George White's Scandals Series

Dancer-turned-impresario George White presented his popular series of revues called the Scandals between 1919 and 1939. The thirteen shows emphasized dancing and new songs, as opposed to the visual opulence of the Ziegfeld Follies. George Gershwin, Richard Whiting, and the team of DeSylva, Brown, and Henderson were among the songwriters whose work was featured in George White's Scandals.

George White's Scandals, Fox (1934). *Screenplay:* Jack Yellen. *Score:* Ray Henderson, Jack Yellen, etc. *Directors:* George White, Thornton Freeland, Harry Lachman. *Choreographer:* George Hale. *Cast:* Alice Faye, Rudy Vallee, Jimmy Durante, Gregory Ratoff, Cliff Edwards, Dixie Dunbar, Richard Carle, Gertrude Michael. *Songs:* Hold My Hand; Oh, You Nasty Man; Sweet and Simple; Every Day Is Father's Day with Baby; My Dog Loves Your Dog; Picking Cotton.

George White's 1935 Scandals, Fox (1935). *Screenplay:* Jack Yellen, Patterson McNutt. *Score:* Jack Yellen, Joseph Myer, Herb Magidson, etc.

Director: George White. *Cast:* Alice Faye, George White, James Dunn, Lyda Roberti, Eleanor Powell, Cliff Edwards, Arline Judge. *Songs:* According to the Moonlight; Oh, I Didn't Know; You Belong to Me; It's an Old Southern Custom; I Got Shoes, You Got Shoesies; I Was Born Too Late.

George White's Scandals of 1945, RKO (1945). *Screenplay:* Hugh Wedlock, Howard Snyder, etc. *Score:* Sammy Fain, Jack Yellen, etc. *Director:* Felix Feist. *Choreographer:* Ernest Matray. *Cast:* Jack Haley, Joan Davis, Margaret Hamilton, Philip Terry, Martha Holliday. *Songs:* Life Is Just a Bowel of Cherries; Liza; I Wake Up in the Morning; Wishing; Who Killed Vaudeville?; Bolero in the Jungle.

Girl Crazy
Alvin Theatre, 14 October 1930 (272 performances). *Book:* Guy Bolton, John McGowan. *Score:* George and Ira Gershwin. *Director:* Alexander Leftwich. *Choreographer:* George Hale. *Cast:* Allen Kearns, Willie Howard, Ginger Rogers, Ethel Merman, William Kent. Lew Parker. *Songs:* I Got Rhythm; Embraceable You; I'm Bidin' My Time; But Not for Me; Could You Use Me?; Sam and Delilah.

RKO (1932). *Screenplay:* Herman Mankiewicz. *Score:* George and Ira Gershwin. *Director:* William A. Seiter. *Choreographer:* Busby Berkeley. *Cast:* Bert Wheeler, Robert Woolsey, Mitzi Green, Eddie Quillan, Stanley Fields, Dorothy Lee, Kitty Kelly. *Songs:* I Got Rhythm; Embraceable You; But Not for Me; Could You Use Me?; Sam and Delilah.

MGM (1943). *Screenplay:* Fred Finklehoffe. *Score:* George and Ira Gershwin. *Directors:* Norman Taurog, Busby Berkeley. *Choreographers:* Charles Walters, Busby Berkeley. *Cast:* Mickey Rooney, Judy Garland, Rags Ragland, Robert Strickland, Tommy Dorsey, Gil Stratton, June Allyson, Nancy Walker. *Songs:* I Got Rhythm; Embraceable You; I'm Bidin' My Time; But Not for Me; Fascinating Rhythm; Could You Use Me?; You've Got What Gets Me.

When the Boys Meet the Girls, MGM (1965). *Screenplay:* Robert E. Kent. *Score:* George and Ira Gershwin, etc. *Director:* Alvin Ganzer. *Choreographer:* Earl Barton. *Cast:* Harve Presnell, Connie Francis, Sue Anne Langdon, Fred Clark, Frank Faylen, Joby Baker, Louis Armstrong, Liberace. *Songs:* I Got Rhythm; Embraceable You; I'm Bidin' My Time, But Not for Me; Treat Me Rough; When the Boys Meet the Girls; Mail Call; Listen People.

Godspell
Cherry Lane Theatre, 17 May 1971 (2,651 performances). *Book:* John-Michael Tebelak. *Score:* Stephen Schwartz. *Director:* John-Michael Tebelak. *Cast:* Stephen Nathan, David Haskell, Sonia Manzano, Johanne Jonas, Jeffrey Mylett, Lamar Alford, Robin Lamont. *Songs:* Day by Day; All for the Best; By My Side; Save the People; All Good Gifts; Turn Back, O Man; We Beseech Thee; Light of the World.
    Columbia (1973). *Screenplay:* David Greene. *Score:* Stephen Schwartz. *Director:* David Greene. *Choreographer:* Sammy Bayes. *Cast:* Victor Garber, David Haskell, Robin Lamont, Katie Hanley, Lynn Thigpen, Jeffrey Mylett, Joanne Jonas, Jerry Sroka, Gilmer McCormick, Merrell Jackson. *Songs:* Day by Day; All for the Best; By My Side; Save the People; All Good Gifts; Turn Back, O Man; Beautiful City; Light of the World.

Golden Dawn
Hammerstein Theatre, 30 November 1927 (184 performances). *Book:* Otto Harbach, Oscar Hammerstein. *Score:* Emmerich Kalman, Otto Harbach, Oscar Hammerstein, Herbert Stothart. *Director:* Reginald Hammerstein. *Choreographer:* Dave Bennett. *Cast:* Louise Hunter, Paul Gregory, Robert Chisholm, Marguerita Sylva, Olin Howland, Barbara Newberry, Gil Squires. *Songs:* We Two; Dawn; When I Crack My Whip; My Bwana; Jungle Shadows; Here in the Dark.
    Warner (1930). *Screenplay:* Walter Anthony. *Score:* Herbert Stothart, Emmerich Kalman, Otto Harbach, Oscar Hammerstein, etc. *Director:* Ray Enright. *Choreographer:* Larry Ceballo. *Cast:* Vivienne Segal, Walter Woolf King, Noah Berry, Lupino Lane, Alice Gentle, Dick Henderson. *Songs:* My Heart's Love Call; Whip Song; Africa Smiles No More; Dawn; My Bwana; We Too; In a Jungle Bungalow; No More.

Good News
46th Street Theatre, 6 September 1927 (551 performances). *Book:* Laurence Schwab, B. G. DeSylva. *Score:* Ray Henderson, B. G. DeSylva, Lew Brown. *Director:* Edgar MacGregor. *Choreographer:* Bobby Connolly. *Cast:* Mary Lawlor, John Price Jones, Zelma O'Neal, Gus Shy, Inez Courtney. *Songs:* The Best Things in Life Are Free; Good News; The Varsity Drag; Just Imagine; Lucky in Love; He's a Ladies Man.

MGM (1930). *Screenplay:* Frances Marion. *Score:* Ray Henderson, B. G. DeSylva, Lew Brown, etc. *Directors:* Nick Grinde, Edgar Mac-Gregor. *Choreographer:* Sammy Lee. *Cast:* Stanley Smith, Mary Lawlor, Bessie Love, Cliff Edwards, Lola Lane, Dorothy McNulty (Penny Singleton), Thomas Jackson. *Songs:* Good News; The Varsity Drag; Students Are We; If You're not kissing Me; Gee But I'd Like to Make You Happy; He's a Ladies Man.

MGM (1947). *Screenplay:* Betty Comden, Adolph Green. *Score:* Ray Henderson, B. G. DeSylva, Lew Brown, Roger Edens, etc. *Director:* Charles Walters. *Choreographers:* Robert Alton, Charles Walters. *Cast:* June Allyson, Peter Lawford, Patricia Marshall, Joan McCracken, Ray McDonald, Mel Tormé. *Songs:* The Best Things in Life Are Free; Good News; The Varsity Drag; Just Imagine; Pass That Peace Pipe; The French Leson; Lucky in Love; Be a Ladies Man.

Grease

Eden Theatre, 14 February 1972 (3,388 performances). *Book and Score:* Jim Jacobs, Warren Casey. *Director:* Tom Moore. *Choreographer:* Patricia Birch. *Cast:* Barry Bostwick, Carole Demas, Adrienne Barbeau, Timothy Myers. *Songs:* Freddy, My Love; Summer Nights; Beauty School Dropout; There Are Worse Things I Could Do; It's Raining on Prom Night; Look at Me, I'm Sandra Dee; Greased Lightnin'; We Go Together.

Paramount (1978). *Screenplay:* Bronte Woodard. *Score:* Jim Jacobs, Casey Warren, etc. *Director:* Randal Kleiser. *Choreographer:* Patricia Birch. *Cast:* John Travolta, Olivia Newton-John, Stockard Channing, Didi Conn, Jeff Conaway, Eve Arden, Frankie Avalon, Joan Blondell, Sid Caesar, Lorenzo Lamas. *Songs:* Grease; Freddy, My Love; Summer Nights; Beauty School Dropout; There Are Worse Things I Could Do; Hopelessly Devoted to You; You're the One That I Want; Look at Me, I'm Sandra Dee; Greased Lightnin'; We Go Together.

Guys and Dolls

46th Street Theatre, 24 November 1950 (1,200 performances). *Book:* Abe Burrows. *Score:* Frank Loesser. *Director:* George S. Kaufman. *Choreographer:* Michael Kidd. *Cast:* Robert Alda, Sam Levene, Isabel Bigley, Vivian Blaine, Stubby Kaye, Pat Rooney Sr., Johnny Silver.

Songs: Luck Be a Lady Tonight; Adelaide's Lament; If I Were a Bell; A Bushel and a Peck; The Oldest Established; Guys and Dolls; Sit Down, You're Rockin' the Boat; I've Never Been in Love Before; Marry the Man Today; Take Back Your Mink; My Time of Day.
   Goldwyn/MGM (1955). *Screenplay:* Joseph L. Mankiewicz. *Score:* Frank Loesser. *Director:* Joseph L. Mankiewicz. *Choreographer:* Michael Kidd. *Cast:* Marlon Brando, Frank Sinatra, Jean Simmons, Vivian Blaine, Stubby Kaye, Robert Keith, Johnny Silver, Sheldon Leonard. *Songs:* Luck Be a Lady Tonight; Adelaide's Lament; If I Were a Bell; The Oldest Established; Guys and Dolls; Sit Down, You're Rockin' the Boat; I've Never Been in Love Before; Marry the Man Today; Take Back Your Mink; Pet Me, Poppa; My Time of Day; Adelaide; A Woman in Love.

Gypsy
Broadway Theatre, 21 May 1959 (702 performances). *Book:* Arthur Laurents. *Score:* Jule Styne, Stephen Sondheim. *Director-choreographer:* Jerome Robbins. *Cast:* Ethel Merman, Jack Klugman, Sandra Church, Maria Karnilova, Paul Wallace, Lane Bradbury, Jacqueline Mayro. *Songs:* Let Me Enterain You; Together, Wherever We Go; Everything's Coming Up Roses; Some People; Small World; Mr. Goldstone; All I Need Is the Girl; If Momma Was Married; You Gotta Have a Gimmick; Rose's Turn; Little Lamb.
   Warner (1962). *Screenplay:* Leonard Spigelgass. *Score:* Jule Styne, Stephen Sondheim. *Director:* Mervyn LeRoy. *Choreographer:* Robert Tucker. *Cast:* Rosalind Russell, Karl Malden, Natalie Wood, Paul Wallace, Betty Bruce, Ann Jillian, Faith Dane. *Songs:* Let Me Enterain You; Everything's Coming Up Roses; Some People; Small World; Mr. Goldstone; All I Need Is the Girl; If Momma Was Married; You Gotta Have a Gimmick; Rose's Turn; Little Lamb.

Hair
Biltmore Theatre, 29 April 1968 (1,750 performances). *Book:* Gerome Ragni, James Rado. *Score:* Galt MacDermot, Gerome Ragni, James Rado. *Director:* Tom O'Horgan. *Choreographer:* Julie Arenel. *Cast:* Gerome Ragni, James Rado, Lynn Kellogg, Steve Curry, Melba Moore, Shelley Plimpton, Lamont Washington, Diane Keaton, Sally Eaton.

Songs: Aquarius; Let the Sunshine In; Good Morning, Starshine; Easy to Be Hard; Hair; Ain't Got No; I've Got Life; Frank Mills.

United Artists (1979). *Screenplay:* Michael Weller. *Score:* Galt MacDermot, Gerome Ragni, James Rado. *Director:* Milos Forman. *Choreographer:* Tywla Tharp. *Cast:* Treat Williams, John Savage, Beverly D'Angelo, Annie Golden, Don Dacus, Dorsey Wright, Cheryl Banes, Laurie Beechman, Melba Moore, Nell Carter, Charlotte Rae, Nicholas Ray. *Songs:* Aquarius; Let the Sunshine In; Good Morning, Starshine; Easy to Be Hard; Hair; Ain't Got No; I've Got Life; Frank Mills.

Half a Sixpence
Broadhurst Theatre, 25 April 1965 (512 performances). *Book:* Beverly Cross. *Score:* David Heneker. *Director:* Gene Saks. *Choreographer:* Onna White. *Cast:* Tommy Steele, Polly James, James Grout, Carrie Nye, Ann Shoemaker, Grover Dale, Will McKenzie. *Songs:* If the Rain's Got to Fall; Half a Sixpence; Money to Burn; She's Too far Above Me; Flash, Bang, Wallop!

Paramount (1967). *Screenplay:* Beverly Cross. *Score:* David Heneker. *Director:* George Sidney. *Choreographer:* Gillian Lynne. *Cast:* Tommy Steele, Cyril Ritchard, Julia Foster, Penelope Horner, Grover Dale. *Songs:* If the Rain's Got to Fall; Half a Sixpence; Money to Burn; She's Too Far above Me; Flash, Bang, Wallop!

Heads Up!
Alvin Theatre, 11 November 1929 (144 performances). *Book:* John McGowan, Paul Gerard Smith. *Score:* Richard Rodgers, Lorenz Hart. *Choreographer:* George Hale. *Cast:* Barbara Newberry, Jack Whiting, Victor Moore, Betty Starbuck, Ray Bolger, John Hundley, Robert Glecker, Lew Parker, Janet Velie. *Songs:* A Ship without a Sail; Why Do You Suppose?; My Man Is on the Make; It Must Be Heaven.

Paramount (1930). *Screenplay:* John McGowan, Jack Kirkland. *Score:* Richard Rodgers, Lorenz Hart, Victor Schertzinger. *Director:* Victor Schertzinger. *Choreographer:* George Hale. *Cast:* Charles "Buddy" Rogers, Margaret Breen, Victor Moore, Helen Kane, Helen Carrington, Gene Cowing. *Songs:* A Ship without a Sail; My Man Is on the Make; If I Knew You Better.

Hedwig and the Angry Inch
Jane Street Theatre, 21 February 1998 (857 performances). *Book:* John Cameron Mitchell. *Score:* Stephen Trask. *Director:* Peter Askin. *Choreography:* Jerry Mitchell. *Cast:* John Cameron Mitchell, Miriam Shor. *Songs:* Origin of Love; Angry Inch; Wicked Little Town; Tear Me Down.

New Line (2001). *Screenplay:* John Cameron Mitchell. *Score:* Stephen Trask. *Director:* John Cameron Mitchell. *Choreographer:* Jerry Mitchell. *Cast:* John Cameron Mitchell, Andrea Martin, Michael Pitt, Miriam Shor. *Songs:* Origin of Love; Angry Inch; Wicked Little Town; Tear Me Down.

Hello, Dolly!
St. James Theatre, 16 January 1964 (2,844 performances). *Book:* Michael Stewart. *Score:* Jerry Herman. *Director-choreographer:* Gower Champion. *Cast:* Carol Channing, David Burns, Charles Nelson Reilly, Eileen Brennan, Jerry Dodge, Sondra Lee. *Songs:* Hello, Dolly!; Put on Your Sunday Clothes; Before the Parade Passes By; It Takes a Woman; So Long, Dearie; It Only Takes a Moment; Ribbons down My Back; Motherhood; Dancing.

Fox (1969). *Screenplay:* Ernest Lehman. *Score:* Jerry Herman. *Director:* Gene Kelly. *Choreographer:* Michael Kidd. *Cast:* Barbra Streisand, Walter Matthau, Louis Armstrong, Michael Crawford, Marianne McAndrew, Danny Lockin, E. J. Peaker, Tommy Tune, Joyce Ames. *Songs:* Hello, Dolly!; Put on Your Sunday Clothes; Before the Parade Passes By; It Takes a Woman; So Long, Dearie; It Only Takes a Moment; Ribbons down My Back; Love Is Only Love; Dancing.

Hellzapoppin'
46th Street Theatre, 22 September 1938 (1,404 performances). *Sketches:* Ole Olsen, Chic Johnson. *Score:* Sammy Fain, Charles Tobias, etc. *Director:* Edward Duryea Dowling. *Cast:* Ole Olsen, Chic Johnson, Barto and Mann, Hal Sherman, Ray Kinney. *Songs:* Fuddle Dee Duddle; It's Time to Say Aloha; Boomps-a-Daisy; Abe Lincoln.

Universal (1941). *Screenplay:* Nat Perrin, Warren Wilson. *Score:* Gene de Paul, Don Raye, etc. *Director:* H. C. Potter. *Choreographer:* Nick Castle. *Cast:* Ole Olsen, Chic Johnson, Robert Paige, Jane Frazee,

Lewis Howard, Martha Raye, Mischa Auer, Hugh Hubert. *Songs:* Watch the Birdie; What Kind of Love Is This?; Heaven for Two; You Were There; Hellzapoppin'; Putting on the Dog; Waiting for the Robert E. Lee.

Higher and Higher
Shubert Theatre, 4 April 1940 (104 performances). *Book:* Gladys Hurlbut, Joshua Logan. *Score:* Richard Rodgers, Lorenz Hart. *Director:* Joshua Logan. *Choreographer:* Robert Alton. *Cast:* Jack Haley, Marta Eggert, Shirley Ross, Leif Erickson, Lee Dixon, Robert Chisholm, Billie Worth, Hollace Shaw, Robert Rounseville. *Songs:* It Never Entered My Mind; Mornings at Seven; How's Your Health?; Nothing but You; From Another World; Disgustingly Rich; Ev'ry Sunday Afternoon.

RKO (1944). *Screenplay:* Jay Dratler, Ralph Spence. *Score:* Jimmy McHugh, Harold Adamson. *Director:* Tim Whelan. *Choreographer:* Ernest Matray. *Cast:* Frank Sinatra, Jack Haley, Michele Morgan, Leon Errol, Victor Borge, Mary Wickes, Barbara Hale, Mel Tormé, Dooley Wilson. *Songs:* A Lovely Way to Spend an Evening; The Music Stopped; I Couldn't Sleep a Wink Last Night; It's a Most Important Affair; I Saw You First; Boccherini's Minuet in Boogie; You're on Your Own.

Hit the Deck!
Belasco Theatre, 25 April 1927 (352 performances). *Book:* Herbert Fields. *Score:* Vincent Youmans, Clifford Grey, Leo Robin. *Director:* Alexander Leftwich. *Choreographer:* Seymour Felix. *Cast:* Louise Groody, Charles King, Stella Mayhew, Brian Donlevy, Madeline Cameron, Jack McCauley. *Songs:* Hallelujah; Sometimes I'm Happy; Why, Oh, Why?; Looloo; Join the Navy; Harbor of My Heart.

RKO (1930). *Screenplay:* Luther Reed. *Score:* Vincent Youmans, Clifford Grey, Leo Robin, etc. *Director:* Luther Reed. *Choreographer:* Pearl Eaton. *Cast:* Jack Oakie, Polly Walker, Roger Gray, Frank Wood, Harry Sweet, Marguerita Padula, June Clyde. *Songs:* Hallelujah; Sometimes I'm Happy; Why, Oh, Why?; More Than You Know; I Know That You Know; Keeping Myself for You.

Follow the Fleet, RKO (1936). *Screenplay:* Dwight Taylor, Allan Scott. *Score:* Irving Berlin. *Director:* Mark Sandrich. *Choreographers:* Hermes

Pan, Fred Astaire. *Cast:* Fred Astaire, Ginger Rogers Randolph Scott, Harriet Hilliard, Lucille Ball, Astrid Allwyn, Joy Hodges, Tony Martin, Betty Grable. *Songs:* Let's Face the Music and Dance; I'm Putting All My Eggs in One Basket; We Saw the Sea; Let Yourself Go; I'd Rather Lead a Band; But Where Are You?; Get Thee behind Me, Satan.
Hit the Deck!, MGM (1955). *Screenplay:* Sonia Levien, William Ludwig. *Score:* Vincent Youmans, Clifford Grey, Leo Robin, etc. *Director:* Roy Rowland. *Choreographer:* Hermes Pan. *Cast:* Tony Martin, Jane Powell, Debbie Reynolds, Vic Damone, Russ Tamblyn, Walter Pidgeon, Ann Miller, Gene Raymond, Kay Armen, J. Carroll Naish. *Songs:* Hallelujah; Sometimes I'm Happy; More Than You Know; Keeping Myself for You; Why, Oh, Why?; Join the Navy; Ciribiribin.

Hold Everything
Broadhurst Theatre, 10 October 1928 (413 performances). *Book:* B. G. DeSylva, John McGowan. *Score:* Ray Henderson, B. G. DeSylva, Lew Brown. *Choreographer:* Sam Rose, Jack Haskell. *Cast:* Jack Whiting, Ona Munson, Bert Lahr, Betty Compton, Victor Moore, Nina Olivette, Frank Allworth. *Songs:* You're the Cream in My Coffee; Too Good to Be True; Don't Hold Everything; To Know You Is to Love You.
Warner (1930). *Screenplay:* Robert Lord. *Score:* Joe Burke, Al Dubin. *Director:* Roy Del Ruth. *Choreographer:* Larry Ceballos. *Cast:* Joe E. Brown, Winnie Lightner, Georges Carpentier, Dorothy Rivier, Sally O'Neil, Edmund Breese. *Songs:* Take It on the Chin; Girls We Remember; Isn't This a Cockeyed World; When Little Red Roses Get the Blues for You; All Alone Together; Physically Fit.

How to Succeed in Business without Really Trying
46th Street Theatre, 14 October 1961 (1,417 performances). *Book:* Abe Burrows. *Score:* Frank Loesser. *Director:* Abe Burrows. *Choreographer:* Bob Fosse. *Cast:* Robert Morse, Rudy Vallee, Bonnie Scott, Virginia Martin, Charles Nelson Reilly, Ruth Kobart, Sammy Smith. *Songs:* I Believe in You; The Company Way; Brotherhood of Man; Rosemary; Grand Old Ivy; A Secretary Is Not a Toy; Paris Original.
Mirisch/United Artists (1967). *Screenplay:* David Swift. *Score:* Frank Loesser. *Director:* David Swift. *Choreographers:* Dale Moreda, Bob Fosse. *Cast:* Robert Morse, Rudy Vallee, Michele Lee, Anthony

Teague, Maureen Arthur, Murray Matheson, Sammy Smith, Ruth Kobart. *Songs:* I Believe in You; The Company Way; Brotherhood of Man; Rosemary; Grand Old Ivy; A Secretary Is Not a Toy; Paris Original.

I Married an Angel

Shubert Theatre, 11 May 1938 (338 performances). *Book:* Richard Rodgers, Lorenz Hart. *Score:* Richard Rodgers, Lorenz Hart. *Director:* Joshua Logan. *Choreographer:* George Balanchine. *Cast:* Dennis King, Vera Zorina, Vivienne Segal, Walter Slezak, Audrey Christie, Charles Walters. *Songs:* I Married an Angel; Spring Is Here; At the Roxie Music Hall; I'll Tell the Man in the Street.

MGM (1942). *Screenplay:* Anita Loos. *Score:* Richard Rodgers, Lorenz Hart, etc. *Director:* W. S. Van Dyke. *Choreographer:* Ernest Matray. *Cast:* Jeanette MacDonald, Nelson Eddy, Edward Everett Horton, Binnie Barnes, Reginald Owen, Douglass Dumbrille, Janis Carter. *Songs:* I Married an Angel; Spring Is Here; At the Roxie Music Hall; I'll Tell the Man in the Street; Aloha Oe; Now You've Met the Angel; A Twinkle in Your Eye.

Irene

Vanderbilt Theatre, 18 November 1919 (670 performances). *Book:* James Montgomery. *Score:* Harry Tierney, Joseph McCarthy. *Director-choreographer*: Edward Royce. *Cast:* Edith Day, Walter Regan, Bobbie Watson, John Litel, Dorothy Walters, Eva Puck. *Songs:* Alice Blue Gown; Castle of Dreams; Irene; The Last Part of Ev'ry Party; Skyrocket.

RKO (1940). *Screenplay:* Alice Duer Miller. *Score:* Harry Tierney, Joseph McCarthy. *Director:* Herbert Wilcox. *Choreographer:* Aida Broadbent. *Cast:* Anna Neagle, Ray Milland, Alan Marshal, Roland Young, Billie Burke, May Robson, Arthur Treacher, Doris Nolan. *Songs:* Alice Blue Gown; Castle of Dreams; You've Got Me Out on a Limb; Irene; There's Something in the Air; Sweet Vermosa Brown.

Jesus Christ Superstar

Mark Hellinger Theatre, 12 October 1971 (720 performances). *Book:* Tim Rice. *Score:* Andrew Lloyd Webber, Tim Rice. *Director:* Tom O'Horgan. *Cast:* Jeff Fenholt, Ben Vereen, Yvonne Elliman, Barry Dennen, Paul Ainsley, Bob Bingham. *Songs:* Superstar; I Don't Know How to Love Him; Everything's Alright; Hosanna; King Herod's Song; What's the Buzz?

Universal (1973). *Screenplay:* Melvyn Bragg, Norman Jewison. *Score:* Andrew Lloyd Webber, Tim Rice. *Director:* Norman Jewison. *Choreographer:* Robert Iscove. *Cast:* Ted Neely, Carl Anderson, Yvonne Elliman, Josh Mostel, Larry Marshal, Barry Denham, Bob Bingham. *Songs:* Superstar; I Don't Know How to Love Him; Everything's Alright; Hosanna; King Herod's Song; What's the Buzz?

Joseph and the Amazing Technicolor Dreamcoat
Entermedia Theatre, 18 November 1981 (747 performances). *Book:* Tim Rice. *Score:* Andrew Lloyd Webber, Tim Rice. *Director-choreographer:* Tony Tanner. *Cast:* David James Carroll, Cleavon Little, Jesse Pearson; replaced by Bill Hutton, Laurie Beechman, Tom Carder for Broadway. *Songs:* Any Dream Will Do; Close Every Door; One More Angel in Heaven; Those Caanan Days; Go, Go, Go Joseph; Benjamin Calypso.

TV (1999). *Screenplay:* Tim Rice. *Score:* Andrew Lloyd Webber, Tim Rice. *Director:* David Mallet. *Choreographer:* Dean McKerras. *Cast:* Donny Osmond, Maria Friedman, Ian McNeie, Robert Torti, Richard Attenborough, Joan Collins. *Songs:* Any Dream Will Do; Close Every Door; One More Angel in Heaven; Those Caanan Days; Go, Go, Go Joseph; Benjamin Calypso.

Jumbo
Hippodrome Theatre, 16 November 1935 (233 performances). *Book:* Ben Hecht, Charles MacArthur. *Score:* Richard Rodgers, Lorenz Hart. *Directors:* John Murray Anderson, George Abbott. *Choreographer:* Allan K. Foster. *Cast:* Jimmy Durante, Donald Novis, Gloria Grafton, A. P. Kaye. *Songs:* The Most Beautiful Girl in the World; My Romance; Little Girl Blue; Over and Over Again; The Circus Is on Parade.

MGM (1962). *Screenplay:* Sidney Sheldon. *Score:* Richard Rodgers, Lorenz Hart, Roger Edens. *Director:* Charles Walters. *Choreographer:* Busby Berkeley. *Cast:* Jimmy Durante, Doris Day, Martha Raye, Stephan Boyd, Dean Jagger, Grady Sutton. *Songs:* The Most Beautiful Girl in the World; My Romance; Over and Over Again; The Circus Is on Parade; Sawdust, Spangles and Dreams.

The King and I

St. James Theatre, 29 March 1951 (1,246 performances). *Book:* Oscar Hamerstein. *Score:* Richard Rodgers, Oscar Hammerstein. *Director:* John Van Druten. *Choreographer:* Jerome Robbins. *Cast:* Gertrude Lawrence, Yul Brynner, Doretta Morrow, Dorothy Sarnoff, Larry Douglas. *Songs:* Shall We Dance?; Getting to Know You; Hello Young Lovers; We Kiss in a Shadow; Something Wonderful; I Whistle a Happy Tune; I Have Dreamed; A Puzzlement; My Lord and Master.

Fox (1956). *Screenplay:* Ernest Lehman. *Score:* Richard Rodgers, Oscar Hammerstein. *Director:* Walter Lang. *Choreographer:* Jerome Robbins. *Cast:* Deborah Kerr, Yul Brynner, Rita Moreno, Martin Benson, Terry Saunders, Rex Thompson. *Songs:* Shall We Dance?; Getting to Know You; Hello Young Lovers; We Kiss in a Shadow; Something Wonderful; I Whistle a Happy Tune; I Have Dreamed; A Puzzlement.

Kismet

Ziegfeld Theatre, 3 December 1953 (583 performances). *Book:* Charles Lederer, Luther Davis. *Score:* Alexander Borodin, Robert Wright, George Forrest. *Director:* Albert Marre. *Choreographer:* Jack Cole. *Cast:* Alfred Drake, Doretta Morrow, Richard Kiley, Joan Diener, Henry Calvin, Steve Reeves. *Songs:* Stranger in Paradise; Baubles, Bangles and Beads; And This Is My Beloved; Night of My Nights; Sands of Time.

MGM (1955). *Screenplay:* Charles Lederer, Luther Davis. *Score:* Alexander Borodin, Robert Wright, George Forrest. *Director:* Vincente Minnelli. *Choreographer:* Jack Cole. *Cast:* Howard Keel, Ann Blyth, Vic Damone, Dolores Gray, Monty Woolley, Sebastian Cabot. *Songs:* Stranger in Paradise; Baubles, Bangles and Beads; And This Is My Beloved; Night of My Nights; Sands of Time.

Kiss Me, Kate

New Century Theatre, 30 December 1948 (1,070 performances). *Book:* Bella and Samuel Spewack. *Score:* Cole Porter. *Director:* John C. Wilson. *Choreographer:* Hanya Holm. *Cast:* Alfred Drake, Patricia Morison, Lisa Kirk, Harold Lang, Jack Diamond, Harry Clark, Ananelle Lee, Lorenzo Fuller. *Songs:* Wunderbar; So in Love; Another Op'nin', Another Show; Too Darn Hot; Brush Up Your Shakespeare; Always True

to You in My Fashion; I Hate Men; Where Is the Life That Late I Led?;
Were Thine That Special Face.
MGM (1953). *Screenplay:* Dorothy Kingsley. *Score:* Cole Porter. *Director:* George Sidney. *Choreographers:* Hermes Pan, Bob Fosse. *Cast:* Howard Keel, Kathryn Grayson, Ann Miller, Tommy Rall, Keenan Wynn, James Whitmore. *Songs:* Wunderbar; So in Love; From This Moment On; Too Darn Hot; Brush Up Your Shakespeare; Always True to You in My Fashion; I Hate Men; Where Is the Life That Late I Led?; Were Thine That Special Face.

Knickerbocker Holiday
Ethel Barrymore Theatre, 19 October 1938 (168 performances). *Book:* Maxwell Anderson. *Score:* Kurt Weill, Maxwell Anderson. *Director:* Joshua Logan. *Choreographers:* Carl Randall, Edwin Denby. *Cast:* Walter Huston, Ray Middleton, Jeanne Madden, Richard Kollmar, Robert Rounseville, Howard Freeman. *Songs:* September Song; How Can You Tell an American?; It Never Was You; There's Nowhere to Go but Up.
   United Artists (1944). *Screenplay:* David Boehm, Roland Leigh, Harold Goldman. *Score:* Kurt Weill, Maxwell Anderson, etc. *Director:* Harry Joe Brown. *Cast:* Charles Coburn, Nelson Eddy, Constance Dowling, Johnnie "Scat" Davis, Richard Hale, Shelley Winters, Ernest Cossart, Otto Kruger. *Songs:* September Song; There's Nowhere to Go but Up; Love Has Made This Such a Lovely Day; Holiday; One More Smile.

Lady, Be Good!
Liberty Theatre, 1 December 1924 (330 performances). *Book:* Guy Bolton, Fred Thompson. *Score:* George and Ira Gershwin. *Director:* Felix Edwardes. *Choreographer:* Sammy Lee. *Cast:* Adele and Fred Astaire, Jayne Auburn, Walter Catlett, Alan Edwards, Cliff Edwards, Kathlene Martyn. *Songs:* Fascinating Rhythm; Oh, Lady, Be Good!; Hang onto Me; So Am I; The Half of It, Dearie Blues; Little Jazz Bird.
   MGM (1941). *Screenplay:* Jack McGowan, Kay Van Riper, John McClain. *Score:* George and Ira Gershwin, Jerome Kern, Oscar Hammerstein, etc. *Director:* Norman Z. McLeod. *Choreographer:* Busby Berkeley. *Cast:* Ann Sothern, Robert Young, Eleanor Powell, Lionel Barrymore, John Carroll, Red Skelton, Dan Dailey. *Songs:* Fascinating

Rhythm; The Last Time I Saw Paris; Lady Be Good; You'll Never Know; Your Words and My Music.

Lady in the Dark

Alvin Theatre, 23 January 1941 (467 performances). *Book:* Moss Hart. *Score:* Kurt Weill, Ira Gershwin. *Directors:* Hassard Short, Moss Hart. *Choreographer:* Albertina Rasch. *Cast:* Gertrude Lawrence, Macdonald Carey, Danny Kaye, Victor Mature, Bert Lytell. *Songs:* My Ship; The Saga of Jennie; Tschaikowsky; This Is New; Girl of the Moment.
Paramount (1944). *Screenplay:* Frances Goodrich, Albert Hackett. *Score:* Kurt Weill, Ira Gershwin, etc. *Director:* Mitchell Leisen. *Choreographer:* Billy Daniels. *Cast:* Ginger Rogers, Ray Milland, Warner Baxter, Barry Sullivan, Jon Hall, Mischa Auer. *Songs:* The Saga of Jenny; Girl of the Moment; One Life to Live; This Is New; Dream Lover.

Let's Face It!

Imperial Theatre, 29 October 1941 (547 performances). *Book:* Herbert and Dorothy Fields. *Score:* Cole Porter. *Director:* Edgar MacGregor. *Choreographer:* Charles Walters. *Cast:* Danny Kaye, Eve Arden, Benny Baker, Vivian Vance, Mary Jane Walsh, Nanette Fabray, Edith Meiser, Jack Williams. *Songs:* Ace in the Hole; Farming; Melody in 4-F; Let's Not Talk about Love; Ev'rything I Love.
Paramount (1943). *Screenplay:* Harry Tugend. *Score:* Cole Porter, etc. *Director:* Sidney Lanfield. *Cast:* Bob Hope, Betty Hutton, Eve Arden, Phyllis Povah, ZaSu Pitts, Dave Willock, Cully Richards. *Songs:* Let's Not Talk about Love; Let's Face It!; Who Did? I Did.

Li'l Abner

St. James Theatre, 15 November 1956 (693 performances). *Book:* Norman Panama, Melvin Frank. *Score:* Gene de Paul, Johnny Mercer. *Director-choreographer:* Michael Kidd. *Cast:* Peter Palmer, Edith Adams, Stubby Kaye, Charlotte Rae, Howard St. John, Tina Louise, Julie Newmar, Grover Dale. *Songs:* (Don't That Take the) Rag Offen the Bush; Namely You; Jubilation T. Cornpone; If I Had My Druthers; The Country's in the Very Best of Hands.
Panama (1959). *Screenplay:* Norman Panama, Melvin Frank. *Score:* Gene de Paul, Johnny Mercer. *Director:* Melvin Frank. *Choreographers:*

Michael Kidd, Dee Dee Wood. *Cast:* Peter Palmer, Leslie Parrish, Stubby Kaye, Joe E. Marks, Stella Stevens, Howard St. John, Tina Louise, Billie Hayes, Julie Newmar. *Songs:* (Don't That Take the) Rag Offen the Bush; Namely You; Jubilation T. Cornpone; If I Had My Druthers; The Country's in the Very Best of Hands.

Little Johnny Jones
Liberty Theatre, 7 November 1904 (52 performances). *Book and Score:* George M. Cohan. *Director:* George M. Cohan. *Cast:* George M. Cohan, Jerry Cohan, Ethel Levey, Donald Brian, Helen Cohan. *Songs:* The Yankee Doodle Boy; Give My Regards to Broadway; Life's a Funny Proposition after All; They're All My Friends; A Girl I Know.
Warner/First National (1929). *Screenplay:* Adelaide Heilbron. *Score:* George M. Cohan, etc. *Director:* Mervyn LeRoy. *Cast:* Eddie Buzzell, Alice Day, Robert Edeson, Edna Murphy. *Songs:* The Yankee Doodle Boy; Give My Regards to Broadway; Painting the Clouds with Sunshine; Go Find Somebody to Love; My Paradise.

Little Nellie Kelly
Liberty Theatre, 13 November 1922 (276 performances). *Book and Score:* George M. Cohan. *Director:* George M. Cohan. *Choreographer:* Julian Mitchell. *Cast:* Elizabeth Hines, Charles King, Robert Pitkin, Georgia Caine, Arthur Deagon, Frank Parker, Barrett Greenwood, Jack Oakie. *Songs:* Nellie Kelly, I Love You; You Remind Me of My Mother; Till Good Luck Comes Rolling Along; The Voice in My Heart.
MGM (1940). *Screenplay:* Jack McGowan. *Score:* George M. Cohan, Roger Edens, etc. *Director:* Norman Taurog. *Cast:* Judy Garland, George Murphy, Charles Winninger, Douglas MacPhail, Arthur Shields, Rita Page. *Songs:* Nellie Kelly, I Love You; It's a Great Day for the Irish; Singin' in the Rain; Danny Boy; A Pretty Girl Milking Her Cow.

A Little Night Music
Shubert Theatre, 25 February 1973 (600 performances). *Book:* Hugh Wheeler. *Score:* Stephen Sondheim. *Director:* Harold Prince. *Choreographer:* Patricia Birch. *Cast:* Len Cariou, Glynis Johns, Hermione Gingold, Patricia Elliot, Victoria Mallory, Mark Lambert, Laurence Guittard, D. Jamin-Bartlett. *Songs:* Send in the Clowns; Now-Later-Soon;

The Miller's Son; A Weekend in the Country; You Must Meet My Wife; Remember?; The Glamorous Life; Liaisons; Every Day a Little Death; It Would Have Been Wonderful.

Sascha-Wein-New World (1978). *Screenplay:* Hugh Wheeler. *Score:* Stephen Sondheim. *Director:* Harold Prince. *Choreographer:* Patricia Birch. *Cast:* Elizabeth Taylor, Len Cariou, Hermione Gingold, Lesley-Ann Down, Diana Rigg, Laurence Guittard, Chloe Franks. *Songs:* Send in the Clowns; Now-Later-Soon; A Weekend in the Country; You Must Meet My Wife; Remember?; The Glamorous Life; Liaisons; Every Day a Little Death; Love Takes Time; The Letter Song; It Would Have Been Wonderful.

Little Shop of Horrors
Oprheum Theatre, 27, July 1982 (2,209 performances). *Book:* Howard Ashman. *Score:* Alan Menken, Howard Ashman. *Director:* Howard Ashman. *Choreographer:* Edie Cowan. *Cast:* Lee Wilkof, Ellen Greene, Hy Anzell, Franc Luz. *Songs:* Little Shop of Horrors; Somewhere That's Green; Suddenly Seymour; Grow for Me; Skid Row; Feed Me; Dentist.

Geffen (1986). *Screenplay:* Howard Ashman. *Score:* Alan Menken, Howard Ashman. *Director:* Frank Oz. *Choreographer:* Pat Garrett. *Cast:* Rick Moranis, Ellen Greene, Vincent Gardenia, Steve Martin. *Songs:* Little Shop of Horrors; Somewhere That's Green; Suddenly Seymour; Grow for Me; Skid Row; Feed Me; Dentist; Mean Green Mother from Outer Space.

Lost in the Stars
Music Box Theatre, 30 October 1949 (273 performances). *Book:* Maxwell Anderson. *Score:* Kurt Weill, Maxwell Anderson. *Director:* Rouben Mamoulian. *Cast:* Todd Duncan, Leslie Banks, Inez Matthews, Warren Coleman, Julian Mayfield. *Songs:* Trouble Man; Lost in the Stars; Cry the Beloved Country; Stay Well; Train to Johannesburg; Thousands of Miles.

American Film Theatre (1974). *Screenplay:* Alfred Hayes. *Score:* Kurt Weill, Maxwell Anderson. *Director:* Daniel Mann. *Choreographer:* Paula Kelly. *Cast:* Brock Peters, Paul Rogers, Melba Moore, Clifton Davis, Raymond St. Jacques, Paula Kelly, Alan Weeks, Jitu Cumbuka. *Songs:* Trouble Man; Lost in the Stars; Cry the Beloved Country; Bird of Paradise; Train to Johannesburg.

Louisiana Purchase
Imperial Theatre, 28 May 1940 (444 performances). *Book:* Morrie
Ryskind, B. G. DeSylva. *Score:* Irving Berlin. *Director:* Edgar MacGregor. *Choreographer:* George Balanchine. *Cast:* William Gaxton, Victor
Moore, Vera Zorina, Irene Bordoni, Carol Bruce, Nick Long Jr. *Songs:*
It's a Lovely Day Tomorrow; Louisiana Purchase; What Chance Have I
with Love?; You're Lonely and I'm Lonely; Fools Fall in Love; Outside
of That I Love You.
  Paramount (1942). *Screenplay:* Jerome Chodorov, Herbert Fields.
Score: Irving Berlin. *Director:* Irving Cummings. *Cast:* Bob Hope, Victor Moore, Vera Zorina, Irene Bordoni, Dona Drake, Andrew Tombes,
Ray Walburn, Maxie Rosenbloom. *Songs:* It's a Lovely Day Tomorrow;
Louisiana Purchase; You're Lonely and I'm Lonely; Take a Letter to
Paramount Pictures.

Mame
Winter Garden Theatre, 24 May 1966 (1,508 performances). *Book:*
Jerome Lawrence, Robert E. Lee. *Score:* Jerry Herman. *Director:* Gene
Saks. *Choreographer:* Onna White. *Cast:* Angela Lansbury, Beatrice
Arthur, Jane Connell, Frankie Michaels, Charles Braswell, Jerry Lanning. *Songs:* Mame; If He Walked into My Life Today; We Need a Little Christmas; Bosom Buddies; My Best Girl; Open a New Window; It's
Today; That's How Young I Feel.
  Warner (1974). *Screenplay:* Paul Zindel. *Score:* Jerry Herman. *Director:* Gene Saks. *Choreographer:* Onna White. *Cast:* Lucille Ball,
Beatrice Arthur, Robert Preston, Jane Connell, Bruce Davison, John
McGiver, Kirby Furlong, Doria Cook, Joyce Van Patten. *Songs:*
Mame; If He Walked into My Life Today; We Need a Little Christmas; Bosom Buddies; My Best Girl; Open a New Window; It's Today;
Loving You.

Man of LaMancha
ANTA Theatre, 22 November 1965 (2,328 performances). *Book:* Dale
Wasserman. *Score:* Mitch Leigh, Joe Darion. *Director:* Albert Marre.
Choreographer: Jack Cole. *Cast:* Richard Kiley, Joan Diener, Irving Jacobson, Robert Rounseville, Ray Middleton. *Songs:* The Impossible
Dream; To Each His Dulcinea; Man of LaMancha; Dulcinea; What

Does He Want of Me?; I Really Like Him; I'm Only Thinking of Him; Little Birl, Little Bird.
  United Artists (1972). *Screenplay:* Dale Wasserman. *Score:* Mitch Leigh, Joe Darion. *Director:* Arthur Hiller. *Choreographer:* Gillian Lynne. *Cast:* Peter O'Toole, Sophia Loren, James Coco, Harry Andrews, John Castle, Brian Blessed, Julie Gregg, Ian Richardson. *Songs:* The Impossible Dream; To Each His Dulcinea; Man of LaMancha; Dulcinea; I Really Like Him; I'm Only Thinking of Him; Little Birl, Little Bird.

Maytime
Shubert Theatre, 16 August 1917 (492 performances). *Book:* Rida Johnson Young. *Score:* Sigmund Romberg, Rida Johnson Young. *Director:* Edward Temple. *Choreographer:* Allan K. Foster. *Cast:* Peggy Wood, Charles Purcell, William Norris, Ralph Herbert, Gertrude Vanderbilt. *Songs:* Will You Remember?; The Road to Paradise; Jump Jim Crow; Dancing Will Keep You Young.
  MGM (1937). *Screenplay:* Noel Langley. *Score:* Sigmund Romberg, Rida Johnson Young, Herbert Stothart, Robert Wright, George Forrest, etc. *Director:* Robert Z. Leonard. *Cast:* Jeanette MacDonald, Nelson Eddy, John Barrymore, Herman Bing, Harry Davenport, Billy Gilbert, Lynne Carver, Tom Brown, Leonid Kinskey, Walter Kingsford. *Songs:* Will You Remember?; Ham and Eggs; Carry Me Back to Old Virginny.

Me and My Girl
Marquis Theatre, 10 August 1986 (1,420 performances). *Book:* L. Arthur Rose, Douglas Furber, Stephen Fry. *Score:* Noel Gay, L. Arthur Rose, Douglas Furber. *Director:* Mike Ockrent. *Choreographer:* Gillian Gregory. *Cast:* Robert Lindsay, Maryann Plunkett, Timothy Jerome, George S. Irving, Jane Connell, Jane Summerhays, Timothy Jerome, Justine Johnson. *Songs:* The Lambeth Walk; Me and My Girl; Once You Lose Your Heart; Leaning on a Lamppost.
  The Lambeth Walk, MGM (1939). *Screenplay:* John Paddy Carstairs, etc. *Director:* Albert De Courville. *Cast:* Lupino Lane, Sally Gray, Seymour Hicks, Enid Stamp-Taylor, May Hallatt, Wilfrd Hyde-White, Noah Howard. *Songs:* The Lambeth Walk; Me and My Girl; Once You Lose Your Heart; Leaning on a Lamppost.

Mexican Hayride
Winter Garden Theatre, 28 January 1944 (481 performances). *Book:* Herbert and Dorothy Fields. *Score:* Cole Porter. *Directors:* Hassard Short, John Kennedy. *Choreographer:* Paul Haakon. *Cast:* Bobby Clark, June Havoc, Wilbur Evans, George Givot, Luba Malina, Edith Meiser, Paul Haakon, Corinna Mura. *Songs:* I Love You; There Must Be Someone for Me; Sing to Me, Guitar; Count Your Blessings; Abracadabra.
Universal (1948). *Screenplay:* Oscar Brodney, John Grant. *Director:* Charles Barton. *Cast:* Bud Abbott, Lou Costello, Virginia Grey, Luba Malina, John Hubbard, Pedro de Cordoba, Tom Powers, Fritz Feld.

Murder at the Vanities
New Amsterdam Theatre, 12 September 1933 (207 performances). *Book:* Earl Carroll, Rufus King. *Score:* Richard Myers, Edward Heyman, etc. *Director:* Earl Carroll. *Choreographer:* Chester Hale. *Cast:* Pauline Moore, James Rennie, Beryl Wallace, Naomi Ray, Billy House, Jean Adair, Lisa Gilbert, Bela Lugosi, Olga Baclanova, Woods Miller. *Songs:* Sweet Madness; Me for You Forever; Fans; You Love Me; Virgins Wrapped in Cellophane.
Paramount (1934). *Screenplay:* Carey Wilson, Joseph Gollomb, Sam Hellman. *Score:* Arthur Johnston, Sam Coslow. *Director:* Mitchell Leisen. *Choreographers:* Larry Ceballos, LeRoy Prinz. *Cast:* Carl Brisson, Kitty Carlisle, Jack Oakie, Victor McLaglen, Dorothy Stickney, Gertrude Michael, Donald Meek, Gail Patrick. *Songs:* Cocktails for Two; Live and Love Tonight; Where Do They Come from Now?; Lovely One.

Music in the Air
Alvin Theatre, 8 November 1932 (342 performances). *Book:* Oscar Hammerstein. *Score:* Jerome Kern, Oscar Hammerstein. *Directors:* Jerome Kern, Oscar Hammerstein. *Cast:* Katherine Carrington, Al Shean, Walter Slezak, Natalie Hall, Reinald Werrenrath, Tullio Carminati, Nicholas Joy, Marjorie Main. *Songs:* I've Told Ev'ry Little Star; There's a Hill Beyond a Hill; The Song Is You; In Egern on the Tegern See; And Love Was Born; We Belong Together; I'm Alone; I Am So Eager; One More Dance.

Fox (1934). *Screenplay:* Howard Young, Billy Wilder. *Score:* Jerome Kern, Oscar Hammerstein. *Director:* Joe May. *Choreographer:* Jack Donohue. *Cast:* John Boles, Gloria Swanson, Douglass Montgomery, Al Shean, Reginald Owen, June Lang, Joseph Cawthorn, Fuzzy Knight, Marjorie Main. *Songs:* I've Told Ev'ry Little Star; There's a Hill beyond a Hill; We Belong Together; I'm Alone; I Am So Eager; One More Dance.

The Music Man
Majestic Theatre, 19 December 1957 (1,375 performances). *Book:* Meredith Willson, Franklin Lacey. *Score:* Meredith Willson. *Director:* Morton Da Costa. *Choreographer:* Onna White. *Cast:* Robert Preston, Barbara Cook, David Burns, Iggie Wolfington, Pert Kelton, Eddie Hodges, Buffalo Bills. *Songs:* Till There Was You; Seventy-Six Trombones; Goodnight, My Someone; Marian the Librarian; Trouble; Rock Island; Lida Rose; It's You; My White Knight; Shipoopi; Gary, Indiana.
Warner (1962). *Screenplay:* Marian Hargrove. *Score:* Meredith Willson. *Director:* Morton Da Costa. *Choreographer:* Onna White. *Cast:* Robert Preston, Shirley Jones, Buddy Hackett, Paul Ford, Hermione Gingold, Pert Kelton, Ronnie Howard, Buffalo Bills. *Songs:* Till There Was You; Seventy-Six Trombones; Goodnight, My Someone; Marian the Librarian; Trouble; Rock Island; Lida Rose; Being in Love; Shipoopi; Gary, Indiana.

My Fair Lady
Mark Hellinger Theatre, 15 March 1956 (2,717 performances). *Book:* Alan Jay Lerner. *Score:* Frederick Loewe, Alan Jay Lerner. *Director:* Moss Hart. *Choreographer:* Hanya Holm. *Cast:* Rex Harrison, Julie Andrews, Stanley Holloway, Robert Coote, John Michael King, Cathleen Nesbit. *Songs:* I've Grown Accustomed to Her Face; I Could Have Danced All Night; On the Street Where You Live; Wouldn't It Be Loverly?; Get Me to the Church on Time; The Rain in Spain; Show Me; A Hymn to Him; Without You.
Warner (1964). *Screenplay:* Alan Jay Lerner. *Score:* Frederick Loewe, Alan Jay Lerner. *Director:* George Cukor. *Choreographer:* Hermes Pan. *Cast:* Rex Harrison, Audrey Hepburn, Stanley Holloway, Wilfred Hyde-White, Jeremy Brett, Gladys Cooper, Theodore Bikel. *Songs:* I've

Grown Accustomed to Her Face; I Could Have Danced All Night; On the Street Where You Live; Wouldn't It Be Loverly?; Get Me to the Church on Time; The Rain in Spain; Show Me; A Hymn to Him; Without You.

Naughty Marietta

New York Theatre, 7 November 1910 (136 performances). *Book:* Rida Johnson Young. *Score:* Victor Herbert, Rida Johnson Young. *Director:* Jacques Coini. *Choreography:* Pauline Verhoeven. *Cast:* Emma Trentini, Orville Harrold, Marie Duchene, Peggy Wood, Edward Martindel. *Songs:* Italian Street Song; Ah! Sweet Mystery of Life; Tramp! Tramp! Tramp!; I'm Falling in Love with Someone; 'Neath the Southern Moon.

MGM (1935). *Screenplay:* John Lee Mahin, Frances Goodrich, Albert Hackett. *Score:* Victor Herbert, Rida Johnson Young. *Director:* W. S. Van Dyke. *Choreography:* Chester Hale. *Cast:* Jeanette MacDonald, Nelson Eddy, Frank Morgan, Elsa Lanchester, Douglass Dumbrille, Marjorie Main, Joseph Cawthorn, Akim Tamiroff, Cecilia Parker. *Songs:* Italian Street Song; Ah! Sweet Mystery of Life; Tramp! Tramp! Tramp!; I'm Falling in Love with Someone; Chansonette; 'Neath the Southern Moon.

The New Moon

Imperial Theatre, 19 September 1928 (509 performances). *Book:* Oscar Hammerstein, Frank Mandel, Laurence Schwab. *Score:* Sigmund Romberg, Oscar Hammerstein. *Director:* Edgar MacGregor. *Choreographer:* Bobby Connolly. *Cast:* Evelyn Herbert, Robert Halliday, William O'Neal, Gus Shy, Max Figman. *Songs:* One Kiss; Softly, As in a Morning Sunrise; Stouthearted Men; Lover, Come Back to Me; Wanting You; Marianne.

MGM (1930). *Screenplay:* Sylvia Thalberg, Frank Butler. *Score:* Sigmund Romberg, Oscar Hammerstein. *Director:* Jack Conway. *Cast:* Grace Moore, Lawrence Tibbett, Adolphe Menjou, Roland Young, Gus Shy, Emily Fitzroy. *Songs:* One Kiss; Stouthearted Men; Lover, Come Back to Me; Wanting You; Marianne.

MGM (1940). *Screenplay:* Jacques Deval, Robert Arthur. *Score:* Sigmund Romberg, Oscar Hammerstein. *Director:* Robert Z. Leonard.

Choreographer: Val Raset. *Cast:* Jeanette MacDonald, Nelson Eddy, Mary Boland, George Zucco, Richard Purcell, Grant Mitchell, H. B. Warner. *Songs:* One Kiss; Softly, As in a Morning Sunrise; Stouthearted Men; Lover, Come Back to Me; Wanting You; Marianne.

No No Nanette
Globe Theatre, 16 September 1925 (321 performances). *Book:* Otto Harbach, Frank Mandel. *Score:* Vincent Youmans, Otto Harbach, Irving Caesar. *Director:* H. H. Frazee. *Choreographer:* Sammy Lee. *Cast:* Louise Groody, Charles Winninger, Wellington Cross, Josephine Whittell, Georgia O'Ramey, Mary Lawlor, John Barker. *Songs:* Tea for Two; I Want to Be Happy; No No Nanette; Too Many Rings around Rosie; Where Has My Hubby Gone? Blues; You Can Dance with Any Girl at All.

First National (1930). *Screenplay:* Howard Emmett Rogers. *Score:* Vincent Youmans, Otto Harbach, Irving Caesar, etc. *Director:* Clarence Badger. *Choreographer:* Larry Ceballos. *Cast:* Bernice Claire, Alexander Gray, Bert Roach, Lilyan Tashman, ZaSu Pitts, Louise Fazenda, Lucien Littlefield. *Songs:* Tea for Two; I Want to Be Happy; No No Nanette; Dance of the Wooden Shoes; As Long as I'm with You; Dancing to Heaven.

RKO (1940). *Screenplay:* Ken Englund. *Score:* Vincent Youmans, Otto Harbach, Irving Caesar. *Director:* Herbert Wilcox. *Choreographer:* Larry Ceballos. *Cast:* Anna Neagle, Richard Carlson, Victor Mature, Helen Broderick, Roland Young, ZaSu Pitts, Tamara, Eve Arden, Billy Gilbert. *Songs:* Tea for Two; I Want to Be Happy; No No Nanette; Where Has My Hubby Gone? Blues; Take a Little One-Step.

Oklahoma!
St. James Theatre, 31 March 1943 (2,212 performances). *Book:* Oscar Hammerstein. *Score:* Richard Rodgers, Oscar Hammerstein. *Director:* Rouben Mamoulian. *Choreographer:* Agnes de Mille. *Cast:* Alfred Drake, Joan Roberts, Bette Garde, Celeste Holm, Joseph Buloff, Howard Da Silva, Lee Dixon, Joan McCracken. *Songs:* Oh, What a Beautiful Mornin'; The Surrey with the Fringe on Top; People Will Say We're in Love; Oklahoma; I Cain't Say No; Kansas City; Many a New Day; Pore Jud; Out of My Dreams; All er Nothin'; Lonely Room; The Farmer and the Cowman.

Magna/Fox (1955). *Screenplay:* Sonia Levien, William Ludwig. *Score:* Richard Rodgers, Oscar Hammerstein. *Director:* Fred Zinnemann. *Choreographer:* Agnes de Mille. *Cast:* Gordon MacRae, Shirley Jones, Charlotte Greenwood, Gloria Grahame, Eddie Albert, Gene Nelson, Rod Steiger. *Songs:* Oh, What a Beautiful Mornin'; The Surrey with the Fringe on Top; People Will Say We're in Love; Oklahoma; I Cain't Say No; Kansas City; Many a New Day; Pore Jud; Out of My Dreams; All er Nothin'; The Farmer and the Cowman.

Oliver!

Imperial Theatre, 6 January 1963 (744 performances). *Book and Score:* Lionel Bart. *Director:* Peter Coe. *Cast:* Clive Revill, Georgia Brown, Bruce Prochnick, Willoughby Goddard, Hope Jackman, Danny Sewell, David Jones, Barry Humphries. *Songs:* Consider Yourself; As Long as He Needs Me; Food, Glorious Food; Who Will Buy?; Where Is Love?

Columbia (1968). *Screenplay:* Vernon Harris. *Score:* Lionel Bart. *Director:* Carol Reed. *Choreographer:* Onna White. *Cast:* Ron Moody, Shani Wallis, Mark Lester, Jack Wild, Oliver Reed, Harry Secombe, Hugh Griffith. *Songs:* Consider Yourself; As Long as He Needs Me; Food, Glorious Food; Who Will Buy?; Where Is Love?

On a Clear Day You Can See Forever

Mark Hellinger Theatre, 17 October 1965 (280 performances). *Book:* Alan Jay Lerner. *Score:* Burton Lane, Alan Jay Lerner. *Director:* Robert Lewis. *Choreographer:* Herbert Ross. *Cast:* Barbara Harris, John Cullum, William Daniels, Clifford David, Titos Vandis. *Songs:* On a Clear Day You Can See Forever; Come Back to Me; Hurry! It's Lovely Up Here; On the S. S. *Bernard Cohn;* What Did I Have That I Don't Have?; Melinda; Wait till We're Sixty-Five; She Wasn't You.

Paramount (1970). *Screenplay:* Alan Jay Lerner. *Score:* Burton Lane, Alan Jay Lerner. *Director:* Vincente Minnelli. *Cast:* Barbra Streisand, Yves Montand, Larry Blyden, Bob Newhart, Simon Oakland, Jack Nicholson, John Richardson. *Songs:* On a Clear Day You Can See Forever; Come Back to Me; Hurry! It's Lovely Up Here; Love with All the Trimmings; Go to Sleep; What Did I Have That I Don't Have?; Melinda; He Wasn't You.

On the Town
Adelphi Theatre, 28 December 1944 (463 performances). *Book:* Betty Comden, Adolph Green. *Score:* Leonard Bernstein, Betty Comden, Adolph Green. *Director:* George Abbott. *Choreographer:* Jerome Robbins. *Cast:* John Battles, Betty Comden, Adolph Green, Nancy Walker, Sono Osato, Cris Alexander, Alice Pearce. *Songs:* New York, New York; Some Other Time; Lucky to Be Me; Lonely Town; Come Up to My Place; I Get Carried Away; Ya Got Me.
MGM (1949). *Screenplay:* Betty Comden, Adolph Green. *Score:* Leonard Bernstein, Betty Comden, Adolph Green, Roger Edens. *Director-choreographers:* Gene Kelly, Stanley Donen. *Cast:* Gene Kelly, Frank Sinatra, Vera-Ellen, Jules Munshin, Ann Miller, Betty Garrett, Florence Bates, Alice Pearce. *Songs:* New York, New York; Come Up to My Place; Count on Me; Prehistoric Man; Main Street; On the Town.

On Your Toes
Imperial Theatre, 11 April 1936 (315 performances). *Book:* George Abbott, Richard Rodgers, Lorenz Hart. *Score:* Richard Rodgers, Lorenz Hart. *Directors:* Worthington Miner, George Abbott. *Choreographer:* George Balanchine. *Cast:* Ray Bolger, Tamara Geva, Luella Gear, Monty Woolley, Doris Carson, David Morris. *Songs:* There's a Small Hotel; On Your Toes; Glad to Be Unhappy; Quiet Night; Too Good for the Average Man; It's Got to Be Love; The Heart Is Quicker Than the Eye.
Warner/First National (1939). *Screenplay:* Jerry Wald, Richard Macaulay. *Director:* Ray Enright. *Choreographer:* George Balanchine. *Cast:* Eddie Albert, Vera Zorina, James Gleason, Alan Hale, Frank McHugh, Leonid Kinskey, Donald O'Connor, Gloria Dickson, Queenie Smith.

One Touch of Venus
Imperial Theatre, 7 October 1943 (567 performances). *Book:* S. J. Perelman, Ogden Nash. *Score:* Kurt Weill, Ogden Nash. *Director:* Elia Kazan. *Choreographer:* Agnes de Mille. *Cast:* Mary Martin, Kenny Baker, John Boles, Teddy Hart, Paula Lawrence, Ruth Bond, Sono Osato, Harry Clark. *Songs:* Speak Low; That's Him; I'm a Stranger Here Myself; Foolish Heart; The Trouble with Women; How Much I Love You; West Wind.

Universal (1948). *Screenplay:* Harry Kurnitz, Frank Tashlin. *Score:* Kurt Weill, Ogden Nash. *Director:* William A. Seiter. *Choreographer:* Billy Daniels. *Cast:* Ava Gardner, Robert Walker, Dick Haymes, Eve Arden, Olga San Juan, Tom Conway, Sara Allgood. *Songs:* Speak Low; That's Him; The Trouble with Women; Don't Look Now But My Heart Is Showing.

Paint Your Wagon
Shubert Theatre, 12 November 1951 (289 performances). *Book:* Alan Jay Lerner. *Score:* Frederick Loewe, Alan Jay Lerner. *Director:* Daniel Mann. *Choreographer:* Agnes de Mille. *Cast:* James Barton, Olga San Juan, Marijane Maricle, Tony Bavaar, James Mitchell, Kay Medford. *Songs:* They Call the Wind Maria; I Talk to the Trees; I Still See Elisa; Wand'rin' Star; I'm on My Way; There's a Coach Comin' In; What's Going on Here?; Another Autumn.
   Paramount (1969). *Screenplay:* Alan Jay Lerner, Paddy Chayefsky. *Score:* Frederick Loewe, Alan Jay Lerner, André Previn. *Director:* Joshua Logan. *Choreographer:* Jack Baker. *Cast:* Lee Marvin, Clint Eastwood, Jean Seberg, Harve Presnell, Ray Walston. *Songs:* They Call the Wind Maria; I Talk to the Trees; I Still See Elisa; Wand'rin' Star; The First Thing You Know; Gold Fever; A Million Miles Away behind the Door.

The Pajama Game
St. James Theatre, 13 May 1954 (1,063 performances). *Book:* George Abbott, Richard Bissell. *Score:* Richard Adler, Jerry Ross. *Director:* George Abbott. *Choreographer:* Bob Fosse. *Cast:* John Raitt, Janis Paige, Eddie Foy Jr., Carol Haney. *Songs:* Hey, There; Hernando's Hideaway; Steam Heat; I'm Not at All in Love; Once a Year Day; Seven and a Half Cents.
   Warner (1957). *Screenplay:* George Abbott, Richard Bissell. *Score:* Richard Adler, Jerry Ross. *Directors:* George Abbott, Stanley Donan. *Choreographer:* Bob Fosse. *Cast:* John Raitt, Doris Day, Eddie Foy Jr., Carol Haney. *Songs:* Hey, There; Hernando's Hideaway; Steam Heat; I'm Not at All in Love; Once a Year Day; Seven-and-a-Half Cents.

Pal Joey
Ethel Barrymore Theatre, 25 December 1940 (374 performances). *Book:* John O'Hara. *Score:* Richard Rodgers, Lorenz Hart. *Director:* George Ab-

bott. *Choreographer:* Robert Alton. *Cast:* Gene Kelly, Vivienne Segal, Leila Ernst, June Havoc, Jean Casto, Jack Durant, Van Johnson. *Songs:* Bewitched, Bothered, and Bewildered; I Could Write a Book; You Mustn't Kick It Around; Den of Iniquity; Take Him; Zip; That Terrific Rainbow.

Columbia (1957). *Screenplay:* Dorothy Kingsley. *Score:* Richard Rodgers, Lorenz Hart. *Director:* George Sidney. *Choreographer:* Hermes Pan. *Cast:* Frank Sinatra, Rita Hayworth, Kim Novak, Barbara Nichols, Bobby Sherwood, Hank Henry. *Songs:* Bewitched; I Could Write a Book; Zip; That Terrific Rainbow; My Funny Valentine; The Lady Is a Tramp; There's a Small Hotel.

Panama Hattie

46th Street Theatre, 30 October 1940 (501 performances). *Book:* Herbert Fields, B. G. DeSylva. *Score:* Cole Porter. *Director:* Edgar MacGregor. *Choreographer:* Robert Alton. *Cast:* Ethel Merman, Joan Carroll, Arthur Treacher, James Dunn, Rags Ragland, Pat Harrington, Frank Hyers, Betty Hutton, June Allyson. *Songs:* Let's Be Buddies; I've Still Got My Health; Make It Another Old-Fashioned, Please; I'm Throwing a Ball Tonight; My Mother Would Love You.

MGM (1942). *Screenplay:* Jack McGowan, Wilkie Mahoney. *Score:* Cole Porter, etc. *Director:* Norman Z. McLeod. *Choreographer:* Danny Dare. *Cast:* Ann Sothern, Jackie Horner, Lena Horne, Virginia O'Brien, Red Skelton, Rags Ragland, Ben Blue, Marsha Hunt, Dan Dailey, Alan Mowbray. *Songs:* Let's Be Buddies; I've Still Got My Health; Make It Another Old-Fashioned, Please; Just One of Those Things; Fresh as a Daisy; The Son of a Gun Who Picks on Uncle Sam; Hattie from Panama; Good Neighbors.

Paris

Music Box Theatre, 8 October 1928 (195 performances). *Book:* Martin Brown. *Score:* Cole Porter, Walter Kollo, E. Ray Goetz, etc. *Director:* W. H. Gilmore. *Cast:* Irene Bordoni, Arthur Margetson, Louise Closser Hale, Erik Kalkhurst, Elizabeth Chester, Irving Aaronson and His Commanders. *Songs:* Let's Do It (Let's Fall in Love)!; Two Little Babes in the Wood; Don't Look at Me That Way; The Land of Going to Be; Paris; An' Futhermore.

First National (1929). *Screenplay:* Hope Lorning. *Score:* Al Bryan, Ed Ward. *Director:* Clarence Badger. *Choreographer:* Larry Cebellos.

Cast: Irene Bordoni, Jack Buchanan, Louise Closer Hale, Jason Robards, Margaret Fielding, ZaSu Pitts. *Songs:* Miss Wonderful; Paris; I Wonder What Is Really on His Mind; Crystal Girl; Somebody Mighty Like You.

Porgy and Bess
Alvin Theatre, 10 October 1935 (124 performances). *Book:* DuBose Heyward. *Score:* George and Ira Gershwin, DuBose Heyward. *Director:* Rouben Mamoulian. *Cast:* Todd Duncan, Anne Brown, John W. Bubbles, Warren Coleman, Abbie Mitchell, Ruby Elzy, Georgette Harvey, Edward Matthews. *Songs:* Summertime; Bess, You Is My Woman Now; I Got Plenty o' Nuttin'; It Ain't Neccessarily So; My Man's Gone Now; A Woman Is a Sometime Thing; I Loves You, Porgy; There's a Boat Dat Leavin' for Soon New York; I'm on My Way.
   Columbia/Goldwyn (1959). *Screenplay:* N. Richard Nash. *Score:* George and Ira Gershwin, DuBose Heyward. *Director:* Otto Preminger. *Choreographer:* Hermes Pan. *Cast:* Sidney Poitier (singing dubbed by Robert McFerrin), Dorothy Dandridge (singing dubbed by Adele Addison), Sammy Davis Jr., Brock Peters, Pearl Bailey, Ruth Attaway, Diahann Carroll, Leslie Scott. *Songs:* Summertime; Bess, You Is My Woman Now; I Got Plenty o' Nuttin'; It Ain't Neccessarily So; My Man's Gone Now; A Woman Is a Sometime Thing; I Loves You, Porgy; There's a Boat Dat Leavin' for Soon New York; I'm on My Way.

Present Arms
Mansfield Theatre, 26 April 1928 (155 performances). *Book:* Herbert Fields. *Score:* Richard Rodgers, Lorenz Hart. *Director:* Alexander Leftwich. *Choreographer:* Busby Berkeley. *Cast:* Charles King, Flora LeBreton, Busby Berkeley, Joyce Babour, Franker Woods, Fuller Mellish Jr., Gaile Beverley. *Songs:* You Took Advantage of Me; A Kiss for Cinderella; Blue Ocean Blues; Do I Hear You Saying "I Love You?"
   Leathernecking, RKO (1930). *Screenplay:* Jane Murtin. *Score:* Richard Rodgers, Lorenz Hart, etc. *Director:* Edward Cline. *Choreographer:* Peal Eaton. *Cast:* Irene Dunne, Ken Murray, Benny Rubin, Lilyan Tashman, Eddie Joy Jr., Fred Santley, Ned Sparks, Louise Fazenda. *Songs:* You Took Advantage of Me; A Kiss for Cinderella; All My Life; Shake It Off and Smile; Careless Kisses; Evening Star.

The Ramblers

Lyric Theatre, 20 September 1926 (289 performances). *Book*: Bert Kalmar, Harry Ruby, Guy Bolton. *Score*: Bert Kalmar, Harry Ruby. *Director*: John Harwood. *Choreographer*: Sammy Lee. *Cast*: Bobby Clark, Paul McCullough, Marie Saxon, Willian E. Browning, Jack Whiting, William Sully, Ruth Tester, Georgia O'Ramey. *Songs*: All Alone Monday; You Smiled at Me; Any Little Tune; Like You Do; You Must—We Won't; California Skies.

The Cuckoos, Radio Pictures (1930). *Screenplay*: Chris Wood. *Score*: Bert Kalmar, Harry Ruby, etc. *Director*: Paul Sloane. *Choreographer*: Pearl Eaton. *Cast*: Bert Wheeler, Robert Woolsey, June Clyde, Dorothy Lee, Hugh Trevor, Mitchell Lewis, Ivan Lebedeff, Jobyna Howland. *Songs*: All Alone Monday; I Love You So Much; Knock Knees; Looking for the Limelight in Your Eyes; Dancing the Devil Away; If I Were a Traveling Salesman.

Rio Rita

Ziegfeld Theatre, 2 February 1927 (495 performances). *Book*: Guy Bolton, Fred Thompson. *Score*: Harry Tierney, Joseph McCarthy. *Director*: John Harwood. *Choreographer*: Sammy Lee, Albertina Rasch. *Cast*: Ethelind Terry, J. Harold Murray, Bert Wheeler, Robert Woolsey, Ada May, Vincent Serrano. *Songs*: Rio Rita; The Rangers' Song; If You're in Love You'll Waltz; The Kinkajou; Following the Sun Around.

RKO (1929). *Screenplay*: Russell Mack, Luther Reed. *Score*: Harry Tierney, Joseph McCarthy. *Director*: Luther Reed. *Choreographer*: Pearl Eaton. *Cast*: Bebe Daniels, John Boles, Bert Wheeler, Robert Woolsey, Don Alvarado, Eva Rosita, George Renavent. *Songs*: Rio Rita; The Ranger's Song; If You're in Love You'll Waltz; River Song; The Kinkajou; You're Always in My Arms; Poor Fool.

MGM (1942). *Screenplay*: Richard Connell, Gladys Lehman. *Score*: Harry Tierney, Joseph McCarthy, etc. *Director*: S. Sylvan Simon. *Cast*: Bud Abbott, Lou Costello, Kathryn Grayson, John Carroll, Patricia Dane, Tom Conway, Barry Nelson. *Songs*: Rio Rita; The Ranger's Song; Long Before You Came Along; Brazilian Dance.

Roberta

New Amsterdam Theatre, 18 November 1933 (295 performances). *Book*: Otto Harbach. *Score*: Jerome Kern, Otto Harbach. *Director*: Hassard Short. *Choreographer:* José Limon. *Cast:* Bob Hope, Tamara, Lyda Roberti, Fay Templeton, George Murphy, Sydney Greenstreet, Ray Middleton, Fred MacMurray. *Songs:* Smoke Gets in Your Eyes; Yesterdays; The Touch of Your Hand; Let's Begin; I'll Be Hard to Handle; You're Devastating; Something Had to Happen.

   RKO (1935). *Screenplay:* Jane Murfin, Stan Mintz, Glen Tryon, Allan Scott. *Score:* Jerome Kern, Otto Harbach, Dorothy Fields. *Director:* William A. Seiter. *Choreographers:* Hermes Pan, Fred Astaire. *Cast:* Fred Astaire, Irene Dunne, Ginger Rogers, Randolph Scott, Helen Westley, Victor Varconi, Lucille Ball. *Songs:* Smoke Gets in Your Eyes; Yesterdays; Lovely to Look At; I Won't Dance; Let's Begin; I'll Be Hard to Handle.

   Lovely to Look At, MGM (1952). *Screenplay:* George Wells, Harry Ruby. *Score:* Jerome Kern, Otto Harbach, Dorothy Fields. *Directors:* Mervyn LeRoy, Vincente Minnelli. *Choreographer:* Hermes Pan. *Cast:* Kathryn Grayson, Howard Keel, Red Skelton, Marge and Gower Champion, Zsa Zsa Gabor, Kurt Kasznar. *Songs:* Smoke Gets in Your Eyes; Lovely to Look At; I Won't Dance; I'll Be Hard to Handle; You're Devastating; The Touch of Your Hand.

The Rocky Horror Show

Belasco Theatre, 10 March 1975 (45 performances). *Book and Score:* Richard O'Brien. *Director:* Jim Sharman. *Cast:* Tim Curry, Bill Miller, Abigale Haness, Richard O'Brien, Jamie Donnelly, Boni Enten, Kim Milford, Meatloaf, Graham Jarvis. *Songs:* Time Warp; Science Fiction, Double Feature; Sweet Tranvestite; Hot Patootie.

   The Rocky Horror Picture Show, Fox (1975). *Screenplay:* Richard O'Brien, Jim Sharman. *Score:* Richard O'Brien. *Director:* Jim Sharman. *Choreographer:* David Toguri. *Cast:* Tim Curry, Susan Sarandon, Barry Bostwick, Meatloaf, Jonathan Adams, Nell Campbell, Peter Hinwood. *Songs:* Time Warp; Science Fiction, Double Feature; Sweet Tranvestite; Hot Patootie.

Rosalie

New Amsterdam Theatre, 10 January1928 (335 performances). *Book:* William Anthony McGuire, Guy Bolton. *Score:* George and Ira Gershwin, Sigmund Romberg, P. G. Wodehouse. *Director:* William Anthony McGuire. *Choreographers:* Seymour Felix, Michel Fokine. *Cast:* Marilyn Miller, Jack Donahue, Frank Morgan, Margaret Dale, Bobbe Arnst,

Oliver McLennan. *Songs:* How Long Has This Been Going On?; Say So!; West Point Song; Oh, Gee! Oh, Joy!; Ev'rybody Knows I Love Somebody.

MGM (1937). *Screenplay:* William Anthony McGuire. *Score:* Cole Porter. *Director:* W. S. Van Dyke. *Choreographer:* Albertina Rasch. *Cast:* Eleanor Powell, Nelson Eddy, Frank Morgan, Ray Bolger, Ilona Massey, Billy Gilbert, Edna May Oliver, Reginald Owen, George Zucco, William Demarest. *Songs:* Rosalie; In the Still of the Night; Who Knows?; I've a Strange New Rhythm in My Heart; Spring Love Is in the Air.

Rose-Marie

Imperial Theatre, 2 September 1924 (557 performances). *Book:* Otto Harbach, Oscar Hammerstein. *Score:* Rudolf Friml, Herbert Stothart, Otto Harbach, Oscar Hammerstein. *Director:* Paul Dickey. *Choreographer:* David Bennett. *Cast:* Mary Ellis, Dennis King, Frank Greene, William Kent, Dorothy Mackaye, Eduardo Ciannelli, Pearl Regay, Arthur Deagon. *Songs:* Indian Love Call; The Mounties; Rose-Marie; Totem Tom-Tom; The Door of Her Dreams; Why Shouldn't We?

Rose Marie, MGM (1936). *Screenplay:* Frances Goodrich, Albert Hackett, Alice Duer Miller. *Score:* Rudolf Friml, Herbert Stothart, Otto Harbach, Oscar Hammerstein, etc. *Director:* W. S. Van Dyke. *Choreographer:* Chester Hale. *Cast:* Jeanette MacDonald, Nelson Eddy, Reginald Owen, James Stewart, Allan Jones, Una O'Connor, Alan Mowbray, David Niven, Herman Bing, George Regas, Gilda Gray. *Songs:* Indian Love Call; The Mounties; Rose-Marie; Diana; Totem Tom-Tom; Some of These Days; Pardon Me, Madame.

Rose Marie, MGM (1954). *Screenplay:* Ronald Millar, George Froeschel. *Score:* Rudolf Friml, Herbert Stothart, Otto Harbach, Oscar Hammerstein, Paul Francis Webster, etc. *Director:* Mervyn LeRoy. *Choreographer:* Busby Berkeley. *Cast:* Ann Blyth, Howard Keel, Joan Taylor, Fernando Lamas, Bert Lahr, Marjorie Main, Ray Collins. *Songs:* Indian Love Call; The Mounties; Rose-Marie; I'm a Mountie Who Never Got His Man; Totem Tom-Tom; The Right Place for a Girl; Free to Be Free.

Sally

New Amsterdam Theatre, 21 December 1920 (570 performances). *Book:* Guy Bolton. *Score:* Jerome Kern, Clifford Grey, B. G. DeSylva, P. G.

Wodehouse, etc. *Director-choreographer:* Edward Royce. *Cast:* Marilyn Miller, Leon Errol, Walter Catlett, Mary Hay, Irving Fisher, Stanley Ridges. *Songs:* Look for the Silver Lining; Wild Rose; Whip-Poor-Will; Sally; The Church 'Round the Corner; The Lorelei. Warner/First National (1929). *Screenplay:* Walldemar Young. *Score:* Jerome Kern, Clifford Grey, B. G. DeSylva, etc. *Director:* John Francis Dillon. *Choreographer:* Larry Ceballos. *Cast:* Marilyn Miller, Alexander Gray, Joe E. Brown, T. Roy Barnes, Pert Kelton, Ford Sterling, Maude Turner Gordon. *Songs:* Look for the Silver Lining; Sally; All I Want to Do Do Do Is Dance; Walking Off Those Balkan Blues; What Will I Do without You?

1776

46th Street Theatre, 16 March 1969 (1,217 performances). *Book:* Peter Stone. *Score:* Sherman Edwards. *Director:* Peter Hunt. *Choreographer:* Onna White. *Cast:* William Daniels, Howard Da Silva, Ken Howard, Paul Hecht, Clifford David, Virginia Vestoff, Ron Holgate, Betty Buckley. *Songs:* Sit Down, John; Molassas to Rum; Momma Look Sharp; But Mr. Adams; He Plays the Violin; Cool, Cool, Considerate Men; Is Anybody There?; The Egg.

Columbia (1972). *Screenplay:* Peter Stone. *Score:* Sherman Edwards. *Director:* Peter Hunt. *Choreographer:* Onna White. *Cast:* William Daniels, Howard Da Silva, Ken Howard, Donald Madden, John Cullum, Virginia Vestoff, Ron Holgate, Ray Middleton, Blythe Danner. *Songs:* Sit Down, John; Molassas to Rum; Momma Look Sharp; But Mr. Adams; He Plays the Violin; Is Anybody There?; The Egg.

Shinbone Alley

Broadway Theatre, 13 April 1957 (49 performances). *Book:* Mel Brooks, Joe Darion. *Score:* George Kleinsinger, Joe Darion. *Choreographer:* Rod Alexander. *Cast:* Eddie Bracken, Earttha Kitt, Ross Martin, George S. Irving, Gwen Harmon, Erik Rhodes, Allegra Kent, Jacques D'Amboise. *Songs:* Shinbone Alley; Flotsam and Jetsam; Toujours Gai; A Woman Wouldn't Be a Woman; Come to Mee-ow; Way Down Blues; True Romance.

Allied Artists (1971). *Screenplay:* Mel Brooks, Joe Darion. *Score:* George Kleinsinger, Joe Darion. *Director:* John David Wilson. *Voices:* Eddie Bracken, Carol Channing, Alan Reed, Ken Sanson, Hall Smith.

Songs: Flotsam and Jetsam; Toujours Gai; A Woman Wouldn't Be a Woman; Cheerio My Deario.

Show Boat
Ziegfeld Theatre, 27 December 1927 (572 performances). *Book:* Oscar Hammerstein. *Score:* Jerome Kern, Oscar Hammerstein. *Directors:* Zeke Colvan, Oscar Hammerstein. *Choreographer:* Sammy Lee. *Cast:* Norma Terris, Howard Marsh, Charles Winninger, Helen Morgan, Jules Bledsoe, Edna May Oliver, Eva Puck, Sammy White, Tess Gardella. *Songs:* Ol' Man River; Make Believe; Can't Help Lovin' Dat Man; You Are Love; Bill; Why Do I Love You?; Life Upon the Wicked Stage.
Universal (1929). *Screenplay:* Charles Kenyon. *Score:* Jerome Kern, Oscar Hammerstein, etc. *Director:* Harry Pollard. *Cast:* Laura La Plante, Joseph Schildkraut, Alma Rubens, Otis Harlan, Emily Fitzroy, Stepin Fetchit, Elise Bartlett, Jack McDonald, Jules Bledsoe (voice only). *Songs:* Ol' Man River; Can't Help Lovin' Dat Man; Bill; The Lonesome Road; Deep River; Here Comes That Show Boat; Down South.
Universal (1936). *Screenplay:* Oscar Hammerstein. *Score:* Jerome Kern, Oscar Hammerstein. *Director:* James Whale. *Choreographer:* LeRoy Prinz. *Cast:* Irene Dunne, Allan Jones, Helen Morgan, Charles Winniger, Paul Robeson, Helen Westley, Donald Cook, Queenie Smith, Sammy White, Hattie McDaniel, Harry Barris. *Songs:* Ol' Man River; Make Believe; Can't Help Lovin' Dat Man; You Are Love; Bill; I Have the Room Above Her; Where's the Mate for Me?; Ah Still Suits Me.
MGM (1951). *Screenplay:* John Lee Mahin. *Score:* Jerome Kern, Oscar Hammerstein. *Director:* George Sidney. *Choreographer:* Robert Alton. *Cast:* Kathryn Grayson, Howard Keel, Ava Gardner, Joe E. Brown, William Warfield, Agnes Moorehead, Marge and Gower Champion. *Songs:* Ol' Man River; Make Believe; Can't Help Lovin' Dat Man; You Are Love; Bill; Why Do I Love You?; Life Upon the Wicked Stage; I Might Fall Back on You.

Silk Stockings
Imperial Theatre, 24 February 1955 (478 performances). *Book:* George S. Kaufman, Leueen McGrath, Abe Burrows. *Score:* Cole Porter. *Director:* Cy Feuer. *Choreographer:* Eugene Loring. *Cast:* Hildegarde Neff, Philip

Sterling, Dom Ameche, George Tobias, Gretchen Wyler, Leon Belasco, Henry Lascoe. *Songs:* All of You; Paris Loves Lovers; It's a Chemical Reaction, That's All; Without Love; The Red Blues; Too Bad. MGM (1957). *Screenplay:* Leonard Gershe, Leonard Spiegelgass. *Score:* Cole Porter. *Director:* Rouben Mamoulian. *Choreographers:* Eugene Loring, Hermes Pan, Fred Astaire. *Cast:* Fred Astaire, Cyd Charisse, Janis Paige, Peter Lorre, George Tobias, Jules Munshin, Joseph Buloff, Barrie Chase. *Songs:* All of You; Paris Loves Lovers; It's a Chemical Reaction, That's All; Without Love; Fated to Be Mated; The Red Blues; Too Bad; Stereophonic Sound.

So Long, Letty

Shubert Theatre, 23 October 1916 (96 performances). *Book:* Oliver Morosco, Elmer Harris. *Score:* Earl Carroll. *Director:* Oliver Morosco. *Choreographer:* Julian Alfred. *Cast:* Charlotte Greenwood, Walter Catlett, Winnie Baldwin, Sydney Grant, Ben Linn, May Boley, Frances Cameron, Percey Bronson. *Songs:* So Long, Letty; All the Comforts of Home; Mr. Patrick Henry Must Have Been a Married Man; Pass around the Apples Once Again; Blame It on the Girls.

Warner (1930). *Screenplay:* Arthur Caesar, Robert Lord. *Score:* Grant Clarke, Harry Akst, etc. *Director:* Lloyd Bacon. *Cast:* Charlotte Greenwood, Bert Roach, Claude Gillingwater, Patsy Ruth Miller, Marion Byron, Helen Foster, Grant Withers. *Songs:* So Long Letty; Am I Blue?; One Sweet Little Yes; Let Me Have My Dreams; My Strongest Weakness Is You; Sugar Kane.

Something for the Boys

Alvin Theatre, 7 January 1943 (422 performances). *Book:* Herbert and Dorothy Fields. *Score:* Cole Porter. *Directors:* Hassard Short, Herbert Fields. *Choreographer:* Jack Cole. *Cast:* Ethel Merman, Bill Johnson, Betty Garrett, Paula Lawrence, Allen Jenkins, Betty Bruce, Jed Prouty, Anita Alverez, Bill Callahan,Wiliam Lynn. *Songs:* Hey, Good Lookin'; By the Mississinewah; Could It Be You?; He's a Right Guy; I'm in Love with a Soldier Boy; Something for the Boys; The Leader of a Big Time Band.

Fox (1944). *Screenplay:* Robert Ellis, Helen Logan, Frank Gabrielson. *Score:* Jimmy McHugh, Harold Adamson, Cole Porter. *Director:* Lewis Seiler. *Choreographer:* Nick Castle. *Cast:* Carmen Miranda, Vivian

Blaine, Phil Silvers, Perry Como, Michael O'Shea, Sheila Ryan, Roger Clark, Thurston Hall. *Songs:* Something for the Boys; I'm in the Middle of Nowhere; Wouldn't It Be Nice?; Boom Brachee; I Wish We Didn't Have to Say Goodnight; Samba Boogie.

Song of Norway

Imperial Theatre, 21 August 1944 (860 performances). *Book:* Milton Lazaras. *Score:* Edvard Grieg, Robert Wright, George Forrest. *Directors:* Edwin Lester, Charles K. Freedman. *Choreographer:* George Balanchine. *Cast:* Lawrence Brooks, Irra Petina, Helena Bliss, Robert Shafer, Sig Arno, Alexandra Danilova. *Songs:* Strange Music; Hill of Dreams; Now!; Midsummer's Eve; I Love You; Freddy and His Fiddle; Three Loves.

ABC (1970). *Screenplay:* Virginia and Andrew Stone. *Score:* Edvard Grieg, Robert Wright, George Forrest. *Director:* Andrew Stone. *Choreographer:* Lee Theodore. *Cast:* Toralv Maurstadt, Florence Henderson, Harry Secombe, Frank Poretta, Robert Morley, Edward G. Robinson, Oscar Homolka. *Songs:* Strange Music; Hill of Dreams; I Love You; Freddy and His Fiddle; In the Hall of the Mountain King; Hand in Hand.

Song of the Flame

44th Street Theatre, 30 December 1925 (219 performances). *Book:* Oscar Hammerstein, Otto Harbach. *Score:* George Gershwin, Herbert Stothart, Oscar Hammerstein, Otto Harbach. *Director:* Frank Reicher. *Choreographer:* Jack Haskell. *Cast:* Tessa Kosta, Guy Robertson, Greek Evans, Dorothy Mackaye, Hugh Cameron, Ula Sharon, Bernard Gorcey. *Songs:* Song of the Flame; The Cossack Love Song; Far Away; Midnight Bells; Woman's Work Is Never Done; Wander Away.

First National (1930). *Screenplay:* Gordon Rigby. *Score:* George Gershwin, Herbert Stothart, Oscar Hammerstein, Otto Harbach, etc. *Director:* Alan Crosland. *Choreographer:* Jack Haskell. *Cast:* Bernice Claire, Alexander Gray, Noah Berry, Alice Gentle, Bert Roach, Inez Courtney, Shep Camp, Ivan Linow. *Songs:* Song of the Flame; The Cossack Love Song; When Love Calls; One Little Drink; Petrograd; Liberty Song; Passing Fancy.

The Sound of Music
Lunt-Fontanne Theatre, 16 November 1959 (1,443 performances).
Book: Howard Linday, Russel Crouse. *Score:* Richard Rodgers, Oscar
Hammerstein. *Director:* Vincent J. Donehue. *Choreographer:* Joe Lay-
ton. *Cast:* Mary Martin, Theodore Bikel, Patricia Neway, Kurt Kasznar,
Marian Marlowe, Lauri Peters, Brian Davies. *Songs:* The Sound of Mu-
sic; My Favorite Things; Do-Re-Mi; Climb Ev'ry Mountain; Edelweiss;
Sixteen Going on Seventeen; The Lonely Goatherd; How Can Love
Survive?; So Long, Farewell; No Way to Stop It.
　　Fox (1965). *Screenplay:* Ernest Lehman. *Score:* Richard Rodgers,
Oscar Hammerstein. *Director:* Robert Wise. *Choreographers:* Marc
Breaux, DeeDee Wood. *Cast:* Julie Andrews, Christopher Plummer,
Peggy Wood, Eleanor Parker, Richard Haydn, Charmian Carr. *Songs:*
The Sound of Music; My Favorite Things; Do-Re-Mi; Climb Ev'ry
Mountain; Edelweiss; Sixteen Going on Seventeen; The Lonely
Goatherd; I Have Confidence in Me; So Long, Farewell; Something
Good.

South Pacific
Majestic Theatre, 7 April 1949 (1,925 performances). *Book:* Oscar
Hammerstein, Joshua Logan. *Score:* Richard Rodgers, Oscar Ham-
merstein. *Director:* Joshua Logan. *Cast:* Mary Martin, Ezio Pinza,
Juanita Hall, Myron McCormick, William Tabbert, Betta St. John.
Songs: Some Enchanted Evening; There Is Nothin' Like a Dame;
Bali Ha'i; Younger Than Springtime; This Nearly Was Mine; Happy
Talk; I'm Gonna Wash That Man Right Outa My Hair; Honey Bun;
You've Got to Be Carefully Taught; A Wonderful Guy; A Cockeyed
Optimist.
　　Magna/Fox (1958). *Screenplay:* Paul Osborn. *Score:* Richard
Rodgers, Oscar Hammerstein. *Director:* Joshua Logan. *Choreographer:*
LeRoy Prinz. *Cast:* Mitzi Gaynor, Rossano Brazzi, John Kerr, Ray
Walston, Juanita Hall, France Nuyen. *Songs:* Some Enchanted
Evening; There Is Nothin' Like a Dame; Bali Ha'i; Younger Than
Springtime; This Nearly Was Mine; Happy Talk; I'm Gonna Wash
That Man Right Outa My Hair; Honey Bun; You've Got to Be Care-
fully Taught; A Wonderful Guy; A Cockeyed Optimist; My Girl
Back Home.

Spring Is Here

Alvin Theatre, 11 March 1929 (104 performances). *Book:* Owen Davis. *Score:* Richard Rodgers, Lorenz Hart. *Director:* Alexander Left-wich. *Choreographer:* Bobby Connolly. *Cast:* Glenn Hunter, Lillian Taiz, Charles Ruggles, John Hundley, Inez Courtney, Joyce Barbour, Dick Keene, Lew Parker. *Songs:* With a Song in My Heart; Spring Is Here in Person; Yours Sincerely; Baby's Awake Now; Red Hot Trumpet; Why Can't I?

First National (1930). *Screenplay:* James A. Starr. *Score:* Richard Rodgers, Lorenz Hart, etc. *Director:* John Francis Dillon. *Cast:* Bernice Claire, Alexander Gray, Ford Sterling, Lawrence Gray, Louise Fazenda, Inez Courtney, Frank Albertson, Natalie Moorhead. *Songs:* With a Song in My Heart; Spring Is Here in Person; Yours Sincerely; I Married an Angel; Rich Man, Poor Man; Baby's Awake Now; Cryin' for the Carolinas; Have a Little Faith in Me.

Strike Up the Band

Times Square Theatre, 14 January 1930 (191 performances). *Book:* Morrie Ryskind. *Score:* George and Ira Gershwin. *Director:* Alexander Leftwich. *Choreographer:* George Hale. *Cast:* Bobby Clark, Paul Mc-Cullough, Blanche Ring, Doris Carson, Jerry Goff, Dudley Clements. *Songs:* Strike Up the Band; I've Got a Crush on You; Soon; I Mean to Say; Mademoiselle in New Rochelle.

MGM (1940). *Screenplay:* John Monks Jr., Fred Finklehoffe. *Score:* George and Ira Gershwin, Roger Edens, etc. *Director-choreographer:* Busby Berkeley. *Cast:* Mickey Rooney, Judy Garland, June Preisser, Paul Whiteman, William Tracy, Ann Shoemaker, Larry Nunn. *Songs:* Strike Up the Band; Our Love Affair; Nobody; Do the La Conga; The Drummer Boy.

The Student Prince of Heidelberg

Jolson's 59th Street Theatre, 2 December 1924 (608 performances). *Book:* Dorothy Donnelly. *Score:* Sigmund Romberg, Dorothy Donnelly. *Director:* J. C. Huffman. *Choreographer:* Max Scheck. *Cast:* Howard Marsh, Ilse Marvenga, George Hassell, Greek Evans, Roberta Beatty. *Songs:* Deep in My Heart, Dear; Golden Days; Drinking Song; Serenade; Just We Two; Come, Boys, Let's All Be Gay, Boys.

The Student Prince, MGM (1954). *Screenplay:* Sonia Levien, William Ludwig. *Score:* Sigmund Romberg, Nicholas Brodszky, Dorothy Donnelly, Paul Francis Webster. *Director:* Richard Thorpe. *Cast:* Edmund Purdom (singing dubbed by Mario Lanza), Ann Blyth, Louis Calhern, Edmund Gwenn, S. Z. Sakall, John Williams, Evelyn Varden. *Songs:* Deep in My Heart, Dear; Golden Days; The Drinking Song; Serenade; I Walk with God; Beloved; Summertime in Heidelberg; Come, Boys, Let's All Be Gay, Boys.

Sunny

New Amsterdam Theatre, 22 September 1925 (516 performances). *Book:* Otto Harbach, Oscar Hammerstein. *Score:* Jerome Kern, Otto Harbach, Oscar Hammerstein. *Director:* Hassard Short. *Choreographers:* Julian Mitchell, David Bennett. *Cast:* Marilyn Miller, Jack Donahue, Mary Hay, Clifton Webb, Joseph Cawthorn, Ciff Edwards, Paul Frawley, Pert Kelton. *Songs:* Who?; Sunny; D'Ye Love Me?; Let's Say Goodnight Till It's Morning; Two Little Bluebirds.

Warner/First National (1930). *Screenplay:* Humphrey Pearson, Henry McCarty. *Score:* Jerome Kern, Otto Harbach, Oscar Hammerstein. *Director:* William A. Seiter. *Choreographer:* Theodore Kosloff. *Cast:* Marilyn Miller, Joe Donahue, Lawrence Gray, O. P. Heggie, Inez Courtney, Barbara Bedford. *Songs:* Who?; Sunny; D'Ye Love Me?; I Was Alone; Two Little Bluebirds.

RKO (1941). *Screenplay:* Sig Herzig. *Score:* Jerome Kern, Otto Harbach, Oscar Hammerstein. *Director:* Herbert Wilcox. *Choreographers:* Aida Broadbent, Leon Leonidoff. *Cast:* Anna Neagle, John Carroll, Ray Bolger, Edward Everett Horton, Grace and Paul Hartman, Helen Westley, Benny Rubin, Frieda Inescort, Muggins Davies. *Songs:* Who?; Sunny; D'Ye Love Me?; Two Little Bluebirds.

Sweet Adeline

Hammerstein's Theatre, 3 September 1929 (234 performances). *Book:* Oscar Hammerstein. *Score:* Jerome Kern, Oscar Hammerstein. *Director:* Reginald Hammerstein. *Choreographer:* Danny Dare. *Cast:* Helen Morgan, Charles Butterworth, Irene Franklin, Robert Chisholm, Violet Carlson, Max Hoffman Jr. *Songs:* Why Was I Born?; Here Am I; Don't Ever Leave Me; Some Girl Is on Your Mind; 'Twas Not So Long Ago.

Warner (1935). *Screenplay:* Erwin Gelsey. *Score:* Jerome Kern, Oscar Hammerstein. *Director:* Mervyn LeRoy. *Choreographer:* Bobby Connolly. *Cast:* Irene Dunne, Donald Woods, Hugh Hubert, Ned Sparks, Joseph Cawthorn, Wini Shaw, Louis Calhern, Phil Regan. *Songs:* Why Was I Born?; Here I Am; Don't Ever Leave Me; 'Twas Not So Long Ago; We Were So Young.

Sweet Charity
Palace Theatre, 29 January 1966 (608 performances). *Book:* Neil Simon. *Score:* Cy Coleman, Dorothy Fields. *Director-choreographer:* Bob Fosse. *Cast:* Gwen Verdon, John McMartin, Helen Gallagher, Thelma Oliver. *Songs:* If They Could See Me Now; I'm a Brass Band; Big Spender; There's Gotta Be Something Better Than This; Where Am I Going?; Baby Dream Your Dream.

Universal (1969). *Screenplay:* Peter Stone. *Score:* Cy Coleman, Dorothy Fields. *Director-choreographer:* Bob Fosse. *Cast:* Shirley MacLaine, John McMartin, Chita Rivera, Ricardo Montalban, Sammy Davis Jr., Paula Kelly, Stubby Kaye. *Songs:* If They Could See Me Now; I'm a Brass Band; Big Spender; There's Gotta Be Something Better Than This; Where Am I Going?; My Personal Property.

Sweethearts
New Amsterdam Theatre, 8 September 1913 (136 performances). *Book:* Harry B. Smith, Fred De Gresac. *Score:* Victor Herbert, Robert B. Smith. *Director:* Fred Latham. *Choreographer:* Charles Morgan Jr. *Cast:* Christie MacDonald, Thomas Conkey, Ethel Du Fre Houston, Tom McNaughton, Edwin Wilson. *Songs:* Pretty as a Picture; Sweethearts; Angelus; Jeanette and Her Little Wooden Shoes; Every Lover Must Meet His Fate.

MGM (1938). *Screenplay:* Dorothy Parker, Alan Campbell, Noel Langley. *Score:* Victor Herbert, Robert B. Smith, Robert Wright, George Forrest. *Director:* W. S. Van Dyke. *Choreographer:* Albertina Rasch. *Cast:* Jeanette MacDonald, Nelson Eddy, Frank Morgan, Mischa Auer, Ray Bolger, Terry Kilburn, Reginald Gardiner, Herman Bing, Douglas McPhail, Gene Lockhart. *Songs:* Pretty as a Picture; Sweethearts; Summer Serenade; Wooden Shoes; Every Lover Must Meet His Fate; On Parade.

Take a Chance
Apollo Theatre, 26 November 1932 (243 performances). *Book:* B. G. DeSylva, Laurence Schwab, Sid Silvers. *Score:* Richard A. Whiting, Nacio Herb Brown, Vincent Youmans, B. G. DeSylva, etc. *Director:* Edgar MacGregor. *Choreographer:* Bobby Connolly. *Cast:* Jack Haley, Ethel Merman, Jack Whiting, Sid Silvers, June Knight, Mitzi Mayfair, Oscar Ragland. *Songs:* Rise 'n' Shine; Eadie Was a Lady; You're an Old Smoothie; Should I Be Sweet?; Turn Out the Lights.
    Paramount (1933). *Screenplay:* Lawrence Schwab. *Score:* Richard A. Whiting, Nacio Herb Brown, Vincent Youmans, B. G. DeSylva, etc. *Directors:* Lawrence Schwab, Monte Brice. *Cast:* Lillian Roth, James Dunn, Cliff Edwards, June Knight, Charles "Buddy" Rogers, Lilian Bond. *Songs:* Rise 'n' Shine; It's Only a Paper Moon; Should I Be Sweet?; New Deal Rhythm; Come Up and See Me Sometime; Turn Out the Lights.

This Is the Army
Broadway Theatre, 4 July 1942 (113 performances). *Score:* Irving Berlin. *Directors:* Ezra Stone, Joshua Logan. *Choreographers:* Robert Sidney, Nelson Barclift. *Cast:* Ezra Stone, Burl Ives, Gary Merrill, Julie Oshins, Robert Sidney, Alan Manson, Earl Oxford. *Songs:* This Is the Army, Mr. Jones; I Left My Heart at the Stage Door Canteen; Mandy; I'm Getting Tired So I Can Sleep; Oh, How I Hate to Get Up in the Morning; The Army's Made a Man of Me.
    Warner (1943). *Screenplay:* Casey Robinson, Claude Binyon. *Score:* Irving Berlin. *Director:* Michael Curtiz. *Choreographers:* LeRoy Prinz, Robert Sidney. *Cast:* George Murphy, Joan Leslie, Ronald Reagan, Charles Butterworth, George Tobias, Rosemary DeCamp, Dolores Costello, Una Merkel, Ezra Stone, Earl Oxford. *Songs:* This Is the Army, Mr. Jones; I Left My Heart at the Stage Door Canteen; We're on Our Way to France; God Bless America; I'm Getting Tired So I Can Sleep; Oh, How I Hate to Get Up in the Morning; The Army's Made a Man of Me; With My Head in the Clouds.

Too Many Girls
Imperial Theatre, 18 October 1939 (249 performances). *Book:* George Marion Jr. *Score:* Richard Rodgers, Lorenz Hart. *Director:* George Abbott.

Choreographer: Robert Alton. *Cast:* Marcy Westcott, Hal LeRoy, Mary Jane Walsh, Desi Arnaz, Eddie Bracken, Richard Kollmar, Van Johnson. *Songs:* I Didn't Know What Time It Was; Give It Back to the Indians; Love Never Went to College; All Dressed Up (Spic and Spanish); I Like to Recognize the Tune.

RKO (1940). *Screenplay:* John Twist. *Score:* Richard Rodgers, Lorenz Hart. *Director:* George Abbott. *Choreographer:* LeRoy Prinz. *Cast:* Lucille Ball, Richard Carlson, Ann Miller, Eddie Bracken, Frances Langford, Hal LeRoy, Van Johnson. *Songs:* I Didn't Know What Time It Was; Love Never Went to College; All Dressed Up (Spic and Spanish); You're Nearer; Heroes in the Fall.

Top Banana

Winter Garden Theatre, 1 November 1951 (350 performances). *Book:* Hy Kraft. *Score:* Johnny Mercer. *Director:* Jack Donohue. *Choreographer:* Ron Fletcher. *Cast:* Phil Silvers, Judy Lynn, Eddie Hanley, Rose Marie, Jack Albertson, Bob Scheerer, Lindy Doherty, Joey and Herbie Faye. *Songs:* If You Want to Be a Top Banana; Only If You're in Love; I Fought Every Step of the Way; The Man of the Year This Week; A Word a Day; My Home Is in My Shoes; Sans Souci.

United Artists (1954). *Screenplay:* Hy Kraft. *Score:* Johnny Mercer. *Director:* Alfred E. Green. *Choreographer:* Ron Fletcher. *Cast:* Phil Silvers, Judy Lynn, Danny Scholl, Rose Marie, Jack Albertson, Johnny Coy, Joey and Herbie Faye. *Songs:* If You Want to Be a Top Banana; Only If You're in Love; I Fought Every Step of the Way; The Man of the Year This Week; A Word a Day; My Home Is in My Shoes; Sans Souci.

The Unsinkable Molly Brown

Winter Garden Theatre, 3 November 1960 (532 performances). *Book:* Richard Morris. *Score:* Meredith Willson. *Director:* Dore Schary. *Choreographer:* Peter Gennaro. *Cast:* Tammy Grimes, Harve Presnell, Cameron Prud'homme, Edith Meiser, Mony Dalmes, Christopher Hewitt. *Songs:* I Ain't Down Yet; I'll Never Say No to You; Belly Up to the Bar, Boys; Colorado, My Home; Are You Sure?

MGM (1964). *Screenplay:* Helen Deutsch. *Score:* Meredith Willson. *Director:* Charles Walters. *Choreographer:* Peter Gennaro. *Cast:* Debbie

Reynolds, Harve Presnell, Ed Begley, Kack Kruschen, Hermione Baddeley. *Songs:* I Ain't Down Yet; I'll Never Say No to You; Belly Up to the Bar, Boys; Colorado, My Home; He's My Friend.

Up in Central Park
New Century Theatre, 27 January 1945 (504 performances). *Book:* Herbert and Dorothy Fields. *Score:* Sigmund Romberg, Dorothy Fields. *Director:* John Kennedy. *Choreographer:* Helen Tamiris. *Cast:* Wilbur Evans, Maureen Cannon, Betty Bruce, Noah Berry, Maurice Burke, Robert Rounseville. *Songs:* Close As Pages in a Book; April Snow; Carousel in the Park; When You Walk in the Room; The Big Back Yard.
Universal (1948). *Screenplay:* Karl Tunberg. *Score:* Sigmund Romberg, Dorothy Fields. *Director:* William A. Seiter. *Choreographers:* Helen Tamiris, Karl Tunberg. *Cast:* Deanna Durbin, Dick Haymes, Albert Sharpe, Vincent Price, Tom Powers, Thurston Hall, Hobart Cavanaugh, Howard Freeman. *Songs:* Carousel in the Park; When You Walk in the Room; Oh Say, Do You See What I See?

The Vagabond King
Casino Theatre, 21 September 1925 (511 performances). *Book:* Brian Hooker, Russell Janney, W. H. Post. *Score:* Rudolf Friml, Brian Hooker. *Director:* Max Figman. *Choreographer:* Julian Alfred. *Cast:* Dennis King, Carolyn Thomson, Max Figman, Herbert Corthell. *Songs:* Only a Rose; Song of the Vagabonds; Hugette Waltz; Love Me Tonight; Love for Sale; Some Day; Nocture.
Paramount (1930). *Screenplay:* Herman J. Mankiewicz. *Score:* Rudolf Friml, Brian Hooker, etc. *Director:* Ludwig Berger. *Cast:* Dennis King, Jeanette MacDonald, Lillian Roth, O. P. Heggie, Warner Oland, Lawford Davidson, Arthur Stone, Thomas Ricketts. *Songs:* Song of the Vagabonds; Hugette Waltz; Love Me Tonight; Love for Sale; Some Day; If I Were King; Mary, Queen of Heaven.
Paramount (1956). *Screenplay:* Ken Englund, Noel Langley. *Score:* Rudolf Friml, Brian Hooker, etc. *Director:* Michael Curtiz. *Choreographer:* Hanya Holm. *Cast:* Oreste Kirkop, Kathryn Grayson, Rita Moreno, Walter Hampden, Cedric Hardwicke, William Prince, Leslie Nielsen. *Songs:* Only a Rose; Song of the Vagabonds; Hugette Waltz; Watch Out for the Devil; This Same Heart.

Very Warm for May
Alvin Theatre, 17 November 1939 (59 performances). *Book:* Oscar Hammerstein. *Score:* Jerome Kern, Oscar Hammerstein. *Directors:* Vincente Minnelli, Oscar Hammerstein. *Choreographers:* Albertina Rasch, Harry Losee. *Cast:* Jack Whiting, Grace McDonald, Eve Arden, Hiram Sherman, Frances Mercer, Donald Brian, Richard Quine, Hollace Shaw, Avon Long, Max Showalter. *Songs:* All The Things You Are; Heaven in My Arms; In the Heart of the Dark; In Other Words; That Lucky Fellow; Seventeen.

Broadway Rhythm, MGM (1944). *Screenplay:* Dorothy Kingsley, Harry Clork. *Score:* Jerome Kern, Oscar Hammerstein, Gene de Paul, Ron Raye, Ralph Blane, Hugh Martin, etc. *Director:* Roy Del Ruth. *Choreographers:* Robert Alton, Jack Donohue. *Cast:* George Murphy, Ginny Simms, Lena Horne, Nancy Walker, Ben Blue, Gloria DeHaven, Charles Winninger, Kenny Bowers, Eddie Anderson. *Songs:* All the Things You Are, Milkman, Keep Those Bottles Quiet; Brazilian Boogie; Somebody Loves Me; Irresistible You; Who's Who in Your Love Life?; Pretty Baby; Oh You Beautiful Doll; What Do You Think I Am?

West Side Story
Winter Garden Theatre, 26 September 1957 (732 performances). *Book:* Arthur Laurents. *Score:* Leonard Bernstein, Stephen Sondheim. *Director:* Jerome Robbins. *Choreographers:* Jerome Robbins, Peter Gennaro. *Cast:* Larry Kert, Carol Lawrence, Chita Rivera, Art Smith, Mickey Calin, Kem LeRoy, Lee Becker Theodore, David Winter. *Songs:* Tonight; Maria; Somewhere; Gee, Officer Krupke; America; Cool; I Feel Pretty; A Boy Like That; I Have a Love; Something's Comin'; One Hand, One Heart.

Mirisch/United Artists (1961). *Screenplay:* Ernest Lehman. *Score:* Leonard Bernstein, Stephen Sondheim. *Directors:* Robert Wise, Jerome Robbins. *Choreographer:* Jerome Robbins. *Cast:* Natalie Wood, Richard Beymer, Rita Moreno, George Chakiris, Russ Tamblyn, Simon Oakland, John Astin, David Winter, Eliot Feld, Anthony Teague. *Songs:* Tonight; Maria; Somewhere; Gee, Officer Krupke; America; Cool; I Feel Pretty; A Boy Like That; I Have a Love; Something's Comin'; One Hand, One Heart.

Where's Charley?
St. James Theatre, 11 October 1948 (792 performances). *Book:* George Abbott. *Score:* Frank Loesser. *Director:* George Abbott. *Choreographer:* George Balanchine. *Cast:* Ray Bolger, Allyn McLerie, Byron Palmer, Doretta Morrow, Horace Cooper, Paul England, Jane Lawrence, Cornell MacNeil. *Songs:* Once in Love with Amy; Make a Miracle; My Darling, My Darling; At the Red Rose Cotillion.; The New Ashmolean Marching Society and Students' Conservatory Band.
Warner (1952). *Screenplay:* John Monks Jr. *Score:* Frank Loesser. *Director:* David Butler. *Choreographer:* Michael Kidd. *Cast:* Ray Bolger, Allyn McLerie, Robert Shackleton, Mary Germaine, Horace Cooper, Howard Marion Crawford, Margaretta Scott. *Songs:* Once in Love with Amy; Make a Miracle; My Darling, My Darling; At the Red Rose Cotillion; The New Ashmolean Marching Society and Students' Conservatory Band.

Whoopee
New Amsterdam, 4 December 1928 (379 performances). *Book:* William Anthony McGuire. *Score:* Walter Donaldson, Gus Kahn. *Director:* William Anthony McGuire. *Choreographers:* Seymour Felix, Tamara Geva. *Cast:* Eddie Cantor, Ruth Etting, Paul Gregory, Ethel Shutta, Tamara Geva, Frances Upton. *Songs:* Makin' Whoopee; Love Me or Leave Me; Until You get Somebody Else; I'm Bringing a Red Red Rose.
Goldwyn/United Artists (1930). *Screenplay:* William Conselman. *Score:* Walter Donaldson, Gus Kahn. *Director:* Thornton Freeland. *Choreographer:* Busby Berkeley. *Cast:* Eddie Cantor, Eleanor Hunt, Paul Gregory, Ethel Shutta, John Rutherford, Spencer Charters, Chief Caupolican. *Songs:* Makin' Whoopee; My Baby Just Cares for Me; I'll Still Belong to You; Stetson; A Girl Friend of a Boy Friend of Mine.

The Wiz
Majestic Theatre, 5 January 1975, (1,672 performances). *Book:* William F. Brown. *Score:* Charlie Smalls. *Director:* Geoffrey Holder. *Choreographer:* George Faison. *Cast:* Stephanie Mills, Tiger Haynes, Andre De Shields, Ted Ross, Hinton Battle, Clarice Taylor, DeeDee Bridgewater, Mabel King. *Songs:* Ease on Down the Road; Be a Lion;

262 ~ Musicals Directory

Home; If You Believe; Slide Some Oil to Me; He's the Wizard; Don't Nobody Bring Me No Bad News; Believe in Yourself. Universal (1978). *Screenplay:* Joel Schumacher. *Score:* Charlie Smalls, Quincy Jones. *Director:* Sidney Lumet. *Choreographer:* Louis Johnson. *Cast:* Diana Ross, Nipsey Russell, Michael Jackson, Ted Ross, Richard Pryor, Lena Horne, Mabel King, Theresa Merritt. *Songs:* Ease on Down the Road; Be a Lion; Home; If You Believe; Slide Some Oil to Me; He's the Wizard; Don't Nobody Bring Me No Bad News; Believe in Yourself; Is This What Feeling Gets?; End of the Yellow Brick Road.

The Wonder Bar
Nora Bayes Theatre, 17 March 1931 (76 performances). *Book:* Irving Caesar, Aben Kandel. *Score:* Robert Katscher, Irving Caesar. *Director:* William Millison. *Choreographer:* Albertina Rasch. *Cast:* Al Jolson, Patsy Kelly, Arthur Treacher, Rex O'Malley, Wanda Lyon, Vernon Steele, Al Segal. *Songs:* Trav'lin' Alone; Good Evening, Friends; The Dance We Do for Al; Something Seems to Tell Me; The Dying Flamingo; Valse Amoureuse.

Wonder Bar, Warner/First National (1934). *Screenplay:* Earl Baldwin. *Score:* Harry Warren, Al Dubin. *Director:* Lloyd Bacon. *Choreographer:* Busby Berkeley. *Cast:* Al Jolson, Dolores Del Rio, Dick Powell, Kay Francis, Ricardo Cortez, Hugh Herbert, Guy Kibbee, Henry O'Neill, Hal LeRoy. *Songs:* Wonder Bar; Don't Say Goodnight; Why Do I Dream These Dreams?; Vive La France; Goin' to Heaven on a Mule.

Yokel Boy
Majestic Theatre, 6 July 1939 (208 performances). *Book:* Lew Brown. *Score:* Sam Stept, Lew Brown, Charles Tobias. *Director:* Lew Brown. *Choreographer:* Gene Snyder. *Cast:* Buddy Ebsen, Judy Canova, Dixie Dunbar, Phil Silvers, Jackie Heller, Mark Plant, Lois January, Ralph Riggs, Lew Hearn. *Songs:* Comes Love; It's Me Again; Let's Make Memories Tonight; I Know I'm Nobody; I Can't Afford to Dream; The Ship Has Sailed.

Republic (1942). *Screenplay:* Russell Rouse, Isabel Dawn. *Score:* Sam Stept, Lew Brown, Charles Tobias, etc. *Director:* Joseph Santley. *Cast:* Eddie Foy Jr., Roscoe Karns, Albert Dekker, Joan Davis, Alan Mowbray, Mikhail Rasumny, Lynne Carver, Marc Lawrence. *Songs:* Comes Love; It's Me Again; Let's Make Memories Tonight; I Can't Afford to Dream; Jim Caesar.

Ziegfeld Follies Series
Florenz Ziegfeld produced twenty-one editions of his Follies between 1907 and his death in 1932. They were usually presented in the New Amsterdam Theatre where such stars as Fanny Brice, W. C. Fields, Bert Williams, Eddie Cantor, Will Rogers, Ann Pennington, and Marilyn Miller were featured. The series of revues was also known for its lavish scenic and costume design and opulent production numbers celebrating the American beauty. Among the songwriters to provide numbers for the Follies were Irving Berlin, Sigmund Romberg, Rudolf Friml, George Gershwin, Victor Herbert, and Jerome Kern. There were a few Ziegfeld Follies after 1932, but these were just revues that paid to use the Ziegfeld name.

Ziegfeld Follies, MGM (1946). *Sketches:* Harry Turgend, Billy K. Wells, George White, David Freedman. *Score:* Harry Warren, Arthur Freed, Roger Edens, Ralph Freed, George and Ira Gershwin, etc. *Directors:* Vincente Minnelli, George Sidney, Robert Lewis, etc. *Choreographers:* Robert Alton, Eugene Loring, Charles Walters, etc. *Cast:* Fred Astaire, Gene Kelly, Judy Garland, Fanny Brice, Victor Moore, William Powell, Lena Horne, Kathryn Grayson, Lucille Bremer, Keenan Wynn, Cyd Charisse, Red Skelton, Esther Williams. *Songs:* This Heart of Mine; Love; Limehouse Blues; The Babbitt and the Bromide; Madame Crematon; Here's to the Girls.

Screen to Stage

Beauty and the Beast
Disney (1991). *Screenplay:* Linda Woolverton. *Score:* Alan Menken, Howard Ashman. *Directors:* Gary Trousdale, Kirk Wise. *Voices:* Paige O'Hara, Robby Benson, Jerry Orbach, Richard White, Angela Lansbury, David Ogden Stiers. *Songs:* Beauty and the Beast; Belle; Be Our Guest; Gaston; Something There.

Palace Theatre, 18 April 1994 (still running). *Book:* Linda Wolverton. *Score:* Alan Menken, Howard Ashman, Tim Rice. *Director:* Robert

Jess Roth. *Choreographer:* Matt West. *Cast:* Susan Egan, Terrence Mann, Burke Moses, Gary Beach, Tom Bosley, Beth Fowler, Heath Lamberts. *Songs:* Beauty and the Beast; Belle; Be Our Guest; Human Again; If I Can't Love Her; Gaston; Something There; Me.

Footloose

Paramount (1984). *Screenplay:* Dean Pitchford. *Score:* Kenny Loggins, Dean Pitchford, etc. *Director:* Herbert Ross. *Choreographer:* Lynne Taylor-Corbett. *Cast:* Kevin Bacon, Lori Singer, Dianne Wiest, John Lithgow, Christopher Penn, Sarah Jessica Parker, Elizabeth Gorcey. *Songs:* Footloose; Let's Hear It for the Boy; Holding Out for a Hero; Somebody's Eyes; Almost Paradise; The Girl Gets Around.

Richard Rodgers Theatre, 22 October 1998 (708 performances). *Book:* Dean Pitchford, Walter Bobbie. *Score:* Tom Snow, Dean Pitchford, etc. *Director:* Walter Bobbie. *Choreographer:* A. C. Ciulla. *Cast:* Jeremy Kushnier, Jennifer Laura Thompson, Stephen Lee Anderson, Dee Hoty, Catherine Cox, Tom Plotkin, Stacy Francis. *Songs:* Footloose; Let's Hear It for the Boy; Holding Out for a Hero; Somebody's Eyes; Almost Paradise; The Girl Gets Around; Learning to Be Silent; Heaven Help Me.

42nd Street

Warner (1933). *Screenplay:* James Seymour, Rian James. *Score:* Harry Warren, Al Dubin. *Director:* Lloyd Bacon. *Choreographer:* Busby Berkeley. *Cast:* Ruby Keeler, Warner Baxter, Bebe Daniels, Dick Powell, Guy Kibbee, Ginger Rogers, George Brent. *Songs:* Forty-Second Street; Shuffle Off to Buffalo; Young and Healthy; You're Getting to Be a Habit with Me.

Winter Garden, 25 August 1980 (3,486 performances). *Book:* Michael Stewart, Mark Bramble. *Score:* Harry Warren, Al Dubin. *Director-choreographer:* Gower Champion. *Cast:* Jerry Orbach, Wanda Richert, Tammy Grimes, Lee Roy Reams, Carole Cook, Joseph Bova. *Songs:* Lullaby of Broadway; Forty-Second Street; Shuffle Off to Buffalo; Young and Healthy; You're Getting to Be a Habit with Me; We're in the Money; About a Quarter to Nine; Shadow Waltz; Dames; Go into Your Dance.

Gigi

MGM (1958). *Screenplay:* Alan Jay Lerner. *Score:* Frederick Loewe, Alan Jay Lerner. *Director:* Vincente Minnelli. *Cast:* Leslie Caron, Mau-

rice Chevalier, Louis Jourdan, Hermione Gingold, Eva Gabor, Isabel Jeans. *Songs:* Gigi; Thank Heaven for Little Girls; I Remember It Well; I'm Glad I'm Not Young Anymore; The Night They Invented Champagne; She Is Not Thinking of Me; The Parisians; Say a Prayer for Me Tonight; It's a Bore.
    Uris Theatre, 13 Nobember 1973 (103 performances). *Book:* Alan Jay Lerner. *Score:* Frederick Loewe, Alan Jay Lerner. *Director:* Joseph Hardy. *Choreographer:* Onna White. *Cast:* Karin Wolfe, Alfred Drake, Daniel Massey, Maria Karnilova, Agnes Moorehead, Truman Gaige. *Songs:* Thank Heaven for Little Girls; I Remember It Well; I'm Glad I'm Not Young Anymore; The Night They Invented Champagne; She Is Not Thinking of Me; The Parisians; Say a Prayer for Me Tonight; It's a Bore; In This Wide, Wide World.

High Society
MGM (1956). *Screenplay:* John Patrick. *Score:* Cole Porter. *Director-choreographer:* Charles Walters. *Cast:* Grace Kelly, Bing Crosby, Frank Sinatra, Celeste Holm, John Lund, Louis Calhern, Sidney Blackmer, Louis Armstrong. *Songs:* True Love; You're Sensational; Well, Did You Evah?; Now You Has Jazz; Who Wants to Be a Millionaire?
    St. James Theatre, 27 April 1998 (144 performances). *Book:* Arthur Kopit. *Score:* Cole Porter, Susan Birkenhead. *Director:* Christopher Renshaw. *Cast:* Melissa Errico, Daniel McDonald, Randy Graff, Stephen Bogardus, John McMartin, Marc Kurdish, Anna Kendrick. *Songs:* True Love; You're Sensational; Well, Did You Evah?; She's Got That Thing; Ridin' High; Who Wants to Be a Millionaire?; Just One of Those Things; Let's Misbehave.

Lili
MGM (1953). *Screenplay:* Helen Deutsch. *Score:* Bronislau Kaper, Helen Deutsch. *Director:* Charles Walters. *Choreographers:* Charles Walters, Dorothy Jarnac. *Cast:* Leslie Caron, Mel Ferrer, Jean-Pierre Aumont, Zsa Zsa Gabor, Kurt Kasznar, Amanda Blake, Alex Gerry, Ralph Dumke, George Baxter. *Song:* Hi-Lili, Hi-Lo.
    Carnival, Imperial Theatre, 13 April, 1961 (719 performances). *Book:* Michael Stewart. *Score:* Bob Merrill. *Director-choreographer:* Gower Champion. *Cast:* Anna Maria Alberghetti, Jerry Orbach, James Mitchell,

Kaye Ballard, Pierre Olaf, Henry Lascoe, Anita Gillette. *Songs:* Love Makes the World Go Round; Always, Always You; Mira; Grand Imperial Cirque de Paris; Yes, My Heart; Beautiful Candy; Direct from Vienna; Humming; Sword, Rose and Cape; She's My Love.

The Lion King

Disney (1994). *Screenplay:* Irene Mecchi, Jonathan Roberts, Linda Woolverton. *Score:* Elton John, Tim Rice. *Director:* Roger Allers, Rob Minkoff. *Voices:* James Earl Jones, Matthew Broderick, Jonathan Taylor Thomas, Rowan Atkinson, Nathan Lane, Whoopi Goldberg, Jeremy Irons, Robert Guillaume. *Songs:* Can You Feel the Love Tonight; Hakuna Matata; Circle of Life; I Just Can't Wait to Be King; Be Prepared.

New Amsterdam, 13 November 1997 (still running). *Book:* Roger Allers, Irene Mecchi. *Score:* Elton John, Tim Rice, Lebo M., Hans Zimmer, etc. *Director:* Julie Taymor. *Choreographer:* Garth Fagan. *Cast:* Samuel E. Wright, Tsidii Le Loka, Jason Raize, John Vickery, Scott Irby-Ranniar, Heather Headley, Kalunana Shuford, Max Casella, Tom Alan Robbins. *Songs:* Can You Feel the Love Tonight; Hakuna Matata; Circle of Life; I Just Can't Wait to Be King; They Live in You; Shadowland; Be Prepared; Endless Night; The Morning Report.

Meet Me in St. Louis

MGM (1944). *Screenplay:* Irving Brecher, Fred Finklehoffe. *Score:* Hugh Martin, Ralph Blane, etc. *Director:* Vincente Minnelli. *Choreographer:* Charles Walters. *Cast:* Judy Garland, Margaret O'Brien, Leon Ames, Mary Astor, Lucille Bremer, Tom Drake, Harry Davenport, Marjorie Main. *Songs:* Meet Me in St. Louis; The Boy Next Door; Have Yourself a Merry Little Christmas; The Trolley Song; You and I; Under the Bamboo Tree.

Gershwin Theatre, 2 November 1989 (253 performances). *Book:* Hugh Wheeler. *Score:* Hugh Martin, Ralph Blane, etc. *Director:* Louis Burke. *Choreographer:* Joan Brickhill. *Cast:* Donna Kane, Courtney Peldon, George Hearn, Milo O'Shea, Betty Garrett, Charlotte Moore, Juliet Lambert, Jason Workman. *Songs:* Meet Me in St. Louis; The Boy Next Door; Have Yourself a Merry Little Christmas; The Trolley Song; Under the Bamboo Tree; Be Anything but a Girl; Wasn't It Fun?; You Are for Loving.

Saturday Night Fever

Paramount (1977). *Screenplay:* Norman Wexler. *Score:* Barry, Robin, and Maurice Gibb. *Director:* John Badham. *Choreographer:* Lester Wilson. *Cast:* John Travolta, Karen Lynn Gorney, Barry Miller, Joseph Cali, Paul Pape, Donna Pescow, Bruce Ornstein. *Songs:* Staying Alive; How Deep Is Your Love; More Than a Woman; Night Fever.

Minskoff Theatre, 21 October 1999 (507 performances). *Book:* Nan Knighton. *Score:* Barry, Robin, and Maurice Gibb, etc. *Director-choreographer:* Arlene Phillips. *Cast:* James Carpinello, Paige Price, Orfeh, Sean Palmer, Paul Castree, Andy Blankenbuehler. *Songs:* Staying Alive; How Deep Is Your Love; More Than a Woman; Night Fever; What Kind of Fool; Open Sesame; Boogie Shoes.

Seven Brides for Seven Brothers

MGM (1954). *Screenplay:* Frances Goodrich, Albert Hackett, Dorothy Kingsley. *Score:* Gene de Paul, Johnny Mercer. *Director:* Stanley Donan. *Choreographer:* Michael Kidd. *Cast:* Howard Keel, Jane Powell, Russ Tamblyn, Tommy Rall, Jeff Richards, Jacques D'Amboise, Marc Platt, Matt Mattox, Virginia Gibson, Julie Newmar. *Songs:* Wonderful, Wonderful Day; Lonesome Polecat; Bless Your Beautiful Hide; Goin' Co'tin'; Spring, Spring, Spring; Sobbin' Women; When You're in Love.

Alvin Theatre, 8 July 1982 (5 performances). *Book:* Lawrence Kasha, David Landay. *Score:* Gene de Paul, Johnny Mercer, Lawrence Kasha, Joel Hirschhorn. *Director:* Lawrence Kasha. *Choreographer:* Jerry Jackson. *Cast:* David-James Carroll, Debby Boone, Lara Teeter, Craig Peralta, D. Scot Davidge, Jeffrey Reynolds, Michael Ragan, Jeff Calhoun. *Songs:* Wonderful, Wonderful Day; Bless Your Beautiful Hide; Goin' Co'tin'; One Man; Sobbin' Women; Love Never Goes Away; A Woman Ought to Know Her Place.

Singin' in the Rain

MGM (1952). *Screenplay:* Betty Comden, Adolph Green. *Score:* Nacio Herb Brown, Arthur Freed. *Director-choreographers:* Gene Kelly, Stanley Donan. *Cast:* Gene Kelly, Debbie Reynolds, Donald O'Connor, Jean Hagen, Millard Mitchell, Cyd Charisse, Rita Moreno, Jimmy Thompson. *Songs:* Singin' in the Rain; You Were Meant for Me; Good

Morning; All I Do Is Dream of You; Make 'Em Laugh; I've Got a Feelin'
You're Foolin'; Fit as a Fiddle.
　　Gershwin Theatre, 2 July 1985 (367 performances). *Book:* Betty
Comden, Adolphe Green. *Score:* Nacio Herb Brown, Arthur Freed. -
Director-choreographer: Twyla Tharp. *Cast:* Don Correia, Mary D'Arcy,
Peter Slutsker, Faye Grant, Melinda Glib, Hansford Rowe, Robert Rad-
ford, Richard Fancy. *Songs:* Singin' in the Rain; You Are My Lucky
Star; Good Morning; Wedding of the Painted Doll; Make 'Em Laugh;
I've Got a Feelin' You're Foolin'; Fit as a Fiddle; Broadway Rhythm.

State Fair
Fox (1945). *Screenplay:* Oscar Hammerstein. *Score:* Richard Rodgers,
Oscar Hammerstein. *Director:* Walter Lang. *Cast:* Jeanne Crain, Dana
Andrews, Dick Haymes, Vivian Blaine, Charles Winninger, Fay Bain-
ter. *Songs:* It Might as Well Be Spring; It's a Grand Night for Singing;
Our State Fair; That's for Me; Isn't It Kinda Fun?; All I Owe Ioway.
　　Music Box Theatre, 27 March 1996 (102 performances). *Book:* Tom
Briggs, Louis Mattioli. *Score:* Richard Rodgers, Oscar Hammerstein.
Directors: James Hammerstein, Randy Skinner. *Choreographer:* Randy
Skinner. *Cast:* John Davisdon, Andrea McArdle, Donna McKecknie,
Kathryn Crosby, Scott Wise, Ben Wright. *Songs:* It Might as Well Be
Spring; It's a Grand Night for Singing; Our State Fair; That's for Me;
Isn't It Kinda Fun?; That's the Way It Happens; All I Owe Ioway; Boys
and Girls Like You and Me; So Far.

Swing Time
RKO (1936). *Screenplay:* Howard Lindsay, Allen Scott. *Score:* Jerome
Kern, Dorothy Fields. *Director:* George Stevens. *Choreographer:* Hermes
Pan. *Cast:* Fred Astaire, Ginger Rogers, Victor Moore, Helen Broder-
ick, Eric Blore, George Metaxa. *Songs:* The Way You Look Tonight;
Pick Yourself Up; A Fine Romance; Never Gonna Dance; Bojangles of
Harlem.
　　Never Gonna Dance, Broadhurst Theatre, 4 December 2003 (84 per-
formances). *Book:* Jeffrey Hatcher. *Score:* Jerome Kern, Dorothy Fields,
etc. *Director:* Michael Greif. *Choreographer:* Jerry Mitchell. *Cast:* Noah
Racey, Nancy Lemenager, Karen Ziemba, Peter Bartlett, Eugene Flem-
ing, Deidre Goodwin, Ron Orbach. *Songs:* Never Gonna Dance; A

Fine Romance; The Way You Look Tonight; I Won't Dance; Pick Yourself Up; Shimmy with Me; I'm Old Fashioned.

Thoroughly Modern Millie
Universal (1967). *Screenplay:* Richard Morris. *Score:* James Van Huesen, Sammy Cahn, etc. *Director:* George Roy Hill. *Choreographer:* Joe Layton. *Cast:* Julie Andrews, Mary Tyler Moore, John Gavin, Beatrice Lillie, Carol Channing, James Fox, Jack Soo. *Songs:* Thoroughly Modern Millie; Jimmy; Jazz Baby; The Tapioca; Baby Face; Do It Again; Poor Butterfly.

Marquis Theatre, 18 April 2002 (still running). *Book:* Richard Morris, Dick Scanlan. *Score:* Jeanine Tesori, Dick Scanlan, etc. *Director:* Michael Mayer. *Choreographer:* Rob Ashford. *Cast:* Sutton Foster, Gavin Creel, Harriet Harris, Marc Kudish, Sheryl Lee Ralph, Angela Christian. *Songs:* Thoroughly Modern Millie; Forget about the Boy; Jimmy; Not for the Life of Me; What Do I Need with Love?; Gimme, Gimme; Ah! Sweet Mystery of Life; I'm Falling in Love with Someone.

Victor/Victoria
MGM (1982). *Screenplay:* Blake Edwards. *Score:* Henry Mancini, Leslie Bricusse. *Director:* Blake Edwards. *Choreographer:* Paddy Stone. *Cast:* Julie Andrews, Robert Preston, James Garner, Lesley Ann Warren, Alex Karas. *Songs:* You and Me; Crazy World; Le Jazz Hot; Gay Paree; Chicago, Illinois; The Shady Dame from Seville.

Marquis Theatre, 25 October 1995 (734 performances). *Book:* Blake Edwards. *Score:* Henry Mancini, Leslie Bricusse, Frank Wildhorn. *Director:* Blake Edwards. *Choreographer:* Rob Marshall. *Cast:* Julie Andrews, Tony Roberts, Michael Nouri, Rachel York. *Songs:* Paris by Night; Crazy World; You and Me; Le Jazz Hot; Louis Says; Living in the Shadows; Chicago, Illinois, Almost a Love Song; If I Were a Man.

APPENDIX A

~

Nonmusical Films That Were Turned into Broadway and Off-Broadway Musicals

Film	Broadway Musical
All About Eve (1950)	*Applause* (1970)
The Apartment (1960)	*Promises, Promises* (1968)
The Baker's Wife (1938)	*The Baker's Wife* (1976)
Big Deal on Madonna Street (1958)	*Big Deal* (1986)
The Blue Angel (1930)	*Poussé-Café* (1966)
Buona Sera, Mrs. Campbell (1969)	*Carmelina* (1979)
The Captain's Paradise (1953)	*Oh, Captain!* (1958)
Carnival in Flanders (1934)	*Carnival in Flanders* (1953)
Dona Flor and Her Two Husbands (1978)	*Savara* (1979)
8 1/2 (1963)	*Nine* (1982)
The Full Monty (1997)	*The Full Monty* (2000)
Georgy Girl (1966)	*Georgy* (1970)
Hail the Conquering Hero (1944)	*The Conquering Hero* (1961)
Hairspray (1988)	*Hairspray* (2002)
King of Hearts (1967)	*King of Hearts* (1978)
La Cage aux Folles (1978)	*La Cage aux Folles* (1983)
La Strada (1954)	*La Strada* (1969)

Film	Broadway Musical
Lilies of the Field (1963)	Look to the Lilies (1970)
Little Shop of Horrors (1960)	Little Shop of Horrors (1982)
Madame Rosa (1977)	Roza (1987)
A Man of No Importance (199x)	A Man of No Importance (2002)
Marius (1931), Fanny (1932), César (1936)	Fanny (1954)
Miracle on 34th Street (1947)	Here's Love (1963)
Never on Sunday (1960)	Illya, Darling! (1967)
Nights of Cabiria (1957)	Sweet Charity (1966)
Ninotchka (1939)	Silk Stockings (1955)
Nothing Sacred (1937)	Hazel Flagg (1953)
Passione D'Amore (1981)	Passion (1994)
The Producers (1968)	The Producers (2001)
The Quiet Man (1952)	Donnybrook! (1961)
Seventh Heaven (1937)	Seventh Heaven (1955)
Smile (1975)	Smile (1986)
Smiles of a Summer Night (1955)	A Little Night Music (1973)
Some Like It Hot (1959)	Sugar (1972)
Summer of 42 (1971)	Summer of 42 (2001)
Sunset Boulevard (1950)	Sunset Boulevard (1994)
Sweet Smell of Success (1957)	Sweet Smell of Success (2002)
Urban Cowboy (1980)	Urban Cowboy (2003)
Villa! Villa! (1934)	We Take the Town (1962)
The World of Henry Orient (1964)	Henry, Sweet Henry (1967)

APPENDIX B

∼

Nonmusical Plays That Were Turned into Movie Musicals

Play	Movie Musical
The Admirable Crichton (1902)	*We're Not Dressing* (1934)
Ah, Wilderness! (1933)	*Summer Holiday* (1948)
The Country Girl (1950)	*The Country Girl* (1954)
Gigi (1951)	*Gigi* (1958)
The Gold Diggers (1919)	*Gold Diggers of Broadway* (1929)
The Jazz Singer (1925)	*The Jazz Singer* (1927)
Magnolia (1923)	*Mississippi* (1935)
My Sister Eileen (1940)	*My Sister Eileen* (1955)
Parfumerie (1937)	*In the Good Old Summertime* (1949)
The Philadelphia Story (1939)	*High Society* (1956)
The Pirate (1942)	*The Pirate* (1948)
Le Prince Consort (19??)	*The Love Parade* (1929)
Sailor, Beware! (1933)	*The Fleet's In* (1942)
Three Blind Mice (1938)	*Moon over Miami* (1941), *Three Little Girls in Blue* (1946)
Yentl, the Yeshiva Boy (1974)	*Yentl* (1983)

APPENDIX C

~

Academy Award–
Winning Musicals

The following movie musicals based on Broadway shows were nominated for the Best Picture Oscar. The winners are in bold.

1934	*The Gay Divorcee*
1935	*Naughty Marietta*
1956	*The King and I*
1961	***West Side Story***
1962	*The Music Man*
1964	***My Fair Lady***
1965	***The Sound of Music***
1968	***Oliver!***
1968	*Funny Girl*
1969	*Hello, Dolly!*
1971	*Fiddler on the Roof*
1972	*Cabaret*
1977	*Evita*
2002	***Chicago***

APPENDIX D

~

Tony Award–Winning Musicals

The following Broadway shows based on movie musicals were nominated for the Best Musical Tony Award. The winners are in bold.

1980	**42nd Street**
1989	*Meet Me in St. Louis*
1994	*Beauty and the Beast*
1997	**The Lion King**
2002	**Thoroughly Modern Millie**

~

Bibliography

Abbott, George. *Mister Abbott*. New York: Random House, 1963.

Alpert, Hollis. *Broadway: 125 Years of Musical Theatre*. New York: Arcade, 1991.

Altman, Rick. *The American Film Musical*. Bloomington: Indiana University Press, 1987.

Atkinson, Brooks. *Broadway*. Rev. ed. New York: Macmillan, 1974.

Aylesworth, Thomas G. *Broadway to Hollywood*. New York: Gallery Books, Smith, 1985.

Banham, Martin, ed. *The Cambridge Guide to Theatre*. New York: Cambridge University Press, 1992.

Baral, Robert. *Revue: The Great Broadway Period*. Rev. ed. New York: Fleet, 1970.

Barrios, Richard. *A Song in the Dark: The Birth of the Musical Film*. New York: Oxford University Press, 1995.

The Best Plays. 83 eds. Editors: Garrison Sherwood and John Chapman (1894–1919); Burns Mantle (1919–1947); John Chapman (1947–1952); Louis Kronenberger (1952–1961); Henry Hewes (1961–1964); Otis Guernsey Jr. (1964–2000); Jeffrey Eric Jenkins (2000–2002). New York: Dodd, Mead, 1894–1988; New York: Applause Theatre, 1988–1993; New York: Limelight, 1994–2002.

Block, Geoffrey. *Enchanted Evenings: The Broadway Musical from* Show Boat *to* Sondheim. New York: Oxford University Press, 1997.

Bloom, Ken. *Broadway: An Encyclopedic Guide to the History, People and Places of Times Square.* New York: Facts on File, 1991.

Bordman, Gerald. *American Musical Comedy: From Adonis to Dreamgirls.* New York: Oxford University Press, 1982.

———. *American Musical Revue: From The Passing Show to Sugar Babies.* New York: Oxford University Press, 1985.

———. *American Musical Theatre: A Chronicle.* 3d ed. New York: Oxford University Press, 2001.

———. *American Operetta: From H.M.S. Pinafore to Sweeney Todd.* New York: Oxford University Press, 1981.

Bordman, Gerald, and Thomas S. Hischak. *The Oxford Companion to American Theatre.* 3d ed. New York: Oxford University Press, 2004.

Botto, Louis. *At This Theatre.* New York: Applause, 2002.

Bradley, Edwin M. *The First Hollywood Musicals.* Jefferson, N.C.: McFarland, 1996.

Druxman, Michael B. *The Musical from Broadway to Hollywood.* New York: Barnes, 1980.

Engel, Lehman. *The American Musical Theater: A Consideration.* New York: CBS Legacy Collection, 1967.

Ewen, David. *New Complete Book of the American Musical Theatre.* New York: Holt, 1976.

Everett, William A., and Paul R. Laird, eds. *The Cambridge Companion to the Musical.* Cambridge: Cambridge University Press, 2002.

Feuer, Jane. *The Hollywood Musical.* Bloomington: Indiana University Press, 1982.

Fordin, Hugh. *The World of Entertainment: Hollywood's Greatest Musicals.* New York: Avon, 1975.

Ganzl, Kurt, and Andrew Lamb. *Ganzl's Book of the Musical Theatre.* New York: Schirmer, 1989.

———. *Ganzl's Encyclopedia of the Musical Theatre.* 2d ed. New York: Schirmer, 2001.

Gottfried, Martin. *Broadway Musicals.* New York: Abrams, 1980.

———. *More Broadway Musicals.* New York: Abrams, 1991.

Green, Stanley. *Broadway Musicals of the 1930s.* New York: Da Capo, 1982.

———. *Broadway Musicals Show by Show.* 5th ed. Milwaukee, Wisc.: Leonard, 1999.

———. *Encyclopedia of Musical Film.* New York: Oxford University Press, 1981.

———. *Encyclopedia of the Musical Theatre.* New York: Dodd, Mead, 1976.

———. *Hollywood Musicals: Year by Year.* 2d ed. Milwaukee, Wisc.: Leonard, 1999.

———. *The World of Musical Comedy.* New York: Barnes, 1980.

Halliwell, Leslie. *Halliwell's Film Guide*. New York: Harper & Row, 1989.

Hirschhorn, Clive. *The Hollywood Musical*. New York: Crown, 1981.

Hischak, Thomas S. *The American Musical Theatre Song Encyclopedia*. Westport, Conn.: Greenwood, 1995.

———. *The American Musical Film Song Encyclopedia*. Westport, Conn.: Greenwood, 1999.

———. *Boy Loses Girl: Broadway's Librettists*. Lanham, Md.: Scarecrow, 2002.

———. *Film It with Music: An Encyclopedic Guide to the American Movie Musical*. Westport, Conn.: Greenwood, 2001.

———. *Stage It with Music: An Encyclopedic Guide to the American Musical Theatre*. Westport, Conn.: Greenwood, 1993.

———. *Word Crazy: Broadway Lyricists from Cohan to Sondheim*. New York: Praeger, 1991.

Jackson, Arthur. *The Best Musicals from Show Boat to A Chorus Line*. New York: Crown, 1977.

———. *The Musical: A Look at the American Musical Theater*. Englewood Cliffs, N.J.: Prentice Hall, 1980.

Kaplan, Philip J. *The Best, Worst and Most Unusual Hollywood Musicals*. New York: Beekman House, 1983.

Kobal, John. *Gotta Sing, Gotta Dance: A Pictorial History of Film Musicals*. London: Hamlyn, 1971.

Laufe, Abe. *Anatomy of a Hit: Long-Run Plays on Broadway from 1900 to the Present Day*. New York: Hawthorn, 1966.

———. *Broadway's Greatest Musicals*. New York: Funk & Wagnalls, 1977.

Lerner, Alan Jay. *The Musical Theatre: A Celebration*. New York: McGraw-Hill, 1986.

Mandelbaum, Ken. *Not Since Carrie: Forty Years of Broadway Musical Flops*. New York: St. Martin's, 1991.

Mast, Gerald. *Can't Help Singin': The American Musical on Stage and Screen*. Woodstock, N.Y.: Overlook, 1987.

Mates, Julian. *America's Musical Stage: Two Hundred Years of Musical Theatre*. Westport, Conn.: Greenwood, 1985.

Matthew-Walker, Robert. *Broadway to Hollywood: The Musical and the Cinema*. London: Sanctuary, 1996.

McSpadden, J. Walker. *Operas and Musical Comedies*. New York: Crowell, 1958.

Miller, Scott. *Deconstructing Harold Hill: An Insider's Guide to Musical Theatre*. Portsmouth, N.H.: Heinemann, 2000.

———. *Rebels with Applause: Broadway's Groundbreaking Musicals*. Portsmouth, N.H.: Heinemann, 2001.

Mordden, Ethan. *Beautiful Mornin'*: *The Broadway Musical in the 1940s*. New York: Oxford University Press, 1999.

———. *Better Foot Forward: The History of American Musical Theatre*. New York: Grossman, 1976.

———. *Broadway Babies: The People Who Made the American Musical*. New York: Oxford University Press, 1983.

———. *Coming Up Roses: The Broadway Musical in the 1950s*. New York: Oxford University Press, 1998.

———. *The Hollywood Musical*. New York: St. Martin's, 1981.

———. *Make Believe: The Broadway Musical in the 1920s*. New York: Oxford University Press, 1997.

———. *One More Kiss: The Broadway Musical in the 1970s*. New York: Palgrave–St. Martin's, 2003.

———. *Open a New Window: The Broadway Musical in the 1960s*. New York: Palgrave–St. Martin's, 2001.

Norton, Richard C. *A Chronology of American Musical Theatre*. New York: Oxford University Press, 2002.

Parish, J. R., and Michael R. Pitts. *The Great Hollywood Musicals*. Metuchen, N.J.: Scarecrow, 1991.

Peterson, Bernard L. *A Century of Musicals in Black and White*. Westport, Conn.: Greenwood, 1993.

Salem, James M. *A Guide to Critical Reviews: The Musical, 1909–1989*. Metuchen, N.J.: Scarecrow, 1991.

Sennett, Ted. *Hollywood Musicals*. New York: Abrams, 1982.

———. *Song and Dance: The Musicals of Broadway*. New York: Metro, 1998.

Sheward, David. *It's a Hit: The Back Stage Book of Longest-Running Broadway Shows, 1884 to the Present*. New York: Watson–Guptill Publications–BPI Communications, 1994.

Simas, Rick. *The Musicals No One Came to See*. New York: Garland, 1987.

Smith, Cecil, and Glenn Litton. *Musical Comedy in America*. 2d ed. New York: Theatre Arts, 1981.

Springer, John. *They Sang, They Danced, They Romanced*. New York: Citadel, 1991.

Stern, Lee Edward. *The Movie Musical*. New York: Pyramid, 1974.

Suskin, Steven. *Opening Night on Broadway: A Critical Quotebook of the Golden Era of the Musical Theatre*. New York: Schirmer, 1990.

———. *More Opening Nights on Broadway: A Critical Quotebook of the Musical Theatre, 1965–1981*. New York: Schirmer, 1997.

Swain, Joseph P. *The Broadway Musical: A Critical and Musical Survey*. 2d ed. Lanham, Md.: Scarecrow, 2002.

Taylor, John Russell, and Arthur Jackson. *The Hollywood Musical*. New York: McGraw-Hill, 1971.

Traubner, Richard. *Operetta: A Theatrical History*. Garden City, N.Y.: Doubleday, 1983.

Wilmeth, Don. B., and Tice Miller, eds. *Cambridge Guide to American Theatre*. New York: Cambridge University Press, 1993.

Wlaschin, Ken. *Opera on Screen*. Los Angeles: Beachwood, 1997.

Woll, Allen L. *Black Musical Theatre: From* Coontown *to* Dreamgirls. Baton Rouge: Louisiana State University Press, 1989.

———. *The Hollywood Musical Goes to War*. Chicago: Nelson-Hall, 1983.

Index

~

About the Author

Thomas S. Hischak is a professor of theater at the State University of New York College at Cortland and a member of the Dramatists Guild. He is the author of twelve books on theater, popular music, musical theater, and film musicals, including *Word Crazy: Broadway Lyricists from Cohan to Sondheim* (Praeger, 1991), *American Theatre: A Chronicle of Comedy and Drama 1969–2000* (Oxford University Press, 2001), *The Theatregoers Almanac* (Greenwood, 1997), *Stage It with Music: An Encyclopedic Guide to the American Musical Theatre* (Greenwood, 1993), *Film It with Music: An Encyclopedic Guide to the American Movie Musical* (Greenwood, 2001), *Boy Loses Girl: Broadway's Librettists* (Scarecrow, 2002), and, with Gerald Bordman, the third edition of *The Oxford Companion to American Theatre* (2004). He is also a playwright with over two dozen published plays. He lives in Cortland, New York, with his wife and two children.